Print That Works

The First Step-by-Step Guide That Integrates Writing, Design, and Marketing

Elizabeth Adler

Bull Publishing Company
Palo Alto, California

Copyright © 1991 Bull Publishing Company
Bull Publishing Company
P.O.Box 208
Palo Alto California 94302-0208
(415) 322-2855
ISBN 0-923521-00-3

Distributed to the trade by
Publisher's Group West
4065 Hollis Street
Emeryville, California 94608

**Library of Congress
Cataloging-in-Publication Data**
Adler, Elizabeth (Elizabeth W.)
   Print that works : the first step-by-step guide that
integrates writing, design, and marketing / Elizabeth
Adler.
         p.   cm.
   ISBN 0-923521-00-3 : $23.95
   1. Business communication. 2. Newsletters—
Publishing. I. Title.
HF5718.A325 1990   89-71186
651.7'4—dc20   CIP

Cover Design: John Stoneham
Interior Design: Elizabeth Adler
Design Assistant: Carolyn Hammond, Pony Press
Production Managers: Helen O'Donnell, Detta Penna
Production Assistant: Peter Penna
Art Indexer: Hilary Adler

Text type: Trump Mediaeval
Display type: Helvetica
Composition: Pony Press
Printer: Bookcrafters, Inc.
Paper: Finch Opaque, Basis 60
Illustration and photography credits: page 381.

To my father

Matthew Alexander Fouratt

When I was small he said:

Look closely at the marigold.

Notice the pattern the seeds make

when the petals are gone.

How can this be an accident?

1912 – 1988

◆

Table of Contents

Understanding the Medium	1 Print That Works	3
	2 Your Competitive Edge	15
Getting Organized	3 Planning the Printed Piece	27
	4 The Steps in Producing Print	37
	5 People Involved in Producing Print	43
	6 Getting It Out on Time	53
	7 Watching Your Money	61
Getting and Holding Attention	8 Tailoring the Piece to Your Audience	71
	9 Ideas to Make Your Piece More Interesting	83
	10 Tapping Your Creativity	97
Writing for Printed Materials	11 A Way to Make Writing Easier	117
	12 Guidelines for Reader-Friendly Writing	123
	13 Making Writing More Readable	143
	14 How to Write a Basic Brochure	157
Design for Communication	15 What's Good Design?	173
	16 Basic Design Decisions	185
	17 Understanding Type	201
	18 Color That Works	219
	19 Selecting and Specifying Paper	231
	20 Art and Photography	241
	21 Logos and the Graphic Image	259
Production and Distribution	22 Desktop Publishing	281
	23 Preparation for Printing	307
	24 Printing	319
	25 Distribution Points	335
Everything Else	Worksheets	347
	Resources	367
	Glossary	369
	Illustration and Photograph Credits	381
	Index	389

Sidebars

Understanding the Medium

1 What Is "Print Media"? 6
2 Kinds of Printed Pieces 7
3 The Virtues of Print 20

Getting Organized

4 The Value of Planning 29
5 Questions for Planning 35
6 Steps in Producing Print 41
7 Possible Roles in Print Production 44
8 Building a Strong Print Team 46
9 Getting Good Help 49
10 How to Run a Good Meeting 51
11 Time Guzzlers 54
12 When You Need It "Yesterday" 55
13 Week-by-Week Schedule 56
14 Backwards Schedule 58
15 Timing the Arrival of Your Piece to Advantage 59
16 The Cost of Producing Print: A Checklist 62
17 Getting Estimates from Printers 63
18 Getting Estimates from Subcontractors 64
19 Budget Checklist 67
20 Tips for Tight Budgets 68

Getting and Holding Attention

21 Audience Profile 77
22 Advertising Specialties 84
23 Ideas to Make Your Piece More Appealing 93
24 Using Idea Lists to Spark Your Imagination 107

Sidebars

Writing for Printed Materials

25 Making the Piece Look Easy to Read ... 125
26 Writing Good Titles ... 127
27 Making Writing More Interesting ... 131
28 Adding Interest with Questions ... 133
29 Selecting a Tone for the Writing ... 137
30 Making a Writing Assignment ... 138
31 Writer's Checklist ... 139
32 Guidelines for Reader-Friendly Writing ... 141
33 Red Flags ... 150
34 Communicating Risk ... 151
35 Proofreading ... 152
36 Proofreader's Marks ... 153
37 Editor's Checklist ... 155
38 Which Panel Gets Read First? ... 160
39 Laura's Brochure (A Sample) ... 169

Design for Communication

40 Seventy-six Design Styles ... 183
41 Page Design ... 187
42 Designing a Cover ... 189
43 Interviewing Graphic Designers ... 191
44 Selecting a Graphic Designer ... 193
45 Working with a Graphic Designer ... 195
46 Type Measurements ... 205
47 Describing Type ... 207
48 Some Popular Typefaces ... 209
49 Choosing Type ... 215
50 Comparing Sources of Type ... 216
51 Type Tips ... 217
52 Color Combinations ... 227
53 Color Tips ... 229
54 Specifying Paper ... 233
55 Getting Dummies ... 235

Sidebars

Design for Communication
(continued)

56 Paper Tips and Reminders 237
57 Graphic Devices 249
58 Illustration Styles 256
59 Ideas for Logos 267
60 The Good Ol' Rubber Stamp. 271
61 Quick and Easy Logos 273
62 Inexpensive Logos 275
63 The Logo: Sign or Symbol? 276
64 Logo Evaluation Checklist 277

Production and Distribution

65 Keeping Up with DTP. 289
66 Your Desktop Publishing Needs 290
67 Buying DTP Equipment 291
68 Selecting Software 293
69 Desktop Publishing Reminders 297
70 Desktop Publishing Terms 304
71 Camera-Ready Checklist 315
72 Printing Terms 323
73 Money Saving Tips 325
74 Questions to Ask the Printer 327
75 Things That Go Wrong 331
76 Press Checklist 332
77 Blueline and Color Key Checklist 333
78 Tips for Working with a Printer 334
79 Ways to Distribute Your Piece 339
80 Envelopes 343

Thanks

The thoughts and efforts of many people have gone into this book.
I sincerely appreciate each person's contribution.

- ◆ Pat Anderson
- ◆ Lin Blaskovich
- ◆ David Bull
- ◆ Mia Clark
- ◆ David Collins
- ◆ Susan Cronin-Paris
- ◆ Mary Enderle
- ◆ Robbie Fanning
- ◆ Harriet Fouratt
- ◆ Matthew Fouratt, Jr.
- ◆ David Hannon
- ◆ Hilary Hannon
- ◆ Yuji Honma
- ◆ Betty Kaplan
- ◆ Judith Kemper
- ◆ Suej McCall
- ◆ Nancy Miller
- ◆ Nancy Moss
- ◆ Helen O'Donnell
- ◆ Marty Olsen
- ◆ Susie Richardson
- ◆ Paul Saffo
- ◆ Judy Smith
- ◆ Doug Solomon
- ◆ John Stoneham
- ◆ Edwena Werner
- ◆ Mary Woodrow
- ◆ Linda Weiner
- ◆ Geoff Westerfield

And most of all, thank you, Richard Adler.

Preface

Once I had a job designing letterheads for a large "not-for-profit" institution. I did fancy letterheads, bold letterheads, dignified letterheads, and plain letterheads. The criteria for a successful letterhead was one that looked good *but not too good,* because if it looked too good, it looked too expensive.

As I worked on these good-but-not-too-good letterheads, I wondered if what I did to them really made a difference. Would it matter if I used red ink instead of blue? Was one typeface really better than another? Did it matter whether I used lines, pictures, or graphic squiggles? Was there anything I could do to that piece of paper to increase its impact? And if so, what?

Another time I wrote a column for a newspaper, and the same questions came to mind. What could I do to make the meaning clearer? Would it matter what format I used? Would interviews or quizzes or questions and answers convey the point better?

And I wondered about the people who looked at my design and read my articles. What were they like? Would they respond the same way I did? How could I make my work more interesting and comfortable for them? What marketing wisdom could be applied to the printed piece to make it more appropriate and appealing?

Gradually it became clearer that working successfully with print involves three parts: marketing, writing, and graphic design; and that the whole is indeed greater than the sum of its parts. The whole is *communication.* And the important question about communication in print is *what works?*

So I took a job at a university research project because I wanted to find out what worked in print. There I had the opportunity to try out new formats for printed pieces, and get follow up data on their effectiveness. As this invisible field of "printed materials" emerged and became more and more visible, the importance of an *integrated* approach became evident.

Next I wanted to try out my theories of print communication away from the university, so I developed a print communication program for a corporate setting. All along I'd been going back and forth between the profit and non-profit worlds. In both I observed the people and the politics involved in developing printed materials. This exposure provided valuable insight into the process of producing printed pieces. It helped clarify what goes into making powerful print, and what makes it ineffectual. These observations are woven throughout this book.

There are as many opinions and approaches to developing and producing print as there are personalities to go with them. This book is based on my own day-to-day experiences as an art director, designer, writer, editor, and project director over many years. Trial and error is a good teacher. I have tried many approaches, and I speak confidently of the mistakes that can be made because I've made most of them. There is no single, set, or *right way* to do anything. There is just what works.

For the past several years I have been consulting with different kinds of organizations, and speaking on communication through the medium of print. I have met many people struggling to put out publications that were both effective and affordable. They often ask if there is a book that sums up this integrated approach to print. I didn't know of any, and tried to find one. After some serious looking, I realized there wasn't one. So I wrote this book. I sincerely hope you find it helpful.

Elizabeth Adler
Palo Alto, California
Summer, 1990

Understanding the Medium

1

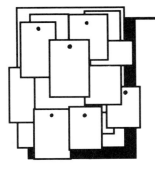

Print That Works

Imagine this: On a large cluttered bulletin board your poster is the one that stands out. On a table full of brochures, yours is the one that gets picked up. In the daily stack of mail, your flyer is the one that gets read. Why? Because it catches the eye, it holds attention, and it's easy to read. People are impressed, persuaded, and inspired to act; they pick up the phone or a pencil. You get your message across.

Possible? Yes! Hard to do? No. Expensive? Not necessarily. It's more a matter of know-how than cost. Just as many expensive brochures get ignored as less costly ones.

Not that money doesn't help, it does. But only if you know what you're doing with it. The success of your printed piece depends more on knowing what is good and what isn't, and what questions to ask at each stage of development. The better you understand the nature of this medium, the better results you can expect to get from using it.

Who This Book Is For

If you use paper to communicate information, this book is for you. It doesn't matter what your printed piece is about—the same ideas can be applied to printed materials with any content, regardless of the topic. (I will use the phrases *printed materials* and *printed pieces* interchangeably throughout this book.)

It also doesn't matter how you produce your printed piece. Effective communication is not determined by the method of preparation. The same principles apply to developing strong printed materials whether you produce them the traditional way or on a computer.

Desktop publishers

Recent technological breakthroughs in desktop publishing have given many more people the opportunity to produce their own publications. The computer is now commonly used to prepare brochures, flyers, newsletters, reports, and many other printed pieces. Users often have no background or training in how to make their printed pieces effective.

Now that the first wave of desktop publishers are familiar with pagemaking programs, fonts, and electronic art, they are discovering that it takes more than dexterity with a mouse to produce a strong printed piece. The technical skills involved with desktop publishing are mechanical—they can be learned relatively quickly from books, classes, and friends. What is more difficult for desktop publishers to learn is what to *do* with the technical skills once they've got them. That's what this book is about.

If you are a desktop publisher, you will be spending more time creating and producing publications than you will be learning how to use computers and software (hopefully!). Say the ratio of time you spend learning technical skills is 20%, and the time you spend employing them is 80%. It's what you do with that 80% that determines whether your message goes into readers' minds or into the trash.

The focus of this book is *the printed piece itself*, not any one of the fields related to it. So it doesn't matter how much (or how little) experience you have had in any particular area. An understanding of the medium involves more than just experience in any single aspect of it, such as writing, design, or desktop publishing.

Whether you are producing printed materials as part of a team, hiring a pro, or doing them entirely on your own, each situation is addressed. This book has been written especially for people in the following environments:

Corporate managers, administrators, and in-house publishing groups

The burden of putting out printed materials often falls on the "in-house" staff, especially as more and more offices get desktop publishing systems. Managers and administrators can now save time and money by producing their own printed pieces. In so doing they eliminate the hassles of depending on others for brochures, newsletter, and reports. *Print That Works* has guidelines, ideas, and suggestions for those putting out print in a for-profit setting.

Non-profit organizations

You may work for a local, county, state, or federal agency, or a hospital or medical group. Or perhaps you work for a school, university, museum or library, or it could be for a political organization, or you may volunteer your time to some organization. Most people in non-profit organizations are dependent on their printed pieces to communicate with their constituency. And most are interested in improving them, especially if there is a way to do so inexpensively. Whatever kind of not-for-profit service you're in, you need print that works.

Small businesses

If you have a small business or are starting your own company, you are probably well aware of the need for print to promote it. A good-looking letterhead, business card, billing form, brochure, and advertisements are all a part of keeping your enterprise alive and thriving. The more effective your printed pieces are, the more you'll profit.

Students

This book is for students in fields related to print, such as graphic design, writing, advertising, journalism, and communications. It provides a comprehensive picture of the entire print production process. It is also for students in fields that depend heavily on printed materials to communicate information. They include areas like marketing and others related to the public, such as public health, public policy, and public relations. As a matter of fact, whatever field you're in, the ability to communicate effectively in print is a real advantage.

The Invisible Medium

What comes to mind when you see the words "printed materials"? Chances are it doesn't send your imagination soaring. Compared with broadcast media, with newer modes of communication like fax machines and electronic mail, and even with newspapers and magazines (a different order of print media), this catch-all category called "printed materials" often fails to elicit a certain—um—electricity.

That's partly because printed materials are a form of print that *works*. "Works" in the sense of "work horse"; of getting a job done. Printed materials are the brochures, newsletters, flyers, proposals, booklets, and reports that keep the day-to-day business of this society humming. They are the everyday link between organizations and the people they serve. Printed materials are the pieces that inform, describe, solicit and advertise; they notify, inquire, remind, and instruct. Printed materials are hard working, but they usually don't evoke much excitement.

And strange as it may seem, I believe this is partly because of the dull-sounding phrase *printed materials*. The development of the medium has been hampered by the lack of something better to call it. In spite of their continuous use by every business and organization, and in spite of the billions of dollars spent on them, nowhere, to the best of my knowledge, are printed materials studied seriously *as a medium*. I know of no place devoted to its understanding or improvement.

Universities offering advanced degrees in communications, for example, offer them in film, television, radio or journalism, but not in "printed materials" (journalism focuses more on newspapers and magazines than on flyers and brochures). It is also possible to learn about writing or design, but these areas are not studied primarily to facilitate communication through printed materials. Printed materials are almost always secondary to something else.

So as printed materials rarely have center stage or the full focus of attention, the potential of this invisible medium often remains unexplored and unrecognized. Printed materials are, nevertheless, print that *works*, and this time I mean "works" in the sense of *being effective*. The focus of this book is the medium of printed materials, how they work, and what makes them effective.

Here, printed materials are untangled from other disciplines and other media. The booklet, the brochure, the catalog, the flyer, and the newsletter are of central interest, and are respected as powerful means of conveying information. In this context, we can look at the printed piece from every angle, and see what makes it succeed or fail. If we are to use this medium to its full potential, we must be able to envision possibilities that go beyond the familiar parameters. The printed piece is a powerful tool for those who know how to use it.

An Integrated Approach

We say on the cover: *Print That Works—The First Step-by-Step Guide That Integrates Writing, Design, and Marketing*. The key word here is *integrates*, because it takes skills and knowledge from several disciplines to make a printed piece really outstanding. With an integrated approach, insights from other fields can be applied to the printed piece to increase its power to communicate. A lot can be learned from psychology or marketing, for instance, about how to make the printed piece more appealing.

An integrated approach calls for print producers to think differently about the way they develop their printed pieces. When writers think more about how their words are formulated to *look* on a page, for example, what they write makes the printed piece stronger. When designers concern themselves with *communication* as much as they do with aesthetics, the piece they design is more likely to fulfill its purpose. When print project directors give thought to marketing and the way they package their information, the piece has more impact. And when everyone involved looks at the printed piece as a vehicle for delivering information, it will be more likely to do so. As McLuhan said, "the medium is the message."

1 | What Is "Print Media"?

Sometimes printed materials are referred to as "print media." "Media" is defined as a means of communication that reaches the general public. So all vehicles of communication such as radio, television, film, newspapers, and printed materials are "media" ("medium" is the singular). This book focuses exclusively on the medium of print, and on printed materials specifically (that is, anything that comes off a printing press with the exception of newspapers and magazines). Thirty different kinds are described in Sidebar 2.

print (print), *v.t.* **1.** to produce (a text, picture, etc.) by applying inked types, plates, blocks, or the like, to paper or other material either by direct pressure or indirectly by offsetting an image onto an intermediate roller. **2.** to reproduce (a design or pattern) by engraving on a plate or block. **3.** to form a design or pattern upon, as by stamping with an engraved plate or block: *to print calico.* **4.** to cause (a manuscript, text, etc.) to be published in print. **5.** to write in letters like those commonly used in print: *Print your name on these forms.* **6.** *Computers.* to produce (data) in legible alphanumeric or graphic form. **7.** to indent or mark by pressing something into or upon (something). **8.** to produce or fix (an indentation, mark, etc.), as by pressure. **9.** to impress on the mind, memory, etc. **10.** to fingerprint. **11.** to apply (a thing) with pressure so as to leave an indentation, mark, etc.: *The horses printed their hoofs on the wet grass.* **12.** *Photog.* to produce a positive picture from (a negative) by the transmission of light. —*v.i.* **13.** to take impressions from type, an engraved plate, etc., as in a press. **14.** to produce by means of a reproduction process: *to print in color; to print unevenly.* **15.** to make an image by means of ink, chemical action, etc., as type, engraved plates, etc.: *This type is too worn to print cleanly.* **16.** to write in characters such as are used in print: *He'd rather print than use longhand.* **17.** to follow the vocation of a printer. **18. print in,** *Photog.* See **burn** (def. 32). **19. print out,** *Computers.* to make a printout of. —*n.* **20.** the state of being printed. **21.** printed lettering, esp. with reference to character, style, or size: *This print is too large for footnotes.* **22.** printed material. **23.** a printed publication, as a newspaper or magazine. **24.** newsprint. **25.** a picture, design, or the like, printed from an engraved or otherwise prepared block, plate, etc. **26.** an indentation, mark, etc., made by the pressure of one body or thing on another. **27.** something with which an impression is made; a stamp or die. **28.** a fingerprint. **29.** *Textiles.* **a.** a design or pattern on cloth made by dyeing, weaving, or printing with engraved rollers, blocks of wood, stencils, etc. **b.** a cloth so treated. **c.** an article of apparel made of this cloth. **30.** something that has been subjected to impression, as a pat of butter. **31.** *Photog.* a picture, esp. a positive made from a negative. **32.** any reproduced image, as a blueprint. **33.** *Motion Pictures, Television.* a positive copy of a completed film or filmed program ready for showing; release print. **34. in print, a.** in printed form; published. **b.** (of a book or the like) still available for purchase from the publisher. **35. out of print,** (of a book or the like) no longer available for purchase from the publisher. —*adj.* **36.** of, for, or comprising newspapers and magazines: *print media.* [1250–1300; (n.) ME *prent(e), print(e), prient(e)* < OF *priente* impression, print, n. use of fem. ptp. of *preindre* to PRESS¹ < L *premere*; (v.) ME *prenten,* deriv. of the n.]

Reproduced by permission from THE RANDOM HOUSE DICTIONARY OF THE ENGLISH LANGUAGE, *Second Edition, Unabridged.* Copyright ©1987 by Random House, Inc.

An integrated approach to printed materials also calls for a look at the *whole process* of print production, step by step, start to finish. Producing a printed piece requires attention to many things. You have to deal with the budget, and know something about the people to whom the printed piece is going. You need an angle so your piece can get and hold attention. You have to get it written, designed, produced, and distributed. And some understanding of the nature of the medium is useful, along with knowledge of the environment into which it goes.

Print That Works is about communication. Everything you do to a printed piece either *enhances* the communication, or becomes *a barrier* to it. How you organize the page, the words you use, the colors, the type, and the paper you choose, the illustrations you include—these are the elements that determine the success of your printed piece.

Ways to Use This Book

This book has been carefully planned to be used in a number of different ways. Here are some of the possibilities:

As a magazine

You can skim through *Print That Works* like a magazine. Or glance through the five pages at the end of this chapter. They have an overview of thirty kinds of printed materials. Look at the pictures and read the captions, or read the sections that catch your attention first or interest you most. You'll be drawn to the parts that address your needs.

As a quick reference

There are 80 sidebars in this book. They have gray screens and consecutively numbered tabs to make them easy to find. Sidebars cover a wide range of topics related to the print production process, from the very beginning (like *Getting Good Help*, Sidebar 9), to the end (like *Ways to Distribute Your Piece*, Sidebar 79). Most contain practical and immediately applicable information. If you need a good opener for a piece you're writing, for instance, Sidebars 26 and 27 suggest possibilities; if you need color ideas for a two color printing job, Sidebar 52 lists many; if you are about to check your piece on the press, Sidebar 76 has a checklist of what to look for. Sidebar 74 has questions to ask printers; 78 has tips for working with them.

For specific information

You don't have to read this book cover to cover. It has seven parts and twenty-five chapters (see the table of contents for an overview). If you are a writer, for example, and you want to know more about design, you can go directly to that part, and read the seven chapters on design. Or you can go directly to Chapter 12, dealing with layout for writers. If you need to select a paper for your printed piece by tomorrow, you can read just the chapter on paper.

If you want some guidelines for evaluating a logo or ideas for ways to come up with one in a hurry, the *Logo Evaluation Checklist* (Sidebar 64) or *Quick and Easy Logos* (Sidebar 61) will help. If you need some clarification on type or inexpensive ways to illustrate a piece you are doing, see *Understanding Type*, page 201, or *Art and Photography*, page 241. If you are producing a brochure to describe your organization, *How to Write a Basic Brochure*, page 157, lays out the steps, and takes you through them. This is one of four chapters in Section 4, *Writing for Printed Materials*.

As a planning tool

You can use this book as a routine planning tool. Reading through the section called *Getting Organ-*

Kinds of Printed Pieces　2

Thirty kinds of printed materials are listed below (placement in these categories is not hard and fast). See pages 9 through 13 for a description of each one.

Business Papers

- Letterheads
- Labels
- Memo Sheets
- Business cards
- Forms and invoices
- Notepads

Information Pieces

- Brochures
- Booklets
- Manuals
- Articles
- Tip sheets
- Menus
- Newsletters
- Directories
- Catalogs
- Data sheets
- Programs
- Binders

Promotion Pieces

- Ads
- Posters
- Post cards
- Flyers
- Calendars
- Ad specialties

Task-Oriented Pieces

- Proposals
- Reports
- Invitations
- Questionnaires
- Presentation folders
- Fund-raising letters

ized will tell you what to do if you haven't produced a printed piece before. If you have, it can serve as a reminder for what needs to be done.

For Ideas

The section called *Getting and Holding Attention* has three chapters, each with ideas, examples, and suggestions for how to get ideas of your own. Go to this section if you are looking for ways to give your piece a competitive edge, or read *Your Competetive Edge*, page 15.

As an introduction or overview

Reading this book straight through, cover to cover, will give you the big picture. If you are a student in a field related to print, you'll get a clearer sense of how it all fits together. If you have little or no background in any of these fields, you will become familiar with them. And if you are investigating desktop publishing, *Desktop Publishing*, page 281, provides an overview.

Sidebars are constructed to be used as is—or copy the ones in the back that will be useful to you. Or use the sidebars as a basis for developing your own, and tailor them to your personal needs.

As a resource book

There are three glossaries in this book. One is specifically for desktop publishing (Sidebar 70); one has printing terms (Sidebar 72), and the third includes terms used throughout the rest of this book (page 369). Words are also defined throughout the text. Sidebars contain reminders and checklists for every aspect of the print production process, and describe such things as how to run a good meeting (Sidebar 10), tips for tight budgets (Sidebar 20), and what you need to say when you specify paper (Sidebar 54). The index will direct you to more specific topics.

However you use this book, keep the piece you are currently interested in in mind as you do. When you see the phrases "printed materials" or "printed piece," substitute the name of what you're planning to produce such as "brochure," "newsletter," "poster," or "ad"—or wherever it fits.

Kinds of Printed Pieces

On the following pages are thirty kinds of printed materials, along with comments and suggestions for each. You can use these pages as reminders of your options: by quickly scanning them, you'll get ideas for different formats you might try. The pieces are grouped by primary function, although several could be placed in other categories as well.

Business Papers

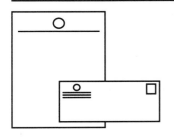

Letterheads
If you're in business of any kind, you need a letterhead with your name, address, phone number, and usually (although not necessarily) a logo. The letterhead creates and maintains your professional image, so it's worth some care. It doesn't have to be fancy, but it does have to look good.

Business Cards
Business cards are handy if not essential for doing business, although some people claim to get along without them. Odd-sized business cards may be fun but cause more frustration than pleasure as they don't fit into wallets or rolodexes. Stick to the standard 2" x 3 1/2", and be sure they're easy to read.

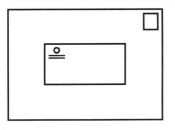

Labels
Labels with your logo, name and address can add class to those big brown envelopes used for mailing unfolded sheets of 8 1/2" x 11" paper. Get labels printed rather than the envelopes themselves—that way you can use the labels on a variety of sizes and on packages as well.

Forms and Invoices
You may need some kind of form or invoice. It can be a version of your letterhead with additional lines and spaces to accommodate your particular copy. In a pinch you can always use your letterhead as a form or invoice. Organize your information so it's crystal clear, and use only as many lines as you really need to help the readability.

Memo Sheets
Memo sheets often look like your letterhead but without the address and phone number. Sometimes called a "banner letterhead," these pieces can serve a number of different functions. They can be used as a cover of a report or a proposal, for an agenda (or for other content) at a meeting or conference, and for informal communications.

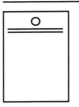

Notepads
Notepads, often 5 1/2" x 8 1/2" (half a standard sheet size), can be a smaller version of the memo sheet, and will be used as much. One characteristic of these handy-sized pads is their tendency to disappear and turn up again on desks in many different places, so you might consider them a subtle form of advertisement for your business or organization.

Promotion Pieces

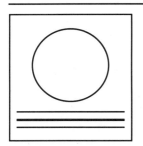

Ads
Advertisements come in a wide range of sizes and prices. Whether you place your ad in the Yellow Pages, a newspaper, or a magazine, be sure to check on details for how to present the final ad, as each media agency has its own set of strict specifications. And double check the deadline—it may be earlier than you think.

Flyers
Flyers—or handbills—are small posters, usually on 8½" x 11" medium to lightweight paper, and printed on only one side. Although flyers have a short life span, they are inexpensive to produce, and can effectively invite, recruit, notify, or announce your event or activity. Keep them simple, use readable type, and avoid illustration unless it's really good.

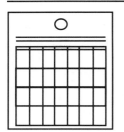

Posters
Of all the printed materials, posters are the ones with the long and noble history as an independent art form. Posters go in and out of fashion, with notable peaks at the turn of the century and in the 60s (they're about due for a comeback). This large, usually illustrated format can powerfully promote your event, your product, or your service.

Calendars
Calendars have long been used as an advertising medium. The advantage of producing a calendar is that its usefulness just about guarantees it will be kept around for a while; the disadvantage is that it can be expensive to produce. But there are ways of doing simplified, single-sheet versions that might be worth some investigation.

Postcards
Postcards have great potential as promotion tools: they can effectively convey a simple message; they can be sent directly to the mailboxes of your audience; they are less expensive to mail than a letter, and several can be sent out sequentially, over time, so the word keeps coming. There is always a way to make good use of them.

Ad Specialities
This is what you call the pens, pencils, magnets, cups, hats, balloons, t-shirts, and odd mix of other items you can order with your name and logo printed on them. Definitely a gimmick but definitely fun, they can promote your cause in a way that's likely to be well received. Look under "advertising specialties" for vendors in the Yellow Pages.

Information Pieces

Brochures

Every organization or business needs a brochure, if only to describe who they are, what they do, and what services or products they offer. Brochures can be any shape or size, but the most common is a standard 8½" x 11" or 14" folded to fit into a number 10 envelope. "Pamphlet" is another name for a brochure.

Newsletters

Newsletters carry information to groups of people with special interests in common and cover just about every topic from health to finance to electric trains. Newsletters appear on a regular basis, and are usually (but not always) 8 pages or less. Readers appreciate stories that are newsy and to the point.

Booklets

Literally "little books," booklets are useful for conveying more detailed or complex information. Consider doing a booklet when you find yourself answering the same questions over and over, or when you want to provide more information than will fit comfortably in a brochure. The most convenient sizes are the standard ones—discuss them with a printer.

Directories

A directory is a booklet listing the names and other relevant information of a particular group of people. If you have a collection of names that would be of interest to others, you might produce a directory as a convenience to them, and put your name and logo on it. You could give it away as a promotion tool, or even sell it.

Manuals

Manuals and handbooks are usually filled with facts and instructions, and serve as a reference. They offer guidance on how to fix things or make them work better on any topic from the car to the human body. Manuals are good for conveying 'how to' information, directions, and guidelines for just about every topic.

Catalogs

Selling through direct mail catalogs is a profitable and growing industry. If you are producing a catalog (or are thinking about developing one), make it as convenient for the reader to use as possible, and include only those photographs or illustrations that make your product look *really* good.

Information Pieces

Articles

Placed in a newspaper, magazine, newsletter, or other format your target audience is likely to see, an article gives you the opportunity to present your case in full. Investigating outlets for an article on your topic or product may be well worth the effort. Writing guidelines are given in Section 4, *Writing for Printed Materials*.

Data Sheets

Data sheets usually include specifications and facts for a particular product, but there's no reason why you couldn't do a data or fact sheet on a service as well. People appreciate a concise summary no matter what your business. And data sheets can be inexpensive enough so that you can update them often.

Tip Sheets

A tip sheet is a single sheet offering tips, advice, and suggestions. Whatever your subject matter, there is probably some kind of tip sheet you could produce that would be of interest to your constituency. Boil your knowledge down to a few concrete suggestions per tip sheet, and use it to inform, educate, and promote your business or organization.

Programs

As the life of a program is short and its purpose quite simple, consider the production of this piece as an opportunity to have some fun in print. Create a format that reflects the nature of the program itself in graphic form. Let your imagination go—the more creative you are, the more memorable the program will be.

Menus

Menus of course are needed only by establishments serving food, but if that's what you do, there's no format more important. Good menus positively reflect the mood and the tone of a particular dining room, and the tastes of the diners they serve. A good menu is also one that's comfortable to hold and easy to read.

Binders

Binders are not exactly a print format, but they are printed on (usually silkscreened), and often hold sheets with information. You can also have the tab sheets printed. The big advantage of binders is that pages can easily be added or removed. Ask a printer for a reference to a binder company, or look under *Screen Printing* in the Yellow Pages.

Task-Oriented Pieces

Proposals

As you need to convince readers of your expertise and professionalism in a proposal, you want it to look good and read well. Wide margins, double-spaced type, and carefully thought through ideas will make your proposal a pleasure to read. Describe needs you propose to fill, what you will do to meet them, goals, costs, and any specific arrangements.

Questionnaires

The layout of a questionnaire can do a lot to invite or discourage response. Make it look easy to fill out: leave enough space for answers (3/8" vertical space is good); make boxes large enough to check, and don't try to cram too much on one page. Write your questionnaire in such a way as to make the analysis easy once you've collected your data.

Reports

Producing a report—whether annually or otherwise, is an opportunity to present your information in a clear, concise, and compelling way. In addition to writing up results, you may also want to describe trends and make recommendations. A good looking, well-written report adds to the credibility of your business or organization, and to yours.

Presentation Folders

Presentation folders are usually 9" x12" folded to accommodate 8½" x11" papers. They are useful at meetings and conferences, for presenting proposals and reports, and for organizing and distributing several printed pieces at once. Pocket and spine sizes vary—get printers' suggestions to produce a folder that meets your needs.

Fund Raising Letters

Fund raising letters are included here as a print format because they are so commonly produced. Everyone appreciates a to-the-point fund raising letter. Say what you want and why as succinctly as possible— a long letter is less likely to get read. Section 3, *Getting and Holding Attention*, will give you ideas to make it interesting.

Invitations

Ready-made invitation stock with matching envelopes come in a variety of sizes, colors, textures, and weights. Choose a color and typeface that will reflect the nature of the event. Call printers or paper companies to get cost estimates, and to find out whether a standard or a custom invitation best suits your needs and budget.

Chapter 2

Your Competitive Edge

Everyone with anything to say or to sell is putting their message in print. And that includes *a lot* of people. At this very moment most organizations from the largest corporate giants to the smallest local groups are preparing something in print. So are department stores, computer stores, supermarkets, and hospitals; so are city, county, state and federal agencies. So are local businesses, schools, museums, and churches; theaters, clubs, political organizations and associations. How many of these printed pieces will really get looked at, let alone *read?*

We're living in an era of information overload. Mailboxes, desk tops, and dining room tables are cluttered with print. There are brochures on company benefits, bank programs, exercise classes, real estate deals, and newsletters and flyers on just about everything. There are newspapers, catalogs, magazines, and reports; directories, guidelines, and school lunch menus.

There is too much to read, too much to respond to, and too much to absorb. This is the media environment today, the arena into which you'll be sending that precious piece of yours. The amount of information available today is expected to double within the next five years, and every five years after that. So there's even more printed pieces headed your way.

DTP: Communication Boon or Future Schlock?

The advent of desktop publishing (DTP)—a system for creating printed materials using a computer and a laser printer on top of your desk—represents a major change in the production of print. It's as great a leap as from handwritten manuscripts to the printing press. Just as the invention of movable type made books more widely available in the fifteenth century, the computer makes "publishing" more widely accessible at the end of the twentieth.

Desktop publishing means that professional-looking pieces can now be produced relatively inexpensively, because the costs of typesetting and paste-up are eliminated. What used to be farmed out can now be done right on the computer screen. "Publishing" is now more affordable, and available to anyone with access to a computer and a laser printer.

Because of the rapid spread of desktop publishing, more print than ever is being generated. Ad agencies, department heads, and project directors are producing more, along with computer users, both inside and outside the office.

Ultimately this is a good thing. The more people

who try their hand at organizing information on a page the better, because in the long run, we'll benefit from the experimentation. Some good publications are likely to be forthcoming—perhaps even some great ones. But in the short run, get ready for the biggest proliferation of what Paul Saffo of California's Institute for the Future calls "laser crud."

In the short run, our environment is likely to be even *more* cluttered with unattractive, unreadable pieces of paper produced by well-intentioned but inexperienced desktop publishers in an attempt to package information. It may be a while before the good ones get good and the bad ones give up (if they do). As someone from Apple Computer said, "we now have the capability of producing a truly ugly page."

The "paperless environment" predicted to accompany the electronic age has failed to materialize; on the contrary, the presence of the computer with its desktop publishing capabilities has resulted in *more* flyers, *more* newsletters, and *more* brochures, not less. Demand for paper has risen dramatically in recent years, not fallen. Now your piece has to be better than ever if it's going to get and hold attention.

The Built-in Edge

If your piece is going to be worth the time, effort, and money you put into it, it's got to be good, and it needs an edge. Some pieces already have a built-in edge. These are the pieces with information that people are *already* anxious to get, such as information about a place they're headed for, or a health problem they have, or a new gadget they buy. If your piece has this kind of built-in edge, you can take advantage of it, and enhance it. (If it doesn't, Section 3, *Getting and Holding Attention*, pages 71–114, will give you lots of ideas for developing one.)

But even when the topic of a printed piece holds great interest for the reader, there is no guarantee that the information will be effectively conveyed. Some print producers unintentionally put up barriers between the reader and the information. They make it difficult for even the most highly motivated audience to get the message. Let me give you two examples:

A few years ago I broke my ankle. It was put in a cast, and I was given two bits of information. One was a booklet called something like "So You Broke a Bone"; the other was a sheet on cast care. As this was my first broken bone and as most medical-related situations interest me, I was anxious to find out what these printed pieces had to say.

But the sheet on cast care was unreadable, let alone comprehensible. It was a disorganized collection of sentences faintly copied on light green paper. And the booklet on broken bones was so obnoxiously cute it would have offended an eleven-year-old. Although I was anxious to "receive" this information, and presumably the producers of these pieces wanted to "send" it (you sometimes wonder), neither piece effectively conveyed its message.

Another example of "high-interest low-impact" print is computer documentation—those shiny booklets that come with a new computer or software package to tell you how to use it. Although the computer itself was brilliantly conceived, developed, and produced, related printed materials often are not. They may look terrific, but they are seldom easy to understand or convenient to use. Why wasn't the same level of creativity, intelligence, and common sense that was used to develop the computer applied to the development of the printed pieces that explain them?

The Untapped Potential for Print

There is lots of room for creativity, intelligence, and the application of common sense to printed materials. Most pieces have the potential for conveying information much more effectively than they currently do.

Because mediocre printed pieces are so common,

we make assumptions about the limitations of the medium. When the possibilities are not recognized or taken seriously, they are neither fully explored nor pushed to their full potential. Experimental use of the medium is practically unheard of.

Often our attitudes toward printed materials are conflicting. On the one hand, our hope for what a printed piece will do is high: we want it to inform, impress, educate, and sell. On the other hand, we usually don't give a printed piece the thought, care, time, or budget that would enable it to meet these expectations. It's a Catch-22. We don't believe printed materials are really effective, so we don't give them the resources they need, so printed materials aren't really effective. It's time to take a new look at this old medium.

The Goal: Communication

The first and most important thing to remember about a printed piece is that *its fundamental purpose is to communicate.* Sometimes producers of print become so caught up in a single aspect of the piece—like the design or the writing or the desktop publishing—that they forget that *getting the message across* is what counts.

A printed piece is a vehicle for carrying information from you to "them." Think of your printed piece as a *package* containing the information you wish to deliver. If this package—your brochure, booklet, newsletter, flyer, or whatever—is one that people are happy to see and want to open, and if it contains information they can readily use, you'll get your message across. The more appealing the package and the more usable the contents, the more effective the communication will be.

The second important thing to remember when you produce a printed piece is to *pay attention to your reader.* Your piece will be more effective if you develop it from the *user's* point of view. That means keeping the reader clearly in mind at all times. When an effort is made to communicate information to readers in a particular target audience, the odds are much better that it will do so.

The Typical Brochure

Let's say a project director of a large organization wants to produce a brochure to describe a new product or program. He or she believes in its virtues, and is anxious to get the word out. The staff agrees a brochure is needed, and everyone anticipates an enthusiastic response.

The director has some ideas in mind about how the brochure should look and some thoughts about what it should say. He or she enlists the aid of a writer and hires a designer. The writer tries to write what the director wants while (understandably) formulating the copy in her own way; the designer attempts to design what the director describes while (understandably) adding his personal style. Too many people (or too few) then review it, and everyone contributes their comments (understandably). The brochure then goes back to the writer, then back to the designer, and then back to the reviewers, who make just a few more changes.

By this time the writer is annoyed and the designer is on overtime. The director's concern now is mainly the budget, and everyone is worried about the deadline. No one has thought the piece through from the user's perspective, and there is no time to test it. The staff is becoming impatient. The brochure is rushed through printing and finally delivered, predictably late. The effort's been made, the time's been given, the money's been spent, and the piece is a disappointment. Five hundred (or five thousand) copies sit on a shelf a year later.

This frustrating, disappointing, time-consuming and expensive process happens over and over again. How can it be avoided?

A major advance in communication was the capability of producing books on printing presses instead of by hand; the ability to create the printed page electronically represents another significant change. The direction it will take remains to be seen.

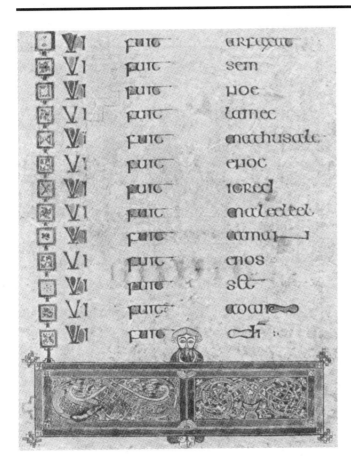

14

Type, graphics and page layout can now be viewed in final form on a computer screen. The puck is a tool for moving or changing elements of the page.

Put One Person in Charge

Developing and producing printed materials is a complex business. It involves a series of sequential steps, each requiring attention to detail and many decisions. If the piece is to be effective, someone needs to stay focused on the overall goal: getting the message across.

But quite often what happens is this: each person involved in the production of the piece (and there can be many) comes to it with a different vision, a different point of view, and a separate agenda. Each well-intentioned person contributes his or her part, separate from everyone else's. When a printed piece tries to incorporate too many ideas and satisfy too many agendas, its ability to communicate is weakened.

But when one person is responsible to see that the piece makes sense as an integrated whole, the ability of the piece to communicate is strengthened. It doesn't matter *who* takes on this role—it can be the director, the writer, the designer, a content expert, or the person paying the bills—so long as *someone* does. And the more that person makes sure the piece is tailored to a particular audience, the more interest that audience will have in the piece.

This doesn't mean that others don't contribute.

This poster, placed on crowded bulletin boards more often than not, has wide white margins. They are intended to set the information off from the clutter of other pieces surrounding it.

The application of expertise from other fields can strengthen the printed piece. Knowledge from three areas are especially helpful: they are marketing, communications, and psychology. Let's take a quick look at each to see what they have to offer:

Marketing

Marketing shows how to define and analyze an audience, and how to test the appeal of the product (your print piece is your "product"). It offers guidance on how to position a piece correctly, and how to get it into the right hands. Marketing also provides methods for testing and evaluating effectiveness, valuable steps rarely taken with printed materials. And marketing often incorporates ideas from both communications and psychology.

Communications

Understanding how we communicate with each other helps make our messages more "receivable." And knowing how to communicate effectively with people of different cultural backgrounds, economic conditions, educational backgrounds, and literacy levels often makes a difference in the effectiveness of the printed piece.

Psychology

The more you know about human behavior, and especially that of your readers, the more powerfully you will be able to persuade them in print. Concepts from behavioral psychology can be especially useful when applied to printed materials. They offer guidance for how to present information, on timing, and on what kinds of formats are likely to work best. Information and ideas from marketing, communications, and psychology will be applied specifically to the printed piece throughout this book.

On the contrary, input from a number of people can enrich and enhance the piece. But the danger is that a printed piece which is *everybody's* baby often ends up as *nobody's* baby. This is less likely to happen when some *one* is in charge. He or she can integrate the ideas of others and keep everyone working toward the same common goal: communication. And the piece that really communicates really has the edge.

Strengthening Print

When people think of what's involved in producing printed materials, they usually think of writing and graphic design. Good writing makes the piece a pleasure to read; bad writing makes it impossible. If your piece isn't read, it can't serve your purpose.

Design creates the critical first impression. If the design is good, it increases the odds that your piece will get picked up and read. If the design is weak, those odds diminish. Design can help readers to get the message. Good writing and design are essential ingredients of an effective printed piece, but it takes more.

3 | The Virtues of Print

The electronic age has resulted in more printed pieces, not less, and competition for peoples' time to read them has increased. Knowing the virtues of print enables you to make the most of it. Here are some questions to ask yourself when you do your next piece:

- What are the maximum numbers of people you can productively reach with this piece?

- As unit costs go down when greater quantities are ordered, what is the largest number of pieces you can realistically use? What quantities represent cost breaks?

- What can you do to your printed piece that would make it more likely to be kept around? (See *Ideas to Make Your Piece More Interesting*, page 83).

- Are there ways you can take advantage of the privacy that print offers?

- Can you do different pieces for different audiences instead of a single general one? How can they be effectively tailored? (See *Tailoring the Piece*, page 71.)

- What is the most effective way to get this piece to your most desired readers? (See *Distribution Points*, page 335.)

- What kind of environment will this piece be going into? What can you do to make it stand out?

- Can this piece be used to reinforce information presented one-on-one, to groups, at events, or on radio or television?

- How can you use this piece to establish and maintain a bond of good will with the people you wish to serve?

QUIT SMOKING

YOU CAN ENJOY A SMOKE-FREE LIFE

Watch the Special Reports on
Action 8 News Hour
Starting at 5:30, February 22
Monday, Tuesday, Wednesday, Thursday, and Friday

KSBW-TV

The Stanford Heart Disease Prevention Program and KSBW-TV 8 will present a series of reports on how to quit smoking. Follow KSBW reporter Gary Lindsey as he looks into different ways to quit, and see how other people are doing it themselves. Quit along with them.

Virtues of the Printed Piece

Printed materials have unique characteristics that can be put to work for you. The more familiar you are with the strengths of the medium, the better advantage you'll be able to take of them. Here are nine "virtues" unique to print.

Printed materials can reach many people

Print is relatively inexpensive compared with other forms of media. You can often reach more people for less money with print.

When quantity goes up, cost comes down

The more copies of a piece you produce, the less each single copy costs. Say it costs $900 to print 500 brochures. That's $1.80 each. If you print 2,500 copies of the exact same piece, it costs $1100, or 44 cents apiece. And if you print 5,000, the cost is $1300, or 26 cents apiece. So the same brochure costs 26 cents when you print 5000, and $1.80 when you print 500. That's $1.54 more per brochure.

*A message is reinforced
when it is carried in more than
one medium. The ad at left announces
a TV special; the pages below are from a quit-
smoking printed piece that carries the same message.*

TUESDAY
DAY TWO

ARE YOU ADDICTED?

Yes, you are probably addicted to nicotine, if your brain needs a steady dose of it to feel "normal."

Smoking can have a soothing effect, but nicotine is really a powerful stimulant. Your brain has learned to rely on it to keep up to speed. That's why most people who quit cold turkey (or "cool turkey") feel very sleepy for a couple of days, as their brain adapts to life without its fix. Then, in a few days, they start to feel "normal" again — without the nicotine.

Because nicotine is addictive, cutting down to three or four cigarettes a day seldom works. That number of cigarettes gives you enough nicotine to keep the addiction going, without providing your brain with enough of the drug to keep it happy. Result: prolonged craving. It's much easier in the long run to cut out cigarettes completely, *and* to avoid nicotine in other forms, such as snuff, pipes, cigars and even the new nicotine gum.

WHAT TO DO TODAY

1. Keep on wrapping a piece of paper around your pack, and making a note of the time and the circumstances every time you have a cigarette.

2. From now on, when you need to buy a new pack, get a different brand. The change of taste will help loosen your ties with cigarettes:

■ Don't pick a brand that's much lower in nicotine. It might make you want to smoke more than usual, to get your usual fix.

3. Change the *way* you smoke. From now on, if you normally smoke right-handed, smoke left-handed. And hold your cigarette between your third and fourth fingers:

■ Everything you can do to disrupt your relationship with cigarettes will help prepare you for the big divorce on Saturday.

WEDNESDAY
DAY THREE

PLANNING FOR THE WEEKEND

Only a few more days of slavery left to go! On Saturday you will be free. Today we suggest that you draw up some plans for the weekend, to help make your liberation as painless as possible.

Remember, the worst of the *physical* addiction should be over by Monday. Just get through the weekend — asleep, if you like — and you'll be well on your way to freedom.

WHAT TO DO TODAY

1. Start making plans for the weekend:

■ Plan to avoid any stressful occasions,and any social occasions where there will be cigarettes available — particularly if there will also be alcohol around to loosen your willpower.

■ Plan to leave time for naps in the afternoons, in case you need them. But also arrange some events that will distract you — like a picnic, or a movie, or a ballgame. Make the arrangements now.

2. If you like to read, get some books out of the library that you won't want to put down:

■ Don't give in to the temptation of starting them today: keep them for Saturday.

3. Think about asking a "buddy" to help you during the quitting process:

■ Ideally, your buddy should be someone who'll quit with you, and is just as determined to make it as you are.

■ Or ask an ex-smoker, who knows what you're going through (but don't pick one of those people who quit without any trouble at all, and can't understand what all the fuss is about).

4. Think about organizing some bets:

■ If you give good odds, promising to pay 20 to 1 if you smoke within a year, the first cigarette would cost you a fortune.

■ Or promise (in writing) that if you smoke in the coming year you will pay $50–$100 to a cause that you hate.

5. Continue to disrupt your smoking by wrapping up your pack, making a note when you smoke, changing brands, and holding the cigarette with the "wrong" fingers.

From now on, only smoke standing up.

Printed materials can be kept

Whereas radio and television messages fly by, printed materials are tangible. People can read just what's relevant to them, and digest the information at their own pace. They can refer back to the piece whenever they want, or pass it on to others.

You can target your message

Printed materials can be tailored to fit the specific needs and interests of a particular target audience. They can then be delivered directly and exclusively to that audience.

Printed materials can be private

Sometimes people are reluctant to come forward for information. This can be especially true when it involves sensitive issues like some related to health or the law. Another advantage of printed materials is that they can be read and reread in private.

Print can be strategically placed

You can place your printed piece wherever your target audience is most likely to be (such as lunch rooms or libraries). *Distribution Points*, page 335, will give you lots of ideas for where that might be.

This guide to medical care presents information in a way that is easy to find and convenient to use. The page is from Take Care of Yourself *by Doctors Vickery and Fries.*

Print can be environmentally tailored

You can help your piece get attention by tailoring it to the environment. For example, if you know that your poster will be on a cluttered bulletin board, you can give it a wide border to make it stand out.

Printed materials support other communication

Handouts, booklets, brochures, flyers, and tip sheets can reinforce information presented one-on-one, to groups, at events, or on radio or television.

Printed materials can help establish a bond

Printed materials can become a tangible bond of good will between you and the people you wish to serve.

Some Good Examples

Take Care of Yourself, a successful self-help medical guide, was revolutionary in the field of home medical guides when it first appeared in the mid 70s. It is easy to follow and comprehensible to the average reader. Graphic charts for common medical problems (one full page each) help users get information quickly and easily. The content is well written, well organized, and clearly identified with large numbers.

Another long-term best seller demonstrates sensitivity to its target audience. *What Color Is Your Parachute, A Practical Manual for Job-Hunters & Career Changers* was first published over twenty years ago, and is now regularly updated and reprinted. Information is presented in a way that is fun to look at, easy to read, and easy to use. The tone is supportive and encouraging for job-seeking readers.

These books take advantage of a natural edge. Written for people who are seeking help, they deliver. No verbal or visual barriers are put between readers and the information they seek. Unlike the pieces I

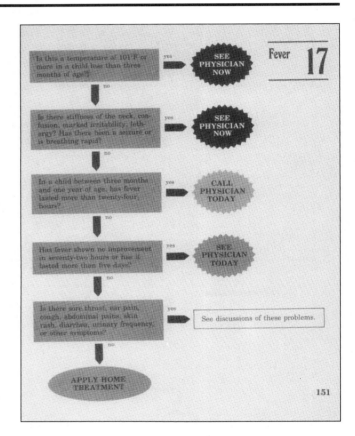

was given for my broken bone, these books are put together in such a way that getting the message is made *easier*, not *harder*. Although these are books and not "printed materials" as we have defined them, the elements that make them work can be applied effectively to any form of print.

IBM's publications for employees (see page 24) are another example of printed pieces that are well-designed and easy to understand. These pieces are noteworthy because printed materials from personnel offices are notoriously frustrating. Some look so overwhelming they get tossed in the trash at a glance. Others make difficult information crystal clear, and so are read. Many other examples of print that works are given throughout the book.

Bolles' What Color Is Your Parachute?,
*below, is an imaginative book of good, practical job
hunting advice written with both compassion and a sense
of humor. These are the very things a job seeker needs most.*

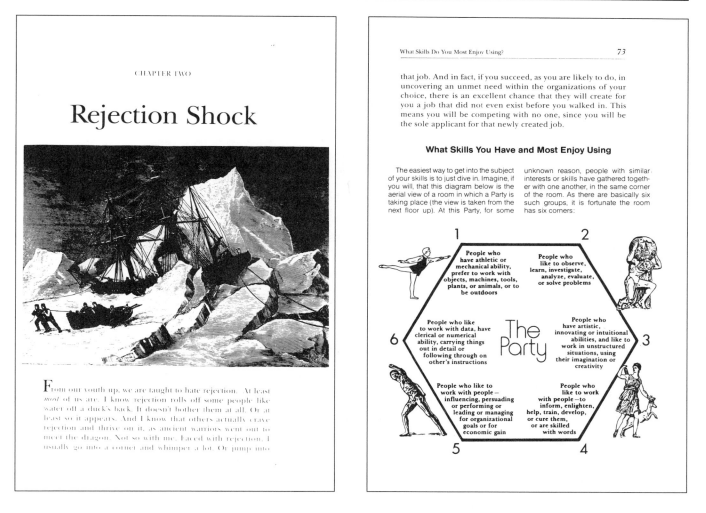

When it comes to weak print, our government is a major offender. It manages to make most of its forms ridiculously difficult to use. We'd all be grateful if someone in Washington paid a little more attention to developing them from the users' point of view.

What You Can Do

In spite of the age of electronic information, we're still flooded with print, and there's no end of it in sight.

Competition for the reader's attention is stiff and getting stiffer, but there are many things you can do to give your printed piece an edge. Here is a summary of the possibilities mentioned in this chapter. More are given in upcoming sections.

- Make the most of pre-existing interest in your subject matter

- Take a fresh look at the medium, and be open to new possibilities

IBM's piece for employees, About Your Company, *is well thought-through and clearly laid out. The tabs are colored, which helps guide readers to sections they are interested in.*

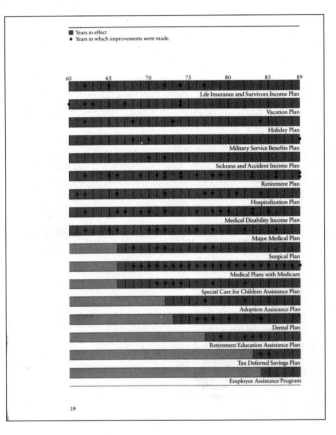

- Keep in mind that the fundamental purpose of a printed piece is *communication*

- Encourage all contributors to focus on that goal

- Think about the printed piece from your reader's point of view

- Put one person in charge of producing it

- Apply knowledge from other areas to print

- Be aware of the "virtues" of the medium, and take advantage of them

- Be on the lookout for good examples of print, and figure out what makes it work

Your Piece Reflects You

Your printed piece is a tangible representation of the expertise, professionalism, and integrity of your organization or business. Each time you produce a new brochure, flyer, newsletter, or other printed piece, you have the opportunity to get the attention of a very important audience—yours. That piece can be a powerful link between you and the people you wish to serve.

The energy, enthusiasm, and skill with which you produce your printed piece is likely to be reflected in the response you get to it. The more understanding and respect you have for your audience, and of the medium you are using to reach them, the more respect your audience is likely to have for you.

Getting Organized

2

Chapter 3

Planning the Printed Piece

You may find yourself developing printed materials without much background or experience in the field. This happens more and more these days as people discover the graphic capabilities of computers, and do their own "publishing" at their desk. A benefits manager, for example, may need to explain company policies; a real estate broker may want to describe his or her services; students may need to advertise their taxi service; city officials may want to clarify new zoning ordinances. People are finding that the most expedient way to get a message across may be to do it themselves.

When printed pieces are developed without a plan, it's usually because producers don't know what is involved or how to go about it. People commonly ask these questions about producing print:

1. How do I develop a plan for producing print? (*Planning the Printed Piece*, page 27)

2. What are the tasks involved? (*The Steps in Producing Print*, page 37)

3. Who does the work? (*People Involved in Producing Print*, page 43)

4. How much time will it take? (*Getting It Out on Time*, page 53)

5. How much will it cost? (*Watching Your Money*, page 61)

The purpose of this section is to help you get organized by answering these questions, and to help save your time, money, and nerves.

Going Public

Starting work on a new printed piece can be exciting: you are about to create something that does not yet exist. This publication will appear in a unique way that only your effort can produce—if someone else was involved instead of you, it would turn out differently. Your personal mark, if not your name, will be on the paper, and unlike so many other efforts, you will have something tangible to show for it.

Once your message is in print, you (and your organization) take on a new legitimacy. Your publication makes your product, service or activity "official" as only the printed word can. But although the prospect of producing a new piece can be exciting, it can also be somewhat intimidating.

Just ask people who produce print regularly. They can always come up with a disaster story (they are such unforgettable experiences): posters were delivered with the headline misspelled, annual reports had key figures reversed, brochures arrived with an important name left off, flyers were printed without a phone number, the color was wrong, the printing was poor, it took twice as long or cost twice as much as it was supposed to.

Whether you are producing a printed piece for the first time or the fortieth, your very best assurance against unhappy surprises is to think the piece through carefully, make a good plan, and get yourself organized.

Developing Your Plan

Each publication you produce is a new venture, aimed at solving a particular problem within the limits of a particular budget and time frame. Like the entrepreneur starting a new business, the creation of your printed piece will require many decisions and attention to detail.

A well-conceived and well-written business plan is central to the success of the entrepreneur. It empowers the entrepreneur to stand by his or her concept with confidence, and enables investors to judge the start-up's potential. The better the plan, the better the chances of success.

Developing a good plan for your printed piece is just as important. It forces you to think your project through step by step, and gives you a clear sense of direction.

The following questions are designed to bring your printed piece more sharply into focus, and help you develop a solid, workable plan to accomplish your goals. You can make use of the questions in several different ways. Answering them yourself will pull your thoughts, ideas, and concerns together; going over them with people one-on-one will elicit valuable input; and using them as points for group discussion will help the piece take shape.

The questions are summarized in Sidebar 5 so that you can copy them conveniently. Or just copy the ones you think will be productive, and add others to them. Or make up your own list of questions. Be sure to go through them separately for *each* printed piece you plan to produce, as the answers for different pieces will bring up different issues.

What Is Your Primary Purpose?

If your printed piece could accomplish just one goal, what would it be? Decide on the single most important purpose for each piece you produce. You should be able to say, for example: "the primary purpose of this newsletter is to keep members of the association updated"; "the goal of this flyer is to get people to come to the meeting"; "the purpose of the poster is to explain the new policy"; "the purpose of this brochure is to sell our new product"; "the purpose of this booklet is to educate the public." When the primary goal of your printed piece is defined, each person working on it can contribute to that end, and you'll have something by which to measure its success.

What Are the Secondary Purposes?

Usually a printed piece has more than one goal. It helps to think each through, and be clear about the order of their importance. When there are two goals of equal importance, you run the risk of accomplishing neither very well. Producers of print who are vague about their priorities have a harder time realizing them. When it is clear as to what's most important and what's of secondary importance, the printed piece comes together better, and is more effective.

Here are some examples of primary and secondary purposes: the primary purpose of a newsletter might be to update its readers; a secondary purpose might be to link people together. The primary purpose of a brochure might be to sell something; a secondary purpose might be to establish a particular kind of reputation. A primary reason for a poster might be to institute a new policy; its secondary purpose could be to inspire enthusiasm for it. And of course another purpose for *all* printed pieces is to create a positive image for the person or organization producing it.

What Is Your Unstated Message?

Since every printed piece you produce conveys an unstated message, whether you intend it or not, you may as well determine what that message will be. The unstated message is whatever *impression* you want to make on your readers. For example, the purpose of a hospital poster may be to let people know that smoking is not allowed, but its message is that smoking is a health hazard. The *purpose* of a retail brochure may be to sell clothes, but the *unstated message* is that the store is for the ultra-trendy. The purpose of a dealer's data sheet may be to make sales, but the message is that this is a first class company.

What Else Can This Piece Do?

A printed piece frequently provides intangible benefits. It can help further your reputation as an expert or leader in a particular field, for example. It can give you more visibility. It can present you as a concerned citizen, a generous company, a reliable business, or a credible organization. A publication can also generate interest around a topic or product you want to promote, whether it is the latest in computer scanners or what's good for your diet. A printed piece can create a positive bond between you and the people you serve. Be aware of these more subtle benefits.

Who Is This Message For?

Who is your target audience? The more you know about your audience, the better able you will be to

The Value of Planning — 4

If you've ever worked on a well-thought-through project, you know what a pleasure it is. And if you've worked on one that's been poorly planned, you know how frustrating it can get. Careful planning makes everyone's job easier. It:

1. Helps you to clarify your goals

2. Enables you to communicate your intentions to others, so you can get feedback early, when adjustments are easier to make

3. Lays out the sequence of tasks to be accomplished

4. Clarifies who has responsibility for what

5. Allows you to prepare better for the work ahead

6. Helps you to anticipate problems before they happen

7. Helps you remember details that might otherwise fall between the cracks

8. Helps you get things done on time

9. Enables you to measure your progress as you go

10. Helps you save money because it helps you avoid mistakes

11. Helps you stay within your budget

12. Helps you stay focused on accomplishing your goal

"speak their language." And that's important because the better you speak their language, the more likely they'll be to get your message.

It is harder to make a printed piece that is developed "for everyone" really appeal to anyone. A piece that appeals to white male corporate executives would probably not make it with Hispanic teenage girls; one generating interest among retired farmers is unlikely to appeal to young urban professionals; one designed for working mothers is less likely to engage college students.

Even when your target audience is broad, there are usually some dominant characteristics you can pick out. Look for common denominators such as location, education, income, taste, age, or interests. Or tailor the piece to the type of person who dominates your audience. Or to the most important subgroup in it. Any way you can customize the piece to your audience will improve it.

How Much Do You Have to Say?

A common urge in developing a printed piece is to want to say it all in one piece. Be selective. Say just what is necessary to get your message across, and no more.

How much you want to say will help determine the kind of printed piece you produce. You may have in mind to do a brochure, but in fact you've got a booklet's worth of information to convey. You may think you've got enough pages to use a spiral binding when actually a stapled piece makes more sense. You may envision a four-page newsletter, but it turns out you'll need eight. Or you may be thinking of doing a poster, but a flyer will accomplish your goals as well.

What Format Will Work Best?

Print producers sometimes get locked in to a format too early—it just doesn't occur to them that there

may be a better "package" to deliver their message. Information headed for a booklet, for example, may be more effectively communicated when it is broken up into separate brochures or tip sheets; copy for flyers may be significantly more effective delivered on post cards; an ad may be more effective in a trade journal than in a newspaper; pages of a directory or manual may work better in a three-ring binder instead of stapled. Don't settle on the final format for your message until you have considered all the options (see Sidebar 2 for ideas). Ask yourself what the *very best* format is to convey your information, and don't settle for less.

How Should This Piece Be Written?

The writing style that is best for your particular piece depends on what would be most appealing and comprehensible to your audience. Among the choices are straightforward factual statements, testimonials, questions and answers, and interviews (more ideas in Sidebar 27). Consider alternative ways to write your message, and get the opinions of your clients or constituency if you can.

What Image Will You Project?

How your piece looks creates an image, for better or worse, and that image enhances or diminishes its overall effectiveness. What image do you want to project? Do you want to look dignified? Friendly? Successful? Serious? Slick? Folksy? Professional? On the cutting edge? Smokey the Bear posters, for example, have a friendly look; museum publications tend to give a more arty or sophisticated impression. Any 'look' can be created by manipulating the elements of graphic design (more on this in the section on design).

One way to come up with a design style that is right for your printed piece is to look at many things in print—books, brochures, magazines, reports, flyers, etc.—and identify pieces that create the kind of image you want to project. Then figure out what design elements go into creating it. (The variable elements in graphic design are: layout, size, art and photography, type, color, and paper.)

What Will Make It Attractive?

Your printed piece will appeal more to your target audience if you give it an angle or theme that relates especially to them. For example, you can use colors that have positive associations for your audience. Or you can add tips or advice relating to your topic that would especially interest them. Or you can include new statistics or data that would grab your audience's attention. The time to start thinking about the possibilities is now (more ideas in Section 3, *Getting and Holding Attention*).

What Are Your Limitations?

Every printed piece has its own set of limitations. The sooner you know what they are, the sooner you can find ways to work around them. Most limits have to do with three things: time, energy, and money. Be hard-headed and realistic about all three at the outset —you'll thank yourself throughout the rest of the project. Let's have a closer look at these limitations.

Time limitations

Needing a piece by a particular date has definite ramifications. When a delivery date is crucial, it's usually wise to postpone exploring anything new. Go with what you know has worked in the past. If you're not sure how to meet the deadlines, consider getting some expert advice—it could save you time and money. When the delivery date is a top priority, you may need to consider producing a more simplified version than

you originally intended. Work with people who are known quantities. Don't try a new writer or designer or printer unless you have to. Be clear with everyone involved as to what your deadlines are, and do what you can to help others meet them. (For more information on time and scheduling, see pages 53–60).

Energy limitations

Energy, unfortunately, is finite. Finding out what you can realistically take on is usually a result of trial and error, with an emphasis on the error. The important question here is: how much of the work can you do yourself, and how much of it can you delegate to others? Somehow we find time and energy for the projects we're most interested in.

Whatever your level of interest in this current piece, evaluate honestly how much energy you have to give to it, and think about who else might be able to take up the slack.

Money limitations

I've known some organizations with no budgetary limits, but not many. If you're working with a less-than-ideal budget (which is usually the case), take heart. Money is *not* the critical component for communicating effectively in print (putting lots of money into a piece does not guarantee success). A limited budget calls for more imagination, so think creatively. Can you make one color look really colorful? (Yes.) Would a flyer serve your purpose as well as a brochure or poster? (It sometimes can.) Does the newsletter need heavy paper? (Sometimes a lighter one is fine.) Sidebar 20 has tips for tight budgets.

Are There Special Requirements?

Think through any special needs for your printed piece as soon as possible—it will save time and trouble later. Answering the following questions will help remind you of some of the most commonly forgotten requirements:

- Whose names must be on this piece?

- What groups must be credited? In what order?

- Who must approve the piece? Who else?

- Does this piece have to fit into a standard size envelope?

- Are there any size restrictions?

- Does this piece have to match or be coordinated with anything else?

- Does it need a logo?

- Should it carry a copyright?

- Will it meet postal requirements?

- What must it weigh to keep the mailing cost down?

What Are the Barriers?

Barriers to the production of a printed piece often come in the form of people. Anything that involves human beings seems to produce politics, and the politics of getting a printed piece produced can be intense, especially when power and egos are involved.

Problems tend to arise when it's unclear who is in charge; when someone doesn't see a need for the piece or has a different purpose for it in mind; when someone expects you to produce something wonderful with little time or money; when someone offers strong opinions but no positive suggestions; when someone doesn't understand the level of complexity, the number of decisions, and the amount of detail involved in print production; or when you have to work with someone who is difficult or not so compe-

tent; and on and on. In these cases the wise print producer anticipates these barriers in advance, and figures out a strategy to get the piece produced with as much harmony and as little hassle as possible.

What Are the Unknowns?

Do you know what quantity to print? Who will write the piece? Design it? Print it? How long will the printing take? When do you want the piece delivered, and where? Is your mailing list ready to go? Do people know their roles? Who has the main over-all responsibility for this piece? Do you know staff vacation plans? Are there other unknowns you can put your finger on? Now is the time to try to identify them.

What Is Its Life Span?

The anticipated life span of a printed piece has implications for both quality and cost. If you must decide which of several pieces to invest in, one criterion to consider is how long the piece will be around. Don't agonize over a piece with a short life span unless it gets high visibility and you're pretty sure it's worth it. Obviously a flyer whose mission is accomplished in a week does not require the amount of time, effort, and money of a catalog to be used for a season, a directory to be used for a year, or a manual to be used for several years. Put your effort into the pieces that will be out there a while, representing you over time.

Another consideration is frequency of use. A menu, catalog, or directory may get repeated use whereas a brochure or report may be looked at just once. You'll probably want a heavier grade of paper for pieces that get handled a lot.

What About Distribution?

What is the best method of distribution to your audience? Think about how to get your printed piece into the right hands while you are planning it. This will give you time to weigh alternatives, and choose the method that will be most effective. There is on-site distribution, which may require getting permissions, a delivery person, and follow-up to make sure the pieces got out the way they were supposed to. There are several classes of U.S. mail which may require investigation. You may want to try more than one method of distribution for your publication, and see which one is most effective. (For more on distribution, see *Distribution Points*, page 335.)

What Else Goes with the Piece?

If your piece is to be mailed, will anything else go along with it? At one time direct mail advertising theory held that the more pieces you put in an envelope, the more successful the mailing would be. It's not that simple; there are too many variables to say for sure. One really well-done card in a standard envelope, for example, would probably do better than a letter, a card, a return envelope, and a brochure that were poorly produced.

On the other hand, sometimes it does make sense to piggyback one piece on another. You might include a separate reply card, envelope, letter, or fact sheet along with a sales catalog, booklet, or brochure. Ask yourself what you'd like most to get in the mail, or better yet, ask members of your audience. Weigh the alternatives, and decide what makes the most sense in each case.

What Action Do You Want Taken?

What do you want people to do as a result of seeing your printed piece? When you lay out specific suggestions for the action you want people to take, you make it more likely to happen. Do you just want people to learn something as a result of having read your publication? Do you want them to make a phone call? Write a letter? Ask questions? Pass something on to someone else? Do you want someone to stop doing one thing or to start doing something else? Would you like people to buy something? Spell out what, where, when, and how. Don't forget to include the important phone number.

Did It Work?

How will you know if your piece has achieved its goals? Although printed pieces are rarely evaluated for their effectiveness after they've been disseminated, you may be interested in finding out how your piece did. Follow-up evaluations offer invaluable direction for future productions. Short of an evaluation, you may want to hold a follow-up meeting of those who were involved in producing the piece. Ask: What went wrong? What went right? How would we do it differently in the future? (See Sidebar 10, *How to Run a Good Meeting*.) Learn what you can from your hard-earned experience. Keep notes and review them before you produce your next piece.

What Else Can You Do?

Studies show that communication is most effective when multiple channels are used to convey the same message. What other methods can you use to achieve your goals?

Should you coordinate the arrival of your print piece with something on television? On the radio? Can you place an ad or an article in a newspaper, a magazine, or a newsletter? Should you hold a press conference? Should a second printed piece deliver a follow-up message? If so, when is the best time to send it? Should it be the same kind of piece or different? Can your message be reinforced with a public (or private) talk? With telephone calls? Reinforcing your message in additional ways can greatly strengthen your case.

Long-Term Planning

If you can plan several printed pieces at once—for a whole campaign or for the upcoming year—so much the better. Long-term planning doesn't mean you are committed eight months from now to actually produce what you plan today, and there are several advantages to laying out a long term plan:

- Long-term planning enables you to put all your pieces into an orderly, coherent, and mutually reinforcing context.

- It can save you money by getting several pieces designed, written, and printed at the same time.

- It allows you to take advantage of upcoming seasons or holidays by relating your printed pieces to them.

- It enables you to piggyback on an event or activity that relates to your topic.

- It gives you time to coordinate the delivery of your message with other media.

- It clarifies the timing of press releases, articles, talks, or conferences.

- It gives you time to coordinate and plan with other businesses or organizations.

- It enables you to reinforce your message consistently in each piece.

Consider going on a retreat to do some long-term planning. Any break from the routine and familiar environment tends to free up thinking and allow for a better flow of ideas, and it's fun. Going somewhere other than the office will help lift morale, generate team spirit, and result in a more inspired plan for your printed pieces. If the budget is tight and you can't afford to rent space at a conference center, club, or hotel, someone's home can work quite well.

If you are working alone on your printed pieces, you might consider treating yourself to a change of scene while you develop your plan. Again, you don't have to go somewhere fancy or expensive—take yourself to a library or a place where they serve good coffee. It can provide the change that leads to fresh and more imaginative ideas.

Developing Your Style

There is no *one way* to plan for printed materials, just as there is no one way to write, design, or produce them. Planning style is personal. People develop their own approach to planning just as they invent their own method of keeping their calendar.

Each time you go through the development and production of a printed piece, you'll find out more about what works for you. Some people like to start off by holding a meeting; others prefer to hole up at home. Some like to sit at a computer; others want a white squeaky board. Some plan most happily on yellow pads; others need their "organizer" notebooks. Still others throw scraps of paper with their thoughts and ideas into file folders. Whatever works.

Learn planning techniques from many people, and try different approaches. As you plan, you can make up your own forms to help you get organized, or take the ones in the back of this book and adapt them to your needs.

If you have trouble getting started on a plan, try making up a list—any list in relation to the piece you are about to produce. It might include the people you need to talk to, ideas for how you want the piece to look, the problems you anticipate, or the questions you have regarding it—anything to get something concrete down on paper.

This sort of list-making gets you thinking about the piece, and helps you to focus on it. You might realize you need to talk to your boss to get support, or to a colleague to get ideas, or to a writer or a designer to ask about their availability. You may decide you want a clean, contemporary look or a warm, friendly one. You may uncover concerns about your work load, your time frame, the budget, or all three. You might realize you need to find out more about mailing rates, or exactly when your piece must be ready. Or you may discover you need more information on your target audience. When you look your list over, it will trigger more thoughts, questions, and ideas. Before you know it, you'll be sketching out a plan.

Planning Alone and with Others

Is it better to plan alone or with someone else? It's probably best to do some of both if you can. The advantage to planning alone is that you can usually get more concentrated thinking done by yourself. But the danger of too much planning alone is that your ideas may become one-sided. Or you may become too attached to them, and find they are harder to change when they come up against new-found limitations or the opinions of others. If you're working on your printed piece alone, run it by friends or relatives to get their response.

Planning with others gives the printed piece the benefit of multiple points of view, and this can make it richer and more interesting. Meetings are usually more productive when you've given the topic some thought beforehand. On the other hand a disadvantage of planning with others is that you can get sidetracked, especially if you haven't thought through your own ideas in advance. And heaven knows it takes longer. A combination of both approaches will benefit your piece most.

Asking Questions

Some of the best planners approach their project with a lot of questions right from the beginning. Asking questions can generate a lot of valuable information,

Questions for Planning   5

To get the most from your printed piece, think it through carefully. Here is a summary of the questions in this chapter to apply to yours. A worksheet version of this sidebar appears on page 348.

1. What is the primary purpose of your piece?
2. What other purposes does it have?
3. What unstated message do you want your piece to convey?
4. What else can this piece do for your organization?
5. Who is your message for?
6. How much do you have to say?
7. What format will work best?
8. How should the piece be written?
9. What image do you want to project?
10. What will make your piece more attractive to your audience?
11. What are your limitations?
12. Are there any special requirements?
13. What are the foreseeable barriers?
14. What are the unknowns?
15. How long will your piece be in use?
16. What is the best method of distribution to your audience?
17. If your piece is to be mailed, will anything else be mailed along with it?
18. What do you want people to do as a result of seeing your piece?
19. How will you know if your piece has achieved its goals?
20. How else can you reinforce your message?

which can save you time and trouble. "Here's what I'm thinking...what do you think?" "Should we produce this piece or that one?" "Now or next Spring?" "How much time can you give to this project?" "Can you think of any other sources of funding?" "What's your experience been with this writer (or that designer or printer)?" "How should we go about this?" "Who else should I talk to?" "What questions should I be asking?"

Ask questions early. In addition to getting valuable input, you're also likely to win support for the piece, as people generally like to give their opinions and be included. Ask questions as part of your basic plan, and as part of every step along the way.

*I*nterest = Energy.

*O*rganization = Time.

. . . Wolfgang Lederer

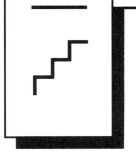

Chapter 4

The Steps in Producing Print

Every printed piece goes through a series of steps as it is produced. The simplest version has just three: writing, then design, then printing. These three steps may well be all you need to know about the sequence of events for producing your piece, especially if it is simple and straightforward, like a postcard or a flyer.

On the other hand, there are times when many more steps are involved, as with a complex newsletter, brochure, or booklet. The piece may also need to be researched, illustrated, pretested, and evaluated for effectiveness after it is distributed. This process could include as many as seventeen steps (they're summarized in Sidebar 6).

Following is a description of what happens at each stage, along with pertinent comments, suggestions, and tips. Some steps—such as design and photography—often happen simultaneously. All of these steps may not be relevant to your current piece, but they are discussed in their entirety, in case you should ever want them.

If you are new to print production, reading through the descriptions of the steps will give you an overview of the whole territory, and perhaps some possibilities you may not have thought of. If you are already familiar with print production, this description offers another perspective, and may give you some new ideas. You can use the outline of steps to help you plan the production of your printed piece, and as a checklist as you go through the process, so that nothing will fall between the cracks.

1. Concept Development

The first step in developing a printed piece is to conceptualize what you would like your piece to be. This is the "dream it up" phase, when you get to use your imagination. Now is the time for loose, fluid brainstorming—the sky's the limit. You will end up with a better piece if you encourage yourself to think big at this stage to shake out all the possibilities. It is easier to carve a big idea down to size later than to pump life into a small one. Decide what you *really* want this piece to be like.

To stimulate your thinking, look at printed materials wherever you find them: in offices, on bulletin boards, at businesses and public agencies, at stores, in waiting rooms, and in your mail box. Look at billboards on the road, programs at concerts or other public events, and flyers posted everywhere.

Perhaps the most stimulating examples are in the books and magazines found in the graphic arts sections of a bookstore, library, or art supply store. Look at books like *Graphis Annual* or art directors' annuals, and magazines like *Communication Arts Annual* and *Print's Regional Design Annual*. They show collections of award-winning designs for print pieces, and are sure to give you ideas. The more you look at good print the more inspired you'll get, and the more fun your project will be.

2. Market Research

Once the piece is conceptualized, next comes market research. It can be an invaluable tool in helping to shape your printed piece.

Let's say you're starting your own business consulting to public agencies, and you want to put together a packet of information describing what you have to offer. You've probably given what you will say quite a bit of thought, which is good; but that's only half the picture. Do you know what people in these agencies are interested in? What information do they need before they hire you? You may want to do some market research. Many a product, service, and printed piece has flopped because it was built on false assumptions. Looking at your piece from your audience's perspective could change the way you present yourself in print.

Say you've been working with a number of clients for several years, and it's time to revise the printed pieces you use with them. Do you know what your clients like and dislike about your current printed materials? Do you know what answers their questions and meets their needs, and what is superfluous? They can probably tell you, if you ask.

Or say you'd like to take your show on the road to different cities or states or countries. Do you know what particularly interests your potential clients, or what needs they have that you might meet? Your piece will be more effective if you find out. Doing some market research can make the difference, so step into the other fellow's shoes.

Imagine your client or constituent reading your piece, and come up with some questions he or she might ask. Then decide what people in your audience would be worth talking to, call them up, and ask them your questions. Market research can be that informal. Or develop a questionnaire or conduct a focus group. Learn as much as you possibly can about your audience's interests and needs before investing in your next printed piece.

3. Content Research

The next step is to pull the information together, so that the copy (the text for the piece) can be written. If you're producing a directory, for example, you need to gather names or other items for it; if you're putting out a newsletter, you need facts for stories; if it's a report, you need data; if it's a brochure, you need information.

You could do both the research and the writing yourself, or just the research and hand it over to a professional writer. Or you could do just the reverse: you do the writing, using information someone else has gathered. Or perhaps a specialist in the field (a "content expert") will supply the facts. Whoever gathers the information for your piece, be sure it's both current and accurate, as your credibility rests on getting it right.

4. Writing

Writing can begin as soon as information is gathered. Some writers like to collect all the information first, then write it up; others go back and forth between research and writing, depending on the complexity of the piece and their individual working styles. *People Involved in Producing Print*, page 43, covers how to find a writer. Section 4, page 115, is devoted to writing for printed materials. It suggests how to make writing easier and more readable, and offers basic guidelines.

5. Copy Approval and Corrections

This is the stage during which all reviewers give their comments to the writer. The writer then makes the necessary adjustments to the copy, and distributes it again for final approval. This process is time-consuming, especially if several people need to review the piece. It is a common cause of schedule delays, so give reviewers a concrete date by which to get their comments back to you. A week is usually reasonable, depending on the circumstances.

6. Editing

Once the content of the piece is approved, the copy should be edited by someone who has editing skills whom you trust and respect. Everyone's writing is improved by a good editing job. An "outsider" as editor is often most helpful. He or she is in the best position to make sure the message is clear. Sidebar 37, an editor's checklist, is on page 155.

7. Proofreading (Copy)

Be sure to get your copy proofread. Give it to someone who is good with detail and mechanics—grammar, spelling, syntax, and so on. Be sure to use your computer spell checker if you have one, but don't count on it exclusively! It will miss typos if they spell a real word (you type "on" when you mean "no," for example); they don't catch repeated words (such as "It it") or words left out; they can't check numbers or punctuation, and they can't make sure letters, words, paragraphs, and sections are in the right order. You'll find proofreader's marks in Sidebar 36, page 153.

8. Design

Although most designers usually don't start to work on the actual design until the copy is close to its final form, most do want to be included at the concept development stage. Bring the designer in at this time. He or she is likely to have good ideas and useful technical advice. Designers are often more valuable sooner rather than later.

There are good reasons why designers like to start on the actual design with finished or near-finished copy. Even the smallest changes in the writing can have a major impact on the layout. Graphic design is a precise art, and adding or deleting words may require quite a bit of rethinking to accommodate the change. So don't expect the real design work to get under way until the copy is pretty much set. It will save you money and time. Sidebar 44 is on hiring a designer; graphic design is covered in Section 5, page 171.

9. Art and Photography

Illustrations can be drawn, art gathered, and photographs taken at any time in the print production process. As the designer (or art director) usually decides what to use and where it will go, this step often takes place after the designer has begun work. Illustrators and photographers will need time to schedule your assignment, so although they may not begin work until the designer tells them what to do, sign them up early. Don't forget to plan time for getting any necessary approvals or permissions for already-created art or photography you intend to use. See *Art and Photography*, page 241.

10. Pretesting

Consider testing the effectiveness of your printed piece before it goes into final form. If you plan to pretest ("market test" as they say in business; they call it "formative evaluation" in academia), hold off on finalizing both writing and design until you've collected all the feedback. See what potential recipients of a fund-raising letter think of it; find out how teenagers react to a booklet for them; ask potential home buyers if the brochure addresses their interests.

The more important the piece, the more important it is to pretest it. Show it to sample members of your audience to get their reaction if you can; if not, show it to anyone whose opinion you respect before going forward. You (or the designer) can prepare a mock-up of your piece. Thanks to desktop publishing, it is now much simpler to prepare a sample for pretesting, and you can more easily make it look like the final product.

11. Design Approval/Corrections

Anyone who must approve the design should see it early on—it's better to get any feedback while it's relatively easy to make changes. Also show the piece to anyone whose opinion is important to you. Build in time for the designer to make adjustments based on the collective response.

12. Preparing the Type

Once the copy is finalized and the design is agreed upon, the words can be set into type. There are two ways to go here: either the type is "set" by a person working on a personal computer ("desktop publishing"), such as an IBM PC or an Apple Macintosh, or it is taken to a "traditional" typesetter.

Traditional typesetting

Specifying the type for a traditional typesetter requires a fair amount of technical skill, and is usually part of the designer's job. If you are not working with a designer and want your copy set into "real" type, call around to find a typesetter who can help you. You can bring in a sample page to show how you would like the type to look, and the typesetter can try to match it. A word of warning: typesetting can be very expensive

(hence the popularity of desktop publishing). Be sure to get cost estimates before work begins. Find out how much corrections and changes will come to *before* they are made; they'll be added on to the original estimate. See *Understanding Type*, page 201.

Desktop publishing

Now that type can be generated on the computer, the designer (whether professional or amateur) can "set the type" on the screen. This means that many type styles, sizes, weights, and column widths can be tried out quickly, easily, and inexpensively. The control is entirely in the hands of the person at the keyboard.

If you don't have desktop publishing equipment or skills "in-house," you can hire it out. Look under *Desktop Publishing* in the Yellow Pages of your telephone book.

Desktop publishing does not provide as many choices of typefaces (fonts) as traditional typesetting, nor is it as sharp. But for many kinds of publications, it looks just fine. See *Desktop Publishing*, page 281.

13. Proofreading (Type)

Once the type has been set (whether traditionally or on a desktop system), get it proofread by someone other than the person who produced it. The purpose of this proofing is to compare the typeset copy with the final written version that was given to the typesetter. It should be set exactly as it was given.

Corrections are to be made at this stage; not *changes*. But that is in an ideal world. Changes are often made on the typeset type, and this is expensive. These changes traditionally cause friction between the writer and the designer. The writer wants to get it right, the designer wants to get it done.

Having been in both roles, I can understand both points of view, and both are valid. Seeing the words in type often triggers the writer's ideas for how to improve them. But making changes at this stage is a royal pain for the designer—it can mean reworking the entire piece. A cooperative attitude and a better understanding of each other's position helps. The writer can try to keep the changes to an absolute minimum; the designer can try to be tolerant of the changes. Another warning: writers' changes increase design and typesetting time. Find out what these changes will do to your schedule and the budget.

14. Paste-up and Checking

Printed pieces with traditionally typeset type need to be pasted-up. Some jobs that are produced via desktop publishing can often be handed to the printer as is (this is becoming more and more the case); others may need to be placed on boards (See *Preparation for Printing*, page 307). It's a good idea to ask your printer how he or she would like the job made ready for printing. Different printers prefer different ways. If you are unclear about the answer, ask to see an example.

Have someone else (in addition to the person who does the paste-up) double-check the camera-ready boards (described in *Preparation for Printing*, page 307). What you turn over to the printer now must be perfect. Changes after this point are expensive.

15. Printing

"Printing" can happen in a number of different ways. You can copy your piece on the office copier, or get it copied at a commercial copy shop. You can take it to a place that does "quick" offset printing, or to a "regular" printer if it is a special or more elaborate job. The cost goes up accordingly.

Pieces that go to a regular printer usually require a "blueline" check. A blueline is a sample of your piece. It shows exactly how it will look when printed, minus color and correct paper. The printer prepares the blueline on photo-sensitive paper (usually blue on white, hence "blueline"). If you're checking a blueline, look for any variations from the boards that you gave to the printer. You may also need to check a color key if the piece has more than one color.

For big jobs, a *press check* may also be necessary. This involves going to the printer's shop to look at samples of the piece as it comes off the press. At this stage you're checking only the most basic things, such as the stock, the color, and the ink coverage. (Sidebar 77 has a blueline checklist; Sidebar 76 has one for a press-check.)

16. Distribution

Distribution is usually the last step of the print production process. If your printed piece is to accomplish the goals you have set for it, it must get into the hands of your intended audience.

If the job is small enough, you can pick it up from the printer yourself. Be sure to ask how many boxes are involved—there can be more than you might expect, and they can be heavy. Or you may want your printed piece delivered to a mailing house to be distributed, or delivered to your office, or delivered partly to your office and partly to "storage."

And by the way, congratulations. Getting a printed piece through all these steps is no small task.

17. Evaluation

Many producers of printed materials do not know what impact their publication has had because there is no follow-up evaluation. Try to do some kind of follow-up on your piece. At the very least hold a debriefing meeting to get the impressions of those who produced it. A better method, of course, is to keep track of how many responses your printed piece brought in, how much enthusiasm it generated, and what your target audience thought of it. There is always something more to learn.

Chapter 5

People Involved in Producing Print

It's hard (if not impossible) to develop and produce printed materials all by yourself. At the very least the process takes two: you and the printer. But you also might perform sixteen of the seventeen steps outlined in Sidebar 6 on your own. Due to desktop publishing more and more people are now writing, designing, and "setting type"—tasks that were formerly done only by professionals.

At the other end of the spectrum, the development and production of a complex printed piece can require the attention and effort of fifty people or more. A new newsletter, for example, might involve many content experts, writers, and reviewers; several groups of people from the target audience for market testing; a creative team of an art director, designer, and photographer; and technical people to carry out production and distribution.

This chapter looks at the development of a printed piece from the project manager's perspective, the person responsible for making the piece happen. But whether you are performing just one of the roles, doing most of them yourself, or directing a cast of thousands, many of them outlined here have to be filled to get a printed piece produced.

If you're thinking of hiring help, it's not too soon to start looking. Finding good people takes time. To get help you need to know:

1. What the tasks are

2. How to find people with skills to do them

3. How to select the best people for the job

Let's look at each of these issues, one at a time.

The Tasks

Decide what tasks need to be accomplished to get your piece produced (it may help to look at the steps in Sidebar 6 and decide which ones are relevant to your project). One of the first decisions you'll need to make is how much of the work to take on yourself, and how much to delegate to others. This, of course, depends on your time, your budget, your skills, and your level of interest in the project.

Carefully think through the best use of your time, and be realistic about your capabilities before you commit yourself. I remember a project director arriving in the office one morning frazzled and exhausted. She'd been up all night trying to put together a simple brochure (with less than satisfying results). I have watched others eagerly start out on the writing or the

7 Possible Roles in Print Production

There are many different tasks in developing and producing printed materials, and the same person often takes on several of them. Define roles clearly to make the best use of your resources.

- Project director
- Marketing director
- Concept developers
- Content experts
- Writer
- Typist or word processor
- Editor
- Art director
- Designer
- Desktop publisher
- Illustrator
- Photographer
- Production Manager
- Typesetter
- Proofreader
- Paste-up person
- Printer
- Consultants
- Gopher
- Approvers
- Funders

design of a piece, only to discover how much skill and hard work is involved. It is not unusual for half-done projects to be turned over to someone else.

If your budget is limited, you may have no choice but to take on tasks you have neither the skills nor the interest in doing. If this is the case, be patient with yourself. It will just take you a little longer than you originally estimated.

Sometimes it appears that you have no choice about who will perform a certain task. There may already be an in-house writer, designer, printer, or other staff person intended to fill a certain role, even though you would prefer not to work with them. Finding competitive costs is often the best way around them. Get permission to go outside by getting estimates that show that the work can be done as quickly (or more quickly) and as inexpensively (or less expensively) outside. It often can. This route can circumvent head-on clashes over personalities and talent.

How to Find the People with Skills

The best way to find the people with the skills you need is through personal connections. People who are recommended to you may or may not work out (check more than one reference), but they usually are a better bet than those you hire cold.

To remind yourself of your connections, use your office Rolodex and your telephone list at home. Go through these names and ask yourself who has anything to do with producing print, or who might know someone who does. Then get on the phone. Help the person you are calling help you by describing:

- What the job is
- The kind of individual you are looking for
- How long you expect it to take
- What you can afford to pay them

You can also use business and social occasions to ask for referrals (it can be a worthwhile topic of conversation in an otherwise unproductive or boring situation.)

If your network fails, you may want to look into public relations firms or ad agencies (it's also good to get a recommendation for one of these if you can). Professional organizations are another good source for names of both individuals and agencies. Or you can try calling the production department of a local newspaper and ask for referrals, or the English or art department of a local school (college level or higher). Or try the Yellow Pages, and ask the people you call for references.

The Best Person for the Job

Some people consistently seem to choose the wrong person for the job. Others consistently choose the right one. The "right one" very often has three outstanding features: talent, conscientiousness, and compatibility (summarized in Sidebar 9, page 49).

Talent can be shown in portfolios or writing samples (do you want your piece to look or sound like what you see?) Experience does a lot to improve talent—does this person have it?

Conscientiousness is important in print production because there are so many details. The ability to anticipate problems ahead of time is valuable; so is the ability to follow through. You also want to work with people you can trust.

Compatibility is another important quality. If you sense friction, working together could be difficult and unpleasant, no matter how talented or conscientious the person is. Notice your comfort level with each candidate.

Weigh these three components carefully, then make your choice. Select the very best people you can. Once you choose them, stand behind them 100%. (See *Making a Writing Assignment*, Sidebar 30; *Inter-*

viewing Graphic Designers, Sidebar 43; *Selecting a Graphic Designer*, Sidebar 44; and *Questions to Ask the Printer*, Sidebar 74.)

The People Who Make It Happen

There are many roles you may need to fill to get your printed piece produced. There are no rules as to who does what. The same person may take on any of the different tasks, and roles frequently overlap. The production of each new printed piece will bring together a different team, even if it's just you and a different printer, or someone new to review your work. Here is a description of each of these roles, along with comments and suggestions related to each.

Project Director

I will refer to the person in charge of getting a printed piece produced as the *project director*. Let's assume it is you. It could be for your company, for your organization, or for yourself.

The project director's role includes both privileges and responsibilities. You get to make the decisions, and you also get the headaches. Ultimately, the praise or blame for the impact your printed piece makes—or doesn't make—belongs to you.

- When you are in the role of director, *direct*. Decide which of the tasks you can take on, and which ones others should do. It is your job to define and clarify each contributors' role.

- The production of a printed piece goes better if you have a plan (discussed in *Planning the Printed Piece*, page 27). As project director, you are responsible for developing it. Include others in the planning process as much as possible. There are several good reasons for doing so: It will promote better working relationships when everyone starts off together, and has a common understanding of

8 Building a Strong Print Team

The process of developing printed materials often requires the effort of several people. If you are responsible for an upcoming newsletter, brochure or other printed piece, the task of pulling the crew together is yours. Under your guidance contributotors can become a highly-efficient team that produces an outstanding product; one that everyone is happy and proud to be a part of. Here are some tips, suggestions, and observations to help make that happen.

- The attitude of the person coordinating the team has a lot to do with how it goes. A positive and enthusiastic approach works best.

- Take advantage of the honeymoon period at the beginning, when everyone is anxious to co-operate. Lay down the ground rules for working together, and build team spirit.

- Meet regularly, and clarify goals, tasks, budgets, and dates.

- It's the team leader's responsibility to make the most of each person's skills, knowledge, and experience, and to keep everyone headed in the same direction.

- Focus on the mutual benefits of creating a first-rate product, and keep the common goal out front.

- Respect each member of the team. Would you give your best if you felt the person in charge didn't respect you?

- Give team members the requisite authority that goes with responsibility.

- Take a cooperative problem-solving approach. Encourage team members to see things from others' perspectives. Reaching an agreement usually involves compromise.

- Minimize tensions: don't exclude anyone from making important decisions. Discourage jealousies and competition by reinforcing individual strengths.

- Don't get upset if you discover a non-contributor on your team. There usually is one. Just notice who it is this time, and don't make a fuss.

- Invest in your team and support it. Help each member look good, and honestly praise all members' efforts. If you come through for them, they'll come through for you.

what is to be achieved. Excluding people from being in on the planning can cause resentment, resulting in apathy or resistance or both; and the earlier that key players are involved, the more likely they are to buy in to the piece. And, with everyone involved early on, ideas tend to evolve faster, and problems surface sooner.

- Pay attention to the budget. This means always keeping the bottom line in mind, and staying on top of estimates and expenses. Let others help you by being responsible for their part of the budget, but be sure to let them know what that amount is.

- Take responsibility for the schedule. Know what is happening with the piece at all times, and keep interested parties updated. It is up to you to keep the project moving along, and to get the piece out on time.

- Don't make assumptions. Don't assume, for example, that the writing won't need another round of editing (it often does); or that designers will also provide the illustration (they may or may not); or that printers will know what you want (they usually don't). Anticipate mistakes or delays before they happen, and see that every base is covered.

- Keep last-minute revisions to a minimum. They are expensive and universally disliked.

- It's your job to see that the piece passes by all the necessary people, and that they get their comments back on time.

- Finally, as project director, you can do a lot to keep working relationships positive. Good leadership makes the print production process enjoyable for everyone, and the result is often a better product. (See Sidebar 8, *Building a Strong Team*, and Sidebar 10, *How to Run a Good Meeting*.)

Marketing Director

The marketing director's job is to figure out the best way to "sell" your product, service, or event. It can also include how to position it in the market place, and how much to charge for it. Another responsibility is to match the product with the right target market. Pilot testing may be involved to help increase the appeal to the particular audience, and follow-up evaluation may be planned to determine its effectiveness. Marketing expertise may be applied to printed materials by a sophisticated professional marketing team (complete with MBAs and PhDs) to map out a full-scale campaign, or by just one person planning a simple self-promotional brochure. (Section 3: *Getting and Holding Attention*, pages 69–114, has more information about marketing.)

Concept Developers

Any number of people can contribute to the conceptualization of a printed piece. The project director, the writer, and the designer usually come up with the ideas, but the printer, colleagues, friends and relatives have also been known to have good ones. Don't underestimate anyone's potential. Although some people may naturally be more creative than others, a well-conducted brainstorming session can make use of everyone's imagination.

Content Experts

Content experts have the special knowledge that's needed for your printed piece. For example, content experts for a newsletter on financial planning might include many kinds of investment specialists; content experts for a brochure on building opportunities might include facilities planners, city officials, and real estate brokers; a flyer with tips on household safety for toddlers could utilize the expertise of pediatricians and early-childhood educators. Often the same person directing the print project is also the content expert.

Writer

The roles of project director and writer are the two that are probably most often combined. If you are writing the piece, don't be intimidated. Writing for printed materials is different from writing high school English papers or novels. Section 4: *Writing For Printed Materials*, pages 115–170, will give you lots of how-to tips and ideas.

Word Processor or Typist

As more and more writers work directly on computers, they often do the typing, word-processing, or data-entry themselves. But sometimes a person fills only this role. When this is the case, the task is often tiring and thankless. The writing may be difficult to follow, highly-detailed or technical, or include lots of charts, graphs, or numbers. Be sure to include this person in the team if you can, and acknowledge the contribution he or she makes.

Editor

The editor's job is to see that the writing of a printed piece communicates the information as well as possible. If you don't use a professional editor, ask someone good at written expression to edit your piece. If you have more than one reviewer, you might ask each one to focus on something different. For example, one editor might just pay attention to mechanics (grammar, spelling, punctuation, and so on); another might concentrate on making sure the message is clear, and offer suggestions for strengthening it. But the ultimate responsibility is the writer's.

Art Director

Art directors (or *creative directors*) help develop the concept and promotion strategy for a printed piece. They develop the "look" of the piece (many art directors are also experienced designers). Art directors usually coordinate and supervise the work of a designer, an illustrator, a photographer, and others, either on staff or sub-contracted, and often serve as a liaison between "the talent" and the project director. Sometimes the art director also has responsibility for the overall production schedule and for the budget.

Graphic Designer

Graphic designers are also called *graphic artists* and *commercial artists*. They have the responsibility for making sure the printed piece simultaneously looks good and communicates effectively. The designer usually works directly with either the project director or the art director. The job typically includes the layout of the piece and specifications for the type, ink colors, paper, and the size. The graphic designer often hires and works with a photographer or illustrator. He or she also usually selects the printer and oversees all aspects of production from beginning to end. A designer's training typically includes an undergraduate degree in design and additional classes in special areas of interest, such as illustration or desktop publishing. Some hold a master of fine arts degree (MFA) in graphic design as well.

Desktop Publisher

The newest role in the development and production of printed materials is *desktop publisher*. These people offer a wide variety of services. Some are freelancers with basic desktop publishing equipment (a computer, page layout software, and a laser printer), technical expertise, and a few classes in design. Other desktop publishers more closely resemble ad agencies and offer a full range of services, including expert design, copy writing, and marketing advice. Many provide computer-generated images as well (for more on this subject read *Desktop Publishing*, page 281). Ask to see examples of the desktop publisher's work. Find out what his or her particular strengths are to see if they match your needs.

Illustrator

If you want first-rate illustrations for your printed piece, go to a professional. The best illustrators are the ones who draw for a living. One very good drawing will strengthen your piece more than many mediocre ones. Resist the urge to use drawings done by friends, colleagues, or relatives unless they are really high caliber.

Clip art (booklets of copyright-free drawings anyone can use) is available for tight budgets. You can find clip art in bookstores and art supply shops. There is also a computer software version of clip art, usually available where software is sold.

The choice of images is getting bigger and better all the time. Be discriminating in your choice of these illustrations. There is a wide range of quality.

Photographer

Nothing conveys a message better than a strong photograph. The better you can describe what you want your picture to communicate, the more it helps the photographer give you what you want. Photographs can be expensive to have taken and get reproduced. They require that the printer do special camera work to prepare them for the press (black and white photos cost considerably less to reproduce than color). Like illustrators, photographers can be found at every ability level and in every price range. An alternative to hiring a photographer to take original pictures is to use stock photographs (described on pages 255–256).

Production Manager

The production manager's job includes a wide variety of tasks, most of which involve some degree of technical detail. This person negotiates prices with subcontractors and vendors, oversees typesetting and printing, keeps schedules, acts as coordinator or liaison among others working on the project, and works as a troubleshooter. The art director or designer fills this role when there is no production manager.

Typesetter

Typesetting is a highly-skilled craft. The best-looking type is set by an experienced typesetter on highly-sophisticated equipment. It gives the typesetter complete control over the look of the type. Better and better typesetting programs and output devices are rapidly becoming more available to the non-professional, but even these take practice and experience to use to full effect. So if you want a top-of-the-line typesetting job, get it set by someone who knows how to do it.

When you go to a pro, you will need to specify the type you want from the typesetter's book. You may

Getting Good Help　　9

No matter what the trade or profession, about 20% of the people are excellent, 20% are awful, and the rest fall somewhere in between. It takes more than ability alone to be good at a job. Here are three qualities to look for when you need help. You may not be able to get them all, but there's no harm in trying.

Talent

Whether you are hiring a writer, designer, illustrator, proofreader, or printer, look for real skill at the task you need performed (ability in other areas is not relevant). Natural talent that has been developed and refined by hands-on experience is best. Study samples of a candidate's work carefully.

Conscientiousness

Producing print involves a lot of detail. Conscientiousness counts. If people don't have it, their share of the work will fall on others (most likely you). Look for someone who can take on responsibility and is willing to do so—the kind of person who anticipates problems and solves them ahead of time. Choose people who can follow through on their own.

Compatibility

There are enough stresses and strains in this world without adding people who create tension. It is easier to get a job done with people with whom you are compatible. It is also more efficient, because you're free to concentrate on the job instead of the personality. Ask yourself how it would feel to work with each candidate. The answer has as much to do with productivity as it does with personal comfort.

also need to *mark up* your copy—that is, write the typesetter's instructions on it. If you don't know how to specify type, you will need the help of a designer or typesetter. Or you might find an example of what you would like your type to look like, and the typesetter can try to match it.

When type is set the traditional way, you sometimes get *readers* (copies of the typeset type for proofreading) on long strips of paper called *galleys*. Copies of these *readers* may be dummied into page layouts. *Repro* copy made from corrected galleys must then be *pasted-up* in its proper position before going to the printer. Or the type may be delivered in the actual page layout.

Proofreader

Experienced print producers are almost fanatical about having their copy proofread—painful experience is once again the reason. Be sure to have your piece proofread by someone other than the writer. Your proofreader doesn't have to be a professional (although it's amazing what a professional proofreader finds), but he or she does have to have a meticulously sharp eye. A good proofreader will check over spelling, grammar, and punctuation. Proofreaders also need to double-check all numbers, watch for inconsistencies, look for broken type (characters that are not completely filled in), and notice if something is missing. Sidebars 35 and 36 are on proofreading.

Paste-up Person

Although pages set by a typesetter still need to be pasted up, those done on a desktop publishing system often don't need to be. Complete paste-up capability is evolving quickly in these systems, even for publications with tricky color registration. So the paste-up person's role is beginning to disappear (although it hasn't yet). Until the production of your piece is com-

pletely computerized—or in case the power fails—it's good to know what's involved.

The paste-up person's role includes pasting (or more often waxing) the type and other graphic elements correctly into position on *the boards* (usually heavy cardboard or *illustration board*), and writing the printers' instructions under the designer's supervision (if the task is not done by the same person). The boards are called *camera-ready* when they are pasted-up perfectly, ready to go to the printer. Sometimes the paste-up person is the graphic designer; sometimes the designer subcontracts this technical work to a *paste-up artist* (odd name—seems like a contradiction in terms).

Printer

The printer makes negatives from your camera-ready sheets or boards. He uses these negatives to make *plates*; the plates go on the press to create the image. He or she will also enlarge or reduce photographs or illustrations so that they fit into specified positions, and *strips* them into the negatives so that they will appear in the correct position on the printed piece. You will have the opportunity to check the work on a *blueline* (Sidebar 77 has a blueline checklist). When the piece is printed and the ink has dried, the printer will *trim* it (cut it to size), and have it collated, perforated, and folded or bound, according to your specifications. The job is then boxed and ready for delivery. (See *Printing*, page 319.)

Consultants

You can hire a consultant in any area of print production, such as writing, design, marketing, or direct mail. Consultants work by the hour, by the day, or by the project. With their advice you can increase the effectiveness of your publication. You can also save at least the amount of their fees by taking their advice on

How to Run a Good Meeting

A True Story: I was once on a two-day retreat with a team of specialists in the psychiatry department of a medical school. By late afternoon of the second day the meeting was still going nowhere. Talkers droned on and wandered off the subject, people doodled on yellow pads, did other work, or otherwise tuned out. Suddenly a woman appeared at an open door, looking for another meeting. She asked the lifeless faces staring at her: "Is this the meeting on Chronic Pain?" The question unleashed hysterical laughter, stunning the inquirer.

A poorly-run meeting is exhausting; a well-run meeting is a pleasure. Make your meetings efficient and productive. Participants will leave energized and satisfied that they've made good use of their time. Here are some tips for running good meetings:

- Prepare an agenda, and circulate it before the meeting.

- Include the time and place of the meeting, and your phone number.

- Ask participants to go over the agenda ahead of time, and to come to the meeting prepared.

- Build in time for updating, new ideas, and free flowing exchanges.

- Meet in a comfortable environment, and set a positive, *work-oriented* atmosphere.

- Ask someone to record the minutes (the job can rotate).

- Start on time, and get right down to business.

- Begin the meeting with the statement: "The purpose of this meeting is . . ."

- Encourage participation by asking for each person's opinion early.

- When discussion strays from the topic, say: "We're off the subject. It is . . ."

- Politely cut off dominating talkers. Don't look at them, and ask to hear from others.

- Break into subgroups for maximum participation; report back to the larger group.

- Stick to the agenda, stay tuned in, and end your meeting on time.

- Make sure participants know when they leave what actions will be taken, by when, and by whom.

- When it's your turn to lead, *lead.* All participants are counting on you to do so.

avoiding expensive mistakes. Hiring and working with a consultant is also a good way to broaden your own education. You can get specific questions answered, and learn in a brief time what otherwise might take you much longer.

If you hire a consultant, prepare ahead to make the best use of the time. Think through questions you want to ask, and collect the examples you want to show. You may want to invite others working on the piece to participate in the consultation.

Gophers

Producing printed materials often requires a lot of running around, so *gophers* are included in this list of roles you may need to fill. The leg work can involve errands like taking the copy back and forth to reviewers, approval people, and proofreaders; getting copies made; picking up supplies, samples, illustrations, scanned images, or *stats* (solid black reproductions called *line art,* such as a logo); and going back and forth to the typesetter, or the desktop publisher, and finally to the printer. The designer often does much of this, but it makes sense to use less skilled (and less expensive) people for these errands if you can.

Approval People

Other people who are involved with producing print are the ones who must approve the piece. This can include anyone from clients, co-producers, funders, co-sponsors, colleagues, to bosses, bosses' bosses, and bosses' bosses' bosses. Wherever you are in the hierarchy, think through carefully whose approval (or endorsement) you need (and want) *before* your printed piece goes to the printer. Overlooking someone can hold up the job, or cause problems later. Because each of these people comes to the piece from a different perspective, they can make valuable suggestions that add to the strength of the piece.

Chapter 6

Getting It Out on Time

When a printed piece is "late," it is often because of a lack of understanding at the outset of how much time is needed. Being able to accurately estimate how long your piece will take to produce will help you to get it out "on time."

To be honest, producing printed materials almost always takes longer than anyone wants it to. One reason is because you can't do it alone. When there are other people involved, you are dependent on them and their schedules. Another reason is because putting out a printed piece involves several steps and many details. Even the simplest flyer has to be thought through, written, typed and/or typeset, laid out, proofread, and reproduced. A complex catalog, newsletter, or booklet that has multiple writers, reviewers, a designer, a photographer or illustrator, and a printer require the time it takes for each person to carry out his or her task, and coordinate it with the others.

And for each additional person involved, there will be additional ideas for how the piece ought to be done, and increased possibilities for misunderstandings. If everyone makes just one mistake, which often happens, the whole production process is held up as each one is corrected. Starting off with a realistic estimate of how long your printed piece will take to produce saves you stress during production and embarrassment when it appears.

Dealing With People Who Don't Understand Why It Takes So Long

If you are producing a printed piece for yourself, you have to pay all the bills. But you're also the boss, so you must justify the schedule only to yourself. If you are working for others, they may not understand why it takes so long to produce.

Anyone who has been through the development and production of a printed piece—even once—has a very different picture of what's involved than someone who hasn't. And often the people who haven't are the ones holding the purse strings. At first they want to know why the piece will take so long; then they want to know what is impeding its progress, and after it's done they want to know why it wasn't out sooner. And they are often the first ones to notice the mistakes that were made because the process was rushed.

Print producers, like most people, usually want to please. They regularly turn themselves into pretzels trying to meet two chronically conflicting goals: turning out a good piece, and meeting the deadline. *Speed; Quality; Low Cost* . . . reads a sign in a print shop . . .*Choose Two.*

11 | Time Guzzlers

There are several circumstances that delay the delivery of the printed piece, and the same ones seem to happen over and over. Be prepared to deal with these regulars.

- Inexperience

- Poor planning

- An unrealistic time schedule

- Undependable or unconscientious people

- Waiting for funding

- An increase in the number of people who must review or approve the piece

- Indecision

- Ambivalence toward the printed piece

- Getting copyrights and permissions

- Anything legal

- Vacations or holidays

- Illness

- Family responsibilities

- Discovering another approval is needed late in the game

- Changing the writing after the design has been worked out

- Any other last minute changes

- Scheduling jobs during peak printing seasons (ask printers what theirs are)

If you are working with or for others who are unfamiliar with the print production process, here are some suggestions for dealing with them:

1. Think through a realistic schedule, so you yourself will be clear as to how much time is actually needed.

2. Explain your schedule as best you can *in the beginning*, and do not commit to a date you have serious doubts about meeting.

3. Build in some extra time for the inevitable surprise setback.

4. Provide all those concerned with regular and frequent updates, so they can follow the progress of the printed piece.

If your bosses, colleagues, or associates are too busy to listen to details, write up a *progress update memo*, date it, and send it to them. You might want to direct copies to everyone connected to the project. These memos can be very useful documents to have. Your update memos will:

- Help you as well as the others to stay on top of production

- Keep the lines of communication open

- Help avoid misunderstandings

- Protect you against someone saying later they weren't informed as to what was happening

- Act as a record and handy reminder of your experience, useful for future pieces

When any task starts taking longer than the time allotted on the original schedule, note it on your update right away, and state its implications for the delivery date. You may want to point out that the amount of time taken up by unscheduled delays (such

When You Need It "Yesterday"

12

You may need to produce a printed piece fast. Whether the rush reflects poor planning or sudden opportunity, now is the time to simplify the process *and work quickly, efficiently, and steadily. Here are some tips to help you get your piece out quickly without going too crazy:*

- Explain the rush situation to everyone involved, from the writer to the printer. Ask for their help and for ideas for how to turn the piece around quickly.

- Keep the number of people involved to a minimum.

- Those with responsibility for the piece now have to shift into high gear. Don't crab about it or pass on the blame; motivate, encourage, and cheer on instead.

- Offer compensation for extra work: comp time if you don't have money, or a promise of the next job; whatever deal you can make in exchange for speed.

- Define the goal of your piece more narrowly, or subdivide your target audience into smaller groups (just focus on older buyers now, for example).

- Limit the content. Less is often more in communication as well as design.

- Use uncomplicated, straightforward writing.

- Keep the design simple and the size standard.

- Use *good* clip art or graphic devices instead of new art or photographs (Sidebar 57).

- Limit yourself to one color or consider one ink on colored paper (Sidebar 52).

- Ask the printer if using an "in-house" paper would save time.

- Keep in mind the Zen expression: "Hasten slowly."

- Warning: If you are regularly rushing to meet deadlines, step back and reexamine the whole situation, including your approach and attitude. People will rally to a call for a rush job once in a while, but not when it's habitual.

as rewriting or last-minute changes) will extend the delivery date by whatever amount of time the delay takes.

Making A Schedule

Who makes and keeps the print production schedule? Typically it is the project director or graphic designer. It usually works best if one person takes on the task, and everyone involved knows who that person is.

The best thing you can do for yourself, for your piece, and for everyone else involved is to be realistic about the time the piece is likely to take to get produced. When you are making up a production schedule, put time on your side. You can never start too soon. The more time that is allowed for ideas to come up, evolve, and get perfected, the stronger your piece will be.

The first thing you need to plan your schedule is a stretch of unbroken time, when you can think without interruption and concentrate on each step. Developing a schedule is too important a task to do piecemeal—that makes it both difficult and risky. Once your timeline is out, other people will be basing their schedules on it, and count on you to maintain it. So wait until you've got a good block of time to think through the schedule. Figure out the questions you need to get answers to, such as when people are

13

Week-by-Week Schedule

Here is a sample week-by-week schedule. It is for a team at a government agency putting out a brochure on women and drug abuse. There is a blank week-by-week schedule on page 350 to use for your own timeline (it can be used again for subsequent updates).

The Piece:	Brochure on Women and Drug Abuse	Date: *1/4/95*
Week of	**Action to be taken**	**By whom**
March 20	Plan brainstorming session to generate ideas	Hilary
	Set time, place, date; notify everyone	Hilary
	Get cost estimates	Hilary
27	Conduct brainstorming session	Jill
	Research and writing	Leah
April 3	Confirm dates; finalize schedule	Hilary
10	Circulate draft to all reviewers	Leah
	Prepare designs with copy for focus group	Allegra
17	Pretest piece	Gita
	Integrate all comments into final writing	Leah
24	Final editing	Chelsea
	Begin design	Allegra
	Begin photography	Erin
	Final copy approval	Hilary
May 1	Present design sketches	Allegra
(and so on)		

available to work, and how long the printing will take. Then write up your schedule so others can read it.

The easiest point to build in time is at the beginning, when everyone involved is most flexible, and dates seem less pressing. It becomes harder and harder to make changes the closer you come to the delivery date. Contributors' tasks are interwoven and interdependent, and they probably have commitments beyond your piece. Furthermore, once a delivery date has been announced, there is pressure to maintain it. In spite of the relief an extended delivery date may bring, it can mean the loss of momentum and morale. Develop a workable schedule in the first place.

The Week-by-Week Schedule

One way to develop a schedule for your printed piece is shown in Sidebar 13. Here's how it works: list all the dates from today until you want your piece finished, in increments of a week, using Monday dates. Put them on the left, each on their own line. Then write out what actions need to be taken, and by whom, next to the week in which they are to happen.

For example, let's say a team of women at a government agency is putting out a booklet on women and drug abuse. The project director is Hilary, Leah is the writer, Chelsea is the editor, Allegra is the designer, Erin is the photographer, Jill is holding a brainstorming session, and Gita is conducting a focus group to pretest the piece. Their schedule might look like Sidebar 13, at left.

The Backwards Schedule

Another good way to develop a schedule for your printed piece is to start backwards, as shown in Sidebar 14. Begin with the date you would like to have your piece in the hands of your audience, and estimate the time each step will take, from the last to the first. That will tell you when you need to begin working.

Let's say, for example, you want a booklet out on September 14. The post office tells you that the mailing will take 4 days, so you want to get it to the post office by September 11, or earlier, depending on when Sunday falls. The printer says printing will take ten working days, which includes time for camera work, printing, drying, and binding. Accounting for weekends and Labor Day, that means your job needs to be at the print shop on August 23. So the work needs to be checked and ready by then.

The designer tells you she needs three weeks for the design, a week to do the paste-up, and a week for typesetting and proofreading. That means she should start designing no later than July 26, and the photographer or the illustrator will begin work shortly thereafter. The copy should be finished as close to this date as possible.

The writer says he'd like a month for research and writing, and he recommends two weeks for the rounds of reviewing, approvals, editing, and proofreading. So the writing must begin six weeks earlier than July 26, which is June 14. You want another two weeks for brainstorming, planning, and gathering estimates, and time to interview members of your target audience. So work on the booklet that you want delivered on September 14 should begin on May 31. If you want to do some research and pretesting, add two weeks for that, and one for making the writing and design adjustments. That brings you to a starting date of May 17. And it's already June 25? You have five choices:

1. Move the delivery date

2. Make the booklet simpler or shorter

3. Find people who *really can* do it faster

4. Spend the next 14 weeks pressuring everybody, including yourself

5. Some combination of the above

14

Backwards Schedule

With this schedule, you start by filling in the date you want your printed piece in the hands of the target audience. Then, by estimating how long each step will take, you fill in the rest of the dates. There is a worksheet version of the backwards schedule on page 351.

The Piece: *Promotion Brochure*

Goal	Time required	Target date
In reader's hands		September 14
Distribution	4 days	September 10
Printing	10 working days	August 23
Proofreading, resetting, check	3 days	August 20
Typesetting	2 days	August 16
Design, photography, illustration	3 weeks	July 26
Research, writing, data entry	4 weeks	June 28
Production schedule, hire help	1 week	June 21
Time and cost estimates	1 week	June 14
Writing and design adjustment	1 week	June 7
Market research and pretesting	2 weeks	May 24
Concept development	1 week	May 17

Timing the Arrival of Your Piece to Advantage

15

Clever timing of the arrival of your printed piece can enhance its success. When you plan your launch date, pay attention to what else might be going on in the lives of your target audience. Coordinating your publication with other events and activities will make it more relevant and more welcomed. Here are some examples.

Can You Tie Your Piece Into a Season?

For winter:
Promoting services such as travel planning, counseling, or winter sports

For spring:
Things relating to houses, gardens, or financial planning services (April 15th)

For summer:
Products or services related to outside activities, beaches, parks, and so on

For fall or the New Year:
Anything that helps people get going and start fresh, like classes or new programs

Can You Tie It Into an Upcoming Event?

To reinforce products or services related to fitness, skill, strength, health, or patriotism:
The winter or summer Olympics

To display flyers or posters:
Fairs, carnivals, and parades

Around the annual Academy Awards:
A message related to entertaining, beauty, glamour, or theater

Can You Tie Your Piece Into An Upcoming Holiday?

For predominantly ethnic populations:
- St. Patrick's Day
- Columbus Day
- Cinco de Mayo
- Martin Luther King's birthday
- Chinese New Year
- Bastille Day
- Rosh Hashanah
- Canada Day

For anything related to the heart or for a young audience:
- Valentine's Day

For issues of government or political interest:
- Patriot's Day
- Fourth of July
- Veteran's Day
- Flag Day
- Lincoln's birthday
- Washington's birthday

For child-related goods or services
- Mother's or Father's Day
- Christmas or Hanukkah
- Halloween
- Beginning of school

Twelve to sixteen weeks, by the way, is a realistic amount of time to develop and produce a booklet (depending, of course, on its length and complexity). The point of taking you through the production of this booklet step-by-step is not only to show you how to do it, but also to underscore how quickly the time gets eaten up. You may want to begin work on your piece earlier than you had imagined.

The Backwards Schedule for a promotion brochure (Sidebar 14) will help you estimate the time it will take to produce your printed piece—it is set up with the steps in reverse order. There is a worksheet on page 351, or develop your own versions.

Reading the schedule from bottom to top will quickly remind you of the tasks involved. If you are pretesting and evaluating your piece, don't forget to add on additional time for these steps.

Experienced print producers can estimate the time their piece requires pretty close to the mark, and the only way to be an experienced print producer is to produce print. Each time you plan a print production schedule, it will be easier to do, and more accurate.

A Miscellaneous Tip

When you are asked when your piece will be out, give as broad an answer as circumstances will permit. Say, for example, the piece will be out "in January" instead of January 1"; "in Summer" instead of "July"; or "later this year" instead of "Fall." That way, your piece might even come out "early."

Chapter 7

Watching Your Money

The planning session is lively and fun. People are saying things like: "This piece is *very* important. It has *got* to be spectacular. We want to knock 'em dead. *Really* make an impression. *Good* design. *Good* quality paper. *Good* color . . ." Then someone asks the question that stops the conversation cold. "How much is this going to cost?"

Whether this conversation takes place in a conference room or in your own head, the issue of cost must be dealt with sooner or later. Producing printed pieces can be expensive. Before going very far with the development of your piece, it's wise to take a close look at your budget, and find out how far it will go.

Past experience may give you some idea of what you might pay for a printed piece, but even when you do exactly the same piece in exactly the same quantity with exactly the same printer, prices have a way of changing, usually upwards. "Ball park" estimates can fall anywhere in the field, so they aren't necessarily helpful, especially if you're working with a tight budget. The most reliable way to find out what your printed piece will cost is to get concrete estimates from the people who know.

A printer is someone you'll need to hire; there may be others as well. To get a full picture of the costs involved in print production, decide who else you want to hire. Other costs include supplies and services. Sidebar 16 has a list of the possibilities.

Once you figure out what you will be paying for, start gathering cost estimates. Estimates take between two and five days; three bids for the same job are generally enough. You can usually pull most of the numbers together within a week. When you request cost estimates, ask for time estimates too.

When you ask people for estimates, be serious about using their services. Figuring out an estimate is time-consuming and hard work. Vendors and subcontractors understandably lose interest when you request them often without coming through with the job. Be sure to look at samples of each freelancer's or vendor's work. Ask for resumes and get and check references. For more on choosing a printing method and a printer, see *Printing*, page 319. Sidebars 43, 44, and 45 will help you choose a designer.

Coming Up With Specifications

In order to give you an accurate price, estimators need to know as much as possible about your piece and the work you would like them to do. But what if you aren't sure yet how many pages there will be, or what quantity you need, or how many colors you want?

16 The Cost of Producing Print: A Checklist

The cost of producing a printed piece often involves more than the printing and your time. You may also need to pay for some of the people, services, or supplies below. Use this list as a reminder of the possibilities.

People	Supplies and Services
☐ Ad agency or P.R. firm	☐ Graphic supplies
☐ Consultant	☐ Software
☐ Writer	☐ Photocopying
☐ Editor	☐ Stats
☐ Secretary	☐ Type
☐ Desktop publisher	☐ Laser or linotronic printing
☐ Art director	☐ Offset printing
☐ Designer	☐ Mailing lists
☐ Illustrator	☐ Mailing house
☐ Photographer	☐ Postage
☐ Typesetter	☐ Delivery
☐ Proofreader	☐ Distribution
☐ Paste-up person	☐ Storage

A worksheet version of this sidebar appears on page 349.

When you don't know, you guess. You have to start somewhere, and people don't always end up producing what they describe the first time around anyway. But come up with something as close as you can. (Detailed information on specifications is covered in *Basic Design Decisions*, page 185.) The closer your guess, the more accurate the estimate will be. As your piece comes into better focus, you can check back with estimators. They will tell you how changes from your original description will influence the price.

Be careful to give each estimator identical specifications so that the prices you get back are comparable. A mock-up of the piece you envision also aids in the communication.

Using the Estimating Forms

Sidebar 17 pulls together information the printer needs to give you an estimate for printing your piece. Sidebar 18 suggests information you may want to gather for each subcontractor (writer, designer, photographer, and so on) you are thinking of hiring. There are estimating forms for both printers and subcontractors to copy and fill in for your projects on pages 352 and 353, respectively. Sidebar 19, a budget checklist, can be used to remind you of what to include, and for adding up your costs.

Printing Estimates

You may want printing estimates for different versions of the same piece. For example, you may request quotes on different quantities, such as 1000, 2000, and 5000 (ask what increments affect price breaks); or for one color of ink and more than one; or for different qualities and weights of paper. Ask printing reps for recommendations—they are knowledgeable and can be very helpful. Use a different estimating form for each version, and identify them as "Version 1," "Version 2," and so on.

Different printers have different presses and equipment. Those who have presses that are most suited to your particular job will be able to print it for less than those who don't. This sometimes accounts for sizable variations in the prices quoted. If an estimate comes back that seems oddly low or oddly high, inquire about it. Ask for the accuracy to be checked if it seems low; ask what is pushing the cost up if it seems high.

By the way, printers can legally deliver 10% over or 10% under the quantity of a job you have requested, so ask them about their policy. If the number you need is critical, ask for a guarantee of that quantity.

Quick Printing

"Quick printing" shops often provide preprinted price sheets that let you do your own estimating. They also have samples of stock (paper) to choose from. One of these shops may be adequate for your job. These businesses are set up to do simple letterheads, business cards, flyers, invitations, brochures, etc; they are *not* set up to do complex pieces that require several colors or halftones (photographs).

For best results, be sure your piece is cleanly laid-out and deliver it with clearly-written instructions. Ask for good solid ink coverage, just as you would in any print shop. And by the way, "quick" printing shops can sometimes be as slow as others as they can get backed up, too. Get your piece in before the very last minute.

Photocopying

If you only need to produce a small quantity of a piece, the least expensive and easiest way to reproduce it may be to copy it. There are now sophisticated copiers in commercial copy shops that do an excellent job. You'll most likely be limited to black "ink," but many shops carry papers of different colors, weights, and textures, or allow you to supply your own. Ask a

---

Getting Estimates From Printers   **17**

Printers need the following information in order to give you a cost estimate for your printed piece. A worksheet version of this sidebar appears on page 352.

- Name

- Phone number

- Name of the piece

- Date

- Quantity

- Size

- Cover stock

- Inside stock

- Number of ink colors

- Number of bleeds

- Number of reverses

- Number of screens

- Number of halftones

- Kind of folding or binding

- Special instructions

- Delivery date requested

Descriptions of these terms are given throughout the book. Check the index for page references.

18 Getting Estimates from Subcontractors

You may need to hire a writer, an editor, a desktop publisher, an art director, a designer, a proofreader, an illustrator or a photographer. If so, it's a good idea to gather the following information on each candidate. Use the worksheet version on page 353 and keep them for future reference.

- Name

- Phone number

- Printed piece

- Date

- Job description

- Time needed

- Dates needed

- Opinion of work

- Person's strengths; weaknesses

- Action taken

- Hourly rate

- Estimated cost for job

- Estimated cost range

- Source of person's name

- References

- Overtime plan

shop employee to tell you about the choices and costs. For more on printing, see page 319.

Pay: By the Hour or By the Job

Printers usually quote a specific price for a job; freelancers charge either by the job or by the hour. I recommend that you request the cost of the entire job. What you really want to know is how much it will cost to get the job done, not what number someone puts next to their time.

Probably the most realistic kind of estimate includes a *range* of prices for the whole job—a certain price if this happens; so much if that happens; at the least it will cost this; at the most it will cost that.

Sometimes people get scared off when they hear an hourly rate that strikes them as high. But if the higher rate is quoted by a more experienced person, as it often is, the rate difference may be made up by more efficient work, with the job taking fewer hours to complete. The person with the lower rate can end up costing you more than the person with the higher rate. And you often get a better product from a more experienced person. Again be sure to ask for the *total range*.

Get the Agreement in Writing

Ask for estimates in writing. When you decide whom to hire, write up a contract or letter of agreement (unless the vendor or freelancer does this for you). Spell out:

- The work to be done

- The starting and completion dates

- The amount of money to be paid

- Payment arrangements

- Anything else needing specification

However informal or trusting your relationship, it is a good idea to have your agreement in writing. It keeps the relationship professional (always wise when work and money are involved). The contract or letter clarifies the understanding for both parties, and can help avoid difficulties later.

Common Budgetary Mistakes

"To be forewarned is to be forearmed" is a good slogan for producing print. There are many opportunities to make mistakes where the print budget is concerned, and mistakes with printed materials can be very expensive. Here are six of the most common problems that have budgetary implications, and suggestions for avoiding them:

1. No Budget Allowance Is Made for Changes

Almost all print producers will end up making *some* changes on their piece during production. They often feel guilty when they do, because they know it is slowing down the process, causing inconvenience to others, and costing more money. But changes are inevitable, even if they do cost time, inconvenience, and money. It may be more realistic (and healthier) to *plan on* making a certain amount of changes, and build in a fudge factor at the outset. When you do make changes (or request that they be made), find out what they will cost *in advance*. You can keep them to a minimum by working a little harder to get it right the first time.

2. Subcontractors Rack Up Additional Hours

Print producers sometimes get a bill for more than the estimate. Here's an example: A designer has estimated the cost of designing a logo for you, and presents you with a sketch. You collect opinions on it, and give it back to the designer to work on with the feed-back. Then someone gets another idea, and the designer works on that. New sketches go back and forth and back and forth, each time with suggestions to make it less symbolic and more realistic, or less realistic and more symbolic, or warmer or more elegant or fatter or thinner. Two months later the bill comes in, considerably higher than the original estimate. You call the designer. He tells you the estimate was based on thirty hours, and he has now worked sixty. This is a difficult moment.

Whose fault is it, and what do you do? The responsibility belongs to both of you. You have the responsibility to be clear as to how much money you will spend; he has the responsibility to let you know when he approaches the limit of his estimate. Fine. He didn't, so what do you do now? If the situation was anticipated in a letter of agreement, it's easy—you go with whatever it says. If not, work out a compromise, and learn from the experience.

You can avoid this difficulty by making it clear to whomever you're working with that he or she *must inform you before* coming to the end of the allotted time. Or if the job is turning out to be more time-consuming than anticipated when the estimate was made, the issue should be raised and the price renegotiated before additional charges are incurred. That way you can decide how to proceed before getting into a pickle. Express your budgetary concerns in the beginning, and agree *up front* how you will handle charges if the work goes beyond what is originally estimated.

3. Spending Money on the Wrong Piece

Don't put out printed pieces by rote. Take the time to think through where you'll get the biggest bang for your buck. It's easy to get sidetracked into putting the lion's share of the budget into relatively unimportant pieces. What is the most important message you want to get across? Who are the most important people to get it to? What piece can most likely do this best? Many a company, group, and individual inadvertently loses sight of these questions, and puts money into the same half-effective pieces over and over.

4. Penny Wise, Pound Foolish

Going with the lowest bidder is not always the smartest thing to do. Cost is one very important variable, but so is quality and reliability. A vendor who takes up an inordinate amount of your time, runs into continuous troubles, or turns out a poor product is no bargain.

5. Thinking Too Small

The budgetary implications for thinking too big are obvious, but thinking too small can also be a mistake. It's important to stay within your budget, but if your message doesn't get across, you've wasted your money, no matter how carefully you handled your dollars. Open-ended brainstorming is important in the beginning regardless of budget; you can cut back later. If you come up with something really exciting—which you're more likely to do when you allow yourself to imagine freely—you may be able to get the right people interested. I have been on many projects for which there is "absolutely no more money." Then the purse-string holder decides something is a good idea, and funds magically appear.

6. Investing Too Much in Promotion

Investing too little in print promotion is a common problem, but so is investing too much. This is an especially dangerous pitfall for entrepreneurs who love graphics. A typical scenario: a man and a woman starting a new business put thousands of dollars and months of effort into a slick brochure and a full-color poster. They become so involved with producing these pieces that time needed elsewhere in the business is lost. Don't misunderstand—good printed pieces definitely contribute to the success of any venture— but not if they deplete energy and funds critical to making an enterprise go.

Using 'Free' Help

Free or volunteer help is often a mixed blessing. It can save you money, but it also has its drawbacks. On the plus side, you may be lucky enough to find skilled, conscientious people to help you with your printed piece—someone (of any age) new to the field , for example, who is looking for an opportunity to break in. That person needs experience, contacts, and pieces for a portfolio, and may be willing to charge you nothing or a reduced fee in exchange for these things. Or a retired or home-centered person may want a change of environment or an interesting project to work on.

On the minus side, free or cut-rate help may be less dependable, less skilled, less experienced, and slower than paid help. Clearly explain the tasks to be done, along with your expectations. Then go with your intuition.

Joint Ventures

Is there someone who would be interested in collaborating with you on producing a piece? Finding a sponsor or co-sponsor for a printed piece can be a cost-saving and worthwhile partnership for both parties involved. You could share the message and the production costs, or the piece could be produced entirely by you and paid for (in part or in whole) by a sponsoring group in exchange for a credit line. If you can come up with a joint venture, you may end up paying half as much—or less—for your printed piece. It also might enable you to put out something twice the size, or to print something more elaborate, or of higher quality, or twice as many (which saves on the unit cost). Some organization may be happy to have you propose the idea.

Showing an interest in the community is good business. It is a common incentive for financial backing in exchange for recognition (often in the form of a credit line). For example, printed pieces for a health promotion program I worked on were sometimes produced jointly by a local television station. The connection may not always be obvious. In the case of the TV station, the belief was that "health sells."

Collaborators or sponsors are limited only by your imagination. A local real-estate company may be interested in co-sponsoring a brochure on housing in your community with an environmental group; some other local business may support a booklet put out by a service club or a social service organization. A county or state agency might want to co-sponsor a publication on computer education or consumer buying; or a consumer organization or a computer company may want to co-sponsor a piece on on-line information for seniors. An ad agency or design house may donate advice or time in exchange for credit. Combinations and possibilities are unlimited.

Sometimes the message can be shared. A landscape architect and a building contractor, for example, might team up to produce an ad for property improvement; a piece on teen suicide prevention could be produced jointly by a school district and a hospital.

Use your network to get a joint or sponsored project going. Think of people you know in business or industry or in service organizations. What ones might be natural collaborators? Who shares a similar interest in your topic or community? Or decide who you would like to work with, and figure out some common denominator.

When you come up with some good candidates, propose a *specific* printed piece to them. This makes the project more concrete, and gives them something real to respond to. Tune in to *their* priorities, and

Budget Checklist 19

Here is a list of expenses commonly incurred in the production of print. You probably won't have all of them, but check through the list to see which ones are relevant to your piece. A worksheet version is on page 349.

Expense	Cost
☐ Writer	$_____
☐ Editor	$_____
☐ Art Director	$_____
☐ Designer	$_____
☐ Desktop publishing	$_____
☐ Illustrator/photographer	$_____
☐ Typesetting	$_____
☐ Proofreading	$_____
☐ Secretarial/typing	$_____
☐ Pretesting/evaluation	$_____
☐ Software/supplies	$_____
☐ Copying/stats	$_____
☐ Paste-up	$_____
☐ Printing	$_____
☐ Mailing/postage/ distribution	$_____
☐ Delivery charges/ storage fees	$_____
☐ Staff time	$_____
☐ P.R. firm or ad agency	$_____
☐ Other	$_____
Total	$_____

20 Tips for Tight Budgets

Tight budgets are as common as the printed pieces they produce. Here are some tips to help you make the most of yours.

- Tell all the people you're working with that the budget is tight. Ask for their suggestions for keeping costs down.

- Give yourself plenty of time. Rush jobs cost more.

- Use your imagination to make up for what is lacking in funds (necessity *is* the mother of invention).

- Think where you might find good free or low-cost help or expertise (a local college, a service club, someone you know?). Offer non-monetary compensation.

- Take an expert to lunch—an hour's worth of a specialist's or consultant's advice may be well worth the price of a sandwich.

- Buy just a small amount of consulting time. It could save you from making expensive mistakes.

- Designers often charge a 10–20% mark-up to oversee printing. You could save this cost if you work with the printer yourself, and pay printing costs directly.

- Use line art (solid ink) rather than halftones (shades of gray, as in photographs or watercolors). They are considerably less expensive to reproduce.

- Don't spend money on a second color unless that color *really* enhances your piece.

- If you want a particular look, ask a designer or printer if there is a way you can get it inexpensively.

motivate them by demonstrating how they will benefit from the co-production. Figure out ahead how much you want them to invest and what you want them to do—they will ask. Offer examples of others who have teamed up before if you can.

Once you are working with a co-sponsoring organization, be sure to show them the copy and design of the piece before it goes to the printer. And double-check to make sure that any credit lines read *exactly* the way sponsors want them to.

The first and foremost advantage of joint venturing in print is cost savings. There is also the potential for producing a stronger, more convincing, and more interesting piece. One disadvantage is that producing a piece jointly can be time-consuming—the more people involved, the more complicated it can get, and the longer it can take to produce. Another disadvantage is that the goals of the joint venturers can turn out to be different, which can raise conflicts and end up muddling your message.

Collaborations go better when problems are anticipated in advance, and each collaborator is sensitive to the other's needs. To work, the joint venture has to be a win/win arrangement for both parties. You'll have to decide on the basis of your goals, your budget, your time, your energy, and your intuition whether or not producing a piece jointly will put you out ahead.

Keeping Track of Your Project

It's worthwhile to set up a budget and production notebook. A three-ring binder works well for keeping forms for estimates, costs, and other information related to the job. Others can get caught up on the project by reading it, and the notebook will be useful in the future. A year from now you may want to know how many pieces you produced, what you paid for them, what paper you used, and who worked on the project. You'll be glad you kept a record.

Getting and Holding Attention

3

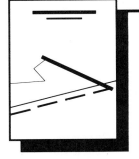

Chapter 8

Tailoring the Piece to Your Audience

Let's say there are four letters waiting for you when you get home, all without a return address. The first letter is addressed to "resident"; the second shows your name printed on an address label; the third has your name typed directly on to the envelope; and the fourth has your name handwritten on it. Which letter are you happiest to see? Chances are you'll be most interested in the one that's handwritten.

Or let's say there are two memos sitting on your desk. You're swamped and have time to read only one. The first memo mentions a project that you are already familiar with; the second one mentions one you've never heard of. Which one do you read? Probably the one with the familiar project.

I'm not suggesting that you address all your printed pieces by hand or produce publications only on topics with which readers are already familiar. But I *am* saying that people are naturally more interested in what relates to them personally. We also prefer what is familiar, because we're more comfortable with the known than the unknown.

So a very powerful way to get and hold the attention of your audience is to tailor your piece specifically to them. When you find a way to relate your product or service directly to your readers, they'll be more interested in it. The better you know your audience, the more powerfully you'll be able to persuade them in print.

The Trend Toward Customization

The trend in marketing these days is toward a more personalized approach—you start noticing it everywhere once you're aware of it. Career counselors recommend individually tailoring resumes to each job you apply for. A major university known for its successful fund-raising campaigns uses different letterheads for different givers: the expensive paper with the embossed design goes to the big donors, copier-grade paper to students, and something in-between for everyone else.

Some mail-order businesses send out several catalogs instead of one, each aimed at a different subgroup. For example, L.L. Bean, the large mail-order business in Freeport, Maine, uses specialty catalogs to appeal to different customers. One is for women, for instance, one for home and camp, another for seasonal sports, and another for fly fishing.

National magazines carry regionally specific ads for different areas of the country. Companies that once invested heavily in nationwide mass marketing campaigns now pay greater attention to ethnic tastes

Tailoring printed pieces to specific target audiences increases interest in them, as these L.L. Bean catalogs demonstrate. One is more likely to be of interest than the others.

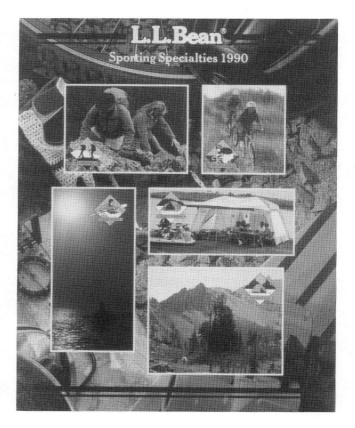

and regional preferences. One giant enterprise has decided to place recipes using its soup in local church bulletins. Why so much interest in tailoring? Because it works.

Madison Avenue or Main Street?

You may not be selling soup, but if you're producing print, you're selling something. If not a product, then perhaps a service, a point of view, or even yourself. It doesn't really matter what the content is, you're still trying to get someone's attention long enough to influence them. Whatever your printed piece is about, the more carefully it is tailored to your audience, the more attention it is likely to get.

Getting and holding the attention of your audience is imperative if you want your piece to have an impact on them. Without it, your effort to inform, persuade, and motivate is wasted. So how do you tailor a piece to your audience? By finding out what will appeal most to *them.*

This does not mean a brochure on counseling services or clean air or day care centers has to look like a Madison Avenue ad for a BMW. That Madison Avenue "look" is just a style, and they use it because they've found that it appeals to prospective BMW owners. That particular style may or may not be right for your audience. If you find out what appeals most to your readers, you can make your piece more attractive to them, whether the style is "Madison Avenue" or "Main Street." Madison Avenue, by the way, is working very hard to figure out what *you* like these days.

Following are twenty questions to help you tune-in to your audience. They include many suggestions and examples that relate to each. Sidebar 21 on page 77 summarizes an audience profile. A worksheet version of Sidebar 21 is on page 354 to fill in with a description of your audience. Let's go through each of the questions now, one by one.

Questions for Tailoring

1. Who Is Your Target Audience?

That is, for whom are you producing this printed piece? Simple enough question, but often not enough attention is paid to the answer. It is easier (and more fun) to develop a good printed piece when you're clear about the answer.

I worked with a group of professionals in a large government agency who do research on environmental hazards. It is their responsibility to communicate their findings, partly so local agencies can comply with the law, and partly so that people can avoid health risks. The agency has many constituencies (scientists, physicians, government officials, and the general public, among others), so they need to get the word out to a broad spectrum of people. The mission of this staff is particularly difficult because they deal with two complex areas: medicine and law. They know their printed pieces could serve their constituency better, but how?

This is a group of good thinkers and writers, but their message became greatly diluted when they addressed it "to everyone." It is not surprising that the staff was frustrated. It was extremely difficult to communicate effectively so long as they approached their audience as one monolithic whole. They needed to focus more closely on each constituent audience. Developing printed pieces for one specific audience at a time is more satisfying, and more successful.

The first step is to recognize the multiple audiences. The second step is to get an accurate picture of the people who make up each target group.

2. Are There More Men or Women?

If your audience is predominantly more male or female, you can feature an aspect of your product or service that will appeal to the dominant gender. If neither

males nor females predominate, consider doing two pieces: one that focuses on women's needs and interests; the other that centers on men's. For example, one clever author wrote a cookbook entitled *Food that Men Like* and then a sequel called *Food that Women Like*. She could have put all of the recipes into the same book and called it *Food that Everyone Likes*, but then which of the three cookbooks would be more interesting to you?

3. How Old Are They?

Different stages in our lives are accompanied by different interests. If your audience is made up of one dominant age group, you can capitalize on it. For example, if you're in real estate in the sun belt, many of your clients may be older retirees. What do older folks want most in a house? The answer to this question could become the basis of an angle for your printed piece, developed to appeal especially to them.

Or if you are advertising a parental stress hotline, what is most on the minds of stressed parents? It's probably something quite different from what's on their teenagers' minds. An effective ad for the teen stress hotline would be quite different from the one for the parents' hotline.

4. Where Do They Live?

Can your audience's living environment provide a way to make your printed piece more appealing to them? Say you're promoting a landscaping service. What are the most popular plants in your client's area? Could you give free tips on their care and maintenance as part of your promotion?

Or say you're part of the U.S. Geological Survey on the West Coast, and earthquake preparedness week is coming up. You want to get people's attention to make them aware of what to do during an earthquake. One thing you might do is to put out a flyer with a map on one side, and information about earthquake safety on the other. The map could show locations shaded in the relative degrees of danger so that residents could see the likelihood of damage during a major quake. This would have a good chance of getting the attention of residents—who can resist looking for his or her house on the map?

5. What Is Their Income Level?

The income level of your audience may suggest where to put the emphasis of your appeal. Say you are a portrait photographer looking for clients. Many families would like portraits, but the amount they can spend on them varies. So you might develop different promotion campaigns to appeal to those in different income brackets.

For example, you could promote your low cost

This map shows relative earthquake danger in San Francisco. It would add interest to a printed piece for residents of that city.

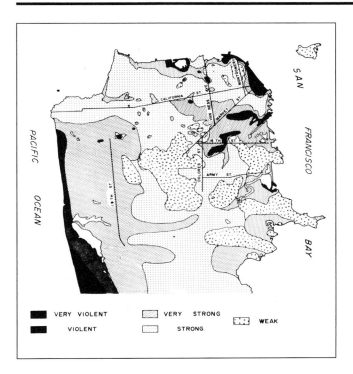

VERY VIOLENT   VERY STRONG   WEAK

VIOLENT   STRONG

version as a "Once in a Lifetime Portrait Package." For people who have more to spend, you might create a broad selection of packages such as "The Birthday Portrait Package," "The "Christmas Portrait Package," "The Graduation Portrait Package," or "The Grandparent Special." Anything that helps potential clients say *this is for me* will make your printed piece stronger.

6. What Is Their Education Level?

How well-educated your audience is could have implications for the vocabulary you use, the length of the sentences you write, and how much illustration you include (pictures are especially helpful in explaining messages to low literacy groups). If, for example, you're targeting people with very little education, take extra care to make your message, your sentences, and your words *short.* But if you're aiming at teachers, for instance (who read a lot), you might say more.

The education level of your audience should however have nothing to do with the *tone* of the piece. Respect the intelligence of *all* your readers, regardless of how much time they've spent in school.

7. What Is Their Knowledge Level?

Knowing your audience's knowledge or skill level in relation to your topic helps you to know where to begin, what to say, and how to say it. It's no use talking computers over the heads of your audience (or under, for that matter). You can't expect parents to stop giving their children aspirin if they are not aware of the danger involved. If your audience is made up of many different skill or ability levels, consider doing shorter, separate pieces aimed at different subgroups rather than a single piece for everyone.

8. How Are They Different?

The less you have in common with your audience, the more careful you must be not to make assumptions. We were doing a low-budget book for Hispanic women, for example, and we needed some inexpensive art. So we got a book of "clip art" (copyright-free illustrations anyone can use) containing attractive Pre-Columbian designs, which we planned to use throughout the book. To us these illustrations looked basically the same—abstract variations on plant and animal themes. We selected several based on their aesthetic appeal to us.

Just before the book went to press we asked the people for whom it was intended to have a look. It's a good thing we did. It turns out that the individual designs had very different connotations to our prospective readers—some positive, others negative. We realized none too soon who should have been select-

Although the folk art, right, may make one impression on you, it may make quite another on the people for whom it is intended.

ing the designs in the first place. Sample your audience's response *before* you send out your piece whenever you can. The less familiar you are with your audience, the more important their feedback is.

9. How Are These People Like You?

The more you have in common with your target audience, the more confident you can be that your piece will hit a responsive chord. If, for example, you're producing a piece that relates to babies, whether it is to promote a nationally available baby food, a day care center, or a line of handmade snowsuits, it helps if you've got one (a baby, that is), because you'll know parents' interests and concerns more intimately. But if you're promoting baby clothes or food or day care and you've never been around a baby, don't worry. Talking with people who have them will give you ideas for how to make the piece relate more personally to them.

10. What Is Their Attitude?

It is helpful to know your audience's attitude toward your topic. If your piece contains information that could be perceived as negative, threatening, or controversial in some way, you must present it carefully. Issues related to the law or to health (such as drug or alcohol abuse, child abuse, abortion or AIDS) can be especially sensitive. These pieces have to be serious and honest enough to make an impression, yet gentle and encouraging enough so that people will be willing to read them.

11. What Is Their Background?

What are the ethnic, religious or cultural traditions of the members of your audience? What events do they take part in? Do they go on big family picnics in the summer or on Labor Day? Will they be at a parade on Chinese New Year, Fourth of July, or Columbus Day? Will they be in front of the TV during football or baseball season? How can you tie your piece in to your audience's interests, festivities, and rituals?

Sometimes there are clues as to how to make your piece more interesting to your audience by focusing on their background (if they have one in common). You might concentrate on some aspect of their common religion, their inherited traditions, or their ethnicity. For example, all ethnic groups have roots to some set of ancient drawings, designs, or patterns— often very beautiful, and *copyright-free*. One example that comes to mind is the ancient Norse art of the Scandinavians. Other examples include the art of the Inuit Alaskans or the Mayan or American Indians, or the images of African tribes or the Pre-Roman British Islanders or the medieval Japanese. What early images relate to the people you serve?

12. What Are Their Values?

Do members of your target audience share a particular value or ethic—such as hard work, or education, or loyalty? These values could be connected with what you are promoting. For example, support for the family is an important value to some cultural groups. In such a case you might emphasize how your product or service benefits the family. Achievement is important to others, so your printed piece might show how your service or product could help those readers get ahead. Or perhaps your service or product reflects something else of importance to your audience. Pointing it out will make what you're offering especially appealing to them.

13. What Are Their Tastes?

Would your audience respond more favorably to a bold, dramatic message or to one that is understated? Would a serious approach work best, or one that is

*Using the kind of imagery
to which your audience is likely
to respond helps get their attention.*

Maternity
and Infant
Care Project

Audience Profile   21

With whom do you wish to communicate? The better you know your audience, the better able you are to do a piece that interests them. This list appears in a worksheet form on page 354.

1. General description

2. Predominantly male or female

3. Age

4. Living environment

5. Income level

6. Education level

7. Skill and knowledge level

8. How they are like you

9. How they are different from you

10. Attitude toward your service or product

11. Background

12. Values

13. Tastes

14. How leisure time is spent

15. What they read

16. Their uniqueness

17. When most likely to get their attention

18. Where most likely to get attention

19. Desired impression

20. Desired action

upbeat or lighthearted? Does a traditional or high-tech look fit them best? Is your audience the glitzy, glossy paper group, or more the textured paper types? Would brilliant jewel tones appeal most, or soft pastel colors, or subtle earth tones? Reflecting your audience's taste makes them more comfortable with your piece, whether it's ornate, streamlined, or punk.

14. How Do They Spend Their Time?

What does your audience do in their free time? Does this group like to tinker with cars? Play tennis? Use metal detectors? Ski? Garden? Bowl? Rent videos? Go on vacation? Is there some way you can make a connection between their favorite pastime and what you're promoting? Could your piece include related suggestions, schedules, or places? If you are promoting your financial counseling service, for example, you might point out that clients might feel more comfortable planning a vacation once they've got their finances under control.

15. What Do They Read?

Audiences are as diverse as the kinds of magazines that are published, and that includes quite a mix: everything from *Ladies Home Journal, Business Week, Mad, Yankee,* and *Scientific American,* to *Reader's Digest, MacUser, Archaeology, Seventeen,* and *People.*

Knowing what your audience likes to read gives you more insight into their preferences. It also clues you in to a writing style that is familiar to them.

16. What Makes The Group Unique?

Do members of your target audience share any unique common denominators? I once developed printed pieces for a beautiful city on the West Coast. Its beauty was a source of great pride to its residents. Whenever possible we included illustrations or photographs of local landmarks and vistas.

Are the people you are addressing particularly proud of anything in their community? Does it have an interesting history? A grand sports arena or some special event? Outstanding architecture? Fine educational institutions? A beautiful landscape or skyline? Any positive connections you can make between something that is unique to your audience and what you are promoting will strengthen your piece.

17. When Can You Get Attention?

What time of day? When during the week? When during the year? Printed materials often demand the thing we have least of—time. Would it be more effective to put out briefer messages during busier times of year, such as fall and December, and pieces with more content when things are slower, like in

If members of your target audience have culteral or ethnic roots in common, it could suggest imagery that is especially attractive to them.

January or the summer? (Sidebar 15 has more ideas.)

Can you find out what day the least amount of mail arrives in your audience's homes? Most of the mail comes to our house on Mondays and Tuesdays; the least on Fridays and Saturdays. If your printed piece arrives on a slower mail day, it has less competition for attention.

18. Where Will the Piece Be Read?

In an office? In the home? In a public place? Sometimes knowing where your printed piece will be read gives you ideas for how to develop it. For example, one audience I was working with said they were most likely to read printed materials in bed before they went to sleep. This gave me the idea that information for this group might be successfully packaged in a booklet with a subtitle like "The Bedside Reader," to suggest bedtime reading. It might also provide an opportunity to give more information than usual, as readers would be comfortably settled in bed with the booklet in their hands (it would have to be lively, though, so it wouldn't put them to sleep).

In contrast, information on a flyer or poster is best when it is brief, as readers are often on their way to somewhere else when they see it.

You may want to make a piece that will be read in an office more business-like. Pieces that go home can be more personal.

19. What Effect Will You Have?

You want your printed piece to have a positive effect, yes, but positive in what way? If you could make just one impression on your audience, what would it be? That you are dependable? Fast? Top quality? Cut rate? Efficient? Experienced? Journalists and the scientific community want up-to-the-minute information. Restaurant goers want the food to taste good. Everyone wants a reasonable price. To increase the odds of capturing the attention of your audience, find out what they want and see if you can offer it.

Answering these and similar questions with your audience in mind will give you a clearer picture of who it is you're communicating with. If you don't have enough answers, you'll know who to ask, and what to ask them.

20. What Do You Want Them to Do?

After reading your printed piece, what do you want people to *do* with it? Pass it on? Keep it for future reference? Throw it away? If you'd like your piece to be passed on to someone else, it's more likely to happen if you suggest it. Make your suggestion concrete (ask them to pass the piece on to a relative, for example, or to someone they know with such-and-such an interest). If you'd like readers to keep the piece, where would you like them to put it? In a

*These brochures all have
the same basic message, but they are
subtly customized to different audiences.*

*This booklet shows a photo of
a family together. It reflects an important
Latino value—appropriate for the audience.*

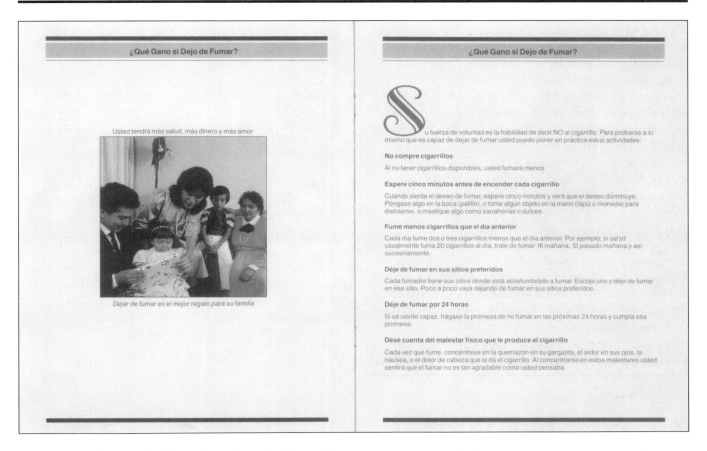

drawer? Desk? Bookshelf? Bulletin board? File cabinet? If you want your printed piece to stay around a while, imagine places where it could be kept, and make specific suggestions.

Audience Sensitivity

It is important to guard against stereotyping. Every group has its own set of cliched images, and they are often offensive to group members, even if they don't seem so to you. Or the images may be outdated, or they just plain don't fit. Go through your piece with your reader's eye, and don't make assumptions.

I once worked on a project that was aimed at two different communities simultaneously. One was thought of as a "cow town," the other was viewed as more sophisticated. There was an assumption that printed materials we developed would reflect these differences. This attitude made me uncomfortable, and I wanted to find out just how different or similar the communities were in relation to the medium of print. So I went to several bookstores in both communities to find out what books were selling best. To everyone's surprise (including mine) people in both communities were reading *exactly* the same books. We made sure there were no "cow town/up town" differences in our printed pieces.

Information in these brochures might have come in a single booklet, but divided into more specific components, they have a better chance of getting attention.

It is also dangerous to make assumptions about peoples' tastes. They are often better (or at least different) than you might assume. Tastes usually reflect where people want to go, not where they are. For example, readers often buy magazines that show lifestyles one step ahead of where they perceive themselves to be. They are more inclined to buy magazines that show the lifestyles to which they aspire rather than the ones they are currently living. Your piece will be more effective if it mirrors your readers' aspirations rather than their reality.

Broad Audiences

I have often been asked about producing one set of materials for a wide range of people. My answer is usually short: do it only if you have to. As with bathrobes, "one size fits all" usually doesn't fit anyone very well. But I also recognize that there are times when you absolutely *must* develop a printed piece for a broad audience and there are simply no realistic alternatives. When this is the case, try asking yourself the following questions:

- Are there predominant types of people in your audience? Can the piece be tailored to them rather than to "everyone"?

- Are there certain people you want to get your message? Does it make sense to focus just on them?

- Can you divide the information up into a series of pieces, send them out sequentially, over time, and target each one primarily to a different sub-group?

- Can you segment your audience *within* the piece, so that people can read just the parts that are relevant to them?

Anything you can do to give your printed piece a distinctive character will help to make it more ap-

pealing. And one of the best ways to give it a distinctive character is to reflect the unique nature of your particular audience. If you do this creatively, your printed piece might just be irresistible.

Chapter 9

Ideas to Make Your Piece More Interesting

As described in the preceding chapter, your printed piece is more likely to get the attention of your audience if you tailor it to them. And like the cherry in the lemonade, it will get even *more* attention if something extra is added to it to make it more appealing. This "value added" something will give your printed piece the edge it needs to compete in today's print environment.

Here are twelve ways to give your printed piece that something extra, along with examples and suggestions for each. They are summarized in Sidebar 23 on page 93 of this chapter.

• Make Your Piece Useful

A printed piece you can *use* as opposed to "just read" will make it more attractive. Tune in to your audience's interests, and figure out a way to tie those interests in to the printed piece in your product or service.

For example, you might include a calendar or a schedule that is of interest to your particular audience. It could be printed as a part of the piece, or go along with it. Perhaps they would be interested in playing dates of a major league ball team, or the schedule for a local little league. Or you might include dates of upcoming computer shows, or your school district calendar. Or perhaps your audience would be interested in theaters or other attractions. Any calendar or schedule that is relevant to your constituency will help attract attention to your piece.

Another way to make your piece useful is to accompany it with tips, advice, or ideas related to the subject you are promoting. For instance I know a woman who owns a chic clothing store. She puts out a very simple handwritten newsletter, usually in sophisticated color combinations (for newsletters anyway) like mauve and gray. She offers tips on the season's fashion trends and hints for updating a wardrobe. Her newsletter is an effective blend of useful information and advertising.

I notice at this very moment that I am writing with a pencil I got from a contractor last year. On it it says "Stevo Smith Carpentry Services" along with his phone number. Turns out I do need some carpentry work done this year. Stevo's pencil stayed around. It is useful, and now it's convenient, because there's his phone number. I'll be giving him a call.

Pencils with names and phone numbers might seem obvious, but pencils with a less common communique may be less so. One year for Christmas I gave my brother some pencils that said "Write Your Sister." You can print any message that is relevant to your organization or business on a pencil.

22 Advertising Specialties

Imaginative use of "advertising specialties" or "business gifts" capture attention and please your recipients. Ordered in large quantities, unit costs can be surprisingly low. Here are some of the kinds of pieces you might have imprinted with your message.

- Napkins
- Balloons
- Pencils
- Decals
- Post-Its
- T-Shirts
- Awards
- Headbands
- Calendars
- Frisbees
- Styrofoam cups
- Shoe laces
- Key tags
- Luggage tags
- Wrist bands
- Rulers
- Balls
- Visors
- Towels
- Tote bags
- Belt buckles
- Glasses

- Hats
- Pins
- Magnets
- Emblems
- Pencils
- Shopping bags
- Mugs
- Bumper stickers
- Buttons
- Yard sticks
- Appliques
- Letter openers
- Pens
- Emblems
- Markers
- Badges
- Playing cards
- Paperweights
- Socks
- Caps
- Ties
- Scarves

The simple handwritten newsletter, below, successfully blends information and advertising. Scarf tips are on the back.

A piece doesn't have to be expensive to be useful. Let's say that bicycle theft is rampant and the police are cracking down. They need a printed piece to get the word out quickly and effectively on a very limited budget. During a brainstorming session officers make lists of who has bikes, where bike-owners tend to be, and what they do. They think: Most bike riders are in school . . . kids in school ara using books . . . books need . . . bookmarks!

The group boils their message down to three strong points and a phone number, and gets thousands of bookmarks printed up. With black ink on a brightly-colored card-weight paper and six bookmarks to a sheet, they are downright cheap. Officers saturate the area. They drop the bookmarks off at schools, libraries, and on store counter-tops throughout the community. This modest format gets the message out quickly and inexpensively. The bookmark makes the message easy to read. It is easy to take along, useful in a book, and convenient to keep.

Or let's say you're trying to cut down on the

*Sheets from this tear-off pad make
blood pressure information easy to convey
and easy to remember. Health professionals
write in patients' numbers and hand the sheet to them.*

Your Blood Pressure Is

120 / 80

WHAT DOES THAT MEAN? The first number gives the blood's pressure against the artery walls while the heart is beating (systolic). The second number is the pressure between beats (diastolic).

WHAT'S OKAY? Below 120/80: Fine. Keep it as low as possible. Between 120/80 and 140/90: Watch it. Get it lower. Above 140/90: The blood can't flow freely through your arteries. You may need a drug to bring the pressure down, otherwise your arteries may be damaged, and you will have a high risk of a heart attack or stroke.

WHAT CAN YOU DO? You can help reduce your blood pressure and keep it low if you cut down on salt, reduce your weight, exercise, and take those pills, if the doctor prescribes them.

♥ Stanford Heart Disease Prevention Program

number of alcohol-related car accidents in a summer resort mountain town. Printing your message on napkins that are served with drinks at local bars would remind people of the dangerous mix of alcohol and mountain roads. Placing them in bars allows you to put the important message in the right place at the right time. If you really want to drive the message

home, it could state the number of alcohol-related accidents in the area. That would be sobering.

There are companies that specialize in printing your name and message on items such as napkins and pencils. To find suppliers of these kinds of things, look in the Yellow Pages of the phone book under *Advertising Specialties* or ask a printer for a recommendation. Call and ask for a catalog. Some of the kinds of pieces you'll find available are listed in Sidebar 22, at left. These "business gifts" may be less expensive than you might think, especially when they are ordered in quantity.

• Make Your Piece Easy to Use

Making your printed piece convenient and easy to use will add to its appeal. An interesting assignment I once had was to figure out a way to help people pay attention to their blood pressure. An even more challenging aspect of the task was to come up with a way to motivate doctors and other medical personnel to educate their patients on the subject. Both of these goals were to be achieved through the use of a *low-cost* printed piece.

Convenience was the key. I developed an inexpensive "blood pressure pad," made up of standard 5-1/2" x 8-1/2" sheets. At the top there was a big blank space for writing patients' blood pressure numbers (such as 120/80), and below there were three short units of information. One explained the numbers, one told what numbers are okay, and one suggested ways to help keep your blood pressure low.

Health professionals could easily fill in the numbers, tear the sheet off the pad, and hand it to their patients. The text reminded them of what points to cover, or they could leave it to the patients to read themselves. Patients left with a sheet that had their blood pressure written on it, and they could go over the information in the comfort of their own home.

Here are some other suggestions for making your

A lighthearted approach makes communicating energy conservation information more interesting for both the sender and receiver.

printed piece convenient and easy to use:

- Make your printed piece easy to open. Brochures that fold one way and then another are awkward to open and cumbersome to hold, especially when they open up to a large size. Ones that you have to hold sideways are less convenient than pieces you hold upright.

- Keep sizes standard. They are more familiar, comfortable to hold, and easier to store.

- If you are thinking of doing a poster, make sure it will fit where you want to post it. Will people be willing to give your poster the amount of space it takes? You may also want to produce a "flyer size" version.

- Consider sending a large postcard instead of a letter. Postcards don't require opening, so your message is immediately in front of the reader.

- Use neatly laid-out and easy-to-read tables of contents and indexes.

- Make sure your printed pieces are placed in convenient locations.

- Put important or regularly-used information in a prominent position.

- Help your readers find what they are after by using clear divisions, running heads, and readable page numbers.

- Feature your phone number on promotion pieces and business stationery.

Make Your Piece Lighthearted

Is there a way you can make your printed piece fun? Let's say you want to produce a piece that helps people lose weight. You know that if they are to be successful, they need to watch what they eat on a daily basis. So you think: what kind of piece might motivate people to monitor their food on a daily basis?

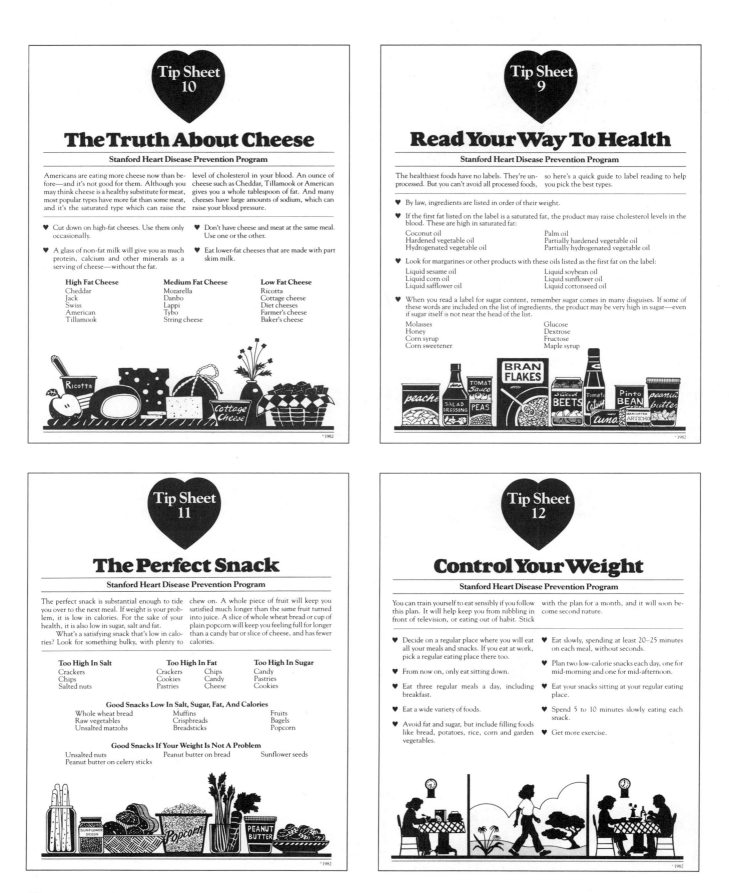

Tip Sheet 10

The Truth About Cheese

Stanford Heart Disease Prevention Program

Americans are eating more cheese now than before—and it's not good for them. Although you may think cheese is a healthy substitute for meat, most popular types have more fat than some meat, and it's the saturated type which can raise the level of cholesterol in your blood. An ounce of cheese such as Cheddar, Tillamook or American gives you a whole tablespoon of fat. And many cheeses have large amounts of sodium, which can raise your blood pressure.

♥ Cut down on high-fat cheeses. Use them only occasionally.

♥ A glass of non-fat milk will give you as much protein, calcium and other minerals as a serving of cheese—without the fat.

♥ Don't have cheese and meat at the same meal. Use one or the other.

♥ Eat lower-fat cheeses that are made with part skim milk.

High Fat Cheese	Medium Fat Cheese	Low Fat Cheese
Cheddar	Mozarella	Ricotta
Jack	Danbo	Cottage cheese
Swiss	Lappi	Diet cheeses
American	Tybo	Farmer's cheese
Tillamook	String cheese	Baker's cheese

° 1982

Tip Sheet 9

Read Your Way To Health

Stanford Heart Disease Prevention Program

The healthiest foods have no labels. They're unprocessed. But you can't avoid all processed foods, so here's a quick guide to label reading to help you pick the best types.

♥ By law, ingredients are listed in order of their weight.

♥ If the first fat listed on the label is a saturated fat, the product may raise cholesterol levels in the blood. These are high in saturated fat:

Coconut oil	Palm oil
Hardened vegetable oil	Partially hardened vegetable oil
Hydrogenated vegetable oil	Partially hydrogenated vegetable oil

♥ Look for margarines or other products with these oils listed as the first fat on the label:

Liquid sesame oil	Liquid soybean oil
Liquid corn oil	Liquid sunflower oil
Liquid safflower oil	Liquid cottonseed oil

♥ When you read a label for sugar content, remember sugar comes in many disguises. If some of these words are included on the list of ingredients, the product may be very high in sugar—even if sugar itself is not near the head of the list.

Molasses	Glucose
Honey	Dextrose
Corn syrup	Fructose
Corn sweetener	Maple syrup

° 1982

Tip Sheet 11

The Perfect Snack

Stanford Heart Disease Prevention Program

The perfect snack is substantial enough to tide you over to the next meal. If weight is your problem, it is low in calories. For the sake of your health, it is also low in sugar, salt and fat.

What's a satisfying snack that's low in calories? Look for something bulky, with plenty to chew on. A whole piece of fruit will keep you satisfied much longer than the same fruit turned into juice. A slice of whole wheat bread or cup of plain popcorn will keep you feeling full for longer than a candy bar or slice of cheese, and has fewer calories.

Too High In Salt	Too High In Fat		Too High In Sugar
Crackers	Crackers	Chips	Candy
Chips	Cookies	Candy	Pastries
Salted nuts	Pastries	Cheese	Cookies

Good Snacks Low In Salt, Sugar, Fat, And Calories

Whole wheat bread	Muffins	Fruits
Raw vegetables	Crispbreads	Bagels
Unsalted matzohs	Breadsticks	Popcorn

Good Snacks If Your Weight Is Not A Problem

Unsalted nuts	Peanut butter on bread	Sunflower seeds
Peanut butter on celery sticks		

° 1982

Tip Sheet 12

Control Your Weight

Stanford Heart Disease Prevention Program

You can train yourself to eat sensibly if you follow this plan. It will help keep you from nibbling in front of television, or eating out of habit. Stick with the plan for a month, and it will soon become second nature.

♥ Decide on a regular place where you will eat all your meals and snacks. If you eat at work, pick a regular eating place there too.

♥ From now on, only eat sitting down.

♥ Eat three regular meals a day, including breakfast.

♥ Eat a wide variety of foods.

♥ Avoid fat and sugar, but include filling foods like bread, potatoes, rice, corn and garden vegetables.

♥ Eat slowly, spending at least 20–25 minutes on each meal, without seconds.

♥ Plan two low-calorie snacks each day, one for mid-morning and one for mid-afternoon.

♥ Eat your snacks sitting at your regular eating place.

♥ Spend 5 to 10 minutes slowly eating each snack.

♥ Get more exercise.

° 1982

*These tip sheets (left) focus on
one topic at a time. They were sent out sequentially,
one every two weeks. The first came with a magnet for posting on
the refrigerator. The piece below has a perforated recipe card at bottom.*

Fish Ideas

There is no trick to fixing really good fish—fish that tastes wonderful and is low in calories, fat and cholesterol. Here's how you do it:

Start with fresh fish, or fish that was frozen while fresh. Look for fish that has shiny skin and no "fishy" odor. If it is dull or has a strong odor, it is probably old. Bake, broil, barbecue or poach the fish. Once it is fried, it is no longer the healthy, low-fat dish it could be. And fish should not be overcooked because that will make it tough. Instead of adding butter to fish, try one of these healthier alternatives:

- A marinade of oil and vinegar with herbs.
- Lemon juice, dill weed, and parsley sprinkled on the fish before cooking.
- A sauce of yogurt with horseradish or yogurt with dry mustard.
- Mild chile salsa spooned over the cooked fish.

Keep an eye out for recipes for fish stews, soups and salads to add variety to your fish dinners.

MONTEREY BAY STEW

For a less-spicy stew, reduce the amount of Worcestershire and pepper by half.

1 Pound fish fillets or steaks	½ Cup chopped celery
½ Cup chopped onion	¼ Cup tomato paste
2 Cups boiling water	1 Tb Worcestershire sauce
1 Can (16 oz) tomatoes or 3 fresh	½ Tsp pepper
tomatoes, chopped	¼ Tsp thyme
1 Cup diced carrots	1 Tb olive oil
1 Cup diced potatoes	

Thaw fish, if frozen, and remove any skin and bones. Cut fish into 1-inch pieces. In a saucepan, heat oil and cook onion until tender. Add

The question rattles around in your head a while . . . daily basis . . . calendar . . . calendar with messages . . . aha! You flash on those little doors, one-a-day, from December first until Christmas. An Advent calendar! Why not produce your own version of an Advent calendar? It could have diet messages (or directions) behind a month's worth of "doors." This printed piece would most likely be kept around, used on a daily basis, and serve as the reminder you want. It would be fun to produce, fun to distribute, and fun to use.

Sometimes a subject cries out for a light-hearted approach. When I was asked to develop an energy conservation campaign for a university, I knew I faced a real challenge. How were we going to get anyone interested in energy conservation—a topic that may be considered—um—dull. The task seemed so impossible it seemed almost funny . . . which made me think of jokes. That made me wonder how to tie jokes in to energy conservation, and that made me think of light bulb jokes (which were popular at the time). So we based the campaign on humor, and decided to deal with the topic very lightly (pun intended).

In the beginning we sent out questionnaires to find out how much people already knew about energy conservation, so we could compare it with what they knew at the end of the campaign. The questionnaire included a pencil with a specially created dinosaur logo on it to help launch the campaign, and to motivate response. We developed stickers that were placed above light switches and on typewriters throughout many buildings. They said things like: "Will the most conscientious, attractive, and/or smart person in the room please turn out the light?" and "Will the last person off the treadmill please turn out the light?" and "OK, it's not your money, but would you please turn off the light anyway? Thanks."

We also printed cups and balloons with energy messages which appeared near coffee machines from time to time. They said things like: (Side one) "The

These blue and white posters appeared one at a time, in sequence. They gave people time to make the transition.

utility bills run about $7,508,951.28 a year, and are rising. Faced with such a huge bill, can you really make a difference by turning off the light? Yes! See side two." (Side two) "When you turn out the light, your friends will copy you. And their friends will copy them. And pretty soon we'll all be working in the dark."

Calendars were also part of the campaign. We produced a new one every season. Printed across different dates were references to activities and events that related specifically to the university community, and to energy conservation. This audience enjoyed the lighthearted approach, and the campaign was more successful because the humor was tailored specifically to them.

Few people can ignore something that is "personalized" to them, whether it involves a sense of humor, a horoscope, or a fortune (did you ever see anyone refuse a fortune in a fortune cookie?) If a lighthearted approach is appropriate for your topic and your audience, you'll get readers.

Tell People What and How

Telling people *how* to do something is often more effective than saying *why* they should do it. Say, for example, a city is concerned about a water shortage. Making concrete suggestions as to exactly how residents can save water will have better results than a generalized request to conserve, or talking about the lack of rainfall. Or telling people the simple steps involved in starting up a computer may be more effective than telling them the computer is easy to get into. Translate your message into practical, usable information that can be acted upon.

Break Information Up

Printed pieces are often ignored because the information they contain looks overwhelming. When printed

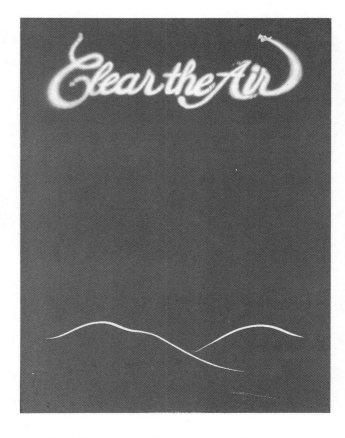

pieces look like they will take too much effort to read, they don't get read. Better to get a few points across than to have many passed over. Dividing information among several pieces and targeting them specifically often works better.

I was once in a situation where I had to get a tremendous amount of information out to a lot of people as quickly as possible. It was at the start of a federally-funded study of a community-based heart disease prevention program. We needed to acquaint residents of 44,000 households with a broad spectrum of health information during one winter, so that the educational interventions could begin immediately in the spring.

It was assumed that we would produce a fat

A matching letterhead comes in handy.
It can be used for memos, announcements,
agendas, policy statements, and, of course, correspondence.

On December 15, Stanford University Hospital
becomes smoke-free. For information call 3-7169.

Please respect our commitment to health.
No smoking is allowed in Stanford University Hospital.

booklet covering topics from exercise to nutrition to smoking cessation to obese children. But it was hard to imagine those currently unsuspecting residents tucking in to a lengthy booklet and absorbing all that information by spring. I knew we needed something special in print if we were to get and hold their attention long enough to make an impression. I wanted whatever we put out to be more interesting, more usable, and more likely to get read than a lengthy booklet. I also wanted people to keep the information around. If they kept it around longer, they would become more familiar with it.

One morning before work I was thinking about this problem, as I was headed for the refrigerator door.

I noticed some magnets on it holding up some notes. I thought, *aha*! If we could get our heart health information up on peoples' refrigerator doors, it would be in their environment on a daily basis, and that way they'd become familiar with the information more quickly. We could give them just a little bit at a time, so it was easy to read, and present new information on a regular basis, so they'd have something new to put up each week. We could mail residents the information and include a heart-shaped magnet, so posting it on refrigerator doors (or anywhere else they pleased) would be easy.

But was I the only one who stuck things up on the refrigerator? We did some research and found out that

*Testimonials don't have
to be made by famous people
or experts to be effective. Those with
whom readers can identify can be as powerful.*

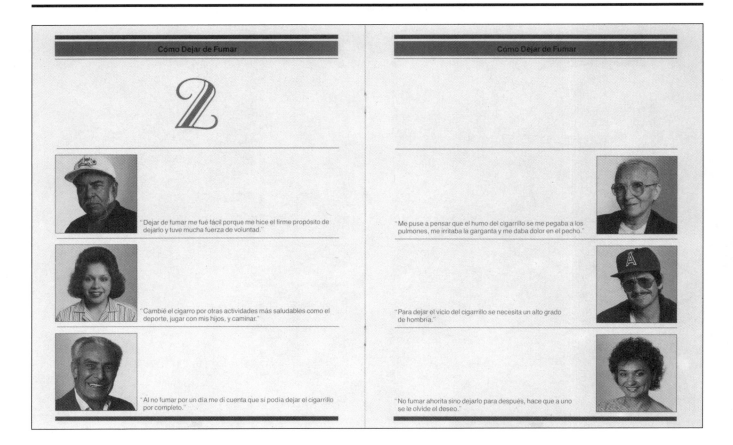

two-thirds of the households had things posted on their refrigerators.

The plan was to divide key information up into a series of useful, do-able tips. We developed a "refrigerator tip sheet program," through which we would mail out one tip sheet a week, over a period of twelve weeks. I sent myself many sheets of paper in the mail, folded in different ways, to see what shape they arrived in, and which ones did best.

The first mailing included a large envelope, a sheet explaining the program, the first tip sheet, and a magnet with the program logo on it. Thereafter, single sheets were folded in half and mailed once a week, for the remaining weeks.

Not everyone at the project was excited about the idea. Nothing like this had been tried before, and there was the usual resistance to something new (no one remembers this part now). But the plan worked. Residents loved the tip sheets. They were anxious to get them, and they read the "bite-sized chunks" of information. People whose houses were accidentally missed in the mailing called to be put on the list. Others called or wrote requesting that the series be sent to friends or relatives in other communities.

Several years later some people still had their tip sheets posted (it was an excellent magnet). We got a lot of information out in three months, and people actually *liked* getting it.

A follow-up evaluation showed that two-thirds of the residents had posted the tip sheets on their refrigerators. I'll always wonder if they were the same two-thirds that had magnets on their refrigerators in the first place.

Another way to present information planned for a large booklet is to divide it into smaller brochures instead. This is particularly effective when some of the information applies more specifically to one group than another.

Information on AIDS, for example, may be more effectively communicated when it addresses drug users, gays, pregnant women, teens, or particular ethnic groups separately, in different printed pieces (rather than in one general one). This way people can identify more easily with the problem and focus on information that really fits their situation. Breaking up information makes it more accessible.

Say It in Different Ways

In one of my attempts to find out what makes print work, I studied the underlying construction of nonfiction books on best seller lists. Several of them had something interesting in common. They presented the exact same information in three different ways: in text form, as a chart, and in an illustration.

Some people "get it" best by reading, others by looking at charts, and still others by looking at pictures. Although I doubt it was done intentionally with this in mind, this made the content more accessible to people with different learning styles. Whatever a person's primary way of absorbing information, it can be reinforced in other ways as well.

Presenting your message in more than one way may be especially important when you must target a broad audience like the general public. This is a good technique to apply to printed pieces when you are concerned that the content may not be understood equally well by everyone.

Ideas to Make Your Piece More Appealing   23

Here are ideas for making your printed piece more interesting. Each is covered in this chapter, and examples are given. The following chapter shows you how to come up with ideas for your particular piece.

- Make your piece useful

- Make your piece easy to use

- Make your piece lighthearted

- Tell people what to do and how to do it

- Break information up

- Say your message in more ways than one

- Give people time to absorb your message

- Use authority

- Make your piece easy to remember

- Keep your message positive

- Keep your message coming

- Offer an award or a certificate

Allow Time to Get Your Message

Most of us don't entirely get a message the first time we hear it. It takes a while for it to sink in, to see how it fits into our lives, and to get used to the idea if it's new. Consider developing a printed piece that gives people time to absorb your message. One project I worked on recently did just that. A hospital was about to prohibit smoking anywhere on the premises. (It might have been any kind of institution.) This was a big step, especially as regular smokers included members of the professional staff. The situation seemed to call for a transition period.

We developed a series of three posters to introduce the plan gradually. To keep production costs down, the posters were all exactly alike, except for the type at the bottom. That could be changed inexpensively. The posters were solid blue with a tiny plane at the top. It drew out in "sky writing" the words "Clear the Air." Two lines at the very bottom indicated local hills (see illustrations on page 90-91).

The first poster had only this illustration. It was placed in all hospital-related buildings, which included a medical school and several clinics. The second poster, put up two weeks later, had words to the effect: "We will be smoke-free as of December 15." The third poster, hung two weeks after that, said effectively: "We are now smoke-free. Please respect our commitment to health." These simple, relatively inexpensive posters gave patients, visitors, nurses, doctors, and other personnel time to adjust to the new policy before it went into effect.

Use Authority

We respond more positively to a printed piece from a credible source. Your message will carry more weight with a quote, statistics, or statements from a reliable source. It might be an expert in the field, a local organization, a famous institution, or the media.

We also feel better about a printed piece when it is endorsed by a respected authority, or by people with whom we can identify. A voice that carries weight does not always have to be one that is well-known.

Sometimes the most "credible source" is a common everyday person, testifying that he or she has the same problems the rest of us do, or that such and such works or is useful or worthwhile. Testimonials worked well in a smoking-cessation piece we did for Latinos in San Francisco. Ordinary people from the Hispanic community were recruited to give their reasons for stopping smoking. The booklet was so well-received that over a million have now been produced and distributed nationwide.

Testimonials have not been used nearly as much (or as well) as they might be in print. There are lots of versions yet to be tried.

Make Your Piece Easy to Remember

We remember information more easily when it is "brought home" to us, and it is more powerfully brought home to us when it is stated specifically and concretely. If educators or insurance companies were to say to parents, for example, "the cost of education is going up," parents might or might not remember it. But if they were to say to them, "by the year 2000 it is likely to cost $100,000 to give your child a four-year college education," they'd be much more likely to remember it.

Or if you are a gardener, for instance, an ad that says "our tools are excellent for the garden" will probably not stick in your mind as well as one that says "our long-nosed hand hoe is excellent for deep-rooted and stubborn weeds."

Of all the printed pieces we looked at on a trip to England, the one I remember best is the one with the map that showed the number of sunny days in each area of the country (Cornwall got the most). Print producers who add this kind of interesting and spe-

*You don't have to wait for a graduation
to use a certificate. Every organization can
find a reason to award one, and they're appreciated.*

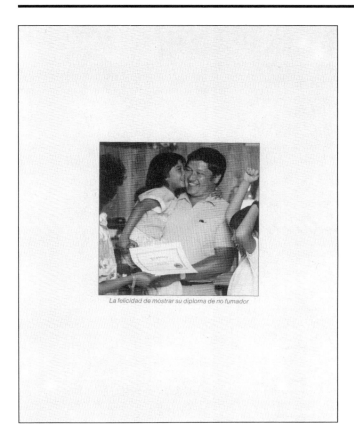

La felicidad de mostrar su diploma de no fumador

cific information to their printed piece will make it considerably more memorable.

Keep Your Message Positive

We respond more positively to positive messages. Saying things in a negative way makes information harder to understand, and casts your topic in a gloomy light. If you're doing an anti-firearm piece, for example, your piece will probably be more effective if it says "people should be free from the fear of getting shot" rather than "people shouldn't own guns." Packaging your message in a positive way is more likely to generate the hoped-for response.

Keep Your Message Coming

One technique mail-order businesses have been using lately is to send out the same catalog more than once in a season. This is because they get more sales after the second catalog appears. People sometimes need time to "get around to it." Whether it is to order socks, send in a subscription, or try a new plumbing service, what gets acted upon these days is usually what is most persistent.

When how-to books come out in a series, the ones in the middle often sell the best. The first ones introduce the series and whet the appetite. The middle ones get bought. The last ones trail off in sales.

How many times have you looked at something offered in print before you made a decision to go for it? To buy a CD, take a class, try a new restaurant, or go to a new movie, for instance. Printed pieces sometimes need to be seen more often than once to be effective. You may have to repeat your message many times before it's really *heard*. So keep it coming.

Offer an Award or a Certificate

A printed certificate with a fancy border is valued by just about everyone (you may not think so until you actually give one to someone). More often than not certificates wind up on walls in such diverse places as the local grocery store, an executive's office, a farm worker's house, and a teenager's bedroom. Is there something you can reward your audience for?

Any kind of certification, special honor, or recognition is appreciated. Can you give an award to the most valued members of your target audience? Can you give one *for excellence* in something? If you have a printing company, for example, you might give an award to your most-valued clients *for outstanding work with the printing trade*. If volunteers help on your project, they would probably welcome a certificate of appreciation.

Bookmarks and postcards are simple, inexpensive, and straight-forward ways to get a message across.

If you do any kind of teaching, or training, awards and certificates are a natural kind of printed piece to use. They acknowledge students' work while they advertise your services. Always be sure to make the certificate out to a *particular individual* if you want it to get hung on the wall.

Or say your business is putting in automatic garage door openers. Perhaps you put a small "certificate" on the inside of every door you install. It could include a space for the owner's name, date of installation, your guarantee, name, and phone number. If someone asks your client for a recommendation, they can easily find your number.

Or if you rent audio-visual equipment, party supplies, contractor's tools, laser printers, or skis, could you reward customers' 100th rental with a certificate, gold seal and ribbon, and perhaps a free rental. It could keep them coming back. Just like the scarecrow in the Wizard of Oz, a certificate makes us all feel more valued.

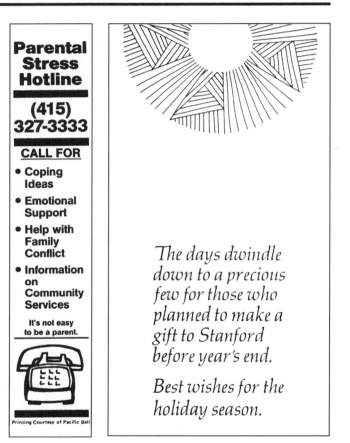

Parental Stress Hotline

(415) 327-3333

CALL FOR

- Coping Ideas
- Emotional Support
- Help with Family Conflict
- Information on Community Services

It's not easy to be a parent.

Printing Courtesy of Pacific Bell

The days dwindle down to a precious few for those who planned to make a gift to Stanford before year's end.

Best wishes for the holiday season.

Chapter 10

Tapping Your Creativity

What makes something seem "new," "clever," "imaginative," or (better yet) "innovative"? A lot has been written on the subject of creativity and the use of the imagination. Theories tend to be long and complex. My own view of it can be stated simply and briefly: creativity is bringing together familiar things that have not been together before. The *unexpected combination* is what creates the impact.

For example, a while ago the *New York Times* ran an article entitled "A New Medium Catches On." The "new" medium is a "magazine billboard." Large bulletin boards (the "billboard") are covered with articles, photographs, and advertisements (the "magazine"). They are hung in waiting rooms, in schools, and on college campuses; topics relate to the environment they're placed in. Future plans include placing them in other types of locations such as convenience stores. This "new medium" has already produced more than $50 million in revenues in a single year; more is expected.

Let's take a closer look at this bright (and lucrative) idea. Here are two familiar things that have been around a while: the magazine and the billboard. When they are brought together, they become a "new medium"—an innovation worthy of description in the *New York Times*. But what exactly is the innovation? It is *the combination*. It is the juxtaposition that is new, not the components.

Or take a dog horoscope poster—a very clever printed piece by Milton Glaser. Again the unusual combination of two familiar things—dogs and horoscopes.

They are combined to create a wonderfully imaginative and funny poster. Whether you look first for the prediction under your sign or your favorite furry beast under it, the piece is instantly engaging.

Another good example of creativity in print is a series of brochures on depression. On the cover is a drawing of Abraham Lincoln and the words: "Depression often attacks the brightest and the best. Lincoln perceived his own recurring sieges of despair. Today, thousands have received help and experience a happier and more productive life."

Inside, on one panel, there are poignant excerpts from Lincoln's letters about his depression. On the other panel is a list of common symptoms of depression ("1. Loss of energy and feeling tired; 2. Erratic sleep patterns and insomnia," etc.). Copy on the back says the problem is common, and suggests what to do if you are feeling depressed.

The power of this innovative brochure comes from the unexpected juxtaposition of two knowns—

*Creators of this brochure
use Lincoln's personal experience
with depression as a means of interesting
readers in the subject. Juxtaposing a respected
leader next to this illness makes a powerful printed piece.*

Depression often attacks the brightest and the best. Lincoln perceived his own recurring sieges of despair.

Today thousands have received help and experience a happier and more productive life.

IN HIS OWN WORDS

"I am now the most miserable man living. If what I feel were equally distributed to the whole human family, there would not be one cheerful face on earth. Whether I shall ever be better I cannot tell; I awfully forbode I shall not. To remain as I am is impossible; I must die or be better, it appears to me." *Excerpt of letter to John T. Stuart, his friend, mentor and law partner, 1841.*

"Although I seem to others to enjoy life rapturously at times, yet when I am alone I am so depressed that I am afraid to trust myself to carry a pocket-knife." *Lincoln, 1837, still grieving the death of Ann Rutledge, 1835.*

COMMON SYMPTOMS

1. Loss of energy and feeling tired.
2. Erratic sleep patterns and insomnia.
3. Decrease in activity with friends, family, job and hobbies.
4. Feeling that life is not worthwhile.
5. Loss of self-esteem and self-doubt.
6. Focus on the past, brooding, a sense of guilt, and thoughts of death.
7. Increase in consumption of alcohol and drugs.
8. Increase in physical pains and complaints.
9. Loss of appetite or overeating.
10. Loss of concentration, indecisiveness and irritability.
11. Overall loss of normal pleasure.

OF DEPRESSION

President Lincoln on the one hand, and depression on the other. Presenting an admired historical figure alongside depression makes the subject more engaging. And the association with Lincoln makes it easier for readers to face their own difficulties. A similar piece was produced using Charlotte Bronte, the author of the classic English novel, *Jane Eyre.*

These pieces bring to mind a poster I did years ago for a museum that illustrates the same point. The title of the show was "Human Concern, Personal Torment." The image on the poster was a large heart with a razor blade dropped into it. The impact of the poster depended on a response to seeing the familiar (the heart and the razor) together in an unfamiliar way.

Where do ideas come from? And more to the point, how do we get them?

Working Toward a Lightning Bolt

Most good ideas don't hit like a bolt of lightning out of the blue; a storm usually brews a while before it hits. In other words, good ideas are often the result of *effort* aimed in a particular direction over time.

Say you want to come up with an interesting angle for a printed piece. Give it some time. The problem has to rumble around in your head a while —a week or two, maybe longer. Your unconscious needs time to turn it over, toss it around, and approach it from different angles. You may need to "sleep on it." Ideas need time to emerge in a variety of ways so that they can change, evolve, and jell. So although an idea may *hit* you like a lightning bolt, getting *the flash* comes neither instantly nor easily. Like most artists

This razor blade dropped into a heart creates an unexpected and disquieting image, one that is right for this poster. It is for an art museum exhibition called "Human Concern/Personal Torment."

This self-promotion Christmas poster gives the reindeer on the familiar yellow road sign a red nose. The unexpected combination of two familiar images—the deer on the road sign and Rudolph—results in a creative piece.

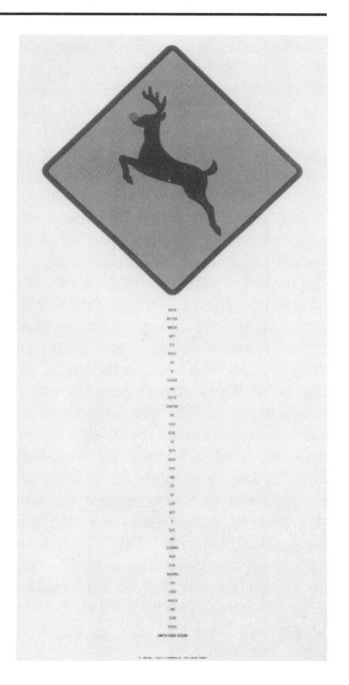

and scientists, we have to earn our breakthroughs.

Perhaps you don't see yourself as particularly creative. Many people just assume they aren't, so they make no attempt to be. With no effort expended, the expectation fulfills itself. You may have heard that good ideas are 10% inspiration and 90% perspiration, but no one mentioned that the perspiration comes first.

Should you hear an inner voice saying "Not me, I'm not creative," switch it off immediately. Tell yourself firmly "I have a *great* imagination. I come up with *fantastic* ideas" (you have to trick that old negative voice). It really isn't necessary to put out any more dull, lifeless pieces that bore you and bore your readers. It helps to use your brain until your imagination kicks in. Read on.

Fish are common, living rooms are common,
and the 50s look is common; combining them unexpectedly
(left) creates an imaginative poster. Below: drawings of 10-year-olds
become increasingly creative when they are given concrete lists to respond to.

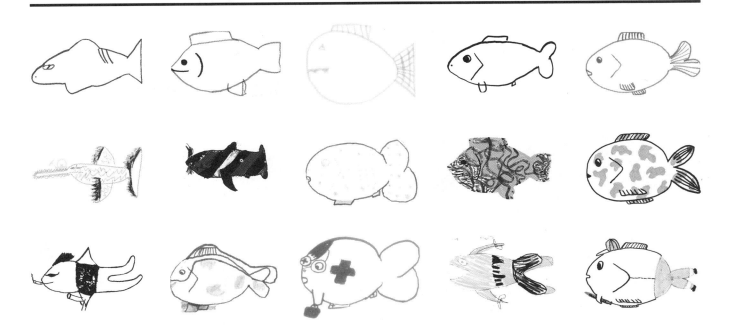

Sparking the Imagination

We all come up with more creative ideas when we have something concrete to respond to, such as a list. For example, when students are asked to draw a fish and are given no other direction, they tend to draw an uninspired, stereotypic fish. But when a list of *kinds* of fish—such as goldfish, shark, angel fish, stingray, guppy, and rainbow trout— are written on the board, drawings become more interesting. The list of specific fish jogs the students' memory and sparks their imagination. They come up with something "more creative."

When another list is added to the board—say one that names the parts of fish, like gills, fins, scales, mouth, and tail, the imagination reaches further. Adding a third list—describing fish with words such as translucent, blobby, sharp-toothed, sleek, pretty, and ferocious, or one that includes the kinds of water fish swim in such as stream, lagoon, lake, river, pond, and

ocean—the drawings become even more interesting and inspired.

Now if the assignment were to create an *imaginary* fish, and students were given lists with kinds of vegetables, animals, plants, or insects, even more ideas would be triggered. Lists of patterns—such as polka dots, stripes, plaids, calicoes, and geometrics—generate truly innovative results. When a familiar pattern (say, plaid) is combined with a familiar something else (like fish), or when a famous person (such as Lincoln) is juxtaposed next to a human condition (like depression), we call the results creative.

Using Idea Lists

Now granted, a newsletter or a brochure is not a fish, but the way to come up with a more imaginative one is the same. If you develop lists of things that relate to your particular printed piece (the equivalents of the list of kinds of fish, water, patterns, etc.), you will

Here the familiar shape of a Christmas tree is made of unexpected objects, creating a unique image. This card says "Wishing you a maintenance-free Christmas. European Auto Techniks."

The yellow stripe on the road is a common sight; so is an annual report. A report cover with a road stripe on it is not. The unusual juxtaposition makes this an appropriate and effective image.

come up with some pretty interesting possibilities. The process of making the lists and mixing and matching the items on them will spark your imagination.

But first you must make up the lists (that's the perspiration); then the idea presents itself (that's the inspiration). Writing lists gives your ordinary mind something concrete to do while your creative mind warms up. But what do you make lists *of*? You make lists of the information already in your head. Emptying it out on paper opens up your mind and clears some space for your imagination.

But what information? You may remember that in Chapter 2, *Your Competitive Edge*, I said that successful communication involved three components:

- You (the sender, or the product or service you represent)

- Your printed piece (the package, your "message vehicle")

- Them (the receivers, members of your target audience)

The strong image on the Kennedy/King memorial concert poster is created by the juxtaposition of one black and one white note. The rest of the poster is red, white, and blue.

By combining the step-by-step building of a snowman with the home-town team, creators of this Denver Sunday Post *cover came up with a highly imaginative image.*

These three components provide an excellent basis for writing good lists.

To generate your lists, focus on each of these three categories—your product or service, your printed piece, and your target audience—one at a time. Write down whatever you know about each category. You can also "free associate" by writing whatever comes to mind in relation to each topic.

Do your audience first, as everything flows from them. Sidebar 24 suggests things to write about your audience. Sidebar 21 will also help.

Next concentrate on your product or service. This will help you pull together your thinking about what it is you are offering, and help you come up with ideas for how to promote it. Sidebar 24 helps you focus on what it is you are offering.

Finally, make some lists about the piece itself. This can give you new ideas for different formats and modes of distribution. When you have made up several lists, try combining items from different ones. Your own creative piece will emerge, uniquely suited to your particular audience.

The designer features an unusual collection of smiles and teeth in this promotion piece for a dentist. The imaginative brochure demonstrates a creative approach to its subject.

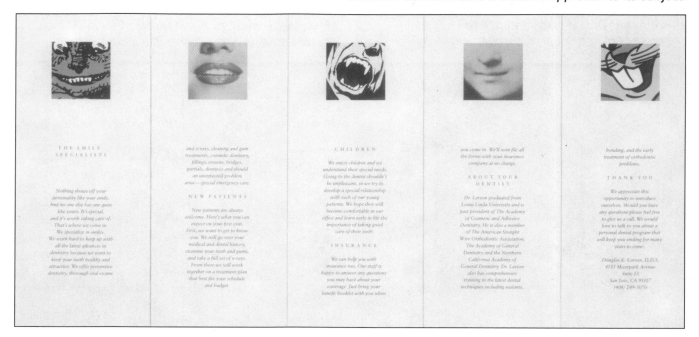

The Evolution of a Printed Piece

Let's go through this process together, from making up the lists to the creation of an actual piece. We'll take Laura Richards and her new business as an example.

Laura Richards has been working at a job she doesn't like for several years. On the side, she has fixed up a few houses, and found that her "cosmetic repairs" have significantly improved their value. Laura spruced the houses up with simple but tastefully chosen paint, carpets, fixtures, window coverings, skylights, decks, and landscaping. People tell her she's good at it, and she loves to do it. Laura would like to establish her own property improvement business, and she's decided to go for it.

Laura is calling her new business *Laura Richards Property Improvement.* She has calculated that her effort can earn back two to four times the amount of the cost of the improvement. Now she needs printed pieces to help her get established. But *what* printed pieces?

Laura starts by making lists. On the next few pages are the ones that she wrote, and the ideas that were generated as a result of making them. The lists are based on topics in Sidebars 21 and 24 (pages 77 and 107). Topics from Sidebar 24 are in boldface italic. They are followed by Laura's lists. My comments are in the column on the left.

Laura's Idea Lists

Your Target Audience

If you're having trouble filling out this list/questionnaire, it may be important to find out more about your potential audience before going further. The more you know about them the better ideas you'll come up with for your printed piece.

Potential clients (in order of priority)

- Realtors
- Builders
- Home sellers
- Developers
- Home owners
- Contractors
- Anyone

Client characteristics (do one client at a time)

Realtors

- **General description:** predominantly female, 30–55, living locally
- **Income**: $40,000 and up
- **Education:** four-year college, real estate license
- **Skill and knowledge level:** knowledgeable in relation to property improvement; business smarts; shrewd; sharp eye; know home market
- **How are they like you:** entrepreneurs; ambitious; interested in houses
- **How are they different:** flashier; more emphasis on show of wealth
- **Attitude toward your service:** open and willing to give it a try; have to be convinced the investment is worth it
- **Background:** mainly white middle and upper middle class
- **Values:** family; money
- **Tastes:** Good taste; decorator-y; the surface look of things
- **Leisure time:** Family vacations; weekends away; college sports; alumni associations; parties
- **Uniqueness**: independent; want flexible schedule; entrepreneurial spirit; often use home office as well as one at work site
- **When are you most likely to get their attention:** at their slow season: Thanksgiving through the holidays; winter
- **Impression you want to make:** that my service can really benefit them
- **Desired action you want them to take:** call and give me a try

Builders

- **General description:** predominantly male, 30–55, living in newer housing
- **Income**: $50,000 and up
- **Education:** some college; junior college; not expensive schools
- **Skill and knowledge level:** think they know what sells; have own opinion of what's good and bad; hit on formula and to stick to it; reluctant to change
- **How are they like me:** not much in common

- **How are they different:** they don't know how to make living space really desirable; don't understand taste
- **Attitude toward my service:** Skeptical; difficult to convince
- **Background:** White lower middle to middle class
- **Values:** conservative
- **Tastes:** expensive cars, big trucks
- **Leisure time:** glitzy hotels, drinkers, RVs and campers, TV watchers
- **Uniqueness:** entrepreneurial; willing to jump in, take chances, make it work
- **Time most likely to get attention:** Most likely to need help: spring, summer
- **Impression you want to make:** Pique their curiosity
- **Desired action you want them to take:** Call and try service

- Realtors are more likely to be open to trying the service
- Builders would be harder to interest
- I have more in common with the realtors: they're predominantly female, they tend to be entrepreneurial, ambitious and independent; we have education, values, and tastes in common. So I could probably work more comfortably and therefore more effectively with them. That should increase the likelihood of my success.
- Realtors are directly in touch with many home sellers at a time. Their commission is directly proportional to what their clients get for their houses. So it is likely that both the realtor and the client would benefit from my service.

As a result of filling out these audience profiles, it was clear to Laura who her best audience was. She decided to stop here and focus on realtors for the time being. Her thinking was as follows:

Where they go
- Office
- Open houses
- House tours
- Real estate-related meetings
- Conferences
- Home

Creating this list gave Laura some ideas as to how to distribute her printed pieces

Where they'll pay attention to the piece
- In their offices
- In professional publications
- At a meeting
- At a conference
- At home

It occurred to Laura that she might volunteer to do a presentation at a meeting or conference, and pass out her printed pieces there.

Using Idea Lists to Spark Your Imagination

24

Your Audience

Come up with ideas for your printed piece by focusing on your audience. Use each entry below as a heading for a sheet of paper, or use the worksheets on pages 355–357.

- Potential clients
  (Put them in order of priority)

- Client characteristics
  (use audience profile questions, Sidebar 21)

- Where they go

- Where they'll pay attention to the piece

- When they'll pay attention to the piece

- Design styles most likely to appeal (see Sidebar 40 for possibilities)

- Writing tones most likely to appeal (see Sidebar 29 for possibilities)

Product or Service

Concentrating on your service or product will give you ideas for your printed piece. This information can provide the content for a strong descriptive brochure.

- Benefits to users
  (What it will do for them)

- Features
  (What's good about your product or service)

- Components of your product or service
  (What goes into it)

- Experience, authority and expertise
  (Why someone should trust you and your product or service)

Your Printed Piece

Think about your piece in relation to the issues below. Combine your responses with ones on your other lists, and you will discover some interesting possibilities.

- Ways to make the piece personally relevant

- Ways to make it useful

- Ways to add authority

- Ways you can suggest what to do or how to do it

- Ways you can motivate your audience to respond

- Ways you can break your information up

- Ways to make your piece easy to remember

- Ways to make the piece easy to get

- Ways to keep your message coming

- Possible formats

Laura realized a good time to launch her campaign would be during the holidays, as that is when the home real estate market is slowest. This would naturally lead in to their most active sales time—spring and summer.

When they'll pay attention to the piece
- Thanksgiving through winter best (slow season)
- Spring next best (that's when the action is)

Design styles most likely to appeal
(Refer to Sidebar 40 for possibilities)
- Tasteful
- Classic
- Understated
- Clean
- Simple
- Refined
- Chic
- Sophisticated

Writing tones most likely to appeal
(Refer to Sidebar 29 for possibilities)
- Professional
- Honest
- Direct

Your Service or Product

Laura felt she could:

Laura could improve interior and exterior space through use of:

The information from this section was useful in developing the copy for the printed piece.

Benefits to users
(What it will do for them)
- Evaluate the property potential
- Add value to any property
- Come up with imaginative (yet practical) ideas to improve the property
- Develop a distinctive look for each property
- Maximize the best features and minimize the flaws
- Maximize the look for the minimum cost
- Find the right people and the right materials at the right price
- Organize and oversee the improvements
- Carry jobs successfully through to completion
- Troubleshoot
- Keep accurate books

Features
(What's good about the product or service)
- Improves value
- Work is done quickly
- Reasonable rates
- Convenient for clients

Components of your service or product
(What goes into it)
- Paint
- Carpets
- Tile
- Windows
- Window coverings
- Doors
- Kitchen fittings
- Skylights
- Decks
- Fences
- Bathroom fittings
- Trim and detail
- Plants
- Flowers
- Landscaping
- Whatever else it takes

Experience, authority, and expertise
(Why someone should have confidence in you)
- Design and management of several remodel and landscape jobs, start to finish
- Background and experience in design
- Contacts with good painters, carpenters, electricians, etc.
- Love of property improvement

Your Printed Piece

Laura wanted her piece to:

What you want the piece to do for you

- Grab the eye
- Not look like junk or bulk mail
- Announce the business
- Create a positive image
- Get realtors to call Laura Richardson Property Improvement
- Become known in the real estate community

Possible formats

- Brochure
- Letter
- Fact sheet
- Post card
- Poster
- Flyer

By scanning her list of target audience characteristics (Sidebar 21), Laura came up with the following ways to tailor her piece. One list often helps to generate another.

Ways to make the piece relevant to this group

- Something to do with women and work
- Something to do with travel or getaway weekends
- A quote on decoration from some well respected decorator
- A quote on property improvement from someone in the business (a local person?)
- Something to do with independence or an entrepreneurial spirit
- Something relating to good taste
- Something realtors can give to *their* clients

Laura thought: what are people who are about to sell their houses interested in? What's on their minds? If I were selling my house, what would be on my mind? What do these people need to know? She realized realtor's clients would be interested in things like:

Ways to make the piece useful

- Something useful realtors can give to their clients
- Something that these clients would be interested in—such as local information
- Holding garage sales
- Getting ready to show the house
- What to plant for a "big quick show"
- Tips on packing
- Tips on moving
- How to move pets
- Settling the new home
- Finding your way around the new location

Now Laura is hitting on something.

Ways to make it authoritative

- Get a written endorsement of someone in the field

In addition to generating ideas for her printed piece, Laura is also coming up with ideas for ways to promote her business.

Each business, service, or product is different. There will be some ways that don't apply to your situation. Not all ideas are going to be equally good. But better too many than too few.

Now an interesting idea is coming to Laura. On another list she identified these seasons as good times to deliver her message; now she's combining it with the idea of post cards (from her "possible formats" list) and with the idea of sending information a little at a time.

Laura is now beginning to be able to visualize a piece that would be appealing to this audience.

As Laura's ideas evolve she comes up with a cost-effective way of making them happen.

Now Laura has yet another idea: She is imagining herself actually going to a realtors' meeting and giving out her printed piece. This is a very powerful way to get a message across. Handing out your printed piece in person reinforces what you have to say, and what you to have say will be reinforced in your printed piece.

- Statements from people whose houses I've done
- Offer to do a realtor's house free in exchange for a written endorsement if satisfied

Ways to suggest what to do or how to do it
- Can't think of anything

Ways to motivate your audience to respond
- Offer a discount to the first two realtors who call
- Give a plaque that says this is a Richards-improved house

Ways you can make the piece lighthearted
- Can't think of anything. Wrong approach for this group.

Ways to break up information
- Send realtors information a little at a time
- Send them a post card every month starting around Thanksgiving when the housing market slows way down. Post cards could continue into the busy seasons as a reminder of the service.

Ways to make your piece easy to remember
- The piece will be memorable if it has useful information on it
- The piece will be memorable if there are quotes by satisfied customers
- It will be easy to remember if it is tastefully done, because it will stand out from the rest
- I could use classy "decorator" colors on my printed piece

Ways to keep your message coming
- Do a post card mailing every month if possible
- Have that be the Laura Richards trade mark
- Do several at once to save time and money

Ways to make the piece easy to get
- Deliver stacks of the post cards to realtors' offices
- Get the names and addresses of realtors and mail them
- Go to real estate meetings and hand them out
- Offer to speak on property improvement at real estate meetings, and hand the printed pieces out after the talk

Once again, the familiar combined in an unfamiliar way results in an imaginative printed piece.

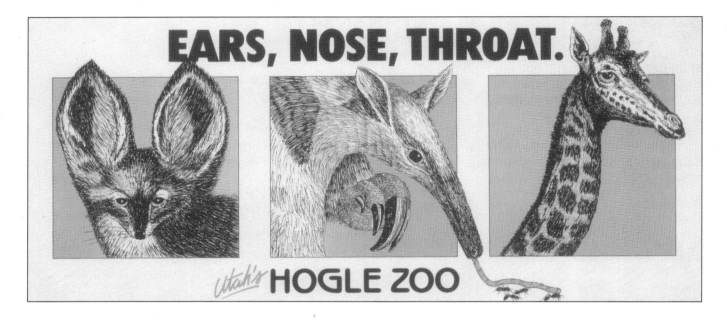

The Emerging Printed Piece

In the effort to come up with an imaginative printed piece to launch her new business, Laura came up with the lists on pages 105–111, and many more ideas than she thought she would. In fact she had more than she knew what to do with.

Of all the ideas that emerged, the one Laura liked best was to develop a printed piece for realtors to give to their clients. Now it was a matter of deciding which of the ideas would appeal most to her clients, and to her clients' clients. Tips about moving? Quick planting? Garage sales? Moving pets? She called a realtor she knew, explained her idea, and asked for some feedback. After Laura explained the possibilities, the realtor said enthusiastically "I want them all!" She had an embarrassment of riches.

Laura decided on the postcard format because it was manageable and inexpensive to produce. She planned to distribute one postcard a month. To make them as cost-effective as possible, she would have several printed up at once and use the same format and design every time, but the content would change monthly.

The Plan

Drawing on information from her lists, Laura came up with the following schedule (my comments are in italic below each month's idea):

November
A postcard introducing the business to prospective clients

Laura decided to do a brief summary of the most outstanding benefits of her service. She could take this information from the list of benefits she'd already made.

December
A simple three-panel brochure to describe the service

The brochure would go out at the end of December, when realtors' work was slow and their post-holiday lives were simpler. It is described in How to Write a Basic Brochure, *page 157.*

January

January's postcard would offer tips on getting the house ready to show

Laura developed a format that would be the same for each month. On side one, she'd put a small amount of copy along with her name and phone number. The content of side two would have a few tips on a different subject every month.

Getting a house ready to sell was something Laura already knew a lot about. She looked forward to writing these.

February

A postcard on preparing for the movers

Laura remembered reading magazine articles on getting ready to move, and she'd also seen books on the subject. She'd spend an evening at the library and the bookstore doing some research and gathering tips.

March

A postcard of tips on moving and pets

She felt she knew her vet well enough to ask him to give her some tips on moving animals. She thought she might also call the airlines to find out about flying them to their new homes.

April

April's postcard would be on tips on the kinds of spring plants that would make a big, quick show

Landscaping was one of Laura's passions—coming up with these tips would be a lot of fun.

If there are areas of knowledge you can sincerely write enthusiastically about, your copy stands a better chance of being interesting.

May

A postcard of tips on garage sales

Laura had had several garage sales, so she felt she would put this one together fairly easily.

As it would now be five months since Laura's brochure went out, she thought she might redistribute it in May, along with her postcard.

June

A postcard on plants to perk up a summer garden quickly

By this time Laura was having so much fun inventing printed pieces she decided to do a year's worth.

July

July's postcard would include tips on how to find a good mover

From her experience of locating building materials and supplies, Laura knew how to make good use of the Yellow Pages. She figured she could come up with moving tips the same way.

August

The postcard for August has tips on settling into a new home

She planned to gather tips from friends, realtors, movers, books, and magazines.

September

A postcard on adding fall color to the house and garden

October

A postcard on getting settled in a new community

Laura thought this could simply be a checklist of the places you need to call to get settled. It would include phone companies, banks, the school district, and so on. There would be blanks or phone numbers after each.

She realized that once she had the postcards printed, she could use them over and over. She could also give her printed piece out in "mix and match" batches, or as a whole set.

The next step is for Laura to start writing the copy for her postcards and her brochure. We'll follow the writing in *How to Write a Basic Brochure*, page 157. A sample of the final result is in Sidebar 39.

Your best ideas are waiting to be discovered. Go after your lightning bolt.

Writing for Printed Materials

4

Chapter 11

A Way to Make Writing Easier

I bet you wish whatever it is you have to write was already written. You've got a lot of good company. Well-known performers say they get stage fright; experienced public speakers say they get nervous; great writers say it ain't easy. It's not surprising that the rest of us find it hard to write. And there are more reasons than one.

Why It's So Hard to Write

First, writing makes you *think*. To be able to write something out, you have to be able to *think it through*. Thinking takes *effort*.

Second, when you write something, it usually means that someone is going to *read* what you've written (unless it's your journal, and even then, who knows). Your words go before others, and are judged. In that sense writing is like public speaking, most people's number one fear. Writing is hard to do because you're afraid you'll make a fool of yourself. You'll say it wrong. You'll expose your ignorance. You'll look dumb. These same fears are shared by the performer and the public speaker.

On top of that, if writing has been difficult for you in the past, facing the blank sheet (or screen) may make you freeze up. Psychologists say that success builds on success and failure builds on failure. If you've had difficulty writing in the past, how can you make a downward spiral go up? Sounds like a Zen *koan*—a question that is unanswerable until you are enlightened, but you have to be enlightened to have the answer.

So writing is difficult for at least three reasons:

- It takes hard work to figure out what to say and how to say it

- It takes courage to ward off the fear of criticism

- It takes persistence to be successful. To write well, you have to be able to think well, be brave (or driven), and persevere

Given these noble attributes (which we may have in greater or lesser supply), what can we do to make writing easier (or at least less painful)?

A Way to Make Writing Easier

A framework helps. Here is one structure that may make the process more enjoyable. It is made up of six major steps: 1. Collect Your Ideas, 2. Schedule Your Time, 3. Organize Your Outline, 4. Decide on the Message, 5. Turn on the Flow, and 6. Finish it Up. Following is a description of each of these steps.

1. Collect Your Ideas

The further ahead you know about your writing assignment, the better. Many writers say "you can't turn it on and you can't turn it off." If that's the case, the more time you have before the piece is due, the more "turned on" time you'll have.

Once you take on a writing assignment, your subconscious starts to work on the piece even if "you" don't. Ideas for your brochure, newsletter, ad, or report can hit you while you're driving somewhere, or at a meeting, or cooking dinner. Or during a wedding, or eating lunch, or in the middle of the night. Don't lose these gems! Start collecting them. Jot them down as they come to you. Don't think you'll remember them later because you probably won't. Make a place to collect them, such as a file folder, a notebook, or a section in the back of your calendar.

Let's say Matthew, a city planner in Michigan, is developing a brochure to promote his seminar on rural town planning. At the ballgame he remembers a statistic he wants to include, so he writes it down on a wrapper, and sticks it into a folder marked "Brochure" when he gets home. The next week Matthew discusses his seminar plans while at a friend's house for dinner. Later that evening he jots down features of his seminar—ideas that came out of the discussion with his friend.

Matthew copies articles at work and adds them to the folder along with thoughts for titles and openers. While riding his bike he comes up with people who might write him an endorsement; their names get tossed into the folder too. One night he has trouble sleeping, so he gets up and writes out more ideas for his brochure. All of these go into the folder, along with his bio.

On the weekend Matthew writes out a description of his target audience and does some research at the library. He adds this to the folder. After a few weeks of jotting notes, the folder is full. Now he has a valuable store of ideas, and he has something concrete upon which to base his writing.

Collecting your ideas over time has several advantages. First, they tend to be your best. Gathered without pressure, as they occur to you, these ideas are likely to be your most "authentic." They give your writing a richness and a depth that it would otherwise not have. When your thoughts are collected at different times and in many states of mind, your writing is fuller; more comprehensive. You're less likely to get those same ideas if you just sit down to write.

Second, gathering ideas over time makes it easier to *begin* writing, because you've got something to start with. And third, writing based on several ideas and more evolved thinking is more interesting to read. Give it a try.

2. Schedule Your Time

Writing is easier when you have a block of uninterrupted time; the longer the better. I know how hard that is to come by, but the alternative is stress and frustration. It's worth making the time.

In fact, writing *demands* uninterrupted time. If you have small children, don't even *try* to write while they're up and about. It activates their antennae to be extra needful, and it frazzles your nerves.

Trying to write in an office can be just as difficult. There are questions, phone calls, and visits. Colleagues can smell it too (so-and-so is just in there writing—good time to stop by for a chat).

So get out of the office. Stay home from work (if no one else is at home). Or get out of the house. Go out first thing in the morning or right after dinner. Go to an empty office or a coffee shop or a library, or borrow a quiet spot at a friend's house. Get hold of your self-discipline and find the time and place you need.

When the time arrives, get some sharp pencils and paper clips, a pad of paper, and your notes. Go to your "thoughtful spot," and proceed to the next step.

3. Organize Your Outline

Once you've carved out the time, you'll probably feel some pressure to make the most of it (this is a common experience among writers). Let's take a nice, calm, orderly approach. All you have to do is one thing at a time, step by step.

- First, go through the notes you've collected (we'll call them "idea notes"), and group them by topic.

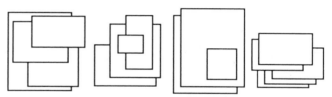

Idea notes: your collection of notes, organized into stacks by topic.

- Then make a topic sheet for each topic. For each topic that comes up in your notes, write that topic on the top of a separate, blank page. For example, one of Matthew's topics that comes up several times has to do with why people should hire him, so he writes the heading "Expertise" on one topic sheet. Other information has to do with what is good about the seminars he is offering; he calls that topic sheet "Features." And his idea notes that have to do with what clients will gain from his presentations he titles "Benefits."

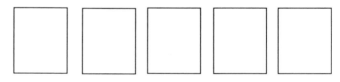

Topic sheets: take the topic from each stack of idea notes, and write that topic as the heading of a blank sheet of paper.

- Then clip the idea notes themselves to the topic sheets they go with. For instance, Matthew clips his bio and his ideas for names for endorsements on the sheet called "Endorsements." You may have several notes clipped to a single topic sheet.

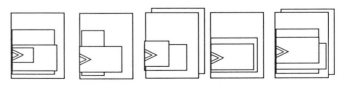

Idea notes and topic sheets clipped together.

- Write the ideas and information from your idea notes on to the appropriate topic sheets.

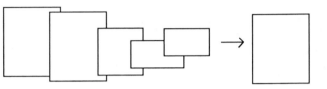

Gather all your ideas from your stack of notes onto the appropriate topic sheet.

- If you have several topics written on the same idea note, go through it and write a topic name beside each entry with a colored pen. (Matthew , for example, had several ideas for different topics on the sheet he wrote up after having dinner with his friend.) Then go through the note and transfer the information on to the right topic sheet.

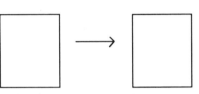

To deal with different topics on the same note, identify them with colored pen; then transfer them to the right topic sheets.

- Sort the topic sheets (with their newly written entries and clipped notes) into some order. It is probably easiest to put them in the same order in which the information will appear in your printed piece. Copy the headings of the topics from your topic sheets on to a clean sheet of paper, and you've got your outline.

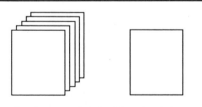

Sort your topic sheets into order. By copying their headings onto a fresh sheet, you've got an outline.

But even more importantly, you've got all your notes gathered and in order, making them easy to write from. If information is missing you'll have to get it, but you'll know where it goes when you do. Now it's just a matter of going through each topic sheet (with its stack of notes), one by one, and writing up the ideas and information they contain. Your outline will guide you easily through the writing.

4. Decide On the Message

Before you write your piece, it's a good idea to step back for a minute and remind yourself of the most important message. Remember the discussion about communication in Chapter 2, *Your Competitive Edge*? To summarize it in a sentence: your printed piece is a vehicle that takes your message from you to "them," your readers. The clearer you are about what you want that message to be, the more likely your printed piece is to deliver that message.

It helps to write it down. Begin with something like "the message I want to get across in this piece is_____"; or "the writing in this piece will be successful if it communicates the following information: 1. 2. 3., . . . (and so on)." If you are writing a report on a program you have just implemented, for example, you might say "the message I want to get across is that this program was highly successful." Back up your message in the report with utilization data and results, and include topics like new trends and recommendations.

In Matthew's case, he might say "what I want to communicate most in my brochure is my level of expertise in rural town planning, and its value to seminar participants." Once you're in touch with the purpose of the piece, you're ready to start the flow.

5. Turn On the Flow

With a clear message in your mind and your notes and outline in order, jump in and write. What you write or how you write doesn't matter; what matters is *that* you write.

Try thinking of yourself as talking instead of writing. Look at your outline and the information on your first Topic Sheet. Write down the information as though you were telling someone about it. Simply tell your story.

Sometimes it helps if you imagine yourself talking to someone in particular. Imagine yourself talking to someone you know, or to one of your readers. Always keep your reader in mind.

Or think of yourself as just putting words down on paper so you'll have something soon to edit. Editing may be easier than writing.

Say it any old way, but get the message down. Let it flow, one sentence after the other. Don't stop. Don't

go back. Keep the pencil moving across and *down* the page. Just concentrate on what you're saying, and keep "talking."

Plan on at least three writing sessions if you can. In each, use a different part of your brain. In the first session, use your *creative mind*; in the second, use your *intelligent mind*; and in the third, use your *mechanical mind*. This way you are free to concentrate on one aspect of the writing at a time.

Creative mind

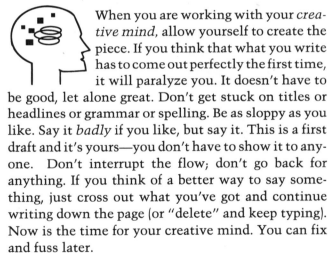

When you are working with your *creative mind*, allow yourself to create the piece. If you think that what you write has to come out perfectly the first time, it will paralyze you. It doesn't have to be good, let alone great. Don't get stuck on titles or headlines or grammar or spelling. Be as sloppy as you like. Say it *badly* if you like, but say it. This is a first draft and it's yours—you don't have to show it to anyone. Don't interrupt the flow; don't go back for anything. If you think of a better way to say something, just cross out what you've got and continue writing down the page (or "delete" and keep typing). Now is the time for your creative mind. You can fix and fuss later.

While you're in "creative" mode, make up titles and invent headlines. Make them descriptive; keep them loose. These are *working* titles and *working* headlines; no need to get them exactly right. Concentrate on the ideas you want to put across, and keep moving.

Using your creative mind is harder when you have high expectations of yourself, especially if it's been a while since you were a child. We forget what it's like to be a beginner. Whenever you use your creative mind, you are a beginner. Each time you sit down to write something new, you are a beginner again. And beginners must allow themselves to make mistakes. That's how they make progress. Let your first draft be a first draft. Be free with it; have fun with it. The work comes soon enough. Once you've got the words on the page, you're in business. Leave the writing and come back to it later if you can.

Intelligent mind

 Once the words are on the page, it's time to apply your intelligence. At a second sitting, go through the piece with your *intelligent mind*. Think about what you're trying to say, and say it. (The next chapter, *Guidelines For Reader-Friendly Writing*, offers concrete principles to help you do this.)

How does the piece *sound*? It may be awful, but at least you've got the rudiments. How is the organization? Look at your outline (or make an outline of what you've written); revise it if necessary. What words are extra? Where can you tighten? Can you rephrase a sentence? Say it better? Make it clearer? How are the headlines? The title? Do they say what you want them to? In the order you want them to? Can you strengthen them? As you work on your writing with your intelligent mind, read the writer's checklist in Sidebar 31, page 139. It is based on the guidelines in the next chapter and will help you critique your own writing.

Mechanical mind

Finally, go through the writing with your mechanical mind, at a third sitting if possible. Before handing it over to someone else, read each sentence out loud in your head to see how it sounds. Reading the sentences as though you were *saying* them points out rough spots quickly. Work with the sentences until they flow smoothly.

Type the piece up (if it isn't typed already), and run it through a computer spelling checker if you have one. Remember that spell-checkers are limited. If you type *fist*, for example, and you meant *first*, it won't get picked up, because *fist* is also a word and the computer (bless its heart) will think it's fine. *Making Writing More Readable*, page 143, covers *mechanical mind* issues. Read through that chapter. Then go through your piece and check for the kinds of issues it raises. When you've done that, hand it over to someone else for feedback.

6. Finish It Up

Here's the writer's dilemma: on the one hand, the more people who respond to your writing, the more input you get, the richer the piece will be, and the fewer mistakes you are likely to make. On the other hand, the more feedback you ask for, the more points of view you have to deal with. And you may get conflicting responses. It will also take you longer to integrate everyone's comments. In addition, the most valuable feedback you get may be from your potential readers, but that usually takes even more time (and more effort) to get. Choose your poison.

Do not allow anything you've written to be printed without someone else going over it. This single step can save you untold grief. If the editor or proofreader misses something too, at least you've got company in misery. Sidebar 37 has an editor's checklist.

Writing is both an art and a craft. The more you do it, the more ways you come up with to make the job easier and more interesting.

Chapter 12

Guidelines for Reader-Friendly Writing

If you are writing the copy for your printed piece, this chapter is for you. Following the guidelines for reader-friendly writing will help make your writing stronger and more interesting. If someone else is writing the piece, this chapter will help you evaluate what's written. Hiring is covered in *People Involved in Producing Print* on pages 43–52; Sidebar 30 has tips for making a writing assignment.

Be Simple and Direct

I believe that the best approach to writing printed materials is a Zen approach: simple and direct, with nothing extra. Why? Because most people read printed materials for information rather than for pleasure. The purpose of a printed piece is not to entertain, as with a novel, or to convey an opinion, as with an essay, or to express a feeling, as with a poem. Its purpose is to do a job. A printed piece is a *working* document, with a mission to accomplish. It is a *business* communication because it helps you to conduct your business. This is as true for a non-profit organization as it is for a profit-making one.

And as with other business transactions, readers appreciate efficiency. Your job as writer of a printed piece is to inform readers as clearly and concisely as possible, and to convince them to take the next step. The "next step" may be simply to form a positive impression of your service or product, or it may be to take some action. In a printed piece, these goals are accomplished best by writing that is simple and direct, with nothing extra.

Make Your Piece Look Easy to Read

It is crucial to the success of your printed piece that it *look* easy to read. People often decide in a single glance whether or not they'll read it. If a brochure or newsletter or flyer looks like it will take too much effort to read, it doesn't get read.

How does the *writer* of a printed piece make it *look* easy to read? Isn't that the designer's job? you might ask. To some extent it is (the designer's contribution to readability is covered in upcoming chapters). But the writer who can imagine text structured in several different ways can boost the appeal of print.

Writing and design are traditionally considered separate tasks. But this causes a problem, because some important considerations fall through the cracks. The most important of these is how the writing is written to look. Making the writing look appealing and comfortable to read is the reponsibility of *both* the writer and the designer.

HealthPrint

Making the Most of Your Time with the Doctor

Using the Phone	Writing it Down	Talking with the Doctor
Knowing how to use the phone can save you time and money. Be prepared to describe your condition accurately and efficiently.	It's a good idea to think through what you want from the doctor *before* you talk. You're more likely to be satisfied if you do.	You have the greatest interest in your health. It is your responsibility—and your right—to make the most of your time with the doctor.

Using the Phone

- If it's an emergency, say so.
- If you're unsure about your need to see the doctor, ask to speak to the nurse, and ask her.
- If you think you'll need extra time with the doctor, request it.
- It's okay to ask what the visit will cost.
- See if a phone conversation can replace a follow-up visit.
- To avoid a wait, call ahead to see if the doctor is on schedule.
- If possible, avoid calling on Monday, the busiest day.

Writing it Down

- Write down your symptoms, such as fever, pain, fatigue, cough, diarrhea, weight change.
- Describe your condition honestly and fully. When is it better? Worse?
- Write down the date of your first symptoms.
- Write down any questions about your condition.
- Write down any medication you are currently using. Include both over-the-counter and prescription drugs.
- Write down any allergies you have, especially to medication.

Talking with the Doctor

- You should be able to ask questions comfortably, and feel satisfied with the answers.
- If you don't understand something, ask the doctor to explain it again.
- When your doctor orders tests, understand what they are for.
- Ask your doctor about alternative treatments, and the risks of each.
- Ask about generics instead of brand-name drugs.
- If you forget to ask something, don't hesitate to call back.

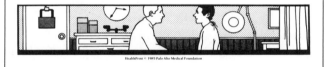

HealthPrint © 1985 Palo Alto Medical Foundation

HealthPrint

The Hidden Costs of Medical Care

We hope you have found this HealthPrint series interesting and useful. Here are some tips to help you get the highest quality health care at a reasonable cost.

1 Make the most of your time with the doctor. If you're unsure about your need to see the doctor, ask to speak to the nurse, and ask her what you should do. Write down symptoms and questions before you talk to the doctor. Use the phone whenever possible. If you don't understand something, ask the doctor to explain it again.

2 Go to the emergency room for life-threatening emergencies: a major injury or a sudden, dramatic change in your health. Don't go for minor injuries or on-going problems. If in doubt, call your doctor for advice. You're more likely to get better care from a doctor you know, so find one you like and trust before an emergency arises.

3 If you are unsure about your need for surgery, get a second opinion. Tell your doctor that you want to feel 100% sure about the need for surgery. Get a second opinion from a family doctor or an internist since a surgeon may be biased toward surgery. Bring a copy of your medical record so tests won't have to be repeated.

4 Buy drugs wisely. When your doctor writes you a prescription, ask if there is an effective generic. As there is no standard price for drugs, call several pharmacies and compare costs. Ask the pharmacist which remedies are best for things like sunburn, diarrhea, constipation, acne, or flu. Some "remedies" are worthless.

5 Avoid unpleasant surprises on your medical bills. Review bills carefully—errors are very common. Know what is and is not covered by your medical insurance. Know the amount of your deductible and copayment. Ask what your doctor or hospital bill will be before you are treated. Find out how your insurance plan works.

6 Compare hospitals' charges, and be aware of alternatives. Hospitals vary in both quality of care and cost; choose a good one when you need it. Keep your stay as short as possible, and avoid hospitals altogether if you can. Get tests and surgery done on an outpatient basis, and use home health services for recovering at home.

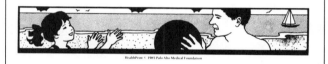

HealthPrint © 1985 Palo Alto Medical Foundation

HealthPrint

Emergency Rooms When to Use Them When to Avoid Them

When to Go	When Not to Go	Be Prepared
If in doubt, call a doctor or an emergency room first for advice. Go to an emergency room immediately for life-threatening conditions such as:	Emergency rooms do not provide the best care for many conditions. And you can wait hours—the most serious cases are treated first. Do *not* go for:	As you are more likely to get better care from a doctor you know, find one you like and trust *before* an emergency arises.

When to Go

- A major injury
- Poisoning
- Convulsions
- Unconsciousness
- Difficulty breathing
- Active bleeding that won't stop with direct pressure
- Chest pain or possible heart attack
- Stupor, drowsiness, or disorientation

When Not to Go

- Sprains
- Infections
- Minor cuts
- Sore throats
- Minor burns
- On-going problems
- Allergies (except reactions to bee stings)

Warning: Your insurance plan may not cover non-emergency treatment at an emergency room.

Be Prepared

- Call your doctor any time you are seriously concerned. This includes nights, weekends, and holidays.
- Keep the numbers of your doctor, friends, ambulance, and taxi by the phone for help or transportation.
- Keep a list of your medications and insurance information in your wallet.
- To find a good doctor, ask friends, relatives, or co-workers for recommendations.

HealthPrint © 1985 Palo Alto Medical Foundation

HealthPrint

How to Avoid Unpleasant Surprises on Your Medical Bills

1 Surprise! You are charged for services you did not receive. *Review bills carefully—errors are very common.* If you have questions about a medical bill, ask for an explanation. On hospital bills, verify the number of days you stayed, which doctors you saw and how often, and the amount and kind of medication or physical therapy you received.

2 Surprise! Your insurance company reimburses you for less than you expected. *Know the basis on which your insurance pays.* Insurance plans often pay only "usual and customary" fees (fees common to your area). If your doctor charges more than what your insurance company considers "usual and customary," you will have to pay the difference in the bill.

3 Surprise! Your insurance company says the care you received is not covered by the policy. *Know what is and is not covered by your medical insurance.* Find out what exclusions and limitations there are in your coverage. Sometimes your insurance company will pay for a more "cost-effective" alternative if it is less than a covered benefit. Get advance approval.

4 Surprise! Your bill is higher than you expected. *Ask what your doctor's bill will be before you are treated.* Don't wait until you're upset about a bill to find out what your doctor charges. Call the receptionist and ask before you see the doctor. When you start with a new doctor, ask what routine services like a physical exam or an office visit will cost.

5 Surprise! Your doctor wants you to pay the bill before your insurance reimburses you. *Know how your insurance plan works.* Submitting claims for reimbursement after you've paid the doctor is standard practice with many insurance plans. If you know in advance that your bill will be large, see if you can work out another arrangement with your doctor.

6 Surprise! You have to pay more than you expected toward your deductible or co-payment. *Know how much of your medical bill your insurance company pays, and how much you pay.* Be sure you know the amount of your deductible (how much you must pay before your insurance begins) and your co-payment (a flat fee or the percentage you must pay).

HealthPrint © 1985 Palo Alto Medical Foundation

Headlines, bullets, and numbers help make these printed pieces for a corporate health program, left, easier to read.

The real test of effective printed materials is neither the excellence of the writing nor the sophistication of the design in themselves, but how well it *communicates the information* it contains. And how well it communicates depends on how well the writing and the design are *integrated*. The arrangement of words a writer uses has a lot to do with how inviting or off-putting the piece looks; how it looks has a lot to do with whether or not people read it. And the person who puts the words together is the writer, not the designer.

As experienced writers know, the same information can be written up in several different ways. For example, it can be presented as solid text with greater or fewer headlines; it can be broken up into longer or shorter paragraphs, or into units with numbers or bullets. Information can be presented in different formats, like questions and answers, or interviews, or testimonials. It can be set off in bullets or sidebars or boxes or charts.

These text arrangements all look different when they are set in type on a page. But the writer usually focuses on the meaning of the words without giving much thought to how the word formulations will look. He or she then hands the copy over to the designer, who is expected to make the piece look easy to read without changing the position of a word.

Writers' roles become integrated with designers' when they pay attention to the *visual impression* a particular arrangement of words will make on the reader. Designers' roles become integrated with writers' when they recognize the writers' part in the look of the piece, and when they help them see alternative arrangements of words.

If you are both writing and designing a printed piece, you've got an advantage. You can write with an awareness of the impact of your word formulations on the design; you can design with a mind to strengthening the meaning of the words. The result will be a piece that really communicates.

Making the Piece Look Easy To Read

25

There are many things that a writer can do to make a piece look inviting. Here are some suggestions for making your printed piece look easy to read:

- Use more headlines

- Use more paragraphs, and make them shorter

- Make your point in fewer words

- Formulate a readable table of contents

- Include an index when practical, and put it where people can find it

- Use bullets when possible

- Use "running heads" (the name of the section on every page)

- Make room for "white" (empty) space

- Keep text units well organized

- Avoid cluttered-looking arrangements of words

- Don't forget page numbers

- More suggestions are covered in *Making Writing More Readable*

Titles that say exactly what the printed piece is about facilitate communication.

Use Good Titles

Your title either enhances the communication of your printed piece or becomes a barrier to it, so give your title some thought. When you write a title, say what the piece is about in a straighforward way. Don't make people *guess* at what's inside as the examples below do (they are taken from real publications). I suspect these writers hoped to pique their readers' curiosity and entice them into reading on. But most simply won't bother.

Examples of weak titles

- Because Your Veterinarian Cares . . .
- It's Your Choice
- Word of Mouth
- If You Could Help Someone See
- What's Your Number?
- Beware the Silent Killer
- Bummed Out Again?
- Is This Our Last Chance?
- Listen with Your Heart
- Information for People of Color
- You are the Most Important Person
- Attention Everyone!
- Guess What?
- Why Work So Hard?
- How Do You Score with the Basic 4?
- Mouse Gene Man
- A Child Alone in Need of Help

THE EXERCISE BOOK

For People Who Don't Exercise

Stanford Heart Disease Prevention Program

There are two kinds of titles that work well. The first is a clear, straightforward, descriptive title that says what the piece is about, such as *How to Get a Bank Loan.* The second kind of title that works is a short, punchy, or clever one, followed by a descriptive subtitle, such as *Happily Ever After: Women's Fiction in Postwar Britain 1945–1960.* There are some examples of good titles on page 127 (these are real ones too). Although some of these are for books, there is no reason why the title of your proposal, brochure, or report

Writing Good Titles   26

The title is an important part of your publication—give it the best one you can. Here are some tips and suggestions for writing good ones:

- Read titles everywhere you go.

- Notice which ones attract your attention, which ones leave you confused, and which ones turn you off.

- Go to a bookstore or library to see many titles quickly.

- Look at titles on lists such as best seller and book award lists. Look for trends, patterns, and ideas.

- When you write your title, say what the piece is about. Make it clear, straightforward, and descriptive.

- Or use a short, punchy, clever title, and follow it by a descriptive subtitle.

- Avoid annoying, controversial, or meaningless titles such as "Diversity/Presence," "Neighborhood Scenes," "Great Surprises," or "What's This?".

- Avoid negative or depressing titles such as "There is a lot to be done," " What's the last thing you'll ever do," or "When one out of five has problems . . ."

- Try some titles out on people (preferably your target audience).

- Choose a title that really does your piece justice.

---

can't be just as clear and interesting. Sidebar 26 has more on writing strong titles.

Examples of strong titles

- Herb Grower and Marketer
- Thirty-Minute Meals
- The Complete Hypercard Handbook
- The Single Parent Household
- Habits Not Diets
- How to Buy a Car
- Town Planning in Massachusetts
- Training Your Cat
- In Search of Excellence
- The Exercise Book: For People Who Don't Exercise
- Senatorial Privilege: The Chappaquiddick Cover-up
- I Can Cope: Learning to Live with Cancer
- Paths of Duty: American Missionary Wives in Nineteenth-Century Hawaii
- The Way Things Work
- A Brief History of Time
- Basics of Birth Control
- Wealth without Risk
- How to Stop Your Dog's Bad Breath

Pay attention to your title. A good one attracts attention. It also makes the piece easier to talk about, and easier to remember.

Keep It Short

We often try to say too much in print. What happens then is that the piece ends up looking crowded, and when it looks crowded, it looks hard to read. When it looks hard to read, it isn't read. So in an attempt to communicate *more* information we often end up communicating *less*.

Decide what is important to say, and say just that. Shorter pieces are less overwhelming and they demand less of the reader. Wordiness can slow readers down, distract them from the main message, and annoy them. Keep your piece as short as you can.

Write Strong Headlines

Headlines, like titles, can be real assets to your printed piece. Make them earn their keep. Write headlines that really *say* something, like the ones in newspapers. That way if readers only skim over your piece you'll still get something across.

For example, instead of saying "Introduction" at the beginning of your printed piece, *describe* what you are introducing: "The Passion for White Water Rafting," for instance, or "Children of the Twenty-first Century." Instead of saying "Background," your headline might read "100 Years of Honest Work," or "It All Started in Chicopee Falls," or "Anne's Early Years in Upstate New York."

The more descriptive your headline, the more you empower it to communicate. To write a good headline, simply describe the piece as vividly as you can. Let's say you are writing a title for a recipe. "Quick Mexican Vegetable Stew" says a lot more than "South-of-the-Border Dinner"; "Dense and Moist Chocolate Cake" communicates more than "Mia's Favorite Dessert." "Cake" is more specific than "dessert"; "dense," "moist," and "chocolate" say more than somebody's favorite ever could. At left are examples of weak headlines, and a stronger version next to them.

Examples of Headlines

Weaker headline	Stronger headline
• Introduction	An Overview of Senior Net
• Background	The Early Years: 1893 - 1914
• Drinking and Driving	Don't Drink and Drive
• Investments	The Widest Range of Investments
• The Chaplaincy	What Chaplains Do
• Ride a Fine Horse	Scenic Trail Rides
• The Mall	Getting to the Mall
• Protection	Protect Yourself from Inflation
• The Program	How the Program Works
• Weight	How to Control Your Weight
• Hitchhikers	Picking Up Hitchhikers is Risky
• CDs	The CD You Can Add to
• Income	Where Our Money Comes from
• More About Food	Good Snacks
• Wagons Roll Along	Family Hay Rides
• Bugs, Bugs, Bugs	Computer Viruses
• What's New?	Charting Model Changes
• Sweet Dreams	How To Sleep Well

Headlines in this brochure are written so that readers get useful information, even if that's all they read.

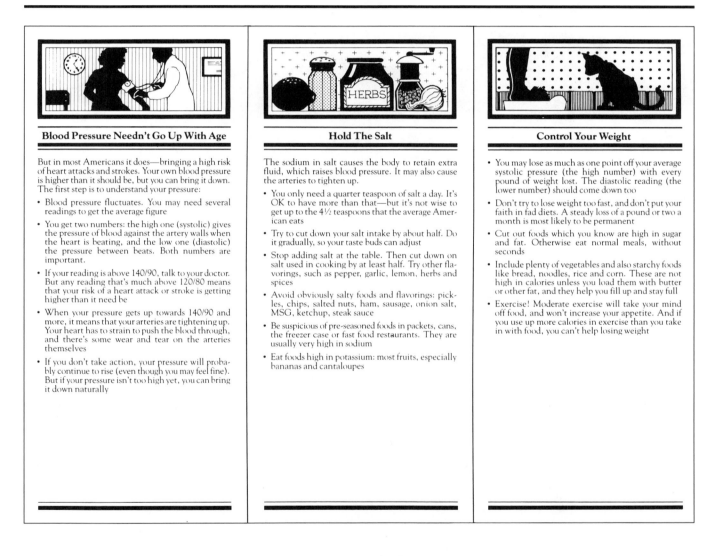

Blood Pressure Needn't Go Up With Age

But in most Americans it does—bringing a high risk of heart attacks and strokes. Your own blood pressure is higher than it should be, but you can bring it down. The first step is to understand your pressure:

- Blood pressure fluctuates. You may need several readings to get the average figure
- You get two numbers: the high one (systolic) gives the pressure of blood against the artery walls when the heart is beating, and the low one (diastolic) the pressure between beats. Both numbers are important.
- If your reading is above 140/90, talk to your doctor. But any reading that's much above 120/80 means that your risk of a heart attack or stroke is getting higher than it need be
- When your pressure gets up towards 140/90 and more, it means that your arteries are tightening up. Your heart has to strain to push the blood through, and there's some wear and tear on the arteries themselves
- If you don't take action, your pressure will probably continue to rise (even though you may feel fine). But if your pressure isn't too high yet, you can bring it down naturally

Hold The Salt

The sodium in salt causes the body to retain extra fluid, which raises blood pressure. It may also cause the arteries to tighten up.

- You only need a quarter teaspoon of salt a day. It's OK to have more than that—but it's not wise to get up to the 4½ teaspoons that the average American eats
- Try to cut down your salt intake by about half. Do it gradually, so your taste buds can adjust
- Stop adding salt at the table. Then cut down on salt used in cooking by at least half. Try other flavorings, such as pepper, garlic, lemon, herbs and spices
- Avoid obviously salty foods and flavorings: pickles, chips, salted nuts, ham, sausage, onion salt, MSG, ketchup, steak sauce
- Be suspicious of pre-seasoned foods in packets, cans, the freezer case or fast food restaurants. They are usually very high in sodium
- Eat foods high in potassium: most fruits, especially bananas and cantaloupes

Control Your Weight

- You may lose as much as one point off your average systolic pressure (the high number) with every pound of weight lost. The diastolic reading (the lower number) should come down too
- Don't try to lose weight too fast, and don't put your faith in fad diets. A steady loss of a pound or two a month is most likely to be permanent
- Cut out foods which you know are high in sugar and fat. Otherwise eat normal meals, without seconds
- Include plenty of vegetables and also starchy foods like bread, noodles, rice and corn. These are not high in calories unless you load them with butter or other fat, and they help you fill up and stay full
- Exercise! Moderate exercise will take your mind off food, and won't increase your appetite. And if you use up more calories in exercise than you take in with food, you can't help losing weight

Put Important Information First

When the most important information is buried in the middle of your printed piece, you risk losing readers before they ever get to it. It's wise to assume that just the first sentence will be read; then just the first paragraph; then just the first page. Choose priorities for your issues, and put the most important ones at the beginning.

Ideally, people will tumble through your writing effortlessly, like falling feathers. This is hard to do when there are lengthy introductions, long explanations, boring backgrounds, chatty overviews, irrelevant histories, letters from presidents, and other nonessential stuff to get through before the meat of the message appears.

This brochure keeps the text to an absolute minimum. It says just what is important to say, and no more.

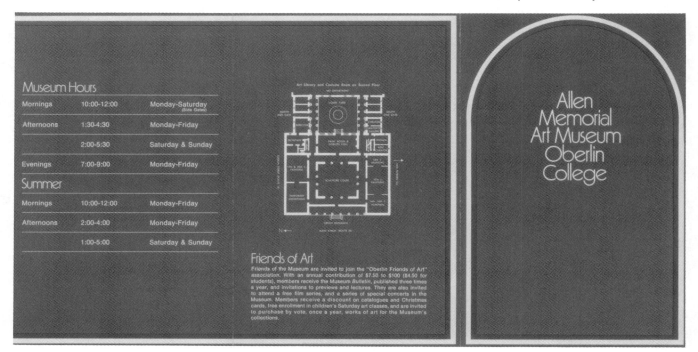

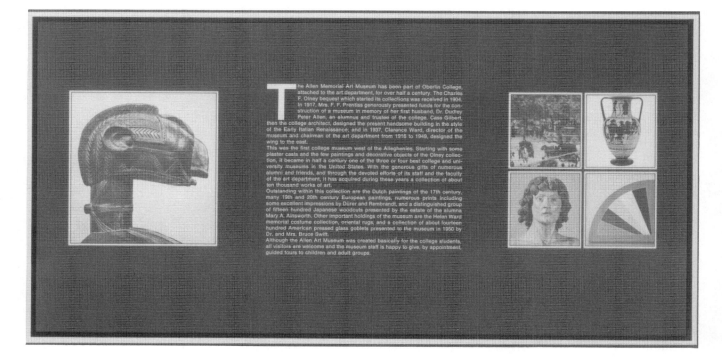

This is especially sad when you've written exactly what your readers are interested in, but they never get to it because of dull or wordy starts. Make the most of that valuable space at the beginning. When you are writing a printed piece, there's no virtue in saving the best for last.

Make Your Writing Interesting

No matter what your topic, there is a dull way to present it and an interesting way. Your writing is stronger when you know your subject well, when you care about it, and when you want to communicate it to others. Get involved—a writer's enthusiasm for the topic comes through. Here are some ways to make the subject you are writing about more interesting—to you as well as to your readers. Begin with a grabber. Start your printed piece with:

A startling fact

Starting your piece with surprising information is a good way to engage your readers. Numbers make startling facts even more dramatic. For instance, you could begin your piece with something like "Within the next ten years, sixty percent of Californians will be Spanish-speaking." Or "One in every four dollars spent in the United States is spent on real estate." Do some research. Look for startling or dramatic data related to your subject. Try reference books or magazine articles related to your topic, or books like *The World Almanac* or the *Guinness Book of World Records*. Reference librarians can be very helpful.

An intriguing question

Another technique is to begin with a question that catches the interest of your reader. Say you're doing a piece for senior citizens. A major concern among the elderly is being able to continue to drive. So starting

Making Writing More Interesting

27

Although some topics are certainly more engaging than others, there is no topic that can't be made interesting. Here are some ways to make your writing more captivating (they are all discussed in this chapter):

Start with a grabber. Begin with:

• A startling fact

• An intriguing question

• A common myth

• An interesting anecdote

• New information

• A slice-of-life

• Interesting comparisons

Use a different format. Try:

• A quiz

• Testimonials

• Questions and answers

• A checklist

• An interview

• Practical tips

Dairy Foods

Week One: Buy whole milk and lowfat. Mix them in equal quantities, and drink that mixture for the first week.

Week Two: Drink lowfat on its own.

Week Three: Mix lowfat and nonfat. Start with one-fourth nonfat, and build up to half, then to three-quarters nonfat.

Week Four: Drink nonfat on its own!

After a few weeks on nonfat, you may find you positively dislike the rich, heavy taste of whole milk. Incidentally, in spite of its name, buttermilk is low in fat, especially when made from nonfat milk (but higher in sodium than regular milk).

YOGURT

Yogurt is as high in fat as the milk it was made from. If it's made from whole milk, it will be full of fat. If it's lowfat and also fruit flavored, it will have enough added sugar to pile on the calories. Plain yogurt, made with nonfat or lowfat milk, is excellent.

BUTTER

There's little to recommend butter, from a nutritional point of view; it's high in cholesterol as well as saturated fat. Margarine is much better—as long as it's not a type that is also high in saturated fat. For more on choosing margarines, see "Hidden Saturated Fat", page 19.

ICE CREAM

Ice cream itself is between 10% and 18% fat by weight depending on how rich it is. Ice milk is a better bet, with only 3 or 4% fat. Sherbet is even better, containing little or no fat, though its sugar content makes it almost as high in calories as regular ice cream.

15

Salt

HOW TO SEASON YOUR FOOD WITHOUT SALT

Meat, Fish, and Poultry

Beef	Bay leaf, dry mustard powder, green pepper, marjoram, fresh mushrooms, nutmeg, onion, pepper, sage, thyme.
Chicken	Green pepper, lemon juice, marjoram, fresh mushrooms, paprika, parsley, poultry seasoning, sage, thyme.
Fish	Bay leaf, curry powder, dry mustard powder, green pepper, lemon juice, marjoram, fresh mushrooms, paprika.
Lamb	Curry powder, garlic, mint, mint jelly, pineapple, rosemary.
Pork	Apple, applesauce, garlic, onion, sage.
Veal	Apricot, bay leaf, curry powder, ginger, marjoram, oregano.

Soups

Bean	Pinch of dry mustard powder.
Milk Chowders	Peppercorns.
Pea	Bay leaf and parsley.
Vegetable	Vinegar, dash of sugar.

Vegetables

Asparagus	Garlic, lemon juice, onion, vinegar
Corn	Green pepper, pimiento, fresh tomato.

continued on the next page

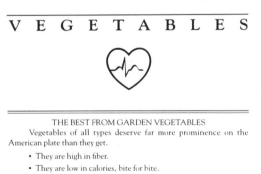

23

Sugar

Low Sugar Cereals

Product	Manufacturer	Total Sugar
Special K	Kellogg	5.4%
Corn Flakes	Kellogg	5.3%
Post Toasties	General Foods	5.0%
Kix	General Mills	4.8%
Rice Chex	Ralston-Purina	4.4%
Corn Chex	Ralston-Purina	4.0%
Wheat Chex	Ralston-Purina	3.5%
Cheerios	General Mills	3.0%
Shredded Wheat	Nabisco	0.6%
Puffed Wheat	Quaker Oats	0.5%
Puffed Rice	Quaker Oats	0.1%

Granola

This is a concentrated breakfast that will help you feel full all morning. The ingredients are available in any supermarket, and it has much less sugar and fat than commercial brands.

3 cups raw wheat germ	1 cup sunflower seeds
2 cups rolled oats	¼ cup oil
1 cup wheat bran	¼ cup brown sugar (or less)
1 cup sesame seeds	1 cup raisins

Preheat oven to 300°, and first toast seeds for 15-20 minutes, stirring often. Grind them in food processor at high speed, or in a blender, ¼ cup at a time. Blend in short bursts, stirring often, until you have a smooth meal. Place all other ingredients, except for raisins, in shallow pan and bake for 45 minutes, stirring every 15 minutes. Add raisins and ground seeds; cool and store covered in refrigerator.

27

V E G E T A B L E S

THE BEST FROM GARDEN VEGETABLES

Vegetables of all types deserve far more prominence on the American plate than they get.

- They are high in fiber.
- They are low in calories, bite for bite.
- They fill you up.
- They are a good source of vitamins and minerals.
- They are inexpensive and easy to prepare.
- They make excellent snacks, as well as accompaniments to the main meal.

To get the most from vegetables, eat a wide variety each week: leafy green types, root types, and vegetables in pods. It's not too much if you eat two at each main meal plus potatoes or some other form of starch (and did you know that a medium potato has no more calories than a large apple?)

40

*Useful and specific
information in this booklet, left, is
organized in ways that are easy to read.*

your piece off with something like "Will this man pass his driving test?" (under a photograph of a representative senior) would be likely to catch the interest of the audience. Ideas for coming up with good questions are given in Sidebar 28.

A common myth

What are the most commonly held myths that relate to the subject you are writing about? They can make an excellent introduction. For example, you might start out with "Bottled water is safer than tap water. Or is it?" Or "They say Americans are the most fit people on earth. But four out of five of them are overweight." Or "Starches are fattening: True or False?" If you write a newsletter or other regularly appearing piece, you could include a "myth of the month." This would be especially effective for subjects around which there are many misconceptions, such as computers or aging or nutrition or bats.

An interesting anecdote

Sometimes the best way to involve a reader is to start off with someone's personal story. A piece for consumers on holiday spending might start off, for instance, with: "Four-year-old Ryan walked into a department store at Christmas-time and said to his brother Rob, 'Can't you just *smell* the toys!'" Or a piece on travel might begin with "Driving in Mexico is always an adventure. The last time Matt and Harriet..." Most of us find a good anecdote seductive. Collect ones that relate to your subject for your printed pieces.

New information

New information draws attention, as newspapers demonstrate. Even using the word "new" seems to make information more appealing. You may as well

Adding Interest with Questions | 28

Beginning your printed piece with a good question can engage readers who might otherwise be lost. Here are some examples of questions that draw readers in. A worksheet version for your piece is on page 360.

1. What is the most common Russian pastime in winter?

2. What do George Washington and Madonna have in common?

3. How many Americans died in Viet Nam?

4. Can you name Queen Elizabeth's four children? Her grandchildren?

5. What is the most expensive vegetable in North Dakota?

6. People from what foreign country own the most property in the United States?

7. What is the best selling article of clothing in New York?

8. At what age is the average person physically strongest?

9. What is silicon?

10. What is the most common age for American men to become fathers?

take advantage of it if you have something new to say.

Let's say you are doing some fund raising for an archaeological dig. You might lead off by describing the latest in archaeological techniques, such as the use of planes with infrared photographic equipment to investigate promising sites.

Or you might say where (or how or why or when) the new technique is being used: in the search for King Solomon's temple in Israel, for example. Or if you are advertising a restaurant you might involve your reader in a headline about the newest trends in eating out, or the most popular food among restaurant diners (which of course you offer).

If you are promoting a kayaking class, you might describe the newest in gear; if you are conducting a campaign against drugs you might quote the latest statistics in your area. There is always something new in every subject, and anything "new" is news.

A slice-of-life

The success of *People* and similar magazines suggests the interest we have in other people's lives. Begin your piece with a "slice-of-life." Common people and everyday situations that readers can relate to have an especially broad appeal. No matter what your topic, there is a way to relate it to some human experience.

If, for instance, you are promoting a shopping service, you could write how "Julia A., with a two-year-old, a demanding job, twenty-five relatives and friends to buy presents for and a holiday to 'produce,' is feeling overwhelmed." More than a few people will be able to relate to that.

Or if you're writing about the older worker, you might begin with "Nancy Arnold's last birthday was a big deal." Readers will want to find out why, which birthday it was, and how close it is to their own. Or if you're selling car telephones you might begin: "Every week Sarah spends Monday through Friday driving between Cambridge and Wellesley . . ."

Interesting comparisons

Another way to make your writing more appealing is to use interesting comparisons. They can be especially helpful if you need to get difficult information across. Say you are writing a piece to reassure an anxious public about contamination from the chemical XYZ. Rather than say it would take so many gallons of XYZ to pose a serious threat, you could say "it would take three swimming pools worth." Or if you are trying to reassure the public about the safety of air travel, you could compare the odds of getting hurt while flying with those of riding in a car.

Or you might compare your product or service this year with last year, or with several years ago. You can also make interesting comparisons between an old version and a new one, or between your service or product and someone else's. People also like to see numbers, rankings, and ratings compared. For a sports-related piece you might compare the number of American Olympic gold medalists with those of other countries, for instance. You can also compare a situation in your city, county, state, or country with that of another. Compare just about anything—from political candidates to television shows to kitchen appliances—and it will interest readers.

Or try an interesting format. Consider:

Testimonials

Testimonials can be very effective. Nationally known figures, local authorities, experts, or just plain folks can be very convincing when they are sincerely behind a service or product. Say you are an employee benefits director with a new benefits package to introduce. You ask several employees to review it ahead, and use their positive comments in a piece that introduces the program to the rest of the workers. Their endorsements are likely to capture more interest and hold more weight than yours. Or if you are a

Boxes are useful in two ways: they visually communicate that action is to be taken, and they can be checked.

NURSES' CHECKLIST

INTERVENTION TRIAL	PREVALENCE SURVEY
NURSE	**NURSE**
☐ 1. Hospital Log	☐ 1. Hospital Log
☐ 2. Biographical Information	☐ 2. Biographical Information
☐ 3. Medical Information	☐ 3. Medical Information
☐ 4. ECG	☐ 4. ECG
☐ 5. Manila mailing envelope	☐ 5. Manila mailing envelope
PATIENT	**PATIENT**
☐ 1. Information for Patients	☐ 1. Information for Patients
☐ 2. Pre-discharge Patient Questionnaire	☐ 2. Pre-discharge Patient Questionnaire
☐ 3. Post-discharge Patient Questionnaire and Cover Note	☐ 3. Post-discharge Patient Questionnaire and Cover Note (Patients returning to work)
☐ 4. Patient Status Report	☐ 4. Postcard re RTW/ Retirement date
☐ 5. Postcard re RTW date	☐ 5. Manila mailing envelope
☐ 6. Map to Welch Road	
☐ 7. Manila mailing envelope	
PHYSICIAN	**PHYSICIAN**
☐ 1. Information for Physicians	☐ 1. Information for Physicians
☐ 2. Cover Letter to Physicians (Intervention Trial)	☐ 2. Cover Letter to Physicians (Prevalence Survey)
☐ 3. Physician Entry Questionnaire and Cover Note	☐ 3. Physician Entry Questionnaire and Cover Note
☐ 4. Regular envelope	☐ 4. Regular envelope

KAISER/STANFORD HE♥RT ATTACK PROGRAM

---

furniture maker, you will generate more interest in your furniture when you quote what a well-known designer had to say about your cabinet, or what a local art critic thought of your table.

A quiz

Another way to make your printed piece interesting to readers (and to yourself) is to come up with a quiz that relates to the subject you are writing about. Readers have a hard time ignoring a quiz, especially when answers give them information about themselves. Any piece that starts out "Test Your Knowledge of ____" (something related to your subject) is likely to draw readers. An antique dealer, for example,

might put out a piece that invites his audience to test its knowledge of old glass: bottles, vases, flasks, paper weights, and so on. Or a municipal energy group might put out a piece that begins "Can you name five ways to keep your house warmer this winter?" Multiple choice answers make tests easier to take.

A checklist

If you can get your readers to "interact" with your printed piece, it will make it more interesting for them. If your job is to establish a particular protocol for nurses, for instance, you can write up what they are to do in several different ways. You can send out a memo in paragraph form, or a step-by-step sheet, or a checklist. The checklist is likely to be the best of the three formats. With boxes to check next to each step, it works *visually* as well as verbally because it communicates that something is to be done. It isn't as important that the boxes actually get checked as it is that people realize there is a procedure to be followed.

Questions and answers

Another good way to engage your readers is to use a question and answer format. It also helps the writer stick to the point, and not write any more than is necessary.

Just about any kind of topic can be written about in questions and answers. Say you want more customers for your bank from the new immigrant population in your area. You might produce a brochure called *Questions and Answers about American Banking.* Include facts about how the banking system works along with the special benefits of banking with you. You may be surprised by the number of long-term residents you get as new customers along with the newcomers.

If you really want to be enterprising, you can have the piece translated into your target audience's native

Tip Sheet 1

Get Ready To Quit

Post this on your refrigerator after you've read the other side.

REMINDER: My quit date will be: _____

♥ From now until Quit Day, keep a piece of paper wrapped around your cigarette pack with a rubber band. Make a note on it each time you smoke. Write down the time of day and the circumstances (for example "on the telephone" or "after dinner"). This may help you cut down, and will help you to stop reaching for a cigarette without thinking about it.

♥ Keep the record sheets and read through them just before you quit. They'll tell you when you most want to smoke, so you can be on your guard at those times.

♥ Practice postponing some of your cigarettes for 15 minutes (rinsing your mouth with mouthwash helps).

♥ Change the way you smoke. For example, stand instead of sitting; smoke with your left hand instead of your right; hold the cigarette between your third and fourth fingers.

♥ Practice relaxation techniques, which will also be useful after you've quit. Sit down and let all your muscles go limp, while your mind focuses on one soothing image, such as leaves blowing in a gentle breeze, or ripples on a lake.

♥ Decide not to smoke in certain places, such as in the car or at your desk.

♥ Take a brisk walk every day. This will get you into training for exercise after you quit, when you'll find it an excellent substitute for smoking.

♥ From now on, buy cigarettes one pack at a time. Change brands each time you buy a pack; choose a brand you don't like.

♥ On the day before Quit Day, read Sheet 2: "Tomorrow's the Day."

Tip Sheet 2

Tomorrow's The Day

Post this on your refrigerator after you've read the other side.

♥ Ask one person to be your special helper—someone you can talk to if you have difficult times.

♥ Do some shopping. Buy substitutes for cigarettes. You don't want to gain weight, so buy plenty of fruit, sugarless gum, fruit juices. Cinnamon sticks and cloves are great; so are raw vegetables such as carrots and celery sticks.

♥ Tell people you come in contact with frequently that you are quitting tomorrow. Ask them to help by not offering you cigarettes.

♥ Before bedtime, put away ashtrays and matches. Destroy any remaining cigarettes.

♥ If possible, arrange to spend tomorrow with non-smokers. Get out of your usual routine. Go to the beach, to a park, to a movie.

♥ Feel good about what you are doing. From the moment you smoke your last cigarette you will be a healthier person, with a greater life expectancy than you ever had before. Sleep well!

♥ First thing tomorrow, read Sheet 3: "You've Quit!"

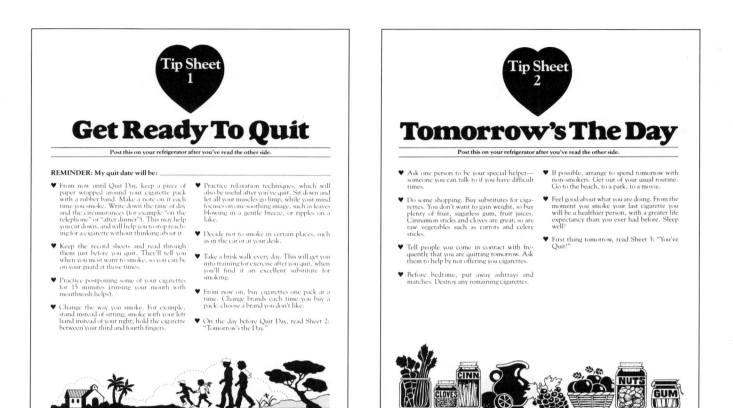

Tip Sheet 3

You've Quit

Post this on your refrigerator after you've read the other side.

If you have an urge to smoke:

♥ Chew something, like a carrot, celery stick, sugarless gum, cinnamon stick, cloves.

♥ Tell your helper or other friends how you are feeling.

♥ Relax completely. Sit down and let all your muscles go limp. Focus your mind on a soothing image.

♥ Breathe very deeply for a few minutes.

♥ Sing (if your family can stand it).

♥ Drink water or juice.

♥ Use a mouthwash after meals.

♥ Take a brisk walk.

♥ Take a nap.

Here are some general suggestions:

♥ Get plenty of exercise, and feel the power come back to your lungs.

♥ Eat regular meals to avoid hunger (which may be mistaken for the desire to smoke).

♥ Try to avoid smokers, especially in social situations where alcohol could weaken your will-power.

♥ Try to avoid tense situations. Keep busy doing things you like.

♥ Don't worry if you are sleepier than usual, or more irritable than usual. These symptoms will pass.

♥ At the end of the week, give yourself your reward (a book, a movie, something for your hobby, something to wear). You've made it!

♥ On your Quit Day plus 7, read Sheet 4: "Staying Free."

Tip Sheet 4

Staying Free

Post this on your refrigerator after you've read the other side.

♥ Watch out for smoking friends. Before you meet these friends, tell yourself, "They may offer me a cigarette, but I won't smoke." Remind them you've quit.

♥ Be especially careful to watch out for moments of tension. If you can't avoid them, prepare for them. Say to yourself beforehand: "I'm probably going to feel tense, but I won't smoke."

♥ If you do have an urge to smoke, time it. It probably won't last long. Urges will now get shorter and less frequent, as time goes by.

♥ If you're afraid of gaining weight, start to cut down on the calories while you exercise more. You're over the worst now, and you don't need to nibble all day.

♥ If you do lapse and have a cigarette, forget it. Start the next day as an ex-smoker again. Don't feel that one failure forces you to go back to your old habit.

♥ Decide on your six-month's reward. Make it a big one: you'll have saved well over $100. You might want a night on the town, an overnight trip, new clothes—whatever your heart desires. Write it down below:

I will have been smoke-free for six months on _____

I will reward myself with _____

Congratulations! Now you are all set to enjoy a long, healthy, happy life.

Information in this smoking "quit kit," left, is boiled down to key tips. They are organized into stages that reflect the quitting process.

language, and print it along side the English translation. This helps them learn English, giving them another reason to read your piece.

An interview

If you're writing a newsletter, an article, a report, or some other piece where it would fit, consider doing an interview. People are often willing (and flattered) to be interviewed, and personal opinions always make a piece more interesting.

Let's say you are writing a progress report for a client who has employed you to conduct a program in her company. A brief interview with Hilary H. in management and another one with Richard A. in operations will make your report more interesting to your employer. It will also make it more credible. Or if you're writing a newsletter—it could be on anything from the stock market to stitchery—consider including a regular interview column. Interviews can be conducted among experts, and among the newsletter readers themselves.

Practical tips

Another thing you can do to make your writing more interesting is to offer tips that relate to your subject.

You might suggest "Five Ways to____" (something relating to your topic, and an appropriate number). For example, if you are promoting your dental practice, you might offer five tips on finding a good dentist under a title like "Five Ways to Evaluate a Dentist."

Or if the purpose of your piece is to get contributions to a fund supporting the arts, it could start off with tips on ways to judge art, how to appreciate music, or how to evaluate a dance performance. Useful tips and advice on your subject placed in an appropriate position can add to the appeal of your printed piece.

Selecting a Tone for the Writing   `29`

Here are some ideas for ways to "flavor" your writing. Whatever style you choose, make sure it has an underlying professional tone. Check one(s) that will appeal most to your particular audience.

- ☐ Direct
- ☐ Light
- ☐ Friendly
- ☐ Fun
- ☐ Witty
- ☐ Honest
- ☐ Serious
- ☐ Strong
- ☐ Authoritative
- ☐ Bold
- ☐ Lively
- ☐ Intimate
- ☐ Punchy
- ☐ Adventuresome
- ☐ Sincere

A worksheet version of this sidebar appears on page 358.

30 | Making a Writing Assignment

You may be turning the writing of your printed piece over to someone else. Before you meet with that person, think through what you want to cover, and collect any missing information. Here are some of the things to discuss with the writer.

- The purpose of the piece

- The approximate length of the piece

- The nature of the target audience

- Sources of background material

- The timeline for the piece

- When the first draft is due

- Who will be reviewing and editing the piece

- How the piece is to be handed in (typed, on disk; number of copies, etc.)

- How much time you expect the writer will put into it

- The amount and schedule of payments

Use a Professional Tone

Good writing has many different tones. For instance, it can be friendly, bold, lighthearted, or serious. (Other possibilities are suggested in Sidebar 29.) Select a tone that is appropriate for your audience. Whatever tone you choose, keep it professional.

"Professional" means clear, concise, and readable; it also means credible. A good example of a professional tone is the one often found in news magazines and newspapers. It is the same kind of language spoken on nightly national news broadcasts. This way of speaking (and writing) is understandable to a large majority of people in many places. A reporting tone works well for most printed pieces. It is business-like yet friendly, informational, yet comfortable. Tones that are too personal, too familiar, or too chatty run the risk of offending or turning off the reader.

Like newscasters' nightly reports, information in printed pieces must be both fresh and accurate. Check names, dates, organizations, and affiliations. Confirm facts and figures. Don't leave out the names of people who should be included, and don't include the names of people who prefer not to be mentioned. Mistakes along these lines can be embarrassing.

Motivate Your Reader

When you are advocating or promoting something in print, don't assume that the reader shares your enthusiasm. Although the benefits or virtues may be obvious to you, they probably won't be to the reader. Describe your topic's attributes as well as possible. Anticipate the readers' questions, including their most basic one, "What's in this for me?" and be sure to answer them.

If you expect someone to respond to your piece, it is important to point out why you think they should. You've got to make your case.

Keep Your Writing Positive

Speak to your readers as you yourself like to be spoken to: in an intelligent, respectful, and positive manner. No one likes complaints or bad news. It's depressing, and putting something in a negative way makes it harder to understand.

Take a positive approach in your writing. If the news *is* bad, include as much of the good side as you honestly can. Say what can be done or is being done to help in an otherwise unfavorable situation. A positive voice is both appealing and reassuring; a cold, condescending, or negative tone is also a turn-off. You can communicate your message without sounding like Pollyanna or Eeyore.

Aim for the Right Level

Have you ever tried to read something in a language you know only slightly? It's frustrating, and you probably gave up. The same thing happens to readers of their own language when a piece is written at the wrong level. It can be too sophisticated, too technical, or too academic; or it can be filled with too much "in house" language. Or it might be too simple, like the brochure I mentioned on cast care.

Hitting the right level is tricky. It is just as easy to assume that your readers know more than they do as it is to assume they know less.

My friend Pat, a psychologist, was putting together a brochure on counseling services and asked me to look at it. Although the services she offered were impressive, they were presented in a way that assumed the reader knew the philosophy behind them. Even if some of them did, others might not. Pat might have cut herself off from potential clients by assuming they understood her approach.

If in doubt, spell it out. To be sure you've hit the right level, get feedback first from your prospective readers.

Writer's Checklist · 31

Before you hand your piece over to someone else to read, go through it one last time to make sure it says what you want it to say. Here is a summary of the guidelines discussed in this chapter.

☐ The piece is simple and direct

☐ The words look easy to read

☐ It has a strong title

☐ The headlines are descriptive

☐ Important information is at the beginning

☐ The piece is interesting

☐ The information is accurate

☐ The tone is positive

☐ It motivates the reader

☐ It is aimed at the right level

☐ Examples are given when needed

☐ There is nothing to date the piece prematurely

☐ The piece is as short as it can be

☐ The piece says what is intended

A worksheet version of this sidebar appears on page 358.

*The brochure below clearly lays
out birth control alternatives. The one at
right has a simple and straightforward title.*

Basics of birth control

PRESCRIPTION METHODS				NON-PRESCRIPTION METHODS			PERMANENT
'The Pill'	Intrauterine Device	Diaphragm	Vaginal Contraceptive Sponge	Condom	Vaginal Chemical Contraceptives: Foam, Suppositories	Fertility Awareness with Abstinence	Sterilization

Use Examples

Examples help to drive a message home. They make the information more concrete, and that helps readers to remember it. Let's say, for example, that Laura Richards is writing some tips for her house sellers' brochure. She could say "Flowers add interest in the yard." Or she could be more specific with "Flowers add interest to shady spots." Or she could add more information like "Flowers such as impatiens and begonias add interest to shady spots." Or she could go even further and say, "Flowers add interest to shady spots: try primroses and forget-me-nots in spring; impatiens and begonias in summer."

**Health Promotion
Print and
Video Materials**

Stanford Center for Research in Disease Prevention

Guidelines for Reader-Friendly Writing

32

Here is a summary of the guidelines for reader-friendly writing. Each is discussed in this chapter, and examples are given.

1. Be simple and direct

2. Make your piece look easy to to read

3. Use good titles

4. Write strong headlines

5. Keep it short

6. Put important information up front

7. Make your writing interesting

8. Keep the tone professional

9. Motivate your reader

10. Keep your writing positive

11. Aim for the right level

12. Use examples

13. Keep the writing timeless

14. Reinforce your writing visually

Maps, charts, diagrams, and similar imagery can add a lot to a printed piece. They are both informative and visually interesting.

Compare this last statement with her first: "Flowers add interest in the yard." The more concrete the example, the more interesting, valuable, and memorable it becomes.

Keep the Writing Timeless

Unless your piece will have a very short life span, keep out anything that could make it sound dated. If you say, for example, that a project will be completed in 1995 and it is 1995, the piece sounds old. And if you give a future date, whatever it is that's supposed to have happened by then may or may *not* have happened. If it hasn't, it will be hard to use the piece.

It is also important to watch the tense. If you say something like "in the future we will be importing techi-widgets," the piece is dated as soon as you're importing techi-widgets. Also think twice about including peoples' names in your piece. Staff turnover is unpredictable. Go through your writing carefully so it includes nothing to prematurely outdate it.

Reinforce Your Writing Visually

As you write, come up with ideas for charts, graphs, illustrations, photographs, or maps to strengthen and reinforce your message. These visual elements can help you present your case more effectively and add interest at the same time. Do not, however, use weak graphics in order to "fill the space." If you do, you could seriously diminish the overall impact of the piece. More on this in *Art and Photography*, page 241.

When a subject seems fuzzy or hard to understand, it more often has to do with the quality of the writing than the difficulty of the subject. If you really want to get your message across, make sure your piece is well written.

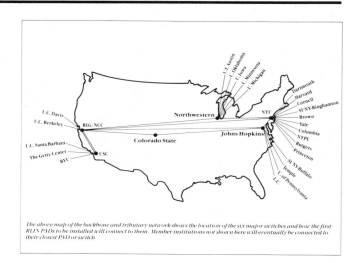

The above map of the backbone and tributary network shows the location of the six major switches and how the first RLIN PADs to be installed will connect to them. Member institutions not shown here will eventually be connected to their closest PAD or switch.

Chapter 13

E
M A H
H E W A
R F C M P S B

Making Writing More Readable

The last chapter offered general guidelines for making your writing reader-friendly while this one goes into more technical detail. It is based on questions that print producers frequently ask in consultations and workshops, including how to work with tables of contents, running heads, indexes, words, and sentences, as well as issues like jargon, technical language, acronyms, and abbreviations. This chapter also covers bullets, levels of heads, and vertical spacing. Although these are designers' concerns, they are of interest to many writers as well.

Later in the chapter Sidebar 33, *Red Flags*, lays out some common mistakes. Sidebar 34 talks about communicating risks to readers. Sidebars 35 and 36 offer tips on proofreading and standardized proofreaders' marks; 37 has an editor's checklist.

There is no single *right way* to write, as far as I'm concerned. The issue in writing for printed pieces is readability, not "right" and "wrong." What counts is getting your message across to your readers, and some ways work better than others. There are no ironclad rules, just continuous experimentation to find out what is most effective with your audience.

Helping Readers Gain Access

You can do a lot to help readers get in to your piece comfortably, and find what they want. The trick is to anticipate how they will read the piece and how they will use it, and to organize the material from their point of view.

You can help orient readers by using a table of contents, running heads, page numbers, an index, headlines, an overview, and a summary whenever they are appropriate for a particular piece. Here are suggestions and comments for each of these:

Table of Contents

You may have noticed the recent trend among some magazines and newsletters to put article titles with page numbers on the cover. It's another sign of the times—not many people have the leisure to read things cover to cover. Whether they are inside or out, tables of contents are helpful. They allow readers to quickly scan the contents of the piece, get an overview, and go directly to what interests them.

But a table of contents is useful only in a piece large enough to need one. I remember one corporate report in which a table of contents (and several other additional pages) made it look silly. This immodest piece had a title page, two pages of credits, a table of

*A section division page and charts
make using this cookbook easier. Large running
heads and page numbers help readers to find their place.*

contents, an "executive" summary, and finally, three pages of text. These were followed by a division page with the name of the next section on it, which was followed by a few more pages of text, and then another division page. The corporate report was too short for all of these pages.

In contrast, newspaper articles are submitted with the absolute minimum number of pages, so that the editor can get right down to the business of editing. Use a table of contents only when it is an asset to your piece. And when you do, make it neat and easy to read.

Running Heads

A running head is the name of the chapter (or section or part) at the top or bottom of every page. It is usually best set in smaller (or otherwise differentiated) type so the reader is not distracted from the main text. Running heads are especially important in long docu-

ments, and they are helpful in those with many different sections. You can put chapter titles on one page, and section or lesser subtopic titles on the facing one.

Page Numbers

Page numbers, sometimes called *folios* in publishing, are essential for readability in booklets, questionnaires, directories, manuals, catalogs, articles, proposals and reports. And page numbers can be equally helpful in brochures, forms, invoices, programs, and menus.

Avoid using "i," "ii," "iii," and so on in opening pages unless you are following a pre-prescribed protocol. This carry-over from academic writing is not appropriate for non-academic pieces. It is confusing for those who are unfamiliar with it, and annoying to some who are. Just start numbering your pages with number 1 on the first right-hand page.

DRESSINGS

OIL AND VINEGAR-BASED DRESSINGS

A number of excellent and healthy dressings are based upon a mixture of about 3 parts oil to 1 part or less of vinegar. You may want to vary the amount of vinegar depending on your taste and the oil used.

ITALIAN DRESSING

²/₃ c vegetable oil; 3 T vinegar; 1 T water; 1 t sugar; 2 t lemon juice; ¼ t garlic powder; 2 drops tabasco hot-pepper sauce; ½ t crushed oregano or basil; ¼ t black pepper. Shake together in jar and chill. Good with cold broccoli.

BASIC FRENCH DRESSING

1 c oil; ⅓ c vinegar or lemon juice, or 3 T of each; 2 T sugar; 1½ t salt; ½ t paprika; ½ t dry mustard; 1 clove garlic. Shake together in jar and chill. Shake well before serving. A basic dressing good on any vegetable salad.

GARLIC DRESSING

1½ c oil; 2 T lemon juice; 2 T vinegar; 2 T finely minced onion, fresh or dehydrated; 1½ t salt; 1 t Worcestershire sauce; dash (⅛ t) white pepper; 2 drops tabasco sauce; ½ t garlic powder or 2 cloves finely minced garlic. Shake together and chill several hours for flavors to blend. Good on tossed vegetable salads or salad of orange and cucumber slices.

LEMON HERB DRESSING

1 c oil; ⅓ c lemon juice; 2 T white vinegar; 1½ T sugar; 1½ t salt; ½ t paprika; ½ t dried salad herbs; 1 clove garlic. Shake well together in jar and chill. Remove garlic. Shake well before serving. Good on broken pieces of spinach; romaine; dandelion greens; or sliced raw mushrooms on endive.

53

CHARTS

INSTANT GUIDE TO HEART HEALTH

FOODS	CHOLESTEROL	SATURATED FATS	SUGAR	SALT	BUYING AND COOKING TIPS
Meat group					This group includes such high protein foods as lentils, dried peas and beans, and eggs. Eat 2 or more servings a day.
Beef, lamb, pork, and veal		•			Buy leanest cuts possible, cook to eliminate fat; don't serve more than once a day.
Ground meat		•			Ask butcher to grind lean meat for you or grind your own. Buy lean ground.
Chicken Turkey					Chicken and turkey are excellent foods; but avoid fat under the skin.
Duck and Goose		•			Wild duck is good; tame ducks and geese very fatty.
Sausage, lunch meats, salami, hot dogs, etc.		•		•	Most of the time eat only about once or twice a week.
Shellfish	•				Eat crab, shrimp, clams, etc. only twice a month.
Fin fish					Fresh, canned, or frozen all excellent.
Eggs	•				Whites are excellent; eat only two to three yolks a week.
Nuts, dried peas, dried beans, lentils					Good, protein foods that can serve as meat substitutes on occasion.
Milk group					Eat 2 or more servings a day.
Milk		•			Choose nonfat ('skimmed') or buttermilk.
Yogurt					Plain, low-fat yogurt is excellent; all yogurt is good for heart health.
Ice Cream	•	•			Substitute sherbet, or imitation ice cream made with oil. Ice milk is not as bad as ice cream.
Cream	•	•			Very high in saturated fat and cholesterol. Avoid it! Use a non-dairy creamer in coffee (one without coconut oil).
Butter	•	•			Very high in saturated fat and cholesterol. Substitute soft margarine.
Cheese	•	•			Use low-fat kinds (like cottage cheese) except on special occasions.

73

Indexes

Index is Latin for *to point out* (as in *index finger*). Indexes and tables of contents serve different, complementary purposes. Tables of contents offer an overview and quick access to particular sections. Indexes provide more detailed references, helping readers locate specific subject matter.

An index is important to include in just about every kind of non-fiction printed piece with any substantial number of pages. It is absolutely essential for publications used for reference.

Such an alphabetical listing of topics, names, and so on—next to the page numbers they appear on in the text—is usually worth the trouble of creating. The index makes information in your manual, catalog, directory, or booklet easily accessible, and assures you that your readers will be able to find what they are after (make sure it is *very* easy to locate).

Headlines

Strong headlines capture the attention of readers, and draw them into the text. How to write good headlines is discussed in the previous chapter, *Guidelines for Reader-Friendly Writing*, beginning on page 123.

Overviews and Summaries

A summary can appear at the beginning of the piece as an *overview* (give it a more interesting name than that), or at the end as a *summary*, or both. They present the substance or general idea of your piece in a brief way.

Be sure that your overview really does give an *over view*. Many don't say anything at all. By the same token, see that your summary really *summarizes* what you have said. Some "summaries" are just last paragraphs with the word *Summary* above them.

This booklet is made more readable through the careful division of information and the use of bullets. Note the generous space for filling in, far right.

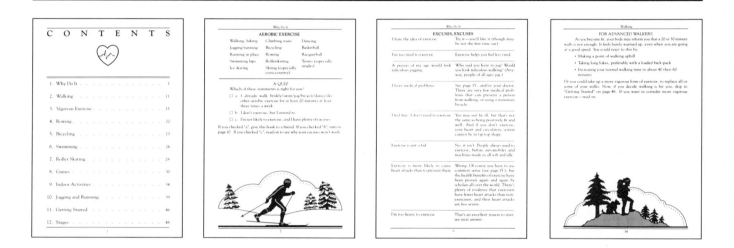

Writing the Text

The text (also called *copy* or *body copy*) is the main part of your printed piece. In writing text, you work with words, sentences, and paragraphs. Bullets sometimes offer an alternative arrangement. Let's have a look at each of these:

Keeping the Words Simple

As a general rule, use the simplest words you can. Instead of *revoked*, for example, say *canceled*, instead of *tariffs*, say *prices*. Often the simplest words have the fewest syllables: use *soon* instead of *presently*, *house* instead of *residence*, *home* instead of *abode*, *stiff* instead of *inflexible*, *rest* instead of *repose*, *jam* instead of *preserves*, better instead of *more advantageous*, *use* instead of *utilize*. If there is a good reason to use the more elaborate word of course do so, but think about it first.

Whether you choose to address your readers as *you*, *we*, or *one*, be consistent. It's distracting to keep switching from one to the other.

Use the *active voice* rather than the *passive voice*—it makes the writing more lively. For example

instead of *People are helped by the program* say *The program helps people*; rather than *The engine can be started by . . .* say *Start the engine by . . .*; instead of *Students are instructed by qualified teachers* say *qualified teachers instruct students*.

Replace long phrases with a single word. For example, rather than saying *show the division between paragraphs* say *separate paragraphs*.

Writing Strong Sentences

Vary sentence lengths. A mix of longer and shorter ones varies the pace and helps keep the reader engaged. Usually one idea per sentence is enough.

Being Aware of Jargon

Jargon is a special language unique to a particular group. Teenagers have their own jargon; so do ethnic groups. There is British English, Canadian English, Australian English, South African English, and American English, and there is regional jargon everywhere. Every trade, scientific, and professional group from printers to inn keepers to bee keepers to surgeons has its own jargon. And so do you and I.

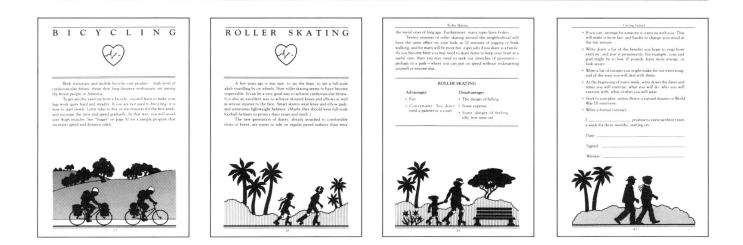

There may be some words that are so familiar to you that you don't think twice about using them—but they may be foreign to others. I once worked with a group of scientists, for instance, who wrote printed pieces for the general public. They often used words like *methodological* and *epidemiologic*—not exactly everybody's household words.

Be aware of your own jargon, and use language that you are sure your readers will understand. Many people don't understand legal terms like *regulatory standard*, *quid pro quo*, or *pro bono*, for example. And although the meanings of words like *outpatient*, *clinical*, or *stupor* are clear to people in the medical community, they may not be to others. Use more commonly understood equivalents when you can: *high blood pressure* instead of *hypertension*, for example; *heart disease prevention* rather than *cardiovascular risk reduction*. Base your word choice on your audience. When in doubt, use the more familiar word or phrase.

Conveying Technical Information

As information becomes more available and scientific and technical fields become more complex, in-terest in these areas is growing. Many people find that they need to convey highly specialized or technical information to readers without a technical background. Today, communicating sophisticated technical information to lay audiences presents one of the greatest challenges to writers of some types of printed materials.

Take instruction manuals for computer programs, for example. It was not so long ago that most of us knew very little about computers. We all needed basic training. But as time goes by and personal computers become more common, the range of knowledge and experience that people have with them becomes greater. The writer often repeats what is obvious to some, and jumps too far ahead for others.

So writers of technical information face two difficult and interrelated challenges: they have to make increasingly complex information understandable to their audiences, and those audiences have increasingly individualized needs. It's not like writing a piece for teenagers on how to drive a car, for example. These readers are approximately all at the same skill level: they don't know how to drive. But people reading about more complex technical areas don't divide up as neatly into *those who know* and *those who don't*.

More often people are at a beginning, intermediate, or advanced stage of understanding, or at one of the many levels in between.

I recently worked with a group of professionals in the field of health policy. They had the particularly difficult task of conveying information relating to medicine and law—both complex areas. On top of that, their audience included a broad mix of people: colleagues in both fields, city, county, and state officials, and "the public."

Writing under these circumstances is especially demanding. Writers must not only translate the content, but they must translate it into several "languages" as well. Colleagues want data, other professionals want budgetary implications, lay audiences want to know how it applies to them, and everyone wants an interpretation, each at his or her own level.

That's the nature of the problem; what about solutions? If you are writing about a technical or complex subject, the first thing to do is to find out about the skill and knowledge level of your audience. If it is diverse, the next thing to do is to break the audience up into sub-groups, and (as much as is realistically possible) do separate pieces for each. If you can focus on a single, cohesive audience, one at a time, you can address each one more effectively. This means putting out more pieces, but you may be able to make each shorter. Each one will be more interesting to the reader, and probably to the writer as well.

Once you've narrowed your audience as much as you can, decide whether it's better to explain your material without using any technical language (in this case you're writing a *translation*), or to use the technical language and define it as you go. The choice depends on your subject and audience.

I know of one study that showed that AIDS information, for example, is communicated more effectively to minority groups using no technical language whatsoever. But in the case of this book, I want to familiarize readers with as much print jargon as possible, so I use it and define it on the spot, e.g. *white* (empty) *space*. If you decide to use technical language, you also may want to include a glossary.

If you're going to err on one side or the other, it's probably better to over-explain rather than under-explain. Assume readers know the least; the alternative is worse. Better to risk offending the more knowledgeable and get the message across than be safely inoffensive and inscrutable. Besides, a little repetition never hurts.

Here are more techniques for communicating technical language effectively:

Take on the role of translator

Pick someone who is intelligent but not familiar with the specialized field about which you are writing—a friend, relative, or colleague, for example. Write as though you are explaining the information personally to him or her. Write as though you are writing in your reader's "native tongue."

Use analogies

Analogies can be very effective in helping readers understand technical information. For example, you might write that "The heat is equivalent to a thousand suns," or "The ratio is the same as one seed to all the seeds in a watermelon," or "The risk is equivalent to smoking 26 packs of cigarettes."

Use visuals

Graphs, charts, maps, photographs, or drawings can also help communicate potentially confusing information. For example, in the chapter called *A Way to Make Writing Easier* (page 117), drawings help to explain how to make idea notes into an outline. Illustrations are especially helpful for those who are less technically and more visually oriented.

*Pictures and color-coded
bars in this table of contents are
matched to sections throughout this booklet.
Long, horizontal lines direct the eye to the right page number.*

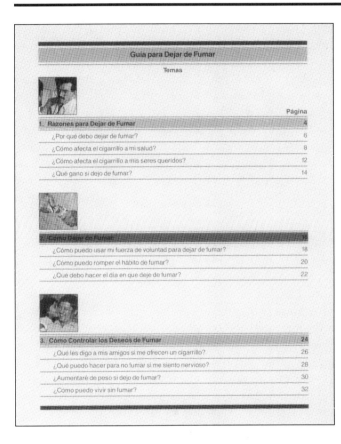

Using Acronyms

Acronyms are names formed by the first letters of a series of words, such as *OPEC* (Organization of Petroleum Exporting Countries) or *HUD* (Housing and Urban Development). If you use an acronym, be sure to say what it stands for the first time you use it. Say, for example, *GUSH (Global Urban Society, Houston) plans to offer a seminar in* . . . . Thereafter you can use the acronym by itself.

If you must use an acronym as a title, be sure its translation sits somewhere close by. I know of a newsletter that uses an acronym for the title on the masthead, and its meaning is nowhere obvious. The appeal of this newsletter would be considerably greater if it had a better title, or if it spelled out directly beneath it what the acronym stood for.

Using Abbreviations

Abbreviations can also trip up readers. Identify any that may possibly be unfamiliar in parentheses after the abbreviation. Say, . . . *ppt (parts per thousand)* for example, or . . . *ROI (return on investment)* or . . . *AAGR (average annual growth rate)* or . . . *CRT (cathode ray tube)*.

Layout for Writers

As I mentioned earlier, writers of printed materials often have questions about basic layout. The following information is directed specifically to them, although it is equally relevant to designers.

Bullets

Bullets are usually solid round dots in front of units in a list. They help readers get information faster (another sign of the times). Bullets make text easier to skim, easier to read, and easier to remember. The

Play it safe

Writers of technical information are often concerned that they will sound condescending to their readers. One way you can avoid a patronizing tone is to start out with *As you probably already know* . . . , or *As you may be aware* . . . . This way readers who do already know what you're talking about won't take offense. Those who don't won't either.

There is no doubt that the communication of highly specialized information is among the most demanding kinds of writing. These techniques can help you get complicated ideas across, but there is no substitute for the extra time and effort this kind of writing requires.

33 | Red Flags

There are several common stumbling blocks to be aware of. These can trip up readers and weaken your point. Notice these "red flags" when they come up in your writing, and see if there are better alternatives.

Red Flag	Comment
Roman numerals	We're not Romans. And more to the point, many people can't read them past 3. Use different levels of heads instead .
Captions	Keep identifying captions (such as "Figure 15") small and inconspicuous on graphs, charts, and maps.
Slashes	"Housing and work" is more readable than "housing/work."
"Should"	"You should . . ." can sound self-righteous and bossy. Get the point across more gently with "You might . . .," "You could . . .," "Consider . . .," or "Have you thought of . . ."
Sounding absolute	Instead of saying "It *causes* problems," say "It *can cause* problems"; instead of saying "This techi-widget works for everyone," say it "*can work.*" The use of "can," a disclaimer, can save you a lot of trouble.
"Very"	Use "very" and other overused words sparingly. Try to come up with more interesting alternatives or drop them—it often makes the sentence stronger. Check a thesaurus for other possibilities.
"However"	"However" sometimes signals an awkward transition or a half-baked thought. Watch for it.

mind can "photograph" a smaller unit of type better than a whole block of it. Break text out into bulleted units whenever it makes sense.

And I mean *whenever it makes sense.* Several years ago I worked with a writer who was what I would call—well—wordy. He loved to chatter on. And on. He lived in a world of privileged isolation, and without the stresses and time pressures his readers had. His writing would have been more appropriate for 19th century British aristocrats than for Type A Americans on the verge of the 21st century. I suggested he try bullets.

After much resistance (in the form of intellectual debate), he rewrote the piece "in bullets." But actually what he had done was to take his copy apart, sentence by sentence, put each one in a list with a bullet in front of it, and add some space above and below. The effect was to string the chatter out *even further.* It didn't work.

Text that is good for bullets is information that makes sense as a list. Anything in a series of three or more can usually be bulleted effectively. Benefits, qualities, features, or characteristics work well. Tips and suggestions also can be effectively conveyed in bullets; so can steps, procedures, agenda items, and anything else that might be numbered instead.

When do you use numbers instead of bullets? If there is a *reason* to number the units, do so; otherwise use bullets. A reason to use numbers? When you mention a number, you may want to use numbers. For example, if you say something like *Here are five reasons why . . .* or *There are seven points . . . .* Bullets are also helpful if you are writing the kind of piece that will be used in a group discussion. They make it easy to refer to a particular item.

In the past bullets were made by the period key of the typewriter, and they have pretty much stayed as solid round dots. There are, however, alternatives. A bullet can be made from any small graphic device such as a square, a triangle, a star, a check, a tiny il-

This simple red and green flyer for a June Strawberry Festival uses strawberry bullets. They both punctuate the main events and decorate the sheet.

Communicating Risk 34

The question of how to write about risks or other potentially disturbing subject matter comes up frequently among some groups of writers. You may be writing about occupational hazards, for instance, or the risks involved with legal or illegal drugs. Or your topic might call for information regarding mountain climbing, hang gliding, trekking, or traveling in countries with serious hazards.

I believe writers have the responsibility of giving readers enough information so that they can make intelligent decisions for themselves. I think the best way to write about risk effectively is honestly. Most of us do want to know what the risks are, straight out. It is important to respect the intelligence of the reader.

But whenever risks are presented, it is also a good idea to tell readers as specifically as possible what they can do to avoid them. Empower readers to take whatever measures are important to to protect themselves. Propose concrete and specific things that they can do. Tell your readers who to call or who to write to get more information. And suggest books or articles they can read.

lustration or logo, and so on. Many computers now have a variety of graphic characters in most font families that can be used as alternative forms of bullets. Or use Zapf Dingbats.

Although the plain bold dot is often best, these options come in handy when you don't have time to design your piece. A triangle instead of a dot, for example, can give an otherwise plain publication some instant style. Print the "triangle bullets" in a color, and you add more interest. Whatever you choose for your bullets, make sure they *enhance* readability rather than detract from it.

Keep the size of the bullet in scale with the type it introduces. A bullet that is too big dominates; one that is too small doesn't catch and direct the eye,

35 | Proofreading

It is just about impossible to catch mistakes on your own writing, so get someone else to proofread what you write. Here are things to watch for when your're proofreading:

☐ Check over each page and reference number carefully

☐ Double-check all other numbers

☐ Mistakes tend to be clustered, so if you find one, be on the lookout for others around it

☐ Make sure the information is in the right sequence

☐ Notice paragraph lengths; note when they're too long (shorter is better)

☐ Check to see if writers' page and section references are accurate

☐ Check spelling

☐ Check grammar

☐ Be sure that brackets, quotes, and parentheses are used correctly

☐ Check punctuation

☐ Watch for repeated words, like "of of"

☐ Look for missing punctuation, like commas or periods

☐ Look for missing words (often small ones like "a" or "the" are left out)

A worksheet version of this sidebar appears on page 359.

which is its purpose. Avoid "empty" bullets—they don't work as well as solid ones. Here is more on bullets (speak of the devil):

- Choose priorities for your bullet units and place them in order of importance, or use a logical order.

- Keep bullet units either all phrases or all sentences consistently.

- Bullet units do *not* need periods unless they are complete sentences.

- This is an example of a bullet unit with two sentences. They have periods at the end of each.

- Three lines is about the maximum for a bulleted unit. If it is longer, you may as well write it as text.

- Notice the vertical spacing in this list of bullets. The lines *within* units are closer; there's more space above and below each entry.

- Notice the horizontal spacing: first the bullet, then *one* space, then the first word beginning with a *capital* letter.

- Notice also that the second line in a unit is flush left with the first line of type above it (not with the bullet).

- Try using bullets in places where you may have not used them before, such as in letters, flyers, and posters.

Bullets can make your printed piece much more readable. Experiment with different kinds, and use them consistently.

Levels of Heads: Defining New Sections

You may need several levels of heads to differentiate sections of your writing and give it a sense of cohe-

This booklet uses a clean layout, triangle-shaped bullets, boldface type, and a section summary to make it more readable.

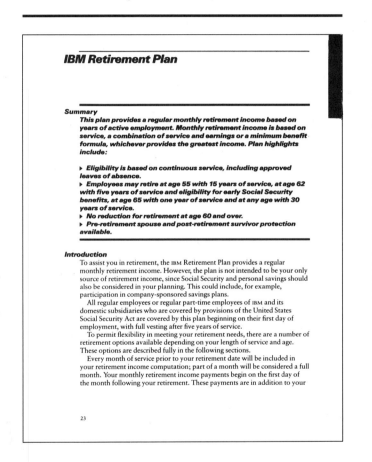

IBM Retirement Plan

Summary
This plan provides a regular monthly retirement income based on years of active employment. Monthly retirement income is based on service, a combination of service and earnings or a minimum benefit formula, whichever provides the greatest income. Plan highlights include:

▶ *Eligibility is based on continuous service, including approved leaves of absence.*
▶ *Employees may retire at age 55 with 15 years of service, at age 62 with five years of service and eligibility for early Social Security benefits, at age 65 with one year of service and at any age with 30 years of service.*
▶ *No reduction for retirement at age 60 and over.*
▶ *Pre-retirement spouse and post-retirement survivor protection available.*

Introduction
To assist you in retirement, the IBM Retirement Plan provides a regular monthly retirement income. However, the plan is not intended to be your only source of retirement income, since Social Security and personal savings should also be considered in your planning. This could include, for example, participation in company-sponsored savings plans.

All regular employees or regular part-time employees of IBM and its domestic subsidiaries who are covered by provisions of the United States Social Security Act are covered by this plan beginning on their first day of employment, with full vesting after five years of service.

To permit flexibility in meeting your retirement needs, there are a number of retirement options available depending on your length of service and age. These options are described fully in the following sections.

Every month of service prior to your retirement date will be included in your retirement income computation; part of a month will be considered a full month. Your monthly retirement income payments begin on the first day of the month following your retirement. These payments are in addition to your

23

sion. Headlines act as guideposts that show which are the broad (or umbrella) topics and which ones come under them. One way to come up with ideas for creating levels of heads for your printed piece is to look at magazines and other publications. It's a good way to see what you like.

Sometimes writers find themselves falling back on the outline style they learned in high school—the one that uses letters as well as numbers. The use of letters with heads is inappropriate for most printed pieces. The sequence of letters is hard to follow past "C," and there are better alternatives. On the next page are nine possibilities created from just one size of type (this is 14 point Helvetica):

Proofreader's Marks · 36

Here are the standard proofreaders' marks, recognizable to both writers and typesetters. The use of a colored pen or pencil makes reading them easier.

Period	⊙	Raise	⊓
Comma	⋀	Lower	⊔
Semicolon	⋀	Begin paragraph	⌐
Colon	:	No paragraph	no ⌐
Apostrophe	⋎	Align horizontal	align
Open quotes	⋎	Align vertical	‖ align
Close quotes	⋎	Center	⏌⌐
Dash	/-/ or ⅟M	Make capitals	Caps
Hyphen	=	caps + lower case	C/lc
Parenthesis	(/)	lower case	lc
Insert	⋀	Small caps	s c
Delete	ℓ	Bold face	bf
Indent	□	Light face	lf
Add space	#	Italic	ital
Ignore change	stet	Roman	rom
Close space	⌒	Broken type	X
Move right	⊐	Spell out	sp. out
Move left	⊏	Wrong face	wf

All caps in boldface

SAMPLE HEADLINE

Caps and lower case (written C/lc), bold, underlined

<u>Sample Headline</u>

C/lc italic, underlined

<u>Sample Headline</u>

C/lc italic

Sample Headline

All caps

SAMPLE HEADLINE

C/lc (this head would sit *directly above* the text)

Sample Headline

C/lc italic in boldface

Sample Headline

C/lc in boldface

Sample Headline

C/lc italic in boldface, underlined

<u>Sample Headline</u>

When any of these heads is *centered* over text, it takes on even more weight. For example, if the headline is centered like this:

Sample Headline

It denotes a higher level than if it were used flush left, like this:

Sample Headline

When you consider that each of the nine versions of heads in the first column can be used either centered or flush left to create different levels of heads, that's eighteen choices from just one size of one typeface. Sometimes the underlined ones don't look good and aren't as readable. Choose the ones that are easiest to read in the typeface you have selected and develop a visually obvious hierarchy for them.

Vertical Space

Leave *more* vertical space between the end of one section and the beginning of the next headline. Leave *less* space between the beginning of a headline and the start of the new text below it. Do this consistently throughout the text. Other things you can do to show a separation within the text are:

- Use horizontal lines (rules) or other graphic devices

- Begin new sections with an initial cap (a letter that is larger than the size of the type, and replaces the first letter of the first word)

- Start off the new section with the first word (or words) in bold face or small caps (see examples in this book, page 186)

Your best choice for differentiating levels of heads will depend on several things: the particular typeface you have chosen, how it looks in relation to your text, and how it looks when it comes out of the particular machine you are using to reproduce it (copier, printer, press, etc.). Experiment. Play around with the possibilities. It's a good way to sensitize and sharpen your eye, and discover new options.

Paragraph Construction

Keep paragraphs short, especially in brochures. Otherwise the reader may become discouraged by too dense a look.

There are several ways to separate paragraphs. They all have advantages and disadvantages—use the one that looks best in your piece. Although this decision is often made by the designer, the writer may also want to consider the alternatives when writing the piece. Here are three possibilities:

1. Keep the first sentence of the first paragraph after a head flush left, and indent all the rest. This is often the choice of designers because an indent doesn't make a "hole" in the first line. Instead the first sentence aligns neatly with the type underneath.

2. The traditional way to handle paragraphs is to indent them consistently throughout the text. Users of this method have convention on their side. How far you indent into the sentence has visual impact—try several variations to see what you like.

3. Instead of indenting, put additional space between paragraphs to separate them. This style can be quite effective, but be aware that it will add to the space needed for your piece.

Editor's Checklist   **37**

Every writer's piece is improved by a good editor. Whether you are having your piece edited or are editing someone else's, here is a checklist to remind yourself of important things to look for.

☐ The piece is clear and understandable

☐ It is well thought out

☐ The piece holds interest

☐ It delivers the intended message

☐ The tone is professional

☐ The grammar is correct

☐ The punctuation is consistent and correct

☐ The spelling is accurate

☐ All numbers have been double checked

☐ All names and addresses have been double checked

A worksheet version of this sidebar appears on page 359.

Getting It Printed

One final detail for writers to pay attention to is the method of reproduction chosen for the piece. The quality of the reproduction greatly affects readability.

Use the best form of reproduction you can afford. Whether your printed piece is reproduced on an inexpensive home copier, a laser printer, or a gravure printing press, be sure you get the best job the machine is capable of giving you (see *Printing*, page 319). Don't let poorly printed copies be a barrier to conveying what you've written. You've worked too hard to jeopardize communication at this stage.

Chapter 14

How to Write a Basic Brochure

There are three printed pieces you need for your service or product: a letterhead, a business card, and a brochure that describes it. These are the essentials. It is difficult to get along with less; more pieces are nice but aren't critical.

A letterhead is important because it makes you (and your organization) official.It can double as a billing form, press release, or other piece when necessary. A business card is important because it helps establish and maintain your network (without the network, there'd be no business). The third piece worth having is a brochure. This is a much more complex piece for the writer, so this chapter is devoted to it.

But first a word on the copy for a letterhead and business card. Keep it to a minimum: your name and title, your organization's name, address, and phone number, and possibly a logo (trademark)—that's all. A letterhead is not the place for a long list of names (they can go on the brochure).

I think a good descriptive brochure is just as important to your service or product as a letterhead and business card. The basic brochure introduces your organization or business to the world, and keeps it alive out there. It is a useful tool for letting people know who you are, and what you have to offer. In its simplest form, a basic brochure does four things. It:

- Describes what you are promoting

- Points out why it is of interest or use to someone else

- Describes the people or organization behind what you are offering

- Says how to find out more

Whether you are managing some segment of a vast industry or a one-person operation selling home-grown herbs, a good descriptive brochure is in continuous use. One of its biggest assets is that it saves time. It answers the questions that you (and other staff members) answer over and over again. Instead of going through the usual litany, you simply put this piece of paper into inquirers' hands and suggest they read it. A well written brochure will answer most of their questions. And it's out there being read while you're doing something else.

Descriptive brochures have lots of other uses. You can enclose them with letters and include them in press kits and presentation folders. You can mail them to large numbers of your target audience. You can take them to meetings and pass them out. You can

*One topic per panel is addressed
in this descriptive brochure. Bold horizontal
lines tie the design into the logo and add visual
interest, eliminating the expense of drawings or photographs.*

THE PROBLEM

It is increasingly apparent that for hundreds of thousands of individuals, we could prevent the suffering that comes from heart disease, injuries, substance abuse, adolescent pregnancy, and certain types of cancer. It is also evident that the most effective solutions to these problems may be found in community-based health promotion programs.

Community residents know best where their own problems lie. They have the motivation, the energy, and the people to get things done. They have close contact with media gatekeepers and other influentials. They have the sensitivity to avoid offending any segment of the population.

However, many communities are held back for lack of:

- Money
- The organizational skills necessary to draw the community together in a productive way
- The experience and technical expertise required to carry out successful health promotion campaigns
- The ability to evaluate programs
- The confidence that they can sustain a major program.

THE SOLUTION

Realizing the potential for change at the community level, The Henry J. Kaiser Family Foundation, with support from other foundations, has launched a national Health Promotion Program that will help communities to tap their own sources of energy.

Communities benefit in two ways:

- The Community Health Promotion Grant Program provides direct funds to selected communities for prevention programs in the fields of substance abuse, heart disease, cancer, injuries, and adolescent pregnancy
- Health Promotion Resource Centers will provide resource materials, technical assistance, and expertise to the funded communities and eventually to other communities interested in health promotion programs

The first of four planned regional Health Promotion Resource Centers was established at Stanford University in 1986, to serve the 13 Western States. In the spring of 1987, 11 Western communities were selected for funding from more than 600 applicants.

PEOPLE

The Health Promotion Resource Center (HPRC) is part of the Stanford Center for Research in Disease Prevention, under the overall direction of John W. Farquhar, M.D. This group has many years of experience in community-based health promotion, including two major studies of heart disease prevention in California communities.

The HPRC has on its staff:

- Health professionals with training in preventive medicine, evaluation, behavioral science, health promotion, public health and community organization
- Media specialists with backgrounds in television and radio, film, public relations, journalism and print
- An information scientist skilled in management of both electronic and paper-based systems

The HPRC also has open lines of communication to consultants from many disciplines at Stanford, and close links with consultants at many other institutions.

OUTREACH

Initially, the HPRC staff will devote most of its outreach energy to providing a range of services to the funded communities, scattered in the Western region between the Arctic Circle and the Mexican border. Certain services will also be made available to other communities. Among the HPRC outreach services will be:

- Personal consultation through community site visits
- Consultation by phone or by mail
- A networking function, with access to community representatives to others with experience in a similar or complementary field
- Presentations on health promotion at workshops and conferences in the Western region
- Catalogues of print and electronic media products available at low cost

The HPRC at Stanford also plans to publish a regular newsletter informing interested readers throughout the West about conferences, materials, and programs in the field of health promotion.

HEALTH PROMOTION RESOURCE CENTER
Stanford Center for Research in Disease Prevention
In Cooperation with The Henry J. Kaiser Family Foundation

---

*Large numbers, alternating in
lilac and turquoise, help readers through
this brochure and act as a decorative element at
the same time. Notice the generous space for writing in Panel 6.*

1
HealthPrint Programs

HealthPrint is an employee education program developed with the American Electronics Association. It teaches employees how to be more cost-conscious health care consumers. HealthPrint Programs help meet all of your employee education needs from cost containment to staying healthy.

A HealthPrint Program consists of eight "tip sheets". They are mailed directly to employees' homes, one a week for eight weeks. This system:

- Puts vital cost containment information directly into employees' hands
- Makes cost containment information interesting to read and easy to use
- Requires no time off from work for employee education
- Provides concrete skills employees need to help change consumer habits
- Makes cost containment information available to the whole family

2
Program 1
Health Care
Getting the Most for Your Money

This HealthPrint Program introduces employees to the need for health care cost containment, and gives them concrete things to do. Tip sheets include:

- **What's Happening in Health Care**
- **The Soaring Cost of Health Care How Much Will You Have to Pay?**
- **6 Ways to Save Money on Your Medical Bills**
- **How to Evaluate Your Medical Insurance**
- **Your Rights and Responsibilities as a Patient**
- **7 Ways to Increase Your Chances of Staying Healthy**
- **How to Find Good Health and Medical Information**
- **Getting the Most for Your Money**

3
Program 2
The Hidden Costs of Medical Care

Once employees understand their role in the cost containment effort, they are ready to learn new ways of using the health care system. Program 2 shows them how. Tip sheets include:

- **The Hidden Costs of Medical Care**
- **Making the Most of Your Time with the Doctor**
- **Emergency Rooms: When to Use and Avoid Them**
- **Dealing With Surgery: How to Get a Second Opinion**
- **Tips on Buying and Using Drugs**
- **How to Avoid Unpleasant Surprises on Your Medical Bills**
- **Good Hospitals; Good Alternatives**
- **Having an Impact on Hidden Costs**

4
What You Get

HealthPrint promotes healthy living while showing employees how to get the highest quality care at the lowest cost. And in the long run, it reduces your company's health care costs.

HealthPrint is an upbeat employee benefit. You can expect that employees will be looking forward to the next HealthPrint Program!

You receive a free "starter kit" with your purchase of a HealthPrint Program. It includes:

- The HealthPrint User's Guide
- Copy and art to introduce HealthPrint in your newsletter
- Posters announcing HealthPrint
- Sample letter explaining the program to employees

We recommend that you begin with Program 1 and follow up with Program 2 (more HealthPrint Programs available soon).

5
Fees and Packages

HealthPrint Programs are priced per employee as follows:

Quantity
Less than 1,000 . . . . $3.25
1,000 - 5,000 . . . . $2.75
More than 5,000 . . . . Special volume discount will be quoted
Sales tax (where applicable) and shipping additional

Special Packages
In addition, special packages are available depending on the size of your company. Price quotes will be provided.

Package 1: Less than 500 Employees
HealthPrint will handle the mailing for you including the postage, mailing house selection, and shipping.

Package 2: 500 - 5,000 Employees
Your return address and logo will be printed on the HealthPrint Programs. HealthPrint will assist in selecting a mailing house and will ship materials.

Package 3: Over 5,000 Employees
Custom designed programs are available. Mailing and shipping can also be done by HealthPrint.

6
How to Order

To order HealthPrint Programs, simply fill out the information in the form below (or call Wanda Kownacki at the AEA: (415) 857-9300 x 334). Return form to:

HealthPrint
Palo Alto Medical Foundation
300 Homer Avenue
Palo Alto, Ca. 94301
or call (415) 321-4121 x 2933 and ask for HealthPrint.

HealthPrint: Call Me
Name:

Company:

Address:

Phone:

HealthPrint is created and developed by Elizabeth Adler. The program is owned by the non-profit Palo Alto Medical Foundation. HealthPrint Programs are being developed in conjunction with the American Electronics Association.

*The use of white space in this brochure
makes it more comfortable to read. Square photographs
placed regularly along the bottom contribute to the clean design. The color
of the initial caps is terra cotta brown, the photos are duotones of terra cotta and black.*

make them available at many kinds of events and gatherings, like conferences, seminars, workshops, luncheons, rallies, classes, fairs, and trade shows. You can leave the brochure behind when you visit a client or member of your constituency (it then becomes a *leave-behind*), and you can give one to your mother so she finally understands what it is you do.

In spite of the many uses of this simple printed piece, there is often resistance to producing one. There is just as much reluctance among people in larger organizations as there is in smaller ones. Many reasons are given, but I think the real one is this: in order to come up with a basic brochure, someone in the organization has to be willing to think through what it's all about. Someone has to be able to describe it, and be willing to *commit* to that description. A good brochure clearly states that commitment. Sometimes people prefer to keep things fuzzy.

Yet the problems the lack of such a piece can create are considerable. The absence of a formally written-up description can keep staff or other inter-

ested parties (such as boards of directors, funders, overseers, and investors) in the dark as to the organization's fundamental role. And if *they* are in the dark, how can clients or the constituency be expected to know? A descriptive brochure provides a common understanding of the organization's goals, and so makes them easier to accomplish. A strong descriptive brochure is a valuable asset to any kind of organization, and is in continuous use.

To get maximum use from your brochure, keep it simple and straightforward. Many people spend vast amounts of time and money on their brochure (usually when it's their first brochure or their first venture, although not always). They become so caught up in it that the brochure becomes the center of attention rather than the project itself.

There are several reasons to keep your brochure simple. First, unless you are a professional writer or designer (or want to be one), you need the lion's share of your time for other things. Second, given the speed with which things change these days, your brochure

38

Which Panel Gets Read First?

One question that comes up frequently in relation to brochures is this: what panel do people read first: the flap panel (Panel 4; see illustration) or the first one on the inside (Panel 1).

As far as I know there have not been any formal studies that answer this question conclusively, but most brochure producers have opinions.

To come up with my own, I watched people open and read countless brochures. What I have observed is that although most people quickly glance at the flap first (Panel 4), they actually start reading the inside far left panel first (Panel 1).

Based on this observation, the most comfortable and natural place to begin your story seems to be Panel 1. The information then flows logically on to the next two panels, Panels 2 and 3. This layout leaves the flap (Panel 4) free for information that more easily stands alone, such as a description of the people who are behind your organization or business.

1 Features	**2** Benefits (Inside)	**3** Action
4 People (flap)	**5** Address (Outside)	**6** Cover

will become outdated before long. If you have invested heavily in it, you will be reluctant to do another one. A simpler, less fancy version frees you to do it over again sooner, and every time you do it over, you do it better.

This chapter describes the fundamental components of a good basic brochure. You can use this structure as a framework, and fill it in with your own content. You can choose from the "mix and match" content modules about to be laid out, and tailor them to suit the needs of your own organization or business.

Basic Format and Content

Following is a description of the simplest and most straightforward version of a brochure that covers the bases sufficiently. It is also the least expensive. More modules (described later) can be added on.

The most economical brochure format is a standard 8-1/2″ x 11″ sheet of paper folded in thirds. If it's convenient, take a sheet of paper now and make yourself a dummy (a three-dimensional sample). It will help you follow along as I describe it.

Hold the paper horizontally and fold it twice, so you have three panels. This gives you a total of six panels, three on one side, and three on the other (see illustration at left). Opened flat, on the "inside," from left to right, you have Panels 1, 2, and 3. Turn the sheet over, to the "outside," you have Panel 4 (the flap), Panel 5 (the address panel), and Panel 6 (the cover), left to right.

As mentioned on the first page of this chapter, there are four principal issues to be covered in a basic brochure. They are:

- Features (the description of the product or service)

- Benefits (the description of its benefits to your clients or constituency)

- People (the description of the people behind the product or service)

- Action (what you want readers to do after reading the piece)

When you add a cover and a mailing address panel, that takes care of the six panels.

Give each topic its own panel on the brochure if you possibly can. It makes the piece easier to read, and it's good discipline for the writer (it keeps the piece from becoming unnecessarily long). If the words don't fill the whole panel, wonderful. The white (empty) space makes the brochure more inviting.

Additional content and panels

Additional panels can be added on to the basic brochure in increments of two—a front and a back. Again I suggest making a sample dummy. Having a model of the piece to work with makes it easier to visualize. Other topics you may want to cover in your descriptive brochure include:

- Background or history

- A description of the current situation, or "the problem"

- A description of what you propose to do about it, or "the solution"

- Descriptions of additional services or products

- Tips or how-tos

- Step-by-step information

Once again, one topic per panel is effective if you can work it out that way. You can always add on more panels if you need to include more information.

A Panel for Fees

You may want one of your panels to include a price list. Panel 5—the address panel—can be used for fees, for instance, if the piece isn't a self-mailer. Or prices can go on Panel 3—the action panel, above the steps you suggest readers take.

There is also an alternative to printing your fees directly on the brochure. You can produce a separate but matching sheet to include fees, the size of the brochure panel, and insert it in the piece. This way you can continue to use the brochure if price information changes before it is outdated. You might also feel freer to change the rates if it doesn't mean reprinting a whole brochure.

Other Inserts

While we're on the subject of inserts, there may be times when you would like to include additional information along with your brochure, such as a map, a schedule, or a specific agenda. You can do this neatly and professionally by printing an insert just as you would for fees (one that matches the brochure panels) described above. It can hold whatever additional information you have.

Laura's Brochure: An Example

In *Tapping Your Creativity*, we went through the process of generating ideas for printed materials to promote Laura Richard's property improvement business. Now we will go through the components of a basic brochure using Laura's piece as an example. My comments are in italics. (If you did the exercises in *Tapping Your Creativity*, you will have most of the copy for your brochure already written.) A small icon at the top of each page shows which panel we are discussing, and Laura's panels are shown at left. (Laura's entire brochure is shown in Sidebar 39 on page 169.)

Sunday, September 24 to Tuesday, September 26, 1989
La Costa Hotel & Spa, Carlsbad, California

**The third annual Agenda may sell out early.
Don't risk being left out of this important conference.
Sign up for Agenda 90 today.**

Mail registration form
with payment to:
Agenda 90
3 Lagoon Drive, Suite 160
Redwood City, CA 94065

Telephone: 415-592-8880
Fax: 415-592-9192
MCI Mail: TBeiers

Participant Information
To help eliminate errors, please include your business card.

Name _____
Title _____
Name on badge _____
Contact _____
Company _____
Address _____
City _____ State _____ Zip _____
Telephone ( ) _____
Fax ( ) _____

Agenda 90 Payment
Payment must accompany registration form. For immediate registration by credit card, please call 415-592-8880. Or fax your reservation form and credit card information to 415-592-9192.

__ Check __ Money order __ MasterCard __ Visa
Make checks payable to Agenda 90.

Card number _____
Expiration date _____
Name as on card _____
Cardholder's signature _____

Conference fee	$1,995
Less PC Letter subscriber discount ($250)	—
(Subscriber discounts are not transferable within companies)	
Less early registration discount ($200)	—
(must be postmarked August 18)	
Total discounts	_____
Conference fee less total discounts	$
Plus hotel deposit	+$ 210
Total enclosed	$

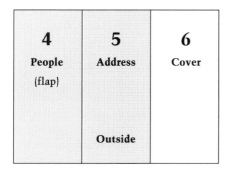

4	**5**	**6**
People (flap)	Address	Cover
	Outside	

**Laura Richards
Property Improvement**

Imaginative, Practical, and Profitable.

A BASIC BROCHURE

The Cover
What words go on the cover of a basic descriptive brochure? The name of your business or organization (this is your "title"), and possibly a short description of it (this is your "descriptive subtitle"). That's all! (For more on titles see page 126). Keep the words on the cover to a minimum unless you have good reasons to do otherwise.

Laura's Cover
The audience for Laura's brochure is local realtors and the home sellers they serve. She put the name of her business,

Laura Richards Property Improvement

on the cover. She also is using a descriptive subtitle (or slogan) that she came up with during the exercises in Chapter 10:

Imaginative, Practical, and Profitable.

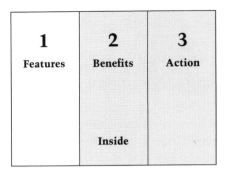

What We Do

We believe that the value of every property can be increased by imaginative and carefully chosen improvements. Each site is evaluated to determine what needs to be added or taken away to increase its market value.

Improvements are made with paint, carpets, and window coverings; new doors, windows, skylights, fittings, tile or trim; and decks, trellises, fences, and landscaping. Our service includes:

• Developing a plan to maximize the property's best features

• Finding the right people and the right materials at the best price

• Organizing and overseeing the improvements

• Keeping accurate books and records

Panel 1: Features

The first thing that people want to know about your organization is what it is you're offering, and the first place they settle in to read is Panel 1. To come up with the features of your product or service, simply describe it, and say what's good about it. Describe your product or service as clearly and succinctly as you can in this panel and mention its outstanding features. If you did the exercise in Tapping Your Creativity *that asked you to list the features and key components of your product or service, you will have most (if not all) of the content for this panel.*

Laura's Features Panel

What We Do

We believe that the value of every property can be increased by imaginative and carefully chosen improvements. Each site is evaluated to determine what needs to be added or and what needs to be taken away to increase its market value.

Improvements are made with paint, carpets, window coverings, new doors, windows, skylights, fittings, tile, trim, decks, trellises, fences, and landscaping. Our service includes:

• Developing a plan to maximize the property's best features

• Finding the right people and the right materials at the best price

• Organizing and overseeing the improvements

• Keeping accurate books and records

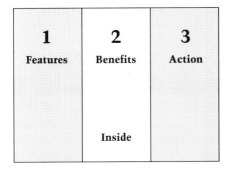

1	2	3
Features	**Benefits**	**Action**
	Inside	

The Benefits to You

Our commitment is to increasing property value quickly, conveniently, and cost-effectively. Our work is:

Tasteful: We can turn tacky into tasteful, dull into distinctive, and good into better. We know popular tastes and trends, and we choose styles, colors, textures, and plantings that maximize appeal and minimize expense.

Fast: We understand the importance of fast turn-around. We stay actively involved with carpenters, painters, plumbers, electricians, and others to get your job done as efficiently as possible.

Convenient: We oversee details: we do the scheduling, managing, and trouble shooting for every job, and carry it through to the end.

Cost-effective: We pay strict attention to the cost of each improvement, and recommend only those that are likely to result in a good return on investment.

Panel 2: Benefits

Once readers know what you are offering, point out its value to them. If you listed the benefits as part of the exercise in Tapping Your Creativity, *you've got the copy for this panel. If not, you can generate it by asking yourself (and others) what the biggest advantages are of your service or product. Give it some thought, and be honest. If you are writing your own piece, you are the expert. If someone else is, ask the person most invested in the organization (it may be you) to describe the benefits to the writer. This may well be your longest panel.*

Laura's Benefits Panel

The Benefits to You

Our commitment is to increasing property value quickly, conveniently, and cost-effectively. Our work is:

Tasteful: We can turn tacky into tasteful, dull into distinctive, and good into better. We know popular tastes and trends, and we choose styles, colors, textures, and plantings that maximize appeal and minimize expense.

Fast: We understand the importance of fast turn-around. We stay actively involved with carpenters, painters, plumbers, electricians, and others to get your job done as efficiently as possible.

Convenient: We oversee details: we do the scheduling, managing, and trouble shooting for every job, and carry it through to the end.

Cost-effective: We pay strict attention to the cost of each improvement, and recommend only those that are likely to result in a good return on investment.

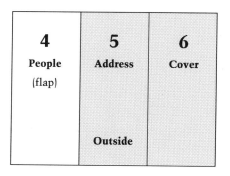

4	5	6
People (flap)	Address	Cover
	Outside	

**Laura Richards
Property Improvement**

Laura Richards, director, is a specialist in property upgrades. She and her assistant, Yudo Halprin, have been improving properties for ten years. Their combined talents and qualifications include: knowledge of space planning and building materials, organizational, managerial, and budgetary experience, and advanced degrees in design.

"Using Laura Richards' services helped me to sell my property for more."
... Sue J.

"These people know how to make a place look a lot better for not a lot of money." ... David H.

"LRPI made so manyimprovements on our house that we didn't want to sell it!"
.... Tom and Gail J.

"Laura and Yudo paid attention to my needs, and they were a pleasure to work with." ... Susie and Jim R.

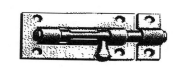

Panel 4: People

Note: This information logically follows along after a description of the features and benefits, but it makes most sense to place it in the flap, Panel 4 (see illustration). It is information that can easily stand alone, and Panel 3 better serves to convey the "action" information.

Now that you've told your readers what you are offering and why they should want it, they'll want to know who is behind it. Readers are wondering if you'll come through with what you promised on Panel 2.

This is where you write up your (or your organization's) credentials. Names of sponsors, funders, and significant others can go here as well. It might include staff names, titles, and degrees; whatever makes sense in your case. On this panel you must offer every assurance you can. If you wrote out your expertise and experience as a part of the Tapping Your Creativity *exercises, you've got the content for Panel 3 too.*

Laura's Credentials Panel

Laura Richards, director, Laura Richards Property Improvement, is a specialist in property upgrades. She and her assistant, Yudo Halprin, have been improving properties for ten years, and have worked on both large and small scale projects. Their combined talents and qualifications include: knowledge of space planning and building materials, organizational, managerial, and budgetary experience, and advanced degrees in design.

"Using Laura Richards' services helped me to sell my property for more."
... Sue J.

"These people know how to make a place look a lot better for not a lot of money." ... David H.

"LRPI made so many good improvements on our house we didn't want to sell it!" ... Tom and Gail J.

"Laura and Yudo paid attention to my needs, and they were a pleasure to work with." ... Susie and Jim R.

1	2	3
Features	**Benefits**	**Action**
	Inside	

Panel 3: Action

Note: The content of this panel logically comes last. Therefore it makes most sense to put it in Panel 3 (on the inside far right panel of the brochure) as this is the last one read.

Everything you have been writing about so far—the features, benefits, and credentials— has been leading up to motivating readers. Now you want them to do something or to think about something in a different way. It might be to change their behavior or their attitude, or to make a phone call, a purchase, or a visit. Whatever action you are hoping for, it is more likely to happen if you concretely suggest it. This is the crucial step; it is the printed piece's equivalent of "closing the deal." Here are examples of the kinds of information this panel could include:

- *A person to call*
- *A phone number*
- *An address*
- *Where to write*
- *What to buy*
- *What to do*
- *What to send in*
- *What changes to make*
- *Suggestions for discussions*
- *How to complete the application*
- *Where to go*
- *How to order*
- *How to register*
- *Whom to pass it on to*
- *Where to put the piece*

Laura's Action Panel

For More Information

Call if you have questions, or to make an appointment for an appraisal. We will be happy to discuss your property with you.

Laura Richards Property Improvement

(425) 326-2346

Or write to us at:

Laura Richards

Property Improvement

9 Pine Hill Road

Maynard, Connecticut 02140

We'll use our imagination, knowledge, and experience to make the most of your property.

For More Information

Call if you have questions, or to make an appointment for an appraisal. We will be happy to discuss your property with you.

Laura Richards Property Improvement

(425) 326-2346

Or write to us at:

Laura Richards
Property Improvement
9 Pine Hill Road
Maynard, Connecticut 02140

We'll use our imagination, knowledge, and experience to make the most of your property.

4	5	6
People	**Address**	**Cover**
(flap)		
	Outside	

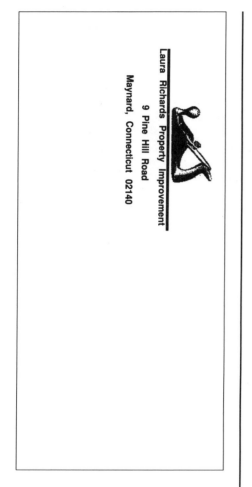

Laura Richards Property Improvement
9 Pine Hill Road
Maynard, Connecticut 02140

Panel 5: Address

This panel is traditionally used for mailing, in which case it includes a return address, postage (often pre-printed), and an address label. Think twice about assigning this space to this purpose. Often people devote this panel to mailing (partly because that's the way it's always been done), and never actually mail the piece out alone. Unless you are sure that the brochure will be used as a self-mailer (without an envelope), don't waste the space!

Often other things go along with the brochure, such as a letter or a booklet. Sometimes the brochure goes in a folder with a proposal, report, or other piece. In this case, you can probably use that panel more advantageously for something else. Furthermore, some print producers feel that a brochure looks classier when it arrives in an envelope, and there are times when it may be more appropriate to send it out in one.

But there is one big advantage to sending a brochure through the mail on its own. When you do, it goes directly into the hands of the recipient, with no envelope in between. If your title is good and your design is strong, why pay extra (for envelopes) to put more paper between your message and the reader? Consider the alternatives, and base your decision on what you think will work best with your audience.

Laura's Brochure (A Sample)

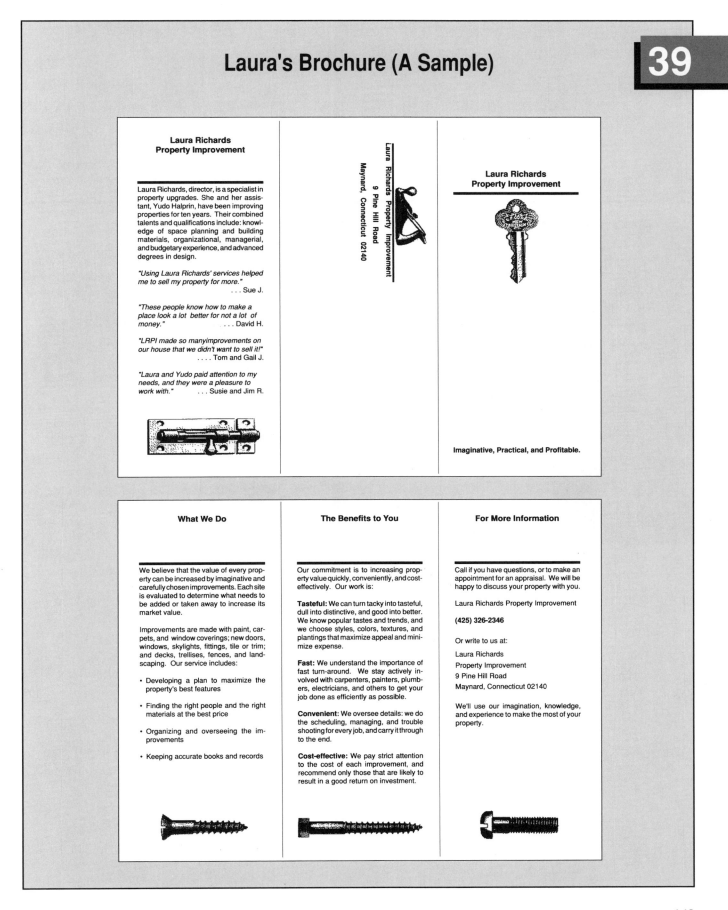

39

**Laura Richards
Property Improvement**

Laura Richards, director, is a specialist in property upgrades. She and her assistant, Yudo Halprin, have been improving properties for ten years. Their combined talents and qualifications include: knowledge of space planning and building materials, organizational, managerial, and budgetary experience, and advanced degrees in design.

"Using Laura Richards' services helped me to sell my property for more."
. . . Sue J.

"These people know how to make a place look a lot better for not a lot of money." . . . David H.

"LRPI made so many improvements on our house that we didn't want to sell it!"
. . . . Tom and Gail J.

"Laura and Yudo paid attention to my needs, and they were a pleasure to work with." . . . Susie and Jim R.

Laura Richards Property Improvement
9 Pine Hill Road
Maynard, Connecticut 02140

**Laura Richards
Property Improvement**

Imaginative, Practical, and Profitable.

What We Do

We believe that the value of every property can be increased by imaginative and carefully chosen improvements. Each site is evaluated to determine what needs to be added or taken away to increase its market value.

Improvements are made with paint, carpets, and window coverings; new doors, windows, skylights, fittings, tile or trim; and decks, trellises, fences, and landscaping. Our service includes:

• Developing a plan to maximize the property's best features

• Finding the right people and the right materials at the best price

• Organizing and overseeing the improvements

• Keeping accurate books and records

The Benefits to You

Our commitment is to increasing property value quickly, conveniently, and cost-effectively. Our work is:

Tasteful: We can turn tacky into tasteful, dull into distinctive, and good into better. We know popular tastes and trends, and we choose styles, colors, textures, and plantings that maximize appeal and minimize expense.

Fast: We understand the importance of fast turn-around. We stay actively involved with carpenters, painters, plumbers, electricians, and others to get your job done as efficiently as possible.

Convenient: We oversee details: we do the scheduling, managing, and trouble shooting for every job, and carry it through to the end.

Cost-effective: We pay strict attention to the cost of each improvement, and recommend only those that are likely to result in a good return on investment.

For More Information

Call if you have questions, or to make an appointment for an appraisal. We will be happy to discuss your property with you.

Laura Richards Property Improvement

(425) 326-2346

Or write to us at:

Laura Richards
Property Improvement
9 Pine Hill Road
Maynard, Connecticut 02140

We'll use our imagination, knowledge, and experience to make the most of your property.

These brochures show the distinctly different feeling that can be created with drawings on a basic brochure. They reflect the different natures of the organizations they represent.

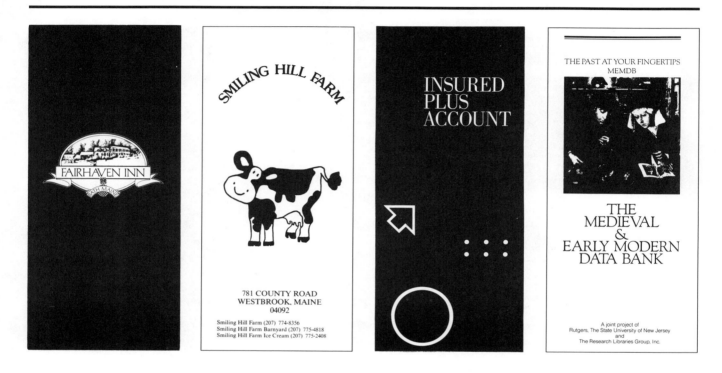

Design for Communication

5

What's Good Design?

According to Webster, to *design* is "to plan the form and the structure artistically and skillfully." *Graphic* means "giving a clear and effective picture." *Graphic design* is the application of type, color, and images to paper—artistically and skillfully—to create a clear and effective whole.

The finest graphic design—like the best art and architecture—is truly magnificent. It is creative and intelligent; it emanates vitality; it is powerful or witty or elegant; it displays stunning technical skill. And most people never see it.

Why? Because the best graphic design is usually found in high-powered businesses, the publishing industry, and in the arts—places where the majority of people are not. In the realms of publishing and the arts, where taste and refinement are priorities, you find exquisitely designed books, magazines, brochures, posters, and announcements. In the world of big business you often see beautiful trademarks, annual reports, booklets, and letterheads. Here the business value of good design is understood, and there is money to pay for it.

The quality of the graphic design that most of us see in our everyday lives is usually not so high. Much of what comes our way is just plain ugly. Brochures, newsletters, flyers, and ads regularly offend the eye with their aggressive design or downright junkiness. The vulgarity of a printed piece is more often commented on than its attractiveness. Good pieces do occasionally appear—a well-designed piece for a city zoo, perhaps, or a good restaurant poster, or a handsome newspaper ad—but these are the exceptions.

The sum total of a person's experience is reflected in his or her taste. With a regular daily diet of graphic schlock and little exposure to the good stuff, it's hard enough to develop discriminating taste, let alone the ability to imagine better possibilities. And it is even harder to create them.

Although the average person may not be aware of good graphic design, there are many producers of print who are (I'll assume you're among them). They want their stationery, reports, booklets, and ads to look as good as possible. The purpose of this section on design, comprised of seven chapters, is to help you raise your graphic design to the highest possible level. But you've got to know what good design is before you can produce it.

So what's good design? Good design is tasteful—people view it with pleasure. Good design is interesting and memorable and attractive—it triggers an idea, creates a mood, or elicits a response. And above all, good graphic design has *style*.

This beautifully designed poster has a very clean layout, very stylized illustrations, and a lot of wit (each drawing represents slang for money: bread, bucks, bills, etc.). The shiny black background sets off the images in dull brown, aqua, and gold.

Recognizing Style

A printed piece has style if you can put the word "very" in front of a positive description of it. A design has style, for example, when you can say it is *very* powerful, or *very* chic, or *very* clever, or *very* trendy, or *very* refined. Or a design that has style might be described as very elegant or very dynamic or very unusual or very clean.

Often the fun of producing a printed piece is in finding a style that suits its audience. As the section called *Getting and Holding Attention* explains, concentrating on the people to whom your piece will go gives you ideas, and makes the piece distinctive.

As graphic designer, you create the style of a printed piece by working with five variables: size, type, color, paper, and images (illustrations, photographs, graphs, and so on). Each of the five elements by itself has a "look." When they are combined skillfully, that "look" becomes *style*.

If you want an old-fashioned looking piece, for example, you might use brown ink, ivory paper, a classic typeface, and 19th century line engravings. If you want a piece that looks *right now*, you might use a splashy script type face in turquoise ink on pale peach paper, and floating squares, zig-zags, dots, and squiggles with shadows.

Finding Inspiration

But say you don't know what style you want—what then? As mentioned above, the first place to look for inspiration is your audience. Every target group has innate characteristics that suggest something; it's a matter of thinking about the audience until the style presents itself. The narrower the audience, the easier to identify the style.

If you need more inspiration, look at examples of the best graphic design, and keep your audience in mind when you do. Whatever style you're after, it

174

Good design is often seen in the corporate world, as exemplified by this brochure for an executive conference for the personal computer industry. Colors are black and cinnamon on a light brownish textured paper. Note the updated version of a woodcut.

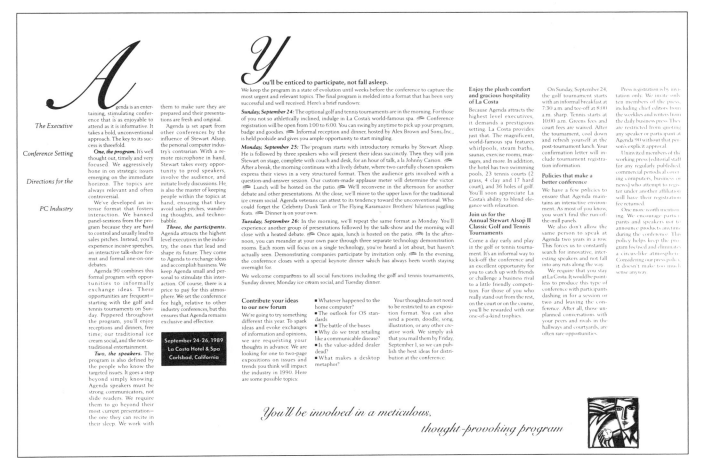

probably has been done before, so you may as well look at award-winning versions.

Where do you find examples of good graphic design? One of the best places to look is in graphic design annuals. Each is a collection of a year's worth of the finest graphic design.

Three good annuals are *Print's Regional Design Annual*, which shows good graphic design from all over the United States; the *Communication Arts* annuals with four separate issues—one each for design, advertising, photographs, and illustrations; and *Graphis Design*. Printed in three languages, *Graphis*

shows design from many parts of the globe. (The Swiss and the Japanese are among the world's best graphic designers.)

There are also art director's annuals and other design collections. Call bookstores, art supply stores, or libraries to see what they've got. If you really want to do some research, you can find design magazines that go back thirty years or more.

Or look at books of art history. People have been deciding how ink should look on paper for almost 2000 years (paper was invented in China in the year 105). The first book printed with movable type in the

Currently popular southwestern images integrate contemporary, Indian, and Mexican design. The one at right is on a T-shirt; the one below is on a box of gourmet sauces.

West was produced in 1455, so there are 500 years worth of type laid out on paper to look at. And there are countless movements and trends in design in the history of art; the ones over the last hundred years are the most applicable to contemporary graphic design.

Don't steal other people's designs, but don't be afraid to let yourself be inspired by them either. Studying the best can teach you a lot about what works. When you look at the design in these publications, notice:

- The style of the piece, and the elements that go into creating it

- The layout (the way the elements are organized)

- The type (the sizes and weights, and their relationship to other elements)

- The colors (what colors enhance certain styles, and work well together)

- The art and photography (what the images are, and how they're used)

- The size and shape of the piece (to see how it contributes to the whole effect)

Use the best art and design to stretch your mind wider; then do your own. As discussed in *Tapping Your Creativity*, (page 97), we can reach deeper into our own imaginations when we have something specific to respond to. Creativity in a void is genius—more than we can reasonably expect when producing a brochure. Everything is based on something else.

Take the popular Southwest style, for instance, exemplified by howling coyotes, cactuses, and strong geometric designs. These "contemporary" images are based on old Indian and Mexican art and craft motifs. They are not the same as the older ones; they evolved from them.

Or take the work of contemporary American artist David Lance Goines. His poster design is original and distinctive, yet reflects his depth of knowledge and interest in many art movements including *Jugendstil* (youth-style), German *art nouveau*.

Or take Laura Ashley's designs. She loved old patterns and prints. Through extensive research she revived, adapted, and reinterpreted many beautiful designs that otherwise would be lost to us.

The best designers usually know their art history. It greatly expands their field of reference and enables them to pull fine imagery from the past into the present. By applying their own sensitivity and individuality to it, they bring it back to life. By translating the imagery into modern design, they give it a contemporary flavor that appeals to our present tastes.

I want to emphasize that I am *not* endorsing copying someone else's design. But neither do I believe that you or I or anyone else can pull good design out of thin air. With literally thousands of years of fine design behind you and perhaps eight weeks before you to get a printed piece produced, you don't always have to start from scratch.

Science and Technology: The Origins of Style

It is interesting (and perhaps surprising) that one of the greatest influences on popular design is science

These refreshing images by David Lance Goines, below, are distinctly contemporary, yet reflect the artist's knowledge of art history.

and technology. New scientific and technological developments have long been a powerful force in shaping what seems attractive to us. Advances in papermaking, ink manufacturing, printing presses, and new processes and products have been changing the look of the printed piece for centuries.

The invention of movable type, for example, changed the look of the book. Soft calligraphic alphabets drawn by hand were replaced by sharp letter forms that suited metal type. The first printed illustrations were carved from wood blocks in the 15th century; these gave way to copperplate engravings in

the 16th and 17th centuries, and they were replaced by photoengraving in the 19th century.

Each technological change brought about new images; each successive image evolved into its own distinctive style. Designers push each technological advance to its artistic limits, whenever they occur. And they dip back into the past for inspiration.

In this century changes have come along extremely fast. Styles, preferences, and tastes in graphic design slide by quickly. Refinements in the air brush influenced design in the 40s. Magic markers, unknown before the 60s, played a role in the of design of that decade; so did new photographic methods of producing type. The result was an explosion of new typefaces

Although Laura Ashley's designs, below, are likely to become associated with the end of this century, they reflect her interest in fine design of past centuries.

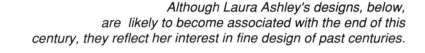

that changed the look of the decade, and of graphic design ever since. And now, in the electronic age of computers, scanners, and laser printers, the style of design is changing again.

There's Nothing New. . .

But for all the new styles, the pattern is old. The cycle goes like this: There is a rebellion against an old, established style. The new revolutionary imagery is seen as a break through, and everyone's excited. Gradually new ideas and innovative designs become familiar. Then the familiar becomes the standard, and a while after that, the brilliant, new, and revolutionary style looks old. Yesterday's new image becomes tomorrow's ageless style. Today it just looks bad. And it will continue to look bad until it's old enough to become classic; then it will reappear again in a new, updated version. Meanwhile a new rebellion is brewing. The cycle repeats itself.

Take Bauhaus style for example. It has had the greatest influence on design in this century. The influence of the Bauhaus, a school of design begun in Germany in 1919, extended to every form of art and architecture. Bauhaus teachers and students explored and experimented with the new industrial technologies and materials of that time (like plastics). What emerged was "modern" style—crisp, clean, and simple forms that were both beautiful and functional. The new look was reflected in architecture, art, ceramics, graphic design, furniture, and sculpture. Some of the finest "contemporary"-looking furniture around today was designed at the Bauhaus in the 20s.

Bauhaus designers grew up in an era dominated by the Victorian style. It was heavy and ornamental and elaborately decorated with frills, curves, and curlicues. It is not surprising that Bauhaus designers went in the opposite direction. Bauhaus style is light, crisp, spare, and clean.

Today's new, fresh-looking styles will be rebelled

This calligraphy from the Book of Kells,
below, was drawn around 800 A.D. The contemporary
birthday card, right, exemplifies renewed interest in hand-drawn
letters—not surprising after centuries of cast metal alphabets.

against too, but the best of them will endure. The cycle goes around again. But the *structure* of good design is timeless.

The understructure of good design is based on *discipline*, and I think discipline is the key to good design: the discipline not to overdo, to resist, and to restrain. In graphic design this means the discipline to stick to one style, and limit the number of typefaces; the discipline to make the most of a few colors and the best of the paper; the discipline to restrict the art to only the best (even when you've got more). And most importantly, good design is based on the discipline to work imaginatively within whatever limitations you face.

This is good news for those on tight budgets: good design does not depend on money. Upcoming chapters will point out ways to use restraint in your design and create good looking pieces, regardless of the amount you have to spend on it.

This outstanding contemporary design combines 30s type, 50s colors (aqua, pink, and gray), and 90s layout and ink (the car and the moon are embossed in silver).

The top two illustrations are on the cover
of a promotion piece for Champion Papers. The style
here integrates a 20s look with our familiar end-of-our-century colors:
peach, teal, and dusty purple. The clean layout, below, from This People *magazine*
is reminiscent of 30s design with its illustration style and widely-spaced headline type.

Woodcuts and woodcut-looking illustrations have been going in and out of vogue regularly since the 1500s. The one on the right was done recently for an annual report cover for Caltrans; the one on the left was done several hundred years earlier.

Current Trends

With this historical perspective, let's look at trends in graphic design today. Recently among the financially well-endowed there's been a tendency to decorate the printed piece opulently (a recycled Victorian approach, perhaps). Slick brochures and other pieces parade in fancy inks and varnishes, expensive papers, foil stamping, die cuts (cut out holes), and uncommon shapes and sizes.

In a graphic euphoria of technology's newest goodies, sometimes the lily gets gilded. And sometimes you can't see the lily for the gilding. Then the

design is lost, not to mention the message. So if you're on a tight budget and can't afford such things, who knows, it may be a blessing in disguise.

Styles around today will also look old before they look classic. What design will we associate with the 90s? Some candidates are emerging: printed pieces with soft, scrawly script next to hard, high tech type; solid bands of color along the edge of a page; computer-generated images alongside slick air brushed ones; updated Soviet and World War II heroic art; floating geometric shapes with shadows; 50s squiggles in colors like aqua and pink; 40s mauves and sage greens, Santa Fe's tans and ivories and peaches; inks

Seventy-six Design Styles

40

Printed pieces have more impact when they have a distinctive style, especially when it is one that suits the target audience. Here is a list of possibilities. Read through it for ideas to fit the piece you're currently working on, or for one you'll be doing in the future.

• Contemporary	• Traditional	• Elegant	• Feminine
• Baroque	• Strong	• Chic	• Art Deco
• Arty	• Understated	• 1990s	• Romantic
• Comic-book	• Old fashioned	• Colorful	• Detailed
• African	• 1940s	• Simple	• Regal
• Clean	• Folksy	• Realistic	• 1960s
• 1920s	• Dignified	• Patriotic	• Urban
• Composite	• Lavish	• Provincial	• Imaginative
• Slick	• French	• Innovative	• Floral
• Clever	• Classic	• California	• Graceful
• Creative	• Dynamic	• Bold	• 1950s
• Sketchy	• Architectural	• Geometric	• Japanese
• Foreign	• Abstract	• Silhouette	• Turn-of-the-century
• Modern	• Decorative	• Professional	• Futuristic
• Business-like	• Designy	• Nautical	• Refined
• Powerful	• Sophisticated	• Authoritative	• Gothic
• Art Nouveau	• Muted	• Rococo	• New Wave
• Hard-edge	• Rich	• Rustic	• Scholarly
• Distinctive	• Masculine	• Southwest	• Lighthearted

Bauhaus designers grew up surrounded by late 19th Century frou-frou (this parlor arm chair is an example). The contemporary-looking Barcelona chair, right, was designed by Mies Van der Rohe in 1929.

Bauhaus designers grew up surrounded by late 19th Century frou-frou (this parlor arm chair is an example). The contemporary-looking Barcelona chair, right, was designed by Mies Van der Rohe in 1929.

in turquoise or teal or brilliant metallic; the look of marble; 90s neon in lime green and hot pink. We'll also come to associate 90s design with the typefaces commonly used by the first desktop computers. And we'll see the development of images that are softer and more human—an instinctive attempt to balance an overload of impersonal electronic images. Whatever today's new look, it will be tomorrow's common style, and fodder for rebellion after that.

Why Good Design?

Some people's interest in graphic design is for the art of it, and that's a good, legitimate interest. My interest in graphic design, however, is not art for its own sake, but for the sake of communication. The purpose of a printed piece is to deliver information efficiently and effectively. Good graphic design is critical to its ability to do so.

Chapter 16

Basic Design Decisions

One of the first (and most important) design decisions print producers make is whether to design a printed piece themselves, or to hire someone else to do it. A closer look at the designer's role, described below, will help you decide whether or not to take on the task. If you decide to hire a graphic designer, see Sidebars 43, 44, and 45, Interviewing, Selecting, and Working with a Graphic Designer.

If you decide to design the piece yourself, you will need to make some preliminary decisions about it so you can get cost estimates from printers. Decisions include things like the size of the piece, how many pages it will have, how it will be folded or bound, and what (if any) special effects or features you would like figured into the estimates (such as scoring, die cutting, embossing, or perforations (pages 189, 192)).

You will also need to decide on a basic layout for your piece. The last section of this chapter discusses the grid and its elements. Grid design involves another set of decisions having to do with margins, columns, and white space. But first things first: who will design your printed piece?

Your Role as Designer

Just as an architect works with concrete, steel, glass, and wood on land, a graphic designer works with type, photographs, and illustrations on paper. Design is putting elements in order—arranging really. If you enjoy organizing and arranging things, you'll like graphic design.

A building is successful when it is good-looking and functions well; so is the printed piece. When it is good-looking, it captures and holds attention. It functions well when you get your point across.

Design can become a barrier to communication. The type may be hard to read, the colors may be unappealing, the size may be awkward, or the arrangement may be cluttered. When faced with these visual offenses, readers don't read. In such cases, the design of a printed piece gets in the way of its success.

At the very least, your job as designer is to keep this from happening. A good design makes conveying a message *more* likely, not *less* likely. And by the way, the information itself should have the spotlight, not the design.

The designer's role is often seen as parallel to the writer's, but actually it is quite different. A writer's job is basically to write; a designer's work usually includes much more than design.

The designer's job involves many details and decisions—hundreds of them. He or she chooses the style of the piece, and each element to pull it off: how to illustrate the piece and where to get the illustrations; which typeface to use and in which weights and sizes; what colors to use, and which of twelve shades to use them in. The designer decides on decorations or borders or boxes or lines, what thickness to put them in, and where to place them. He or she selects from among ten different papers with seven different finishes in twelve shades of white.

Then there are the aesthetic decisions. All elements (the art, the type, the color, and so on) need to be *balanced*. There needs to be *variety*. There needs to be *contrast*. And the designer must *unify* all elements, so they work together harmoniously.

Graphic designers are dependent on others for the successful outcome of their work, so they must maintain good relationships with many people. They must interact effectively with writers, illustrators, typesetters, printers, and so on. A sloppy illustration or a bad printing job, for example, can ruin an otherwise good design.

And contrary to the general impression, the designer makes as many *left brain* (logical) decisions as *right brain* (intuitive) ones. He or she is typically responsible for most (if not all) of the details of production, from beginning to end. So designers are managers. They oversee the piece through each of many successive phases. They monitor deadlines and stay on top of the budget. They select the reproduction method for the printed piece, and they interview and select the typesetter and the printer. Sometimes designers are even involved with distribution.

Designers also do a lot of leg work. They get materials and supplies, drop off photographs, pick up type, make trips to the copy center, bring mock-ups around for approval, go to the Post Office, make deliveries to printers, and do press checks. If you're on the fence as to whether to hire a designer or do the piece yourself, considering what's involved in these errands may help you decide.

Steps in the Design Process

The Steps in Producing Print, page 37, describes all the steps a printed piece goes through from conception through to distribution. The ones most relevant to the graphic designer, simplified and briefly stated here, are:

Conception: This is the creative phase, when you come up with ideas for the design. Base your ideas on the knowledge of your target audience, the content of your piece, and the nature of your product or service. Now imagination counts.

Application: Next you turn your good ideas into rough sketches, so you (and others) can see what you've got. Try many possibilities, and don't put too much effort into a single idea yet.

Feedback: Then collect the responses and opinions of others, and ask for their suggestions.

Adjustment: After you get some feedback, select your best, and make adjustments to the design. Inexperienced designers underestimate the amount of time it takes to make changes and develop a good design. Come to think of it, so do experienced ones.

Production: The final stage involves perfecting the design on the computer (or getting it typeset), getting it proofread, preparing the piece for the printer, checking it over carefully, and guiding it through printing and delivery.

Notice the amount of time spent *creating* the design (the imaginative part) as compared with *producing* it (application, feedback, adjustment, and production). A simple, ordinary brochure can take six to eight weeks to go through these stages. About one fifth of the work is actual design.

Decisions at the Beginning

The amount of money that is available for a printed piece determines the graphic possibilities, so the first thing a designer must deal with is the budget. It determines, for example, how many colors you can use, and whether or not you can afford expensive paper. These options influence your approach to the design, so you need to know the budget before you begin. Which often puts you squarely in a Catch-22 situation.

In order to find out what you can afford, you need to get estimates. For printers to be able to give you useful estimates, you need to give them a description of the piece. And for you to be able to describe the piece, you need to know what you want. How do you know what to ask for when you don't know what you can afford?

You guess. The following sections are included to help you be a better guesser. Printers' estimates will be as accurate as your description, so the more specific you can be, the better. Sidebar 17 summarizes the information you need to give to printers so they can quote you a price (there is a fill-in version on page 352). Estimate-getting is discussed in detail in *Watching Your Money*, beginning on page 61.

So one of the first things to do as you think about your design is to get some requests for estimates out. It's good to know as soon as possible how realistic your concept is. Here are the kinds of things you'll have to make decisions about to get estimates.

The Size of the Piece

Standard trim sizes

The *trim* size is the final size of the piece. Booklets, brochures, reports, and so on are frequently printed on large sheets of paper, and are *trimmed* or cut down to their final size on large paper cutters. When you get an

Page Design 41

If you are designing a booklet, catalog, report, or similar piece, you will design more pages than one. Here are components of a printed piece that may need special attention.

Parts of a Publication

- Covers: outside front and back
- Covers: inside front and back
- Title page
- Credits page
- Copyright page
- Table of contents
- Chapter division pages
- Pages of charts, maps, etc.
- Sidebars
- Appendixes
- Glossary
- Index

Parts of a Page

Page layout involves many decisions. For each of the following elements, you must specify a size and a weight of type, and its precise position on the page. If more than one color is used, you must designate the color of each element. Components on a page may include:

- Title
- Page numbers
- Subheads
- Footnotes
- Captions
- Running heads
- Headlines
- Initial caps
- Introduction
- Body copy

estimate, the printer will want to know your piece's trim size.

Printers often use paper that comes in large, over-sized sheets. To avoid waste, the size of a particular sheet is based on the size most often called for in a particular grade. Printed pieces that deviate from standard size cost more. Odd sizes take more of the printer's time to produce, and you pay for the full sheet anyway. It's a good idea to stick with standard sizes as much as possible, unless there is a good reason to do otherwise. The printer can tell you the most economical trim sizes. Among them are 5-1/2″ x 8-1/2″, 8-1/2″ x 11″, 11″ x 17″, and 22″ x 34″.

Cost is only one reason to use a standard size. Did you ever try to put an odd-sized business card with your others? Or to hold a menu that was so big it knocked half the things off the table when you opened it? Or tack a large poster onto a crowded bulletin board? Or read a printed piece with many folds on an airplane? Annoying potential readers doesn't help your cause.

Filing and storage systems are designed for standard sizes. Oversized pieces take up more space, and there is no convenient place to store them. Under-sized pieces can seem insignificant, and they get lost among other papers. So in addition to saving money, standard-sized pieces are better because they are easier to read, easier to find, and easier to store.

One advantage of an odd size, however, is that it can help to make a printed piece look more distinctive. Although this advantage is often outweighed by the disadvantages just mentioned, an odd-sized piece is sometimes worth doing. You might consider using an odd size for a program, an announcement, an invitation or other piece for a special occasion. A square shape, for example, is especially aesthetically pleasing. You may need to get envelopes custom-made to fit your odd size. There are companies that specialize in this—your printer will know of them.

Some odd sizes are odder than others. Be sure to discuss your ideas about size with a printer before going ahead with the design. Remember to take the reader's convenience and storage options into account as well as the aesthetics.

Length

I recently walked into the first meeting of a group of people who were planning a brochure. An issue was being hotly debated. Some said the piece should have three panels, others said four. But how could anyone know the length before a word of text was written? I suggested getting estimates on both sizes. That way we could get on with first issues first, like the purpose of the piece and who it was to go to.

The length of a printed piece is best determined by the amount of information it is to carry. It's probably wise to get estimates on more than one size in the beginning. Then you'll know whether or not the longer piece is within your budget. If not, write less. Cramming too much into too small a space will work against you.

The Number of Pages

The number of pages in a booklet (catalog, directory, etc.) that is to be saddle-stitched (stapled) must be four or a multiple of four. That's because a flat sheet of paper folded in the middle gives you four surfaces: a front, (open it) a left middle, a right middle, and (close it) a back. If you take a second sheet and fold it in half, and you staple it to the first folded sheet in the middle to form a booklet, you have eight surfaces. Each time you add a new sheet you get four new surfaces. So the number of pages in a booklet to be saddle-stitched is always four or a multiple of four.

Do you count the cover or not when you specify the number of pages? A sharp printer will clarify this point, but don't count on it. Make certain you both understand what is intended. One way to clearly de-

Designing a Cover

42

People do judge books (and all other printed pieces) by their covers. Here are some tips to help you come up with good ones.

- To get ideas for an imaginative cover, hold a brainstorming session (with others or by yourself).

- If your cover also needs to function as an advertisement for the piece, design it with that purpose in mind.

- Ask yourself: how would this cover look as a poster? A good cover is as powerful as a good poster.

- A simple, well-ordered all-type cover in a beautiful color is more impressive than one with weak art or photography.

- Integrate all elements on the cover into a harmonious whole.

- Design your cover to reflect the nature of the contents of the piece.

- Make clear what the reader is to look at first, second, third, and so on.

- Relate the cover design to the design of the inside pages when possible.

- Don't forget to do a good design for the back cover too.

scribe it is to state *the number of pages* you want, *plus cover.* So you might say, for example, the booklet has *16 pages plus cover.*

Sometimes a catalog or booklet cover is made of the same paper as the inside sheets. This is called a *self-cover.* When this is the case, be sure to make that clear. For example you might say a catalog has *forty pages, which includes a self-cover.*

Finishing and Special Effects

Among the early decisions (or educated guesses) the designer makes are technical ones having to do with how the piece goes together, called *finishing*, and whether or not the paper is to be treated in a special way. In order to come up with an accurate estimate, you must describe how the piece is to be folded or bound, and whether or not it is to be scored, collated, or perforated. If you want it to be die cut or embossed you must say so, so that it can be figured into the cost. Here is a brief description of these alternatives.

Scoring

If your piece is printed on heavy stock (paper) and is to be folded, get it *scored*. Scoring is cutting a shallow slice into the paper—not all the way through—along the fold line so that it folds clean and crisp. Without scoring, heavier paper will fold in a broken, ragged edge, which significantly detracts from the look of the piece. Ask if your particular piece needs to be scored. Don't count on someone else to think of it.

Folding and direction

The way a piece folds usually depends on two things: the capabilities of folding equipment available to your printer, and the design. There are several options for folding a printed piece, such as an accordion fold or a gatefold. Ask a printer for advice.

Eye-shaped holes in this cover are die cut (cut out) so that the eyes printed on the sheet underneath show through.

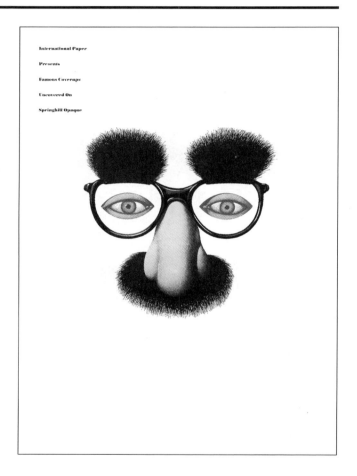

International Paper

Presents

Famous Coverups

Uncovered On

Springhill Opaque

Along with the question of how to fold a piece often comes the question of how to *hold* the piece: "upright" (with the long side vertical) or "sideways" (with the long side horizontal). Holding the piece "upright" is better in most circumstances.

First, if the printed piece is held sideways, it must be *turned* to read it. This is inconvenient.

Second, the majority of printed pieces are designed to be held upright. When several are shown together, they will be displayed upright. The piece that is designed to be held sideways will be going the wrong way in relation to the rest.

Third, if a sideways brochure is folded into panels, you'll have more design headaches. The folds will divide the piece into horizontal panels rather than vertical ones, and vertical ones tend to accommodate type more comfortably. It is certainly possible to design a good-looking printed piece that is held sideways, but it can make your job harder and the reading more awkward.

Now for the exception. Occasionally there is a good reason to design a brochure sideways. For example, when a piece is to be used as both a flyer and a brochure (such as a piece for a political campaign that is handed out and *posted* more than it is mailed), it may make sense to fold it sideways. This is because it will spend most of its life opened up, displaying one full inside page. As one entire page, it will be read vertically. Under these circumstances, it may be better to design the piece as a whole page to be posted rather than as a brochure in panels.

Collating

Collating—putting pages together in order—is done either by hand or by machine. It depends on the size of the job.

Collating will influence the overall cost of your printed piece, so if it needs collating, say so on your printer's estimate sheet.

Binding

There are several methods of holding a printed piece together along its spine (edge). The most common kinds of bindings are:

Stitching

Stitching is the printer's word for stapling. There are basically two kinds. The first is called *saddle stitching* because the staples sit on the spine of the folded paper like someone sitting on a saddle. Most booklets are saddle-stitched. Covers of saddle-stitched pieces are stapled on along with the inside sheets. Saddle stitching is a simple and inexpensive kind of binding.

The second kind of stitching is called side stitching. In this method, sheets are folded and stacked up, and stapled about a quarter of an inch in from the edge. Covers are glued on. Thicker booklets may be side-stitched.

Perfect binding

With this method, sheets are folded and stacked, then glued or sewn together at the spine. Either hard or soft covers may be attached with endsheets and glued to the spine.

There is a maximum number of pages that can be successfully saddle-stitched, and a minimum number of pages that can be perfect bound. Check with a printer before making assumptions.

Wire, plastic, and ring binding

Bindings made of wire, plastic coils, or rings (as in three-ring loose-leaf binding) are called mechanical binding. The big advantage of these bindings is that booklets produced with these methods will lay open and flat. Ring binders have the additional advantage of allowing users to add and subtract pages. Most mechanical bindings come in a surprisingly wide variety of sizes and colors.

The printer can show you samples and give you comparative costs. Ask him or her to advise you on the best choice for your piece.

If you decide to use a three-ring binder, you may want to get something "printed" on the cover. Binder covers are not actually printed; they are silk-screened. Finding a good source for binders and silk-screening is sometimes difficult, as there tends to be a lot of turnover in this business. Ask around for recommendations. You can also look under *Advertising Specialties* in the Yellow Pages. Ask silkscreen vendors for

Interviewing Graphic Designers

43

Instead of designing the piece yourself, you may decide to hire a graphic designer. The more you interview, the more likely you'll be to come up with one that's right for your project. Here are questions to ask.

- What do you consider to be the best piece in your portfolio? Why?

- What aspects of design do you like best?

- Do you use a computer? What kind? Do we have compatible software?

- What services do you provide?

- Do you handle the type?

- Do you prepare camera-ready art?

- Do you oversee production?

- Have you worked with an organization like this before?

- Does my piece interest you?

- How are you with deadlines?

- How do you charge? What is the payment schedule?

- When would you be available to work?

- Can you leave a sample of your work and a resume with me (or send them)?

- Do you have letters of recommendation or references? May I call them?

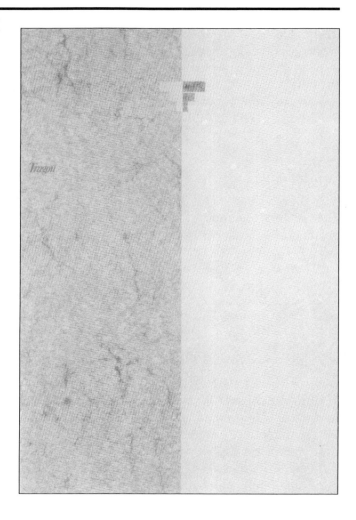

A pattern of small circles are embossed on the right half of this piece. The deco design is brought into the 90s with colors of gray marble, peach, and teal.

references, check them out, and look at samples of their work.

Perforations

Perforations—the small holes punched in a line across a sheet of paper—make it easier to tear out, or a section easier to tear off. If you want your printed piece *perfed*, (the return section of a brochure, for example), say so on your estimating form. You may want to get quotes (estimates) both with and without perforations.

Die cuts

A die cut is a cutout in the surface of the paper; the *die* is the metal piece that does the cutting. Designers often use die cuts on covers so that the sheet of paper beneath shows through. Die cuts are expensive, and they require special attention. There may be occasions when a die cut is exactly what you want, and may be worth the price. Ask how much a die cut will affect the time as well as the cost.

Embossing

Embossing raises the surface of a sheet of paper to form letters, numbers, or other shapes. It is created by pressing a metal die into the paper without cutting through it. The depth of the embossing can range from shallow to quite deep. Printers can show you charts that have different depths. Look at them carefully and specify the depth you want.

Embossing requires heavier paper, and some heavier papers emboss better than others. It's a good idea to get the advice of an experienced printer or paper salesperson. He or she can recommend the best papers for your particular image.

An embossed surface can have ink on it or not. When it has no ink it is called *blind embossing*. Blind embossing is among the more elegant techniques available to the designer. Although it is expensive, do not automatically rule it out. You may want to compare the prices of doing blind embossing with using two or three colors of ink, for example. They may be closer in cost than you'd think. Once you've paid for getting a die made, you can use it indefinitely. So getting a die cast of your logo, for example, or some other regularly used image, could well be worth the exploration.

Selecting a Graphic Designer

44

Here are the kinds of issues to consider after you interview each designer. Fill out the worksheet (page 361) while the meeting is still fresh in your *mind, and attach his or her resume and business card to it. Keep these evaluation sheets. They may come in handy in the future.*

Name: _____   Date: _____

Yes No

___ ___ 1. Does this person have the specific skills you need?

___ ___ 2. Do you like most of the pieces in the designer's portfolio?

___ ___ 3. Would you like your printed piece to look like these?

___ ___ 4. Does the designer have relevant experience?

___ ___ 5. Is this person available when needed?

___ ___ 6. Does the designer charge a rate you can afford? Is it negotiable?

___ ___ 7. Was the designer on time for your interview?

___ ___ 8. Does this person strike you as reliable and conscientious?

___ ___ 9. Would this person fit in with your organization?

___ ___ 10. Would you enjoy working with this person?

Comments: _____

_____

_____

_____

_____

*Margins frame a page, so choose proportions carefully. In illustration **a**, the sides and top are equal; the bottom is larger. In **b**, the sides and bottom are equal, the top is smaller. Illustration **c** has equal sides with a smaller top and a larger bottom. Exactly equal margins, **d**, are less pleasing.*

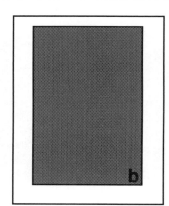
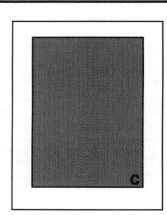
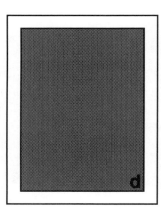

Doing the Layout

Layout is the arrangement of elements (type, art, and graphics) on paper. The goal is to lay them out in a pleasing and functional order, one which requires a minimum of effort to read. A layout with type and images neatly organized is least demanding on the reader. This kind of layout will look easy to read, and when it looks easy to read, it usually looks good.

An orderly, regular sequence is especially important for publications with many pages. When readers can anticipate how the information will be structured on a page before they ever see it, it makes reading easier. A regular, expected sequence allows readers to go from one end of the piece to the other with the least amount of interference. They are free to concentrate on the content, from one page to the next, without having to reorient themselves to a different layout on every page. Each page can have enough variation to keep it from becoming monotonous, but the underlying design remains the same. The structure of this underlying design is called a *grid*.

Creating a Grid

A grid is a pattern or a plan for pages in a printed piece; it is the designer's blueprint for the design. The grid enables a designer to make all pages in a printed piece have a consistent look. It establishes a regular rhythm so that one page flows easily to the next, and makes the text easy to follow.

All illustrations and other graphic matter "hang" on invisible grid lines like clothes on a clothesline (except that they can "hang" from a side or bottom grid line as well as from the top).

In creating a grid, the designer comes up with a set of rules which are maintained throughout the piece. These rules precisely specify all spatial relationships on the page. For example, the bottom, left, and right margins of this book are 4-1/2 picas (about 3/4"); the top is 5 picas. The columns are consistently 20 picas wide (about 3-5/16"); the space between them is 2 picas (about 11/32") consistently. The length and weight of all rules (lines) throughout the book are also specified and kept regular; so is the space above and below all headlines, icons, and pictures.

Computers and page layout programs make creating a grid design easier, faster, and more fun. You can specify the number of columns and the amount of space you want between them, and they appear instantly on the screen.

It's worth the effort to come up with a good grid. Once you've got it you can use the same basic layout on many pieces, and you can use it over time. To fa-

Working with a Graphic Designer

45

Writers, marketing directors, project coordinators, content experts, and others often work with graphic designers. And as in all relationships, things go better when you can see a project from his or her point of view. Here are some suggestions to help make your relationship with a designer a good one.

- Resolve internal staff conflicts about the piece before meeting with the designer.

- Have everything pulled together when you get together: the agenda, your copy, photos, illustrations, and so on.

- Each designer has his or her own distinct style. Be sure that style is the one you want for your printed piece.

- Include designers in the planning process as much (and as soon) as possible. They can give you fresh ideas and technical advice.

- Familiarize the designer with your organization, and discuss what you hope to accomplish with the piece.

- Clarify your agreement in writing, and establish a payment schedule in the beginning.

- Find out how many times you are entitled to use the design (or illustration) you are buying. Negotiate these rights at the outset.

- Changes frequently prolong the designer's work. Discuss compensation that exceeds the original agreement up front.

- Designate one person from your organization to be the contact person with the designer.

- Show the designer samples of printed pieces you like.

- Discuss your logo and style, color, and paper preferences if you have them.

- Go over what must be included in the piece at the outset (logos, names, copyright, etc.).

- Describe any limitations, such as needing to match something else, or fit into an envelope.

- If you are on a tight budget, tell the designer (or illustrator) what you can afford, and ask what he or she can do for that amount.

- Develop a realistic timeline with the designer, write it up, and make sure everyone involved has a copy.

- If there are any changes in either the time schedule or the piece itself, let the designer know as soon as possible.

- If you are dissatisfied with the designer's work, say so (gently). Give him or her the opportunity to improve it.

- Respect the designer's opinion. Presumably he or she knows more about design than you do. Keep in mind that you are partners with a common goal.

The Grid
*This annual report provides
a good example of design based on
a grid (or basic underlying structure). All
pages below are based on the grid at right.*

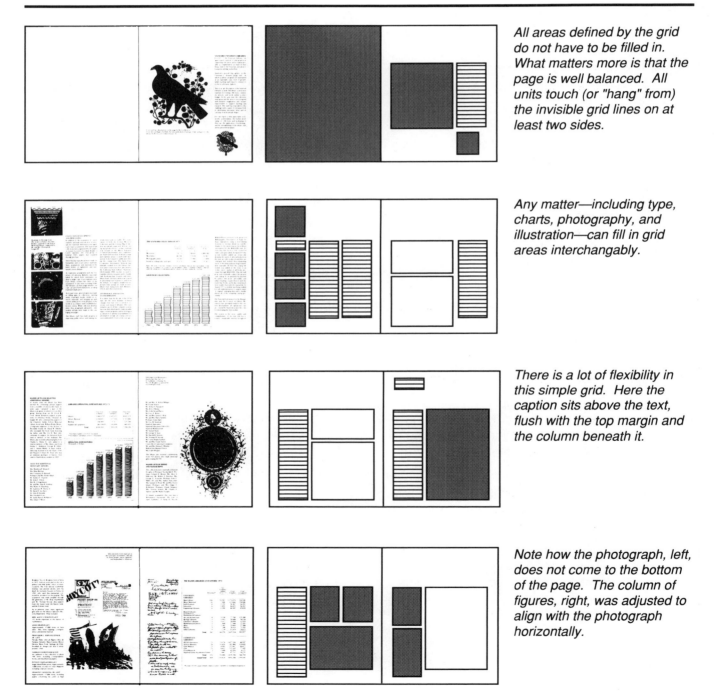

*All areas defined by the grid
do not have to be filled in.
What matters more is that the
page is well balanced. All
units touch (or "hang" from)
the invisible grid lines on at
least two sides.*

*Any matter—including type,
charts, photography, and
illustration—can fill in grid
areas interchangably.*

*There is a lot of flexibility in
this simple grid. Here the
caption sits above the text,
flush with the top margin and
the column beneath it.*

*Note how the photograph, left,
does not come to the bottom
of the page. The column of
figures, right, was adjusted to
align with the photograph
horizontally.*

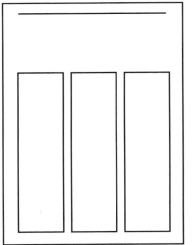

The distance between the top edge of the page and where the image area regularly begins is called the sink.

Type or visual matter can occupy one, two, or three columns at a time.

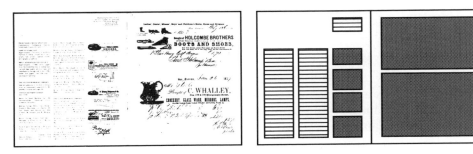

Space above the sink line can hold illustrations, a caption, or it can be left empty. Note that the space between pictures and columns generally remains constant.

All elements relate to the invisible grid. Material can be divided up into small units, or take up the entire image area.

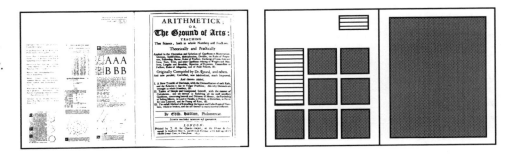

All illustrations do not have to fit squarely within the grid lines. Breaking out of them occasionally makes the design more interesting.

*Each of the printed pieces
below shows the effective use of
white space. Notice how the art, photographs,
and type are carefully balanced within the space.*

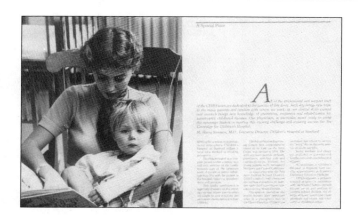
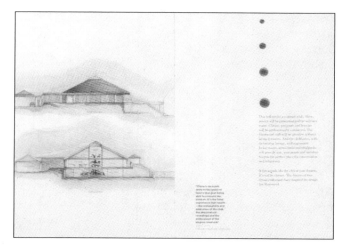

miliarize yourself with grids, look for the design structure on different printed pieces. When you see a publication you admire, find its underlying grid.

When you create a grid, you work with both positive and negative elements on the page. Positive elements are such things as type, photographs, and illustrations (covered later in this Sections 5); negative elements are more abstract, like white space, margins, and columns, discussed below.

White Space

White space is the "negative" or "empty" space on the page, and there is seldom enough of it. "White" space, by the way, can be any color—it's whatever color the background of the printed piece happens to be (it's most often white, hence the name).

Writers often see white space as an empty place to put words; inexperienced designers see it as a hole to be filled. Pros, on the other hand, see white space as a valuable element to the design of the page. To them this "negative" space is positive space—something to be used as a counterpoint to balance other elements. Printed pieces with too little white space are common; pages with too much are rare.

White space contributes both to the function and the beauty of a printed piece. It adds spaciousness, making the piece easier to read. White space is breathing space; a place to rest. It helps keep function and beauty in balance. White space also adds grace, sophistication, and elegance to a page that might otherwise look cluttered.

Use white space as a frame for a unit of type or a drawing or photograph, so they can be seen more clearly. Or use white space to surround some other element and make it stand out dramatically. Don't fill up the space for the sake of filling it up. Use white space *intentionally*.

Margins

Sensitively-designed margins contribute to the overall attractiveness of your printed piece and to the comfort of reading. They make only a small difference (if any) to the budget. Pay attention to the margin widths on your pages, and experiment with different sizes.

Formulas for margins with aesthetically pleasing proportions are shown on page 194. Page numbers and other typographical elements often occur in the margins, so be sure to take these into account when

The margin on the inside (or binding edge) of a page is called the *gutter*. If you want the left and right margins to be equal when the piece is put together, take into account that some of the space may be taken up by the binding (like plastic spiral, for example), and adjust the gutters accordingly. Ask the printer how much additional space you need to leave in the gutter to compensate for the binding.

Columns

Choose column widths that make reading comfortable. Generally, the wider the column gets, the larger the type you need (and the more space between the lines.) Narrower columns can have smaller type (and less space between lines). The amount of space *between* the columns is also important. Too wide a space can make the design unattractive; columns that are too narrow interfere with legibility.

As the designer of a printed piece, you will make many, many decisions. You'll make broad, aesthetic ones—like whether the style should be clean and sparce or decorative and elaborate—to detailed and technical ones, like how a piece folds and goes together, and what size and weight to specify each line

you lay out a page.

To find the most comfortable balance of margins and type, try out typefaces in different column widths on the page (you can do this easily if you have desktop publishing software). Each typestyle requires a different ratio of type to margin for optimum appeal. You don't need to use real copy to test alternative widths, but you do need to use the real typeface.

This effective poster uses a single column of type in a generous margin of white space. It helps the reader to focus on the image and the message.

of type. To do a good job, you must be aware of numerous possiblilities, and know how to choose among them. All the while you have to keep the whole in mind, as the impact of the printed piece depends on the sum of its parts. If you want your piece to have a big effect, you must carefully make a thousand small decisions.

Understanding Type

If you feel anxious at the very mention of the word "type," you are not alone. Typography is a vast and complex subject, and inumerable books have been written to explain it. Many designers, technicians, and craftspeople devote their professional lives entirely to this area of graphics. There is no obvious or easy access point for the beginner—so jump in. Experience is the best teacher.

You can get the basics of type from this chapter, but keep reading and learning. The more familiar you become with it the more confidence you'll have in using it, and the more you will enjoy working with it. So to begin at the beginning . . .

Look at these graphic shapes you are reading—right now, on this page. Look at them for a moment as the sequence of curved, straight, and slanted marks on paper that they are. Really *notice* them. When you "read" these squiggles, your brain instantaneously decodes them into comprehensible information.

This bit of magic is what enables us to communicate in print. These shapes we read are either handwritten or mechanically set. When they're mechanically set, they're called type.

Our alphabet is made up of twenty-six upper case and twenty-six lower case letters, ten numbers, and a miscellaneous assortment of other symbols, such as periods, quotation marks, percentage signs, and foreign language accents. The entire set of characters, all matching in design, is called a *font*. Font is another name for typeface or type style; the names are used interchangeably.

Every font has its own designer and its own history, its own personality and its own unique qualities and characteristics. Each is more or less appropriate for a particular printed piece. You wouldn't want to read this book set in wedding script, for instance, and a wedding invitation wouldn't be as attractive set in ordinary type.

Type strikes us on two levels: on a cognitive level (the decoding part), and on a visual level (the design part). Some designers will work with type on a page for long periods of time with absolutely no idea of *what the piece is about*. They ignore the meaning of the type entirely. They see each font as graphic texture, as a different shade of gray, and as producing a distinctly different visual effect. Designers pay attention to the forms of individual characters: the design of the letter V, for example, may be especially handsome in one font and uninspired in the next, or one typeface may have a strong number 3 while another is weak.

Other people zero in on what the type *says* and have absolutely no idea what the page looks like. For

There is enormous variety in the design of letter forms, creating a wide range of personality in typefaces. There are thousands of designs for each letter and number.

them, the graphic effect is entirely subliminal. If you are going to select good type for your printed piece, you must be able to look at it *both* ways.

When type is used for headlines, it is called *head type* or *display type*. When it is used for the main part of the text it is called *text type* or *body type*. Sometimes the head type is in the same type style as the body type; sometimes it is different. For example in this book the head type is Helvetica, and the body type is Trump.

Selecting Type

Type Style

In the latter part of this century there has been an incredible change in the number of type styles available. Thirty years ago there were perhaps twenty or so common typefaces. Design students could learn the names of the major ones, and become familiar with them. Technological advances in the 60s and 70s triggered an explosion in type design; now there are thousands of styles available. The average designer has a hard time keeping up with *seeing* them all, let alone learning their names.

Many of the new typefaces are based on older classic ones that were carefully designed by highly-skilled craftsmen in previous centuries. It will be interesting to see which of the newer, trendier type designs will stand the test of time. Some will barely last the length of time the designer spent designing them; others will endure and become classics themselves.

Typefaces are grouped into different categories, based on their design. Different typesetters and typesetting books sometimes have their own classifica-

tion systems, which can make it confusing. But boiled down to the most fundamental divisions, there are three categories:

- Serif, with little "feet," a more traditional-looking style:

This is a serif typeface

- Sans (French for "without") serif, with no "feet," a more contemporary looking style:

This is sans serif

- Decorative—everything that doesn't fit into the other two:

This is a decorative typeface

Other categories you may hear mentioned include *Oldstyle* (a classic serif typeface based on Roman letters); *Modern* (styles that were "modern" when they were designed 200 years ago, compared to the styles that preceded them); *Transitional* (an integration of Oldstyle and Modern); *Square Serif* (a type with squared-off serifs); and *Script* (like handwriting).

Type Families

There can be many variations of the same type design within a single typeface. Most typefaces have at least three variations: regular, italic, and bold. Some have more than twenty.

The ordinary type within one family is called *regular*. It is also sometimes called *plain* or *normal* or *medium*. When it is straight it's called *Roman*; when it is slanted it is called *italic*.

There are many versions of the same typeface, as these eight variations of Caslon demonstrate (there are even more). The pages, below, of Instant Lettering® are from Letraset's Graphic Materials Handbook.

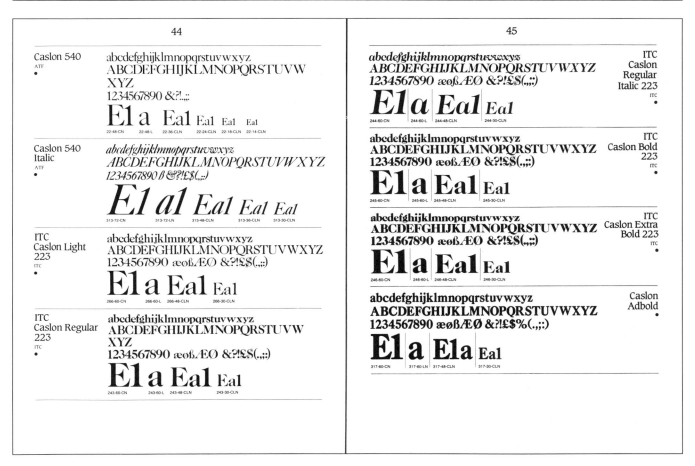

Type may be squished tightly together (called *condensed, compressed* or *compacted*); or it may be pulled apart (called *extended* or *expanded*). The same type may also be available in a very skinny version (called *thin* or *light*) or a fat version (called *bold, demi bold, black,* or *ultra black*). There may be an outline form (which is also called *comstock*), or a *shaded* one (also called *shadow*). And just when you think you've got it, you realize that the shadow version can also come in light or medium or bold, and also in light or medium or bold italic.

In summary, here are some possible variations within the same type style family:

- Italic
- Demi bold
- Condensed
- Bold
- Extra condensed
- Extra bold
- Expanded
- Black
- Extra light
- Shadow
- Light
- Outline
- Medium
- Comstock
- Bold italic
- Extended

It seems that computer technology produces new variations daily. When it comes to type, even the pros

*Kerning is adjusting
the space between characters
so they read more easily and look better.*

are learning continuously. Don't get overwhelmed; just keep noticing what you like, and gradually type will seem more familiar.

Making Use of Variations

As discussed earlier, some fonts come only in regular, italic, and bold. These are fine if you're doing an ad or a flyer, but if you are producing a publication such as a newsletter, more variations within the family come in handy. You may want several variations to create different levels of heads, say for a booklet (a system for heads is described on pages 152–154, in the writing section). And you may need other variations for footnotes, running heads, captions, and so on.

The number of variations within a family is also something to consider when you are choosing a font that will be used for a long time, say for an ongoing project, or at the start of a new business. Does the typeface you are interested in come in extended or condensed, for example? Is there a light version? You may want the flexibility later, if not now.

Look carefully at each variation of type within every family you are considering. All members of a family are not equally strong. Look especially carefully at the italics. Some are readable and good looking; others are weak.

Type Size

The height of a typeface is described in *points*. You might say, for example, that you want a booklet set in 12 point type. The size of a typeface is often chosen from a series of set sizes, such as 10 point, 12 point, 14 point, 24 point, 42 point, and so on.

These odd numbers originally came from the height of the block of wood that the letter originally sat on. (It is interesting to see these now-random sizes on computer screens—they can cause confusion for many desktop publishers.) Now type can be repro-

duced in just about any height you want. If you are creating the type yourself, size possibilities depend on the capabilities of your computer.

One thing that can really trip you up if you aren't aware of it is the fact that *type sizes are not standard*. That is why I said that type is *described* in points rather than *measured* in points. One size in a particular typeface is not necessarily the same size as the same point size in another face. For example, these typefaces are all 12 point:

- *This is 12 point Zapf Chancery*
- **This is 12 point New Century Schoolbook**
- **This is 12 point Helvetica**
- This is 12 point Times
- This is 12 point Garamond

If you hear a debate as to what size type is best for a particular kind of publication, don't pay much attention to it. A 10 point type in one font can actually be the same size as a 12 point type in another, which may again differ in height from a 12 point type in another typeface.

During this century there has been a trend toward using larger and larger type. If you look at a the type in a newspaper from around 1900, you will be struck by how small it is. Glance at newspapers onward through the decades and you'll see that the type seems to be growing! Now with an increasingly older popu-

lation in this country, the trend toward larger type is likely to continue. Body type these days is commonly set in 10, 11, or 12 point, and head type is commonly set in 12 through 24 points.

Most people realize that type can be too small to read comfortably, but not as many realize that type can also be too large. After a certain point, a larger type face used for body copy may be as difficult to read as one that is too small. And titles and headlines are often set larger than they need to be. Heads set in the same size as the text can often work well, so long as they are in bold, and sit above it.

Vertical Space: Leading

When you specify a type face, you have to choose the style and the height of the type, and you also have to specify the amount of space between the lines. The space between the lines is called *leading*, because strips of lead used to be added between rows of metal type to space it out vertically.

The leading, like type, is also described in points. Space between lines of type is measured from the baseline of one line of type to the baseline of the next (see Sidebar 47). One point of leading adds 1 point of vertical space, for example; 4 points of leading gives 4 additional points. Type that has no lead added between rows is said to be *set solid*.

So, for example, when you specify the body type for a newsletter, you might request a 10 point type with 2 points of leading (2 points of vertical space

---

Type Measurements　46

Picas and points are the standard of measure used in typography. Here is a summary of the basics.

- **Picas**
  6 picas = 1 inch
  1 pica = 12 points

- Lines, column widths, and the space between columns are often given in picas, as are page depths.

- **Points**
  72 points = 1 inch
  1 point = .0138" (1/72 of an inch)

- The point is used to describe type size and line spacing (leading).

- Between 5 and 12 points, standard sizes for type go up in 1 point increments (5 point, 6 point, 7 point, etc.).

- Above 12 points, 6 points is often the standard increment (traditional standard sizes are: 14, 18, 24, 30, 36, 42, 48, 60, and 72).

- Computers now produce type in just about any size.

- **The em:**
  The em is the area occupied by the capital letter M in whatever typeface you are using. It will be narrower if you are using a condensed typeface, wider if you use an expanded one. The widths of all characters in an alphabet are designed to relate to the width of the M.

Most fonts come in italic. Some are more handsome and readable than others. Italic is called italic, by the way, because it was first used in an Italian edition of Virgil in 1501.

The Owl and the Pussy-cat went to sea
In a beautiful pea-green boat,
They took some honey, and plenty of money,
Wrapped up in a five-pound note.

The Owl and the Pussy-cat went to sea
In a beautiful pea-green boat,
They took some honey, and plenty of money,
Wrapped up in a five-pound note.

The Owl and the Pussy-cat went to sea
In a beautiful pea-green boat,
They took some honey, and plenty of money,
Wrapped up in a five-pound note.

The Owl and the Pussy-cat went to sea
In a beautiful pea-green boat,
They took some honey, and plenty of money,
Wrapped up in a five-pound note.

The Owl and the Pussy-cat went to sea
In a beautiful pea-green boat,
They took some honey, and plenty of money,
Wrapped up in a five-pound note.

The Owl and the Pussy-cat went to sea
In a beautiful pea-green boat,
They took some honey, and plenty of money,
Wrapped up in a five-pound note.

The Owl and the Pussy-cat went to sea
In a beautiful pea-green boat,
They took some honey, and plenty of money,
Wrapped up in a five-pound note.

The Owl and the Pussy-cat went to sea
In a beautiful pea-green boat,
They took some honey, and plenty of money,
Wrapped up in a five-pound note.

---

added between the lines). The way you say it is *10 on 12*; you write it *10/12*. The 10 is the size of the typeface; the 12 comes from adding the 2 additional points for the space between the lines.

Horizontal Space: Kerning, Letterspacing, and Wordspacing

Kerning, letterspacing, and wordspacing are adjustments in the horizontal line of characters to make words look better and be more readable. Letterspacing is adding space between characters; kerning is subtracting space between them, and wordspacing is spacing out the words in a line of type, either by adding or subtracting space.

As type increases in size, the space between letters looks more and more awkward. That's because the space between letters is mechanically set, not set by eye. These techniques give a printed piece a more even and professional look.

The space between a capital L and T, for example, can look much further apart than the space between an H and B (LT; HB) or an L and a J and an N and an R (LJ; NR), although they are actually the same. That's when kerning comes in handy. The L and T (or L and J) can be brought in closer together so that they look as though they have the same space between them as the H and B (or N and R). In some desktop publishing software letters are kerned automatically; others allow you to do your own kerning. Some do both.

Describing Type

47

Parts of type

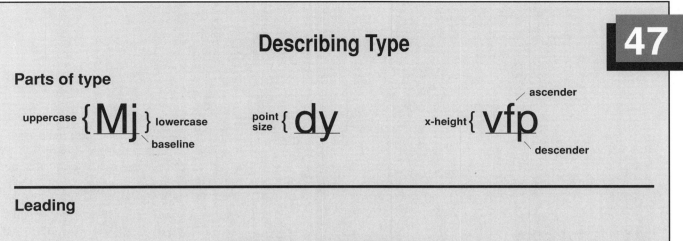

uppercase { **Mj** } lowercase
baseline

point
size { **dy**

x-height { **vfp**
ascender
descender

Leading

The Owl and the Pussy-cat

This is Palatino set 12 /12 ("set solid")

The Owl and the Pussy-cat went to sea
In a beautiful pea-green boat,
They took some honey, and plenty of money,
Wrapped up in a five-pound note.

This is Palatino set 12/13

The Owl looked up to the stars above,
And sang to a small guitar,
"O lovely Pussy! O Pussy, my love,
What a beautiful Pussy you are, You are,
What a beautiful Pussy you are!"

This is Palatino set 12/14

Pussy said to the Owl, "You elegant fowl!
How charmingly sweet you sing!
O let us be married! too long we have tarried:
But what shall we do for a ring?"

This is Palatino set 12/15

They sailed away for a year and a day,
To the land where the Bong-tree grows,
And there in a wood a Piggy-wig stood,
WIth a ring at the end of his nose, his nose
With a ring at the end of his nose.

This is Palatino set 12/16

"Dear Pig, are you willing to sell for one
shilling
Your ring" Said the Piggy, "I will."
So they took it away, and were married
next day
By the Turkey who lives on the hill.
They dined on mince, and slices of quince,
Which they ate with a runcible spoon;
And hand in hand, on the edge of the
sand,
They danced by the light of the moon, the
moon,
They danced by the light of the moon.

This is Palatino set 12/18

The Owl and the Pussy-cat went to sea
In a beautiful pea-green boat,
They took some honey, and plenty of
money,
Wrapped up in a five-pound note.

Poem by Edward Lear (1812–1888)

This column below is an example of ragged right text; the one on the left is justified.

The Column Edge: Justified and Ragged Right

A column of type that has a straight, even, aligned right edge is said to be *justified* or set *flush left and right*. A column of type that has lines ending in different lengths, giving its right edge a "ragged" look, is called *unjustified* or *ragged right*.

Should you use justified or unjustified type? Each of these versions has strengths and weaknesses. Which is better depends on your overall design. Justified columns give a neat, controlled look, and are commonly used for newspapers, magazines, and so on. Ragged right columns have a more informal impression. Justified columns used to give a piece an official or professional look, but that distinction has faded. Designers now use unjustified columns as a design feature, and both justified and ragged columns of type are common. Either can look professional.

Some say that a ragged right (unjustified) column is easier to read because it is less likely to hyphenate words. This may be an important consideration when you have an audience of people whose reading skills are poor. Otherwise both can be readable. Legibility depends more on the the font, the size, and the leading than whether it's justified or ragged right.

Readability

Type legibility is extremely important. When type is hard to read it becomes a serious barrier to communication. If you are in doubt about the readability of a particular font, don't use it. Select a typeface that you yourself find comfortable to read. If someone else chooses one for you that you are uncomfortable with, discuss it. If type is to play a purely decorative role, that is another matter, but that's not usually the case.

Legibility not only depends on the typeface you choose; it also depends on how you specify it (request it to be set). Your sensitivity to size, weight, spacing, and layout *all together* make a difference in the readability of the piece.

Beginners often put too much space between the lines of type in headlines and titles. This makes information harder to get, and it weakens the appearance of both the type and the overall design.

Columns of type that have too much space between letters or words in them are also less readable. Words that are spread out too far create *rivers* (white or empty space flowing through them). In such a case, wordspacing (or letterspacing) is needed to tighten the column up.

By the way, readability also depends on some factors other than type. It depends on your readers' reading ability (or literacy level), their age, their interest in the subject, where they are when they read it, how good the light is, how they're feeling at the moment, and their personal responses to the design, colors, and images you've used with the type. Many of these variables are obviously beyond your control. That is why it's so important to make good decisions about what you *can* control.

Line Length

Horizontal line lengths are measured in picas. There are 6 picas to an inch. The *optimum line length* is the length of a line you can read most easily and quickly, with maximum comprehension and minimum fatigue. Several scientific studies have been conducted to determine optimum line lengths. They tend to be unmercifully detailed, and worse, contradictory. Pursue this line of investigation if it interests you; if not, I think you'll do fine by using your common sense and following these general guidelines:

Be wary of *either* extremely short or extremely long lines. Type is hard to read if the line is too long; it is also hard to read if it is too short. It is

Some Popular Typefaces

Typefaces, like colors and styles, go in and out of vogue. Following is a brief description of some of today's more commonly-used fonts.

The popularity of these particular fonts has been greatly increased due to their availability for desktop publishing.

Palatino: Palatino is a handsome typeface. Its subtle style alone is enough to give a publication character. Palatino was created by Hermann Zapf in the late 40s, and is based on much earlier type designs. Palatino is a highly readable typeface with an especially nice italic (*this is an example of Palatino italic*). Outstanding Palatino characters are C, D, P, Q, R, X, Y, a, e, c, h, m, p, 1, 5, and 8.

Melior: Melior is another typeface designed by Hermann Zapf. His aim was to make a highly readable font, a goal he certainly achieved. Melior's distinguishing characteristic is a square serif, which gives the face a well-balanced, square, and solid look. Printed pieces using Melior reflect this square, solid style. Melior's especially good looking characters include C, O, Q, R, S, a, g, d, 6, 8, and 9.

Helvetica: For over thirty years Helvetica has been one of the most popular typefaces, and for good reason. It is a handsome and very readable type. Each character has a clean design, giving pieces that use Helvetica a crisp, contemporary look. This sans serif type fits together compactly: its x height is large; its ascenders and descenders are short (see Sidebar 47 for definitions). Helvetica has been imitated many times, and appears in slightly changed versions under many different names. It has a large family of variations, which makes it especially appealing. Helvetica was designed by Max Meidinger in 1957. It is named after its country of origin, Switzerland (the Swiss are known for their outstanding graphic design). Especially well-designed characters are B, E, G, P, R, S, a, c, e, 1, 2, 3, 5, 8, and 9.

Times: Times is one of the most widely used typefaces today. It is a good basic all around type, good for just about any kind of publication, and is particularly popular for magazines. It too is highly readable, compact (with a large x height), and has a large family of variations. It was designed over 50 years ago for the *Times of London* by Stanley Morison, and is used world-wide. Individual Times letter forms look good when enlarged to a very large size. Especially distinguished Times characters are C, E, G, M, W, d, e, r, l, and 9.

Optima: Optima is another popular sans serif face. It has a grace and elegance that gives the type a distinction all its own. With thick and thin lines, Optima has a subtle calligraphic look. It is useful for a wide range of publications, and is especially effective for distinguishing a particular piece from others. Optima was also designed by Hermann Zapf. Outstanding characters in Optima are D, G, M, O, X, Z, and the number 7.

Avant Garde: In contrast to Melior's square look, the design of this sans serif typeface is round. It is a distinctive typeface with a definite contemporary flavor, and is better for short units of type and heads rather than for long manuscripts. There is a big difference in the width of the letters—the round ones are considerably wider. Notice, for example, the difference in the words "poem" and "flit." You might think they were from different fonts. This typeface was designed by Tom Carnase and Herb Lubalin in 1970. Especially handsome Avant Garde letters are C, G, O, Q, R, e, g, and p, and the numbers 5 and 6.

A well designed typeface is handsome.
Sometimes a designer will take advantage of
its beauty and use letters and numbers extra large,
as is the case with this elegant annual report, below.

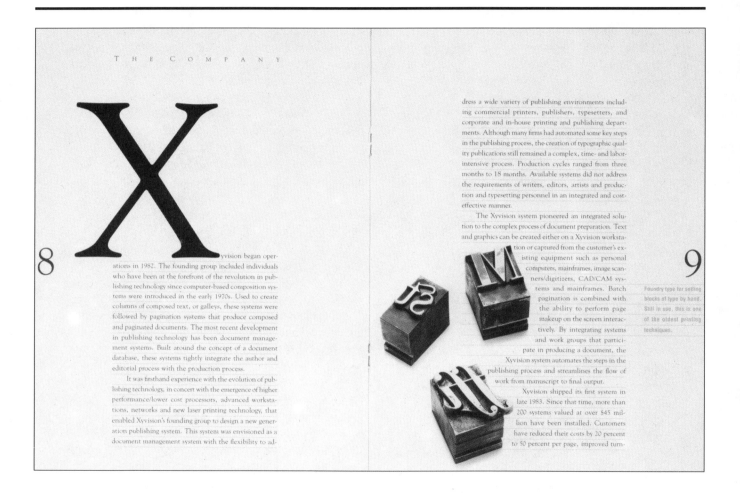

hard to generalize as to what is "too long" and what is "too short"—that depends on your typeface and the height of the characters. In general, the longer the line (or the wider the column), the more vertical space (leading) you need between the lines. In other words, for longer lines (and wider columns), use larger type and more space between the lines. For shorter lines (and narrower columns), use smaller type and less space between the lines.

Try different variations, and see what is most comfortable to you. If you are especially concerned about readability and line length, as you might be for a less-literate audience, you may want to try out some samples on them.

Capital Letters

Capital letters were designed to hook the eye at the beginning of a word, not to spell out entire words. Words set in all capitals are not as easy to read as caps and lower case (abbreviated *C/lc*—See Sidebar 36 for type-specifying and proofreading marks). If you want

*Type does not always
have to be mechanically set,
as exemplified by this poster for a
Texas American Institute of Graphic Arts fund-
raiser. Here it suits the style of the illustration perfectly.*

to use all caps, they work better in headlines or words otherwise set off than with words in text. Also, be aware that words in all caps take up more space.

Alignment

The more zig-zagging in and out the eye has to do along the left margin of a page, the more work it is to read. Lining things up can make reading easier and more comfortable. Keep the number of indents on the left-hand side of a page to a minimum, and keep indents small unless you are using them for a special dramatic effect.

The Number of Fonts to Use

When you ask designers the most common mistake non-professional designers make, they are all in agreement: they use too many typefaces in a single piece. Unless there is *good reason* to do otherwise, keep the number of fonts (and their variations) to an absolute minimum. This may be especially difficult for desktop publishers who have access to many fonts (and there are lots more coming). Too many variations in type make a printed piece look cluttered, less inviting, and harder to read.

If you look at really well-designed pieces, you will see that very few typefaces are used. When there are two, it is often a sans serif head type and a serif body type. There should be a definite purpose for adding more variations to your piece. If you do use more fonts, make sure they *add* to the legibility and look rather than *detract* from it.

Selecting Type

As mentioned earlier, each typeface has its own distinct personality. The more you work with type, the more you notice there seems to be a "right" typeface for every piece. It becomes a matter of considering dif-

This page from Letraset's Graphic Materials Handbook demonstrates the wide range of type styles available today.

ferent ones until you find it. Sometimes it's a process of elimination—rejecting ones that are obviously wrong for a particular piece.

Look, for example, at typefaces on the next page and say to yourself "corporate annual report." Then look at the typefaces and think "invitation to the office Christmas party." Try "letterhead for a new computer company," then "fund-raising letter for an environmental group," then "real estate ad." Typefaces sometimes seem to volunteer themselves.

Sometimes it helps to live with some options for a while. Copy a few possibilities from a type book (or run them out on your printer). Or get some samples set. Try different faces, sizes, and leadings, different headlines, different line lengths, and column widths. Look at columns set both ragged right and justified.

Put the samples up on a wall near you. If it's body copy you are considering, make sure your sample includes enough type so you can really get the feel of it. One usually stands out as right after a while.

Getting the Type Set

Alternatives

The equipment your type is set on makes a big difference in its appearance (see page 216 for comparative output). Get your type set on the highest-quality machine you can afford. Choices usually boil down to either traditional typesetting or typesetting à la desktop publishing. Both are compatible with word-processing software, and accept text either from a disk or telephone modem.

However you get your type set, talk with people experienced with it before the job is done. Typesetters are very knowledgeable and can save you time and money by discussing your job beforehand. If you are using type set on a computer, talk with colleagues, friends, or people at computer stores—anyone willing to share their experience with you.

Traditional typesetting

You will get the highest quality typesetting job if you go to a reliable shop with experienced typesetters and the latest equipment. Skilled craftspeople with highly specialized machines can fine-tune your type so it looks beautiful and reads easily. You will have the broadest selection when you go this route, and you'll get expert advice. And, of course, you will get the biggest bill. It's a good idea to send your copy out for bids; prices can vary widely.

Desktop publishing

With this method of generating type, (as the name suggests), you are the typesetter. Your equipment consists of a computer and one of three output devices: a dot-matrix printer (unsuitable for reproduction), a laser printer, or a linotronic machine. The latter two are available for use at shops called *service bureaus* (or *service centers*). Look under *Copying* or *Desktop Publishing* in the Yellow Pages.

Linotronic type is the top of the line for desktop-published pieces and there are levels of refinement to choose from (See *Desktop Publishing*, page 281). Linotronic output is more expensive than other methods (such as laser printing), but it costs less than traditional typesetting. Although computer-produced type set on a linotronic machine still lacks the quality of type professionally typeset, it is very good, and rapidly getting better. But the fact still remains: the quality of the type is reflected in the cost.

Because it can produce a good looking page for the money, laser printing has quickly become commonplace. It is appropriate for pieces that you want to look nice, but don't want to spend a lot of money on.

If you plan to use a laser-printing service, be sure to have a sample run out so you know what to expect when when the final is produced. Some services insist you do this so they know what the job is supposed to

14

Egyptienne Bold Condensed	● 30-84 pt	66
English Tudor	● 36-60 pt	67
Exeter	● 28-54 pt	68
Falernus	● 20-48 pt	68
Fox	● 36-60 pt	70
Fraktur Bold (Fraktur Bold)	● 24-60 pt	71
Freestyle Script	○ ● 30-60 pt	73
Freestyle Script Bold	● 42-60 pt	73
GALLIA	● 24-48 pt	78
ITC Galliard Black Italic	● 18-48 pt	78
Goudy Extra Bold	○ ● 24-60 pt	81
Goudy Heavyface Condensed	● 30-60 pt	82
Goudy Fancy	● 36-72 pt	82
Goudy Handtooled	● 36-60 pt	82
Goudy Old Style	● 24-48 pt	82
Goudy Old Style Italic	● 24-48 pt	82
Hawthorn	● 36-60 pt	83
Jenson Medium	● 30-72 pt	92
Jenson Extra Bold	● 30-72 pt	92
Juliet	● 30-60 pt	93
Kalligraphia	● 24-72 pt	93
KORNELIA	● 36-54 pt	93
Lazybones	● 42-72 pt	94
Le Griffe	△○ ● 30-84 pt	94
Lectura	● 28-60 pt	95
Lectura Bold	● 28-60 pt	95
LETTRES ORNEES	● 72 pt	95
Locarno Light	● 30-60 pt	95

Locarno Medium	● 30-60 pt	96
Locarno Bold	● 30-60 pt	96
Locarno X-Bold	● 30-60 pt	96
Loose New Roman	● 30-72 pt	96
MANUSCRIPT CAPS	● 42-72 pt	97
Melior	● 18-48 pt	97
Mistral	● 30-60 pt	98
Modern No 20	● 18-144 pt	99
Murray Hill Bold	● 24-72 pt	99
Medison Casual	● 36-72 pt	100
Obliq Light	● 28-54 pt	101
Obliq Medium	● 28-54 pt	101
OCR-A	● 8mm-15mm	101
Old English	△○ ● 18-72 pt	101
Optima	○ ● 16-84 pt	102
Optima Medium	● 18-60 pt	102
Optima Bold	○ ● 18-84 pt	102
Palace Script	△○ ● 18-60 pt	103
Palatino	○ ● 24-60 pt	103
Palatino Italic	○ ● 24-60 pt	103
Palatino Italic Swash Caps	● 24-60 pt	103
Palatino Semi Bold	● 24-60 pt	103
Palatino Ultra Heavy	● 36-72 pt	104
Park Avenue	○ ● 18-48 pt	104
Pendry Script	○ ● 36-60 pt	105
Pepita	● 36-60 pt	105
Perpetua Bold 461	● 30-72 pt	105
Plantin 110	○ ● 24-60 pt	106

Pt Size Range   *Pt Size Range*

Make use of type for its design value
as well as for its meaning. This announcement uses both machine set and handwritten letters.

Script type, strategically placed
next to the marble-like open area, gives
an elegant appearance to this brochure. Three
die-cut holes on the lower right balance the design.

Choosing Type

Choosing type can be mind-boggling, especially if you don't know what you're looking for. It can make you want to close your eyes and point. Here are some tips:

- Read at least a paragraph in each typeface you are considering (choose the one that's most readable)

- Look at the type both as a headline and as a column of text

- Compare the overall style of different typefaces, and decide what impressions they make

- Check the number of variations available in the type families you are considering

- Compare the look of the italics in different fonts for both readability and beauty

- Choose a typeface that suits the nature of your content

- Notice individual character forms, especially the ones you will be using for initial caps or headlines

- If your text calls for lots of numbers, compare the design of the numbers in several typefaces

- If you are going to put headlines and body copy in different typefaces, make sure they are compatible

- Look at x-heights in different typefaces, and compare the heights of ascenders and descenders (See Sidebar 47)

- Notice how the letters sit next to each other; there should be a comfortable fit

---

look like. If you're doing the laser printing yourself, don't expect it to come out perfectly the first time. Some noodling is usually required, so be sure to give yourself some extra time.

A word on computer fonts: every computer comes with a certain number of fonts (called *screen fonts*), which can be supplemented with discretionary software. But just because a font is installed on your computer does not mean it will print out from a laser printer or a linotronic machine. The printer (or output device) you use must have the matching *printer font*. Find out what fonts are available on *the output device* you will be using *before* you make your type selection. Sometimes laser-printing shops will make you a disk of their screen fonts. This will enable you to see on *your* screen exactly what is likely to come out on *their* printer.

For access to laser printers and linotronic equipment, and to computers for that matter, go to a service bureau. Expert help is often available there, so take the opportunity to learn. Ask how you will be charged, and get an estimate before you begin. If you are in the market for a computer, you can try out different machines.

Typewriter

The typewriter is the bottom of the line, but you can make it work when you have to. In fact I have seen some pieces produced on a typewriter that were more effective than comparable material that was typeset. For instance one booklet from a women's shelter in San Francisco was printed on carefully chosen paper and had good line drawings. Although the piece was extremely low budget, typewriter type did not interfere with communication. What is lacking in type style can be made up for with excellent layout—make it neat and clean, and use lots of white space. If you are turning typewritten copy over to someone else to typeset, make sure it is easy to follow.

50   **Comparing Sources of Type**

There are several ways to get your copy turned into type. Some of the most common ones are shown below. Compare them with a sharp eye (especially the last three), and consider the advantages and disadvantages of each in light of your budget.

Typewriter

Look at these graphic shapes you are reading--right now, on this page. Look at them for a moment as the sequences of curved, straight, and slanted marks on paper that they are. Really notice them. When you "read" these squiggles, your brain instantaneously decodes them into comprehensible information.

ImageWriter®

Look at these graphic shapes you are reading—right now, on this page. Look at them for a moment as the sequences of curved, straight, and slanted marks on paper that they are. Really notice them. When you "read" these squiggles, your brain instantaneously decodes them into comprehensible information.

Laser Printer

Look at these graphic shapes you are reading—right now, on this page. Look at them for a moment as the sequences of curved, straight, and slanted marks on paper that they really are. Really notice them. When you "read" these squiggles, your brain instantaneously decodes them into comprehensible information.

Linotronic

Look at these graphic shapes you are reading—right now, on this page. Look at them for a moment as the sequences of curved, straight, and slanted marks on paper that they really are. Really notice them. When you "read" these squiggles, your brain instantaneously decodes them into comprehensible information.

Typesetting Machine

Look at these graphic shapes you are reading—right now, on this page. Look at them for a moment as the sequences of curved, straight, and slanted marks on paper that they really are. Really notice them. When you "read" these squiggles, your brain instantaneously decodes them into comprehensible information.

Rub-on type comes in a wide variety of fonts and colors, and is handy for a distinctive title or initial cap. Below is a sheet of Letraset's Instant Lettering®.

Press Type

For a cover or headlines you can use *rub on* type. It's also called *press type* or *transfer lettering* (it's called *Instant Lettering®* by Letraset). Many handsome type styles are available. They come in a wide variety of sizes from 6 to 192 points. The standard color is black, but sheets are also available in white, red, green, gold, blue, and yellow. You can find it at art supply and stationery stores. A sheet is expensive, however

Type Tips

Here are two of the most common mistakes made with type, along with a quick, easy, and inexpensive way to give a low-cost typesetting job some life.

Warning!

If you had a penny for every type mistake that was caught too late, you could retire. It is very easy to miss errors—both the typesetter's or your own. It is *your* responsibility to go over the type scrupulously before the piece goes to the printer. Read the piece backwards and forwards (literally), and ask others to go over it. For more on proofreading, see Sidebars 35 and 36.

Underlining

I recently saw an article titled "Real Typesetters Don't Underline." That sums it up. Find alternatives to underlining if you can, especially if you are using computer-set type. The lines in underlining often come so close to the letters that it makes both the word and the page look messy. Italics is often a better alternative.

Quick emphasis

If you want certain lines to stand out and you don't have too many printed pieces, you can use a stationery store highlighter, and dash on the color by hand. In addition to the familiar yellow, several other highlighter colors are available, including green, turquoise, orange, and hot pink. These colors come in both fluorescent and regular intensities.

In general, printed pieces work better with fewer typefaces rather than more. Here's the exception: when type is used as a decorative element, as in this lively poster below.

(around $13). It takes practice and care to get the letters on properly, but it can be done. Directions are often given in the catalog from which you select the typeface.

Work Consciously

However you get your type set, stay on top of costs right from the beginning. Surprises are common with typesetting bills. To avoid them, ask for continuous updates in the price as changes are made.

When type is carefully chosen and set, it powerfully enhances your printed piece. Take the time to make your decisions thoughtfully, and get the advice of those with experience. When you see your final product, you'll be glad you did.

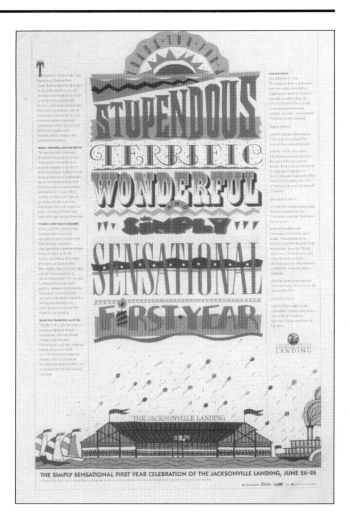

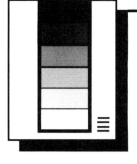

Chapter 18

Color That Works

Would you say there are five hundred colors? Or perhaps a thousand? A million? More. Ten million colors have been recorded as discernible by the human eye at the National Bureau of Standards. Computers can generate more than 16 million. Most people can name about twenty. And when it comes to selecting colors for printing, we tend to name the same ones over and over.

A better understanding of color equips the print producer to be more adventurous, and to make more effective selections. The purpose of this chapter is to expand your view both of color and of printing ink. It will help you choose the colors for your printed piece with more confidence.

Ink on paper, like paint in a room, can have enormous impact. Also like paint in a room, ink on paper is the least expensive way to create visual impact. That impact can help you to convey your message more effectively. The beauty of a color alone may be enough to attract a reader. On the other hand, weak or poorly-coordinated colors can spoil an otherwise good design. The colors you select for your printed piece either *support* communication, or they become *a barrier* to it.

Color preferences are influenced by many factors, one of which is our own individual pair of eyes. Color is light—radiant energy. Our eyes are sensitive to vast differences in the intensity of light, from the brightest sunlight to the dimmest moonlight. Different cones in our eyes are sensitive to different colors: some to red, some to blue, and some to green.

Green light, say from a landscape, activates the green-sensitive cones, which send impulses to the brain. The brain then responds by recreating the landscape, based on the signals it receives. So what we see is the result of the condition of the cones in our eyes, and how we interpret the signals they send. Our interpretation is based on our own personal experience. Since no two of us have exactly the same eyes or exactly the same experience, no two of us see exactly the same thing.

So color preferences are influenced by our experiences, which are stored both consciously and unconsciously. Like pleasant or unpleasant associations with sounds or smells, colors trigger positive or negative responses that skip the brain and go straight to the emotions. The color of a room where you grew up, for example, or your favorite crayon, or the colors in a familiar landscape, or the color of your first car may influence your response to certain colors forever. One color may evoke a pleasant experience; another may make you feel ill. There also may be some genetic

The PANTONE Color Formula Guide is standard equipment among designers and printers. Here are some of the other related products.

PANTONE *Color Formula Guide 747XR (printing ink)*

PANTONE *by Letraset Color Products Selector*

PANTONE *by Letraset Color Overlay Selector*

predispositions to your color preferences, based on the color of your eyes, hair, and the tones in your skin. Color preferences are highly subjective.

Ideally, your printed piece will have colors to which your target audience will have a strong, positive response. You can't do much about the individual experiences of the people in your audience, or the condition of the cones in their eyes, but you *can* tune in to certain commonalities and preferences. They could be cultural, for example, or educational or generation-related. These common denominators give you clues as to which colors are more likely to be appealing to them, and which ones are likely to be a turn off.

I once developed two sets of health-related brochures for a Hispanic population. One set was brilliant red, blue, and yellow; the other was deep green, burgundy, and navy. Everything except the colors was exactly the same. You guessed it—the brightly-colored brochures were greatly preferred (this preference for brilliant colors may reflect the brightly-colored flowers and birds of Central and South America). Interestingly, though, the predominantly non-Hispanic physicians who handed them out preferred the more

subtle and subdued colors (like the ones in the northern European landscape, which reflected their dominant heritage).

Our ideas about what colors we like best are also influenced by the particular time and place in which we live. What looks wonderful to our eye in one environment may not look so good in another. A brilliantly colored shirt that looks outstanding in Hawaii, for example, may look outlandish in Connecticut. Colors that look good in one decade often look awful in the next. Color preferences, like foods, go in and out of fashion. They are more or less appealing in one period or another.

Take the 50s, for example. Avocado and old gold were popular (along with Jello, Spam, and Betty Crocker cakes). In the 60s earth tones and psychedelic hues (and brown rice and homemade bread) were in vogue. Electric and bright primary colors (along with quiche) were popular in the 70s; pastels (and pasta) were in fashion in the 80s.

And the 90s? It's hard to know for sure, but I'm willing to guess. Teal, peach, and turquoise will be popular a bit longer. And you will probably be seeing a lot of magenta, purple, jade, dark green, plum,

PANTONE *by Letraset Color*
Paper Selector/Coated

PANTONE *by Letraset Color*
Paper Selector/Uncoated

PANTONE *by Letraset Color*
Letrafilm Matte Selector

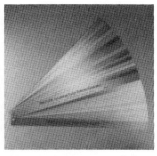

PANTONE *by Letraset Color*
Selector/Graduated

fuchsia, mustard, and olive, and "new" powdery colors like cocoa brown. Fluorescent pinks, oranges, and lime green, along with metallic colors like silvery blue and copper will also be more evident.

One of the most interesting books I've read traced western color preferences back several thousand years. It showed the colors in vogue during Egyptian dynasties, Greek and Roman periods, the Middle Ages, and at the courts of several French kings. It laid out the colors that were popular from colonial times up to the middle of this century.

Cycles of color preferences are repeated, but never in exactly the same palette. Take the moss greens and mauves that were popular in the 1940s for instance. They're back again, but amidst others, such as the powdery brown I mentioned. Or take the pink that went with charcoal gray in the 50s. After being out of fashion in the 60s and 70s, pink has come around again. But this time the pink is with Santa Fe tans and ivories, not charcoal (unless, of course, the designer wants to create a 50s look).

This year again, appliance manufacturers, architects, and clothing designers will gather to pick out the colors for the upcoming season. And like it or not, most of us will be influenced by what they select. We'll see their choices in department stores, restaurants, offices, and hotel lobbies across the country. The "new" colors will strike us as fresh, inspiring,

and filled with vitality. The old ones will look weary and worn, and so will our printed pieces if we use them. Trends in color are worth watching.

Printing Ink

Color in publications comes from paper and printing ink. This ink is usually transparent, which means that you have to use darker inks over lighter papers. The shade of the paper beneath changes the shade of the ink printed on top of it. A blue ink on yellow paper, for example, comes out with a greenish tinge. The same shade of blue will look different on a bright white paper than it looks on ivory paper, and it will look different again printed on red or brown paper.

Inks in colors other than black (which is also considered a color, by the way) cost more. This is because color requires extra work. Color separations must be made from the art boards (discussed in *Preparation For Printing*, page 313). Time is needed for mixing the inks, for making adjustments, and for washing up the press.

Different presses can run different numbers of colors at the same time. There are two-color presses, for example, and four-color presses. Based on the kind of press your piece is run on, an additional color may cost very little extra. Discuss prices for additional colors with printers.

Markers, below, are color-coordinated to the PANTONE Color Formula Guide. They have broad, fine, or ultrafine nibs.

PANTONE®* Colors

Imagine trying to describe the shade of your shirt to someone over the phone. If the person on the other end tried to match your description to a color sample from among several shades, chances are the guess would be wrong as often as it was right. Color is difficult to describe accurately.

On top of that, color changes according to the conditions under which it is seen. The same green ink on a glossy paper, for example, looks different on a textured sheet. Green ink next to blue looks one way; next to orange it looks another. And the same green ink looks different yet again in a dark printing shop and in bright sunlight. The texture of the paper, the color it is next to, and the level of light all influence the way a color looks.

Enter PANTONE colors. When you select colors for your printed piece, you will probably select them from a PANTONE Color Formula Guide. This Guide contains 747 colors plus four process colors (more on that later). The PANTONE MATCHING SYSTEM* has been the international standard for specifying printing ink colors since the early sixties, and it is the most widely used in the printing industry today. It takes the guesswork out of describing color.

Each color is shown both on glossy coated paper (in the first half of the fan book), and then again on uncoated paper (in the second half). Each of the 747 colors has a code number and a formula. The number is followed by a "C" or a "U," which stands for coated or uncoated, reminding you of the type of paper that the color you are looking at is printed on.

The blue ink on the cover of this book, for instance, is PANTONE 286C. The formula beneath this color swatch in the PANTONE Color Formula Guide says it is made up of 12 parts (75%) PANTONE Reflex Blue and 4 parts (25%) PANTONE Process Blue. The red on the cover is PANTONE Red 032 C; (it is a basic premixed color so there is no formula); the yellow is

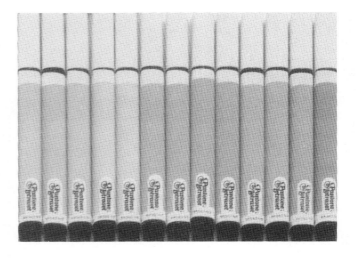

PANTONE 116C (19 parts (97%) PANTONE Yellow, 1/2 part (3%) PANTONE Warm Red). This code enables the printer to duplicate specified colors exactly.

All printers have a PANTONE Color Formula Guide. You can use theirs or buy your own. They are expensive, but they're worth the investment if you do a lot of color specifying.

Other related products are available for design and layout at art supply stores. They include markers in broad, fine, and narrow tips, sheets of coated and uncoated paper, and transparent color overlay sheets. There are also books with perforated swatches for tearing out and attaching to the final art, so that the printer is sure to get the right color. There is a PANTONE Color Tint Selector 747XR that shows colors in tints (lighter shades or "screens" of the colors), as halftones (photographs), and in type, all on both coated and uncoated paper. And there are selector books for color-coordinated papers and overlays. These products are "professionally priced," but they help designers and their clients get a better idea of what the piece will look like before it's printed.

If you can't find the color you want in a PANTONE

222

* Pantone, Inc.'s check-standard trademark for color.

*This postcard of colors
from PANTONE, Inc. advertises the latest
metallic shades of silver and silvery-lavender.*

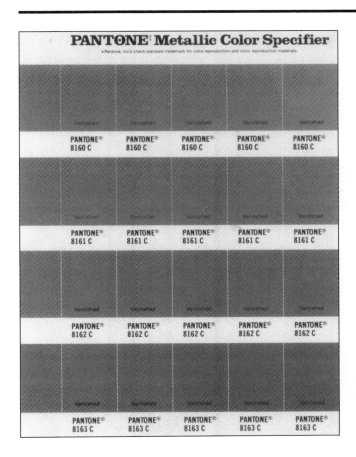

PANTONE Metallic Color Specifier

Publication, it's probably because it isn't there. Until the PANTONE book was updated, many of the "newer" and more popular "designer colors" were not available (a few million more are still missing). There are newer color coding systems with more colors, but they are not as commonly used. It is hard for these systems to break in once a standard has already been established.

If you want to use a color that is not available in the system, you can look for it in something already printed, or mix it yourself (poster paints work well). Bring the sample of what you want in to the printer, and he or she can match it. (Be sure to ask what the ad-

ditional cost will be—it's usually not much.) I've had reds (along with other colors) matched many times, for despite the many shades of red, the one I want just isn't there.

I have also mixed up special colors to be used for logos and trademarks. Printers will match the sample you give them (the larger the better), record the formula for mixing the ink, and give it a name (such as Dick's green). It's then readily available for future use.

Four-Color Process, or Process Color

There are basically two approaches to specifying color for printing. One is by selecting solid colors from the system just described; the other involves four colors, called process color. PANTONE colors are specified mostly when the areas to be printed are solid; four-color, or process color is used when there are continuous shadings as with photographs, or art work like watercolors or pencil sketches.

Process color uses only four colors of ink. Yellow, magenta (a purplish-red), cyan (a turquoise blue), and black. Different sizes and densities of tiny dots in the four colors give the illusion of many colors. They trick the eye into believing the image is in full color. You can see the dots if you look at a full color picture in a magazine under a magnifying glass. Without it, the colors blend and so give the impression of full color. This blending of dots is based on the same principle Impressionist painters like Monet, Renoir, and Seurat were so excited about 100 years ago.

You might think that because process color printing requires only four colors to create a full color look that it would be less expensive than specifying single, solid colors. But because of the precise film work involved, this is not the case. The colors in the art or photographs must be separated into each of the four colors. This process requires time and skill and is relatively costly.

This logo by a Wyoming designer is strong in black and white. The image and the type are "reversed"; the ink "bleeds" to the edge.

If you are going to be using process color printing, work closely with your printer. Although magnificent results are possible, there are limitations to the process, and adjustments are often needed. Look at color proofs and check the images at every stage along the way.

Special Inks

Some truly amazing effects can be created with special inks. You can give your printed piece more interest and punch for relatively little extra by using metallic inks, fluorescent inks, or varnish. Ask a printer to show you samples with these kinds of inks. Discuss the pros and cons of each, and weigh the advantages against the additional cost. Here is a brief description of these inks:

Metallic inks

There are 204 metallic ink colors in the PANTONE Metallic Color System. They come in their own specifier guide.

Metallic inks are made from metallic powders, and work best on coated paper. They give a printed piece a very distinctive look for not a lot extra. In addition to gold, silver, and shades of copper and bronze, there are many other subtle colors including gray blues, steel greens, and silvery reds, browns, pinks, and lavenders.

Fluorescent inks

There are seven brilliant fluorescent colors in the PANTONE Color Formula Guide: lime green, turquoise, yellow, a light and a dark orange, a pink, and a fuchsia. These fluorescent inks emit and reflect light, and are most effective when printed on glossy paper (preferably a bright white). You wouldn't want to read much text in these colors, but they can be effective for special situations when you may want a special look, or when you want to attract attention. Fluorescent inks can be used effectively on posters, announcements, invitations, and flyers, as well as on ad speciality items like hats and tee-shirts. These inks work well as a second color to black.

224

*Different screens of inks in
just two colors give this Christmas card
for a health promotion program a multi-colored
look. The color separations are shown on pages 328–329.*

Varnish

Varnish is an ink that is usually clear, but it also can be tinted. It can be either glossy or dull. Varnish can cover an entire piece, such as the cover, or just certain areas, to create a contrasting sheen (called spot varnish). Varnish also looks best on coated paper.

There are both practical and aesthetic reasons to use varnish on your publication. A varnished surface protects it against fingerprints (it's upsetting to find that your handsome booklet gets covered with fingerprints the first time it's picked up). The most familiar use of varnish is on glossy covers—it's what creates that slick professional look. A varnish "run" through the printing press usually costs the same as an additional color of ink. Discuss possibilities for using varnish on your piece with the printer.

Screen Tints

By using a "screen" of a full color, you can get the look of a second, third, or fourth color for little or no extra cost. This is specified as a percentage of the full color, in increments of 10. For example, if you select red as a full color (which would be 100% red), you can also get it "screened down" to different percentages: an 80% red is just a little lighter red, 40% red looks pink, and 10% red looks pale pink. You indicate on the art work which percentages go where.

Although screens provide many shades of the original color inexpensively, using them really effectively takes skill. The full strength color and its screened versions sometimes don't look good together. And using screens means using a stronger color together with pastels. The effect of clear brilliant blue, for example, can be weakened next to its screened percentages of lighter blue. It's tricky to make red and its screened pinks work well together, or emerald green and its pastel screens. And screens of black can make muddy-looking grays.

If you use screened tints, you will need a tint guide that shows what the different percentages of PANTONE Colors look like when screened. Printers have them; you can also find them in book stores, art supply stores, and libraries. Be sure you like the lighter shades as well as the full color, and, most importantly, that you like them together.

This line image works well in black and white. It would also be effective in one color of ink on a colored paper, in such combinations as those suggested in Sidebar 52.

Reverses and Bleeds

Colors are "reversed" when the background has the ink (usually darker) and the type appears in the color of the paper it's printed on (usually lighter). In this case the usual positive ink impression and negative background are reversed. When the type is "negative," with the background color surrounding it, the type is referred to as being "dropped out" (see illustration on page 224).

A bleed means that the ink goes right to the edge of the sheet. A piece might bleed on one, two, three, or all four sides (as the cover of this book does).

Reverses and bleeds provide an inexpensive way to get a very powerful look. They easily make an ordinary printed piece look more sophisticated and professional. The covers of a handsome series of brochures for a large bank, for example, use just one vivid color in the background, and simple but clean-looking type dropped out. The type appears white (or dropped out) because the piece is printed on white paper. Dropped out type (or images) are whatever color the paper is.

When you use a reverse you may want to set the type in boldface rather than regular. The additional weight of the boldface type will help it to stand out better from the surrounding color. Reverses are effective with small amounts of type (such as on a cover). Body copy set in reverse is harder to read. Designers often compensate for this added difficulty by making the type larger or bolder (or both) when they reverse it.

Selecting Colors

Hue, Value, and Saturation

Sometimes you look at a color and you know it's wrong, but you don't know why. That's when a basic color vocabulary comes in handy. Each color has three distinct, describable qualities. The first is *hue*, which

is interchangeable with the word "color," and means the same thing. The second is *value*, which is how light or dark the color is. The third is *saturation*, which describes the intensity of the color.

So in a situation in which you know something is wrong with a color, the fault could lie in any (or all) of these three areas. The value may be wrong (it could be too dark or too light), or the saturation could be off (it could be too weak or too intense), or the hue could be wrong (the color itself). Seeing color in terms of hue, value, and saturation enables you to evaluate color with greater perception and more accuracy.

Using One Color Effectively

Don't be discouraged if you have only one color to work with. It's not how many colors you have, it's what you do with color that counts. When I give workshops, I like to show examples of printed pieces with

Color Combinations

You may be in a hurry and not have time to give much thought to color. Or you may not have much experience in selecting colors, or just not know where to begin. Here are some color combinations that work. They will save you time, or get you started.

One Ink Color
The second color is paper

- Rust on bright yellow

- Burgundy on gray

- Bright green on bright white

- Silver on white

- Black on light brown

- Avocado on light brown

- Brilliant emerald on yellow

- Charcoal on light gray

- Burgundy on pale blue

- Dark peach on light peach

- Tan on ivory

- Bright pink on pale yellow

- Gray on white

- Deep burgundy on white

- Dusty aqua on pale aqua

- Brilliant red on white

- Black on camel

Two Ink Colors
Best on white paper

- Dusty aqua, mauve

- Brilliant red, black

- Lavender blue, orange

- Deep navy, clear pink

- Bright navy, red

- Dark teal, burgundy

- Turquoise, red

- Bright green, navy

- Sage green, apricot

- Turquoise, coral

- Deep navy, burgundy

- Bright red, lavender blue

- Moss green, brown

- Slate blue, silver-pink

- Spruce green, silver

- Charcoal, camel

- Turquoise, violet

Three Ink Colors
Best on white paper

- Moss green, apricot, brown

- Pale yellow, teal, mauve

- Burgundy, dark green, navy

- Aqua, lavender, pink

- Navy, burgundy, tan

- Teal, yellow-orange, rust

- Teal, red, gold

- Pencil yellow, blue, red

- Turquoise, yellow, orange

- Peach, tan, blue

- Black, hot pink, orange

- Midnight blue, rust, yellow

- Magenta, purple, black

- Black, dark green, red

- Light blue, tan, pink

- Lime, royal blue, black

- Dusty blue, rose, ivory

Black ink on white paper alone can be used effectively, especially when the layout, the type, and the paper are especially chosen to enhance a very black and white look.

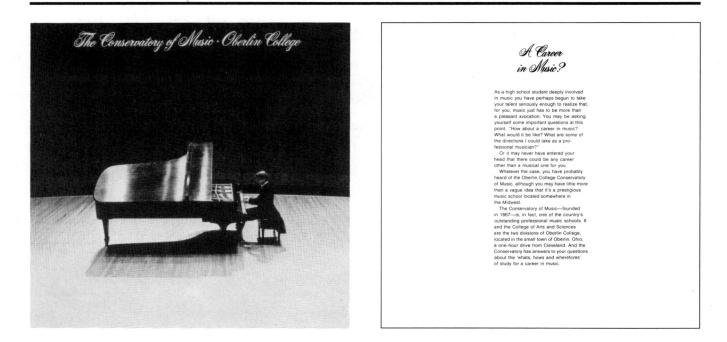

many colors next to others with just one or two. A lot of multi-colored pieces don't have nearly the impact that other one or two color pieces do. When you are limited to just one, make sure it is a *beautiful* color, and that the shade of paper you choose to go with it does the color justice. Sidebar 52 offers some specific suggestions.

Sometimes when people work with just one color they are disappointed with the way the job turns out. When their piece comes off the press they discover there isn't *enough* of the color. This is usually because the color was not used in any large solid areas. If you want one color to have impact, you have to assign it to large enough areas so that it will show. You can use thicker lines or bars rather than thin ones, for example, or you can use a reverse or bleed. These techniques will give your piece a more colorful look.

Black ink by itself can be used very effectively, especially if you think of it as the *color* black and not just as ordinary black printing ink. Use it on bright

white paper, or on a rich creamy ivory. Tell the printer that you want *good ink coverage*, so that the ink is a full-bodied, rich, beautiful black, not a dark gray. Printing on a coated paper (which can be either dull-coated or gloss-coated) will make the black more lively and add to its richness. Varnish on top of the black ink can also make it deeper and more interesting. Or use black ink on a colored paper. If you do, be sure the color of the paper you choose really looks good with black. Some colors combine with black more effectively than others.

Color and Type

A word on choosing colors for type. There are times when colored type works well, especially for titles, and sometimes for headlines. But when body copy is in black and the head above it is in a color, the body copy usually stands out more than the head. This defeats the purpose of the head.

Black headlines are more commanding. They are eminently readable, and always work. Dark colors, such as navy blue, deep green, burgundy, charcoal, and dark brown are also quite readable, especially on white or a light-colored paper. But when maximum legibility is crucial, use black type for the body copy.

Choosing Color Combinations

Choosing colors that go well together is more time consuming (and challenging) than you might think. The more colors you try to put together, the greater the challenge. Any color can look good or bad, depending on what it's next to. An assignment sometimes given in art schools is to select the color you *dislike* the most, and work with it until you find a color that, when next to it, changes your opinion of the color you disliked. The *combination* of colors you choose is as important as choosing any single color.

Colors often seem to work better together when they have some underlying theme that unifies them. For example, earth tones go well together (think of the colors related to the earth—green, brown, rust, gold, granite, sand); so do primary colors (think of a paint box—bright red, purple, blue, green, yellow, and so on); so do pastels (think of Impressionist paintings—pinks, ivories, blues, and lavenders). It is more difficult to use a mix of primary colors and pastels together effectively, or pastels and earth tones (not impossible, just more difficult).

An underlying color theme could have to do with value and saturation as well as with hue. Colors that have the same degree of lightness or darkness work well together; so do colors with similar intensities. Jewel tones like emerald, sapphire, ruby, and amethyst go well together because they have the same degree of vividness. Soft heather grays and mauves and pinks look good together because they share a common lightness. Colors work well together when they are *uniformly* vivid or pale.

Color Tips

Every printed piece you do is an opportunity to experiment with color. Here are some tips to help make it more successful.

- When you are choosing a color for a printed piece that may need to be reproduced on a copier, make sure the color copies well

- Be sure to specify from the right section of the PANTONE Color Formula Guide (the first half shows ink on coated paper; the second half is on uncoated paper)

- Get a sheet of matching paper to see how the color looks over a large area

- For maximum legibility, use strongly contrasting colors

- Ask the printer for good ink coverage

- Notice the colors other people have chosen for their publications

- Collect samples of the ones you like in a file folder

- Sometimes you can give a piece new life simply by updating the colors

- For regularly appearing publications, have one of the colors printed ahead (such as the masthead); then overprint the sheets with text as new editions come out

- When selecting colors, ask yourself: is this the *very best* color for the piece? Do I like it? Will the audience like it?

- If you must choose a color by committee, choose one that at least *someone* really likes (one person's favorite is often better than the group's compromise)

Also, most light and dark *versions of the same color* can look good together. For example, tan ink on pale tan paper works; so does aqua on light aqua paper. If you use this kind of combination, choose the paper first. It's easier to match ink to paper rather than paper to ink.

Colors that are next to each other in the rainbow also work harmoniously together, especially when they are equally light or dark or subdued or intense. Purple looks good with blue, for example, red goes well with orange, orange with yellow, yellow with green, and so on. Warm colors also combine well, and cool colors go well together.

When it comes to putting colors together, nature is the master; we don't improve on it. For an endless source of good possibilities, look at the combinations of colors in nature. Notice the colors in your local landscape, and how they change from season to season. Observe color combinations in fields, forests, deserts, or mountains; or by the ocean; or on the plains. Even the colors in a haphazard pile of stones seem to be carefully coordinated. Or pay attention to the colors at different times of day. One set of colors dominates a foggy morning, and the palette changes by noon. Another comes forth at twilight, and still another in the moonlight.

Color is one of life's pleasures. Whether you are selecting just one or several for your next printed piece, there is no reason why you can't use colors that are striking and beautiful. Try reaching past ordinary red and blue to the millions of others. Or if you *do* use red or blue, make sure they are magnificent shades, or make them *very* red, or *very* blue.

Chapter 19

Selecting and Specifying Paper

Sometimes you just walk into a quick printing shop, look over the papers available, pick one you like, and that's that. But other times selecting the right paper for a printed piece is more of a challenge.

Paper comes in a wide variety of grades, colors, textures, weights, and, finishes. Different mills have their own names for similar papers with similar finishes and colors. So unless you are really familiar with printing papers or unless you are satisfied with what's on the counter, you'll need some help.

Get the advice of someone who works regularly with paper (called *stock* in the trade) and knows it— a graphic designer, an art director, a paper company representative, a printer's rep, or a printer. All of these people have paper samples and swatch books. Printers are especially good to discuss papers with because they are regularly in touch with paper company sales people, and they know which papers work best on their presses.

Criteria for Choosing Paper

There are several criteria upon which to base your choice of paper. How the paper looks, what it will be used for, its cost, opacity, its availability, and how the printed piece will be distributed all must be considered. Later on in this chapter we'll go over how to specify paper (including things like weight, finish, and grade). But first let's have a quick look at the criteria for selecting the right paper for your job.

Purpose

You may need guidance right off the bat as to which kinds are suitable for your particular piece. Paper is manufactured with end-uses in mind, so one consideration is its life span. If the piece is to be around for a while, or if it will be handled frequently, as a directory or catalog might be, it requires paper with qualities different from those required by a flyer.

Look

The paper you choose conveys a subtle message of its own. Not only is the quality of the sheet registered by the eye, it is also felt in the hands. Paper can add distinction and prestige to your piece, or it can weaken the impression. And paper helps convey a mood.

Sometimes it's worth giving up other things to go with a more expensive paper. There are a number of things you can juggle if you really want to use good paper. For example, you might decide to use only one

Heavy paper is used for this 33" long brochure, giving its length added sturdiness. It is for a meeting of database professionals in San Diego.

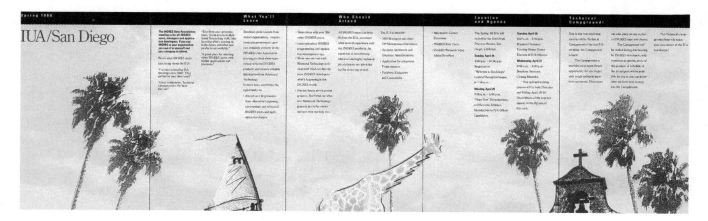

color on a beautiful stock instead of two colors on a less costly one. Or you might choose to use less art (or no art) and count on handsome type and paper for your impact instead.

Start at the high end of the paper spectrum—look at the quality papers *first*. This will train your eye to recognize good paper, and familiarize you with the range. You can always come down. Often you can find less expensive stock that looks very similar to an expensive one. If the paper you like takes you over budget, ask if there is a lower-priced version.

Cost

The cost of paper is not as significant for small jobs as it is for bigger ones. The paper cost per piece remains constant, while other unit costs diminish as print runs increase. But the larger the quantity of a piece you order, the larger the percentage the cost of the paper becomes. So pay especially close attention to paper when you're printing large quantities.

Printers often buy up large amounts of paper and have it available in the shop. This is known as "house stock." House stock is often a good choice for three reasons: first, it's often a higher-quality sheet than you could otherwise get for the money because it was bought in quantity; second, the printer is familiar

with how it handles on the press (its "printability"); and third, it's readily available. Ask about it.

Opacity

Opacity, or "show-through," describes the degree to which you can see the printing on the other side of the sheet. For paper that is to be printed only on one side, opacity doesn't matter. On a sheet that's printed on two sides, it does. Ask to see a printed sample of the sheet if your piece will printed on both sides.

Availability

For a variety of reasons, printers sometimes have difficulty getting a particular paper from the mill that produces it. So before you get too attached to any sheet, check on its availability. And be sure you are looking at current swatch books—sheets, colors, and their names change regularly.

Distribution

If your piece is going to be mailed, pay attention to the *weight* of the papers you are considering. Get a sample made in the same weight, size, and number of pages as your printed piece, and find out what it will cost to

232

mail. A slightly heavier or lighter stock can make a big difference in your total mailing cost.

Specifying Paper

When you specify paper for your printed piece, you need to describe five things: the weight, the name and line of the paper, the grade, the color, and the finish. If the particular paper you select comes in only one color or one finish, you don't need to mention it. Here are some sample specifications (this information is found in paper swatch books):

- 80 lb. Simpson Gainsborough cover, stone blue (Gainsborough sheets all have the same finish, so none is mentioned)

- 60 lb. Warren Lustro dull cover (Lustro sheets are all white, so no color is mentioned)

- 60 lb. Wausau Astrobrights text, Terra green (Astrobrights sheets all have the same finish, so none is mentioned)

Weight

The weight of paper is described in terms of how many pounds one ream (500 sheets) of it weighs when cut into standard size sheets. For example, a 65-pound cover stock means that a ream of it weighs 65 pounds. This is called *basis weight*. This is written 65 lb. or 65#. Sheet sizes are standard within each grade (page 235); they vary from one grade to another. Knowing the standard sheet size allows you (or the printer) to plan a printed piece in a trim size that avoids waste.

Name

Sometimes the name of the paper includes both the name of the paper company and a particular line of papers, like *Strathmore* (the company) *Grandee* (the

---

Specifying Paper 54

Selecting and specifying a good paper often takes more time (and ability) than many people realize. Each of the following characteristics needs to be fully and accurately described. Don't be afraid to ask for help. (Worksheet version: page 362.)

Weight:

Name:

Line:

Grade:

Color:

Finish:

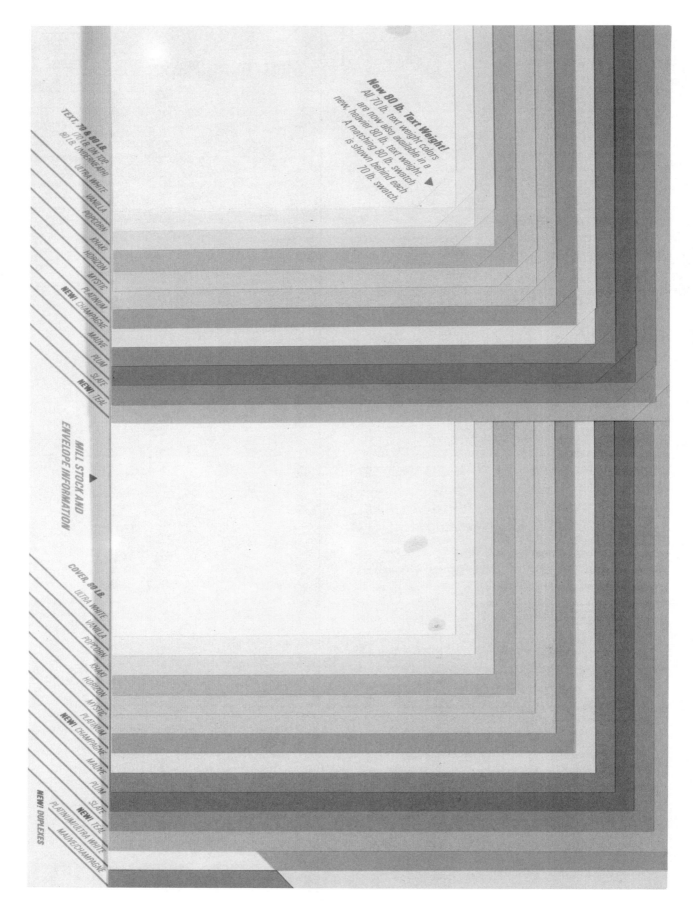

New 80 lb. Text Weight!
All 70 lb. text weight colors are now also available in a new, heavier 80 lb. text weight. A matching 80 lb. swatch is shown behind each 70 lb. swatch.

TEXT, 70 & 80 LB.
(70 LB. ON TOP, 80 LB. UNDERNEATH)
ULTRA WHITE
VANILLA
POPCORN
KHAKI
HORIZON
MYSTIC
PLATINUM
NEW! CHAMPAGNE
MAUVE
PLUM
SLATE
NEW! TEAL

MILL STOCK AND ENVELOPE INFORMATION

COVER, 80 LB.
ULTRA WHITE
VANILLA
POPCORN
KHAKI
HORIZON
MYSTIC
PLATINUM
NEW! CHAMPAGNE
MAUVE
PLUM
SLATE
NEW! TEAL
NEW! DUPLEXES
PLATINUM/ULTRA WHITE
MAUVE/CHAMPAGNE

Paper comes in an amazing array of colors, finishes, weights, and prices. Printers, designers, and paper sales reps can show you samples such as these.

line), or *Beckett* (the company) *Ridge* (the line). Words like *offset* or *opaque* may also be a part of the name of a sheet, like *Hammermill Offset*. Use the entire name and the particular line of papers when you specify stock for printing.

Grade

Paper is organized into grades based on most common use. The grades of paper frequently used by producers of printed materials are cover, bond, text, book, and offset. Each of these grades is a family of papers in itself. Each has its own standard size, range of weights, and variety of colors and textures. Here is a brief description of each of these grades:

Cover

Cover stocks are strong and durable, and come both coated and uncoated. They are used for presentation folders, business cards, invitations, menus, and covers of reports, booklets, catalogs, and so on. Cover stock is often made to match other papers, so that pieces requiring different weights can be coordinated (a letterhead and business card, for example).

Common cover weights are 60 lb., 65 lb., and 80 lb. A few cover stocks are measured in points (for example, .010 inches, or 10 points). Sheets with a different color on each side (with names like *Duplex* or *Two-sheet*) are also available. If you are considering die cutting or embossing (described on page 192), be sure the stock you are interested in is suitable. The standard size of a cover sheet is 20" x 26".

Bond

Bond, or writing paper (also sometimes called ledger, mimeo, and photocopy paper) is used for things like stationery, business forms, flyers, and resumes. This stock is uncoated, and colors are usually light. Surface

Getting Dummies   55

Paper companies sometimes make up samples (called dummies) of your printed piece from the papers you specify. You must describe exactly what you want. (A worksheet version of this sidebar appears on page 363.) Include:

Size:

Number of pages:

Binding or folding:

Inside sheets:

Cover sheet:

Pocket height:

Spine width:

Other special treatment:

Plain black ink can be effective when paper is carefully chosen to enhance it. Brown kraft paper suits these illustrations.

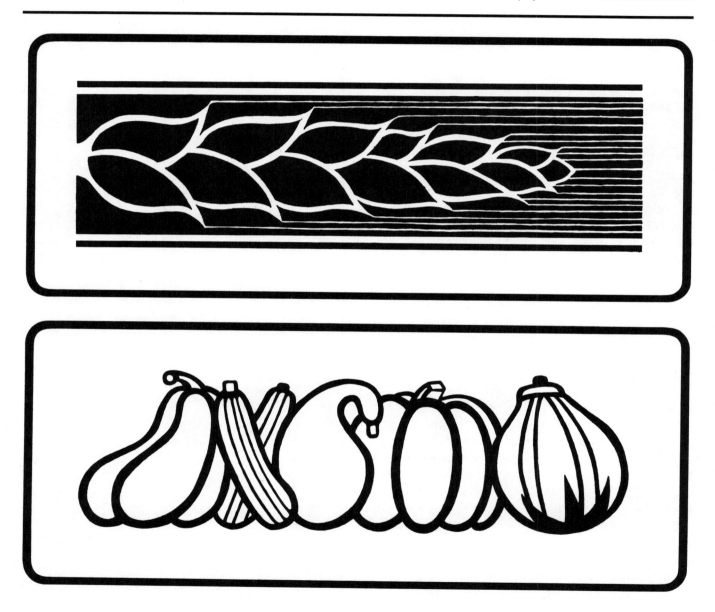

textures include smooth, laid (thin stripes in the same color as the paper), cockle, wove, and linen. Common weights are 20 lb., 24 lb., and 28 lb. Sheets with watermarks and cotton fiber contents (25%, 50%, or 100%) are among the most elegant. Most have matching envelopes and heavier sheets (cover weight) for business cards, presentation folders, report covers, and so on. The standard sheet size is 17" x 22".

Text

Text papers are used for booklets, brochures, reports, announcements, self-mailers, etc. They come in a wide range of colors and finishes. Most text sheets are uncoated and come in vellum, felt, embossed, and smooth finishes. Common weights for text papers are 70 lb., 80 lb., and 100 lb. Text weight papers usually come with matching cover sheets. The standard sheet size is 25" x 38".

Book

Book papers are less expensive than text papers. They can be either coated (gloss-coated and dull-coated) or uncoated. Book papers come in the same weights as text papers, but they are usually white. The range of finishes is not as great as for text papers. Book papers are used for such things as brochures, books, catalogs, and directories. The standard size is 25" x 38".

Offset

These sheets have been especially made for offset presses and are less expensive than others. They come in several colors and finishes, but the choices are not as broad or as interesting as the range of text papers. Offset paper is used for booklets, flyers, and general everyday printing. Common weights are 50 lb., 60 lb., and 70 lb. They sometimes come with a matching cover stock. Standard size is also 25" x 38".

Paper Tips and Reminders

56

Many handsome papers have been made since its invention in China in 105, and among the most beautiful are those for offset printing. Enjoy working with paper. Here are some tips.

- Take time in the beginning to find the right papers for your publications

- Look at many papers before you decide on one

- Once you make a good decision, you can confidently specify sheets from the same family of papers over and over

- When you find a paper you like, ask if there is a comparable one that costs less

- Ask printers about their house stock

- *Feel* the papers you are considering

- Ask to see *printed* samples of the paper that interests you

- Remember that the color of the paper will affect the color of the ink on top of it

- Specify the color of paper by its *specific* name, especially when it's white

- If you come across something printed on a paper you like, bring it to the printer (he or she may be able to match it for you)

- Rely on printers' experience—they usually know what they're talking about

The paper for this business card, left, is bright sparkly white—perfect for the brilliant red and blue inks. The paper samples below it are from a typical swatch book.

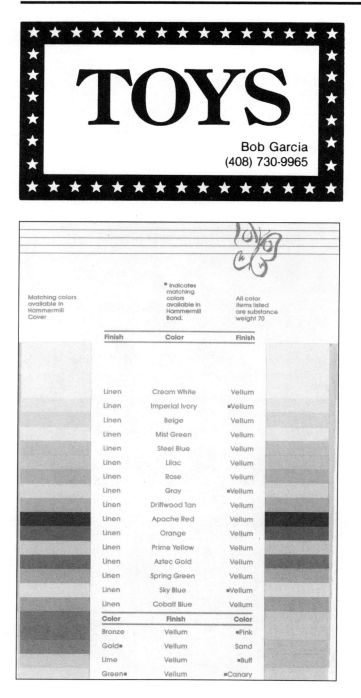

Color

When you specify the color of a paper, be sure to describe it *exactly*. This is especially important with white, as a mill may put out over 100 shades. White sheets have names like bright white, frost, ocean surf, natural white, vanilla, ultra white, glacier, warm white, cream, and popcorn. This year's names may be different from last year's, or the sheet may have been discontinued, so be sure swatch books are current.

Every white has some other color in it. Gather a handful of "white" papers and you'll see the difference: some whites are yellowish-white, some are bluish-white, and others have a grayish cast. You'll also notice the difference in levels of brightness. Choose a white that is compatible with the overall style of your piece and that goes best with the colors that will be printed on top of it. Remember, the shade of the paper affects the color of the ink.

In addition to many whites, printing papers come in a spectacular array of colors. There are many more subtle and intense choices than the goldenrod and pastel blue and green we so commonly see. But most of us will probably use only a small percentage of the beautiful colors available. Because printing ink is transparent, we usually need a white or light colored surface. It provides maximum contrast for reading, and shows off color and photography best.

Colored stock usually costs a bit more. But have a look anyway—the choices (especially in text papers) are truly dazzling. Papers with names like Tahitian Orange, Roman Bronze, Gamma Green, Chocolate Mousse, and Spice Ivory reflect the richness of the colors. Become familiar with the alternatives so you'll have them in mind when you need them.

Finish

Paper for printing comes in a wide range of textures from pebbly rough to glossy smooth. Common names

The texture of the paper can add impact to an illustration. The cover of this booklet on traditional Mexican food is on a bright yellow hopsack-textured sheet.

for finishes are suede, dull, matte, vellum, embossed, antique, luster, gloss, ripple, stipple, and wove.

Stock also comes in coated or uncoated finishes. Coated stock has been coated to give it a fine, smooth surface. Not all coated sheets are high-gloss. They also come in dull and matte finishes as well, and can be coated on just one side. Coated stock is usually white. It gives a slick professional look, and photographs, colors, and black look snappiest on it.

Uncoated stock comes in a magnificent range of colors and textures. These sheets often have a rich and sophisticated look. Neither coated nor uncoated stock is "better." It is more a question of which paper is best suited to your particular piece.

Getting Samples

As you may have discovered when choosing paint for a wall from a tiny paint chip, small samples in swatch books don't always tell you as much as you want to know. You can get paper samples (and the swatch books themselves) either through a printer or directly from the sample department of a paper company (look up paper companies in the Yellow Pages). Some paper companies will make you a sample *dummy* for no charge. This is a very valuable service. Take advantage of it but don't abuse it.

A dummy is a paper sample that is put together to your exact specifications. Getting dummies is a good way to compare sheets you are considering. For example, if you are planning a booklet, you may want to see it made up using two different papers. Or you may want to compare different covers on the same or different inside sheets, or two different sizes. Dummies enable you to really get the *feel* of the sheet as well as the look. They also enable you to show other people what you have in mind.

Give the exact specifications when you order dummies, including the description of binding, or other special treatments. Presentation folders, for example, come with and without pockets. If you want a pocket, you need to specify its height (such as 3"). An example of specifications for a booklet might be:

- Trim size: 8-1/2" x 11"
- Pages: 16 pages plus cover
- Binding: saddle stitched on the 11" side
- Inside: 70 lb. Teton text, ivory
- Cover: 80 lb. Teton cover, indigo

With so many choices for paper, you can see why selecting it can be a time consuming process. It's also a lot of fun—just give yourself enough time to see everything and make a thoughtful decision. Seek the advice of those who know paper best. Keep up with what's new, and explore possibilities beyond what you're used to. That way you're more likely to come up with paper that truly enhances your printed piece.

This clever announcement
and invitation for Planned Parenthood
uses paper bag-like paper. The "bagness" of
the paper is emphasized by the zig-zag cut top edge.

Chapter 20

Art and Photography

Good graphic material is worth going after. Visual imagery catches the eye, holds attention, and lures people through your printed piece. It relieves the monotony of type, motivates people to read the text, and makes the piece more interesting. Images also reinforce your message, and so support communication.

Not long into the development of a printed piece you realize you need something more than type. But what? There are essentially three choices: *graphic devices* (for lack of a better name), *illustration*, and *photography*. Within these categories is a wealth of imagery for every budget, so no printed piece ever need be without visual support. We'll cover each of these three areas in this chapter.

But first some technical information. All printed images are referred to as either *line art* or *halftone*. Line art is an image that is filled in solid and has sharp edges. Halftones are images with a range of shades with many graduated tones (as in photographs and some illustrations). They often have soft or fuzzy edges (examples on the next page).

Halftones are more expensive to reproduce than line art. They require extra camera work, and they also take more time to produce (halftones and four-color process are discussed on page 223).

So all illustrative matter is either line (such as silhouettes or woodcuts), or halftone (such as pencil sketches, watercolors, and photographs). Photographs for the most part are halftones; graphic devices (to be described) are usually line art.

Printers need to know how many halftones you are planning to use in order to give you an accurate cost estimate (line art that is in position on the camera ready boards costs nothing extra). Keep this in mind as you read about the possibilities for visual elements in this chapter, especially if you are on a tight budget. Here are seven tips that apply to *all* visual imagery, whether it's line art or halftone.

1. Avoid Weak Images

No art is better than bad art. The same goes for photographs: no photographs are better than weak ones.

Any picture you use on your printed piece will be taken in at a glance. If the images you use are weak, ugly, or meaningless, they can do more harm to your piece than good. If your pictures are amateurish or if they're inappropriate, they detract from the overall impact. Weak pictures can also reduce the integrity of the publication, and become a barrier rather than a support to communication. So use only what's good. When in doubt, leave it out.

A halftone is any picture that has continuous tone (shades of gray from black to white), such as this photograph of Yosemite below.

2. Use One Style of Art

Mixing styles can be done successfully, but it takes quite a lot of skill. So unless you really know what you're doing, you may be better off using just one kind of art.

Pick a style you like and stick to it. If you use silhouette drawings, stay with silhouettes. If you use fine line drawings, use them consistently throughout. If you use photographs, stay with photographs. If you use an art style from a particular period, such as the 30s, stay with that.

3. Place Elements Carefully

Keep in mind that the purpose of your piece is to communicate information, and a cluttered layout discourages readers. Using a grid (described on page 194) for the placement of illustrations, photographs, and graphic devices helps keep your layout clean. It establishes a regular pattern for the images with built-in opportunities for variation.

Place illustrative material evenly throughout the piece. Use it to draw readers through a publication—right through to the very end.

Line art is solid black and white,
like the ink drawing shown here. Line art
is less expensive to reproduce than halftones.

4. Use Appropriate Illustrations

Select art that goes with your message and suits your audience. If you are using photographs of people, your audience should be able to identify with them. If the piece is for older adults, for example, use photographs of older adults; if it's for sports fans, show sports fans; if it's for Native Americans, use pictures of them.

5. Choose Positive Images

People naturally respond more positively to positive images. They like to see what is possible: what they can do, what they can have, and what they can become. Avoid grim or negative imagery unless you have a concrete reason for using it.

There are occasionally exceptions, as in the case of a smoking-cessation booklet I did awhile ago. People in this particular audience said they wanted pictures of diseased lungs and wrinkled faces to be reminded of the harm smoking does. In this situation negative images were effective, but in general, positive ones are likely to serve you best.

6. Give Yourself Time

So often I hear "if we'd only started earlier..." Finding talent, coming up with images, and getting them right is time-consuming. Plan time for feedback, revisions, retakes, and adjustments. And remember that illustrators and photographers are working on jobs other than yours. They'll need to schedule you in, so set things in motion as soon as you can.

7. Collect Ideas

As you become more and more familiar with your subject area, certain imagery may emerge as being particularly suited to it. You may come across kinds of illustrations or photographs that really fit. Collect these images. Copy good examples out of books, cut them from magazines, and keep booklets, brochures, and newsletters in a file. Save your samples. You'll be glad you have them when it's time to illustrate your next piece. This collection will help to point you in the right direction, or help an illustrator or photographer to better understand what it is you're after.

There are many sources of copyright-free art and graphic devices. Representing the choices is the Dover catalog of clip art books, left, a sampling of rub-on devices from Letraset® below, and computer software from T/Maker's ClickArt®, right, along with examples of electronic output.

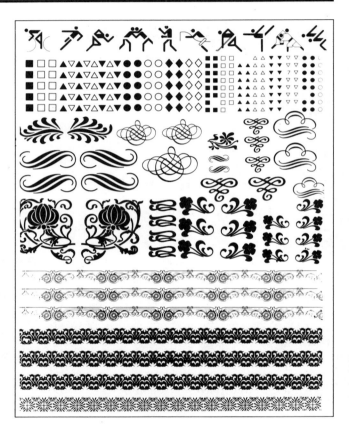

Graphic Devices

When you need something fast, when you want a particular kind of look, or when you can't afford original art or photography, graphic devices are the answer. Graphic devices are all visual elements other than original illustrations and photographs. They include a wide assortment of things, such as typographic ornaments and characters, borders, lines, symbols, and geometric shapes. Graphic devices are also letters and numbers that are used for their graphic effect as much as for their meaning. They are much less expensive than original illustrations and photography, and can be just as effective.

Selections of these images are available on rub-on sheets at art supply stores. An enormous range of borders, letters, tones, patterns, rules, corners, numbers, symbols and illustrations are available. Ask to see the Letraset® catalog, and others if they have them. These kinds of devices are also sometimes available from type books.

Copyright-free graphic devices also can be found in *clip art* books and as software (such as *Click Art®* by T/Maker). Images of every sort are represented. They include everything from nature designs, folk art, ethnic, and primitive art, to textile designs, fashion, sports, business, and religious illustration.

Clip art books are relatively inexpensive. You can

image yourself. If not, you can get an enlargement or reduction of the image you want on copiers with that function, or by getting a *stat* made. A stat (short for photostat) is a photographic copy of line (solid) art. Printers may be able to make them for you, or they can tell you where to get them. Here are some kinds of graphic devices, and suggestions for how to use them in your printed piece. Sidebar 57 summarizes them.

Initial Caps

An initial cap is an enlarged (and sometimes decorated) letter. It replaces the first letter of the first word of a block of type. Initial caps were commonly used as decorative devices in handwritten manuscripts during the middle ages. They are still effective today, and a lot less work to produce.

An initial cap can sit on the same base line as the rest of the line of type, and stick up above the rest of it. Or it can be tucked into lines of text so that it is no higher than the first line of type. Or it can be anywhere in between. Initial caps usually look better when they sit on the same base line as one of the lines of type in the text.

You can use an enlarged letter from the same font as the text, or use one from another font. Typefaces come in every style imaginable. Sometimes just the addition of a stunning initial cap—possibly in a second color—is all the visual enhancement a printed piece needs.

Letters

Enlarged letters can also be used as decorative devices in your publication. Choose letter forms that tie in with the overall design style of your piece. If you are using a question and answer format, you can use an enlarged *Q* for *question* and *A* for *answer*, and place them in the text like initial caps. Compare individual letters in different typefaces: one typeface may have a

find them at bookstores or art supply stores, or you can write to one of the largest publishers for a free catalog: Dover Publications, Inc., 31 East 2nd St., Mineola, NY 11501. Computer clip art is available at stores that carry software.

The *placement* of the graphic device is important to its effectiveness. So is its size. Blowing up an exclamation point to three inches high, for example, gives the symbol a whole new impact. Going in the opposite direction, greatly reduced elements repeated as a pattern (such as your logo or some other tiny illustration) also can be effective.

If you are working on a computer and have the right software, you can easily change the size of the

*A small illustration can be repeated
over and over to create a pattern, either in straight lines
as shown, or set in alternating rows like polka dots. Here the
image creates a decorative pattern for the insides of booklet covers.*

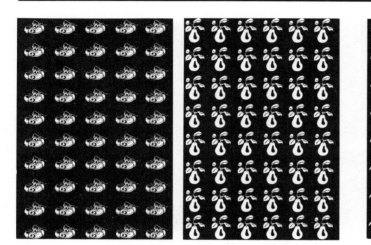

CONTENTS

1. Food for Thought 3
2. Food from Animals 6
3. Eggs 13
4. Dairy Foods 14
5. Hidden Saturated Fat 19
6. Salt 21
7. Sugar 25
8. Carbohydrates 29
9. Fiber 33
10. Protein 35
11. Vegetables 40
12. Eating Out 42
13. A Balanced Diet 44
14. Conclusion 45

beautiful letter A, for example, the next an ugly A. Of course when you are using a Q and an A, you are after the very best looking Q and A you can find. It doesn't matter what the other letters in the typeface look like if you aren't going to be using them.

Numbers

To add visual interest, numbers can be enlarged in the same way as letters. Numbers have the added function of showing viewers what to read first, second, third, and so on, as illustrated in the brochure on page 124. Many numbers are beautifully designed. They can contribute to the look of a printed piece when they are used large enough to really show their design, and when they are positioned well. Numbers can be tucked into text like initial caps, or used as independent elements.

Typographical Characters

Typographical character such as ! @ # $ % ^ " &
* on any keyboard (or ✿ ▲ ✳ ❂ ◆ ▼ ✿ ▲ ✳ ✳ ✳ ✳ ●
❂ ❖ ✦ ☆ ↔ ♣ ⛄ ✄ ✺ ☞ ➡ ☎ ✱ ✐ ✢ ➑ ➊ ʼʼ ❑ ➲ ✿ ☛

➤ ➠ ✚ ✉ ➟ ➪ ♥ ❣ ↔ ¶ → ➢ ❧ ↕ ✖ ❝ from a font called *Zapf Dingbats*) can also be used to add visual interest and strength to a printed piece. Selecting *just one* element and using it consistently throughout the piece is usually most effective. These kinds of graphic devices can be especially powerful when they are enlarged to proportions that relate aesthetically to the rest of the page. Quotation marks can also be blown up to set off a pertinent bit of information. If you use enlarged quotation marks, you will probably want to enlarge the type too. By the way, some quotation marks are much better looking than others.

Typographical Ornaments

There is a typographical ornament that is right for every style and every publication—it's just a matter of looking. The number of typographical ornaments that have been used in printing—some for centuries— is staggering. There are decorative spots, corners, dashes, vignettes, flourishes, brackets, and curlicues of every imaginable kind. They come in a wide range of styles such as art nouveau, art deco, floral, and classic, and can be found in any typesetter's book.

An initial cap is an inexpensive way to add graphic interest to a page. These examples show a variety of placements in relation to the text.

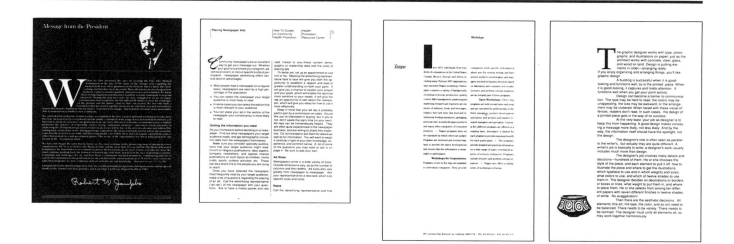

Geometric and Free-Form Shapes

Notice how designers use simple elements to add to the appeal of a printed piece. Something as unpretentious as a small square or circle can make an effective decorative element. A bold triangle in the right spot can give a printed piece distinction. Use bars, stars, circles, diamonds, or hexagonal shapes, etc., large or small, in the background or in the foreground, by themselves, or in patterns or lines. Free-form shapes and squiggles often give a piece a 50s look.

Stripes, Checks, and Polka Dots

These graphic devices can be incorporated effectively into the design of a printed piece as borders, backgrounds, or spot illustrations (but not all together!). They can be powerful, so use them carefully, and be sure they don't detract from the look or legibility of the piece. Use stripes, checks, and polka dots to create patterns for such places as the insides of covers. Or use them as faint backgrounds on mailing panels or covers. But be sure they're *very faint* when something goes on top of them, and don't use them behind text.

Lines or Rules

A tremendous amount can be done with just plain lines alone. Try different numbers of lines (called *rules* in graphics) together, and in different weights (thicknesses) (see page 251). Good design can be created with as little as this. A thick line with a thin one directly above or below it, for example, was used so commonly in the 80s it has practically become a standard device. It was used in every kind of publication, from newsletters to magazines to brochures and booklets. Try out some new combinations.

Variations and permutations of lines are unlimited. Try three together, or one with a row of tiny typographic ornaments beneath it, or one with a row of dots. Put together lines with stars or checks or dollar signs or anything else that suits your piece. Mix, match, and make up your own combinations.

Another popular graphic device that emerged in the 80s was a bar (a very heavy line), either in black or another color, that bled off the edge of a page. Using lines and bars is a very good way to give your printed piece a sophisticated look without going to a lot of trouble, time, or expense.

The design of individual letters, numbers, and other typographic elements is rich and varied. Add style to your printed piece by choosing a character that suits the nature of your content.

Borders

Used with discretion and taste, borders can contribute to the look of a piece. They come in many styles, and there's one for every purpose. Make sure any border you use complements the type and other elements it surrounds. Don't let it overwhelm the page—its purpose is to *enhance*, not dominate.

Symbols

There are many copyright-free symbols, and again, when they are used sparingly and wisely, they can add impact. There are international, architectural, and technical symbols, and symbols for traffic, transportation, and holidays. There are pictures of telephones, computers, flags, snowflakes, and music notes, and symbols for people, sports, home, travel, and transportation, to name a few. A well chosen symbol in the right spot can be very effective.

Logos

Logos can also be used as graphic devices. Blow yours up huge to make a dramatic design, or reduce it down very small and create a pattern with it. Enlarge sections of the logo (if it lends itself to this sort of thing), or make a border out of it by repeating it end to end. Try it in different colors, embossed, and reversed (what's dark becomes light; what's light becomes dark). A good logo by itself is often enough for a clever mind to work with—see what you can do with yours.

Screened Boxes and Alternatives

You often see text set off in a box in publications such as newsletters and catalogs. Sometimes it has a *screen* of a light color behind it. The box can be a very handy device to set information apart, but it can also cause some problems. Screened boxes are very powerful

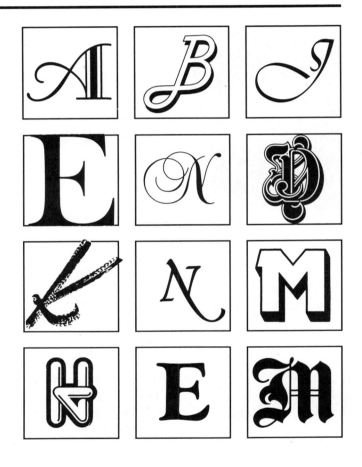

elements on a page. They pull the eye immediately to themselves.

Because screens are set off by themselves, they sometimes demand more attention than they're due. The danger is that they will overshadow the main message on the page. Watch out for this.

Sometimes the *color* of a box weakens an otherwise strong design. This is because the colored backgrounds in boxes are usually *screened* colors—some percentage of a full color on the page (say 30% red). These two colors (the full 100% red color and the 30% screen of red—or, in effect, pink) are often colors that don't look so good together.

Graphic Devices · 57

With an enormous array of graphic devices to choose from, no piece ever needs to be just straight type. They are helpful when you are short on time or money. Some possibilities:

- Initial caps
- Letters
- Numbers
- Typographic characters
- Dingbats
- Typographic ornaments
- Geometric shapes
- Free-form shapes
- Stripes
- Checks
- Dots
- Lines
- Borders
- Symbols
- Logos
- Maps
- Screened boxes
- Charts
- Graphs

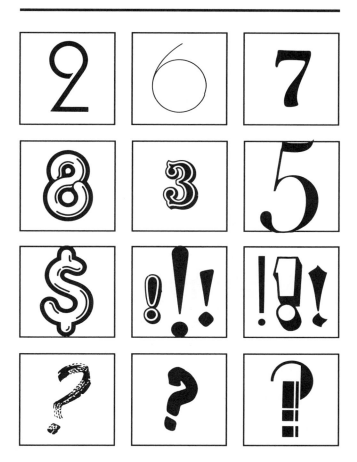

Use boxes carefully, or set the text off in some other way. For example, you can use horizontal lines above and below the text you want to stand out. You don't need the sides of the box. Just the top and bottom of a box can work as well, and are less intrusive. These horizontal lines can be doubled or tripled, or used in a combination of weights. They will help the information stand out without throwing off the page design.

Or you can use a row of small dots, triangles, letters, squares, or some other similar device instead of lines. They often look good in a second color. Another alternative is to dramatically change the size or weight of the type instead of putting it in a box. A section of

Letterforms alone provide the illustration for these publication covers. Note the clever presentation of the"H," left. It is done in cross stitch to go with the title Handcrafted.

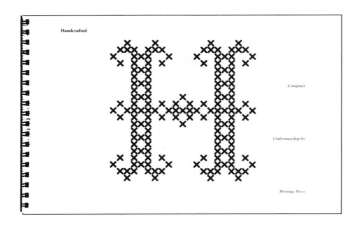

enlarged italics, for example, can be especially effective. If you use them, be sure the font you choose has a well-designed italic. Some are much more handsome than others.

Maps, Graphs, and Charts

Maps, graphs, and charts can make your printed piece more interesting to look at and provide useful information at the same time. If you use them, make them *readable* and comprehensible (it's amazing how many are not).

Make maps large enough so they can be read comfortably. Better to use two graphs, for example, than try to cram too much information into one. Present chart information in a logical and well-organized manner. You may also want to consider blowing up a map, graph, or chart extra large to make it an even more dramatic graphic element.

With so many graphic devices to lighten and enliven your printed piece, a little exploration is sure to be rewarded. The key is be to selective, disciplined, and *not overdo it.* Your piece will communicate the message you want to get across better if it is simple, neat, and clean. A small amount of graphic device goes a long way.

Illustration

By *illustration* I mean *original* illustration, done for a particular printed piece. There is an illustration style to suit every mood, every publication, and every target audience (several are listed in Sidebar 58). To get ideas for illustrations, go to a bookstore, art supply store, or library and ask to see design and illustration annuals. They are collections of the year's best. After you have some idea of what you want, find an illustra-

*Lines alone or in combination
with a number, letter, or graphic element
provide visual relief. At right are simple line
combinations for borders or frames. Below three
horizontal lines and the number 3 decorate the page.*

tor who has a similar style (some graphic designers also illustrate). Finding and hiring help is covered in *People Involved in Producing Print*, page 43.

I have noticed that many illustrators seem to have a flair for drawing either *people* or for drawing *things*. They are rarely equally good at both. If you need drawings of people, be sure that that is where your illustrator's talent lies.

When you work with an illustrator, give him or her as much input as possible about what you're after. If you have something concrete in mind, explain it as fully as you can in the beginning. If you don't, you can explore the possibilities together. Describe the purpose of the piece in which the drawings are to appear, the audience for whom it is intended, and what you hope to accomplish with it. Show the illustrator any pictures that do what you want yours to do. Get the person headed in the right direction and then let go, so the illustrator can do what he or she does best.

Sometimes an illustrator takes a drawing to a near-finished state before you see it. If it turns out to be the wrong image, for whatever reason, you both end up feeling bad. Either the illustrator has to start over again from scratch, or you're stuck with it. On

There is an illustration style to suit every taste.
The two below are line art; the two at left are halftones.
The artist painting is from a clip art book; the rest are original.

the second round the illustrator may be less enthusiastic. *Insist* on seeing *different ideas* in rough form before any one is developed too far.

Don't be afraid to use "common" images. Whether it's the human figure, a Christmas tree, or a heart, it's what the artist does with it that counts.

Illustrators often do the drawings larger than they will appear in final form. This enables them to get in more detail than they could if they worked in the final size. When this is the case, the printer will reduce the artwork and put it in position. Be sure illustrations are carefully marked so they correspond to the appropriate place on the camera-ready art.

When line illustrations are done in the exact size that they will be used, they can be placed directly onto the boards. This is the least expensive way to go because no camera work is required of the printer.

The effect of a photograph changes according to the way it is cropped. Tighter cropping focuses attention more directly on the subject.

Photography

When they're good, photographs engage readers in a way no other image can. Start off with the strongest pictures you possibly can: ones that are sharp, in focus, have good contrast, and good composition. (If you are looking for a photographer, see page 49.)

Getting good photographs is just the first step—how they are used is important too. Their placement, their size, and how they're cropped (cut) will make a difference to their overall effectiveness.

I prefer photographs placed in some sequential order rather than scattered high, low, and everywhere in a piece. The argument for scattered placement is

Sometimes the same photograph can be cropped to fit different space requirements. Or choose a shape that is most aesthetic, or best fits your design. Is one of these formats more interesting to look at than the others?

that it brings the eye to different areas of the page. That's fine, but I think there is a greater advantage to grouping them, or at least placing them in some regular order than can be anticipated. When readers look at photographs, they look at photographs; when they read, they read. So when photos are grouped, or regularly placed, they are easier to look at. *Regular* placement is not the same as *rigid*, however (see grids, pages 194–198). The comfort, convenience, and pleasure of the reader is the uppermost consideration.

The size of a photograph also matters. Sometimes they are just plain too small to do them justice. This is especially true when a photograph contains a lot of "information," such as in a group shot or other busy picture. But keep in mind that a picture has to be

really good to appear large, because the bigger it gets, the more flaws that show.

Clever cropping can make a weak photograph passable and an average photograph look great. Don't be afraid to zoom in on the subject. Outside edges often have no content whatsoever. When they are cropped out, the viewer is not distracted by irrelevant stuff in the background, and the image of interest can appear larger.

Another thing that helps photographs look their best has to do with focal length. Keep it the same on pictures that appear close together. For example, if there are several photos of people, they will look better if they are all consistently either "mug shots," or all shot from the waist up, or all full bodies. Even when you're showing just heads, try to have the same amount of head fill each frame. Similarly, photographs on the same page are usually more effective when they're all shot from the same angle. Either all from above, or all from below, or (my favorite) all straight on.

Another thing to be aware of: when photographs have a strong directional line or thrust, or when they are of people, they will look best *facing inward*, toward the center of the page. Otherwise the eye is directed to the outside edge and off the page. If your photos face the wrong way, simply write *flop* on the edge of the photograph, and the printer will reverse its direction in your publication.

Sometimes a thin rule (line) around a photograph helps its appearance, especially when the edges are light or non-existant. These lines act as a frame, hold the picture in, and help define the space. Again, though, be careful to use a weight of line that does not compete with the photograph.

If you want your black and white photographs to have real richness and depth, consider having them printed as *duotones*. This two-color halftone created from a one-color photograph improves the look of any picture, no matter what the subject. You need to specify two colors unless it is a *double black* duotone. Ask a printer to show you samples.

Warm colors like rust or brown work well with black in duotones, especially on pictures of people. You can use the second color alone in other places in the publication. And by the way, skin tones always look better in warm colors. Avoid blue and green ink on pictures of people.

Stock Photos

Stock photographs are available from agencies that specialize in finding pictures. You request an image, and for a fee they find it for you, and offer you prints

58 Illustration Styles

When you are thinking about art for your publication, consider one of the illustration styles below. If none of these is right, perhaps one will trigger an idea for something that will be.

- Silhouette
- Collage
- Pastel
- Pen and ink
- Wood cut
- Pencil drawing
- Watercolor
- Photographic
- Block print
- Cross-hatch
- Engraving
- Painterly
- Curvelinear
- 3-dimensional
- Air brush
- Computer-generated

- Delicate
- Bold
- Calligraphic
- Realistic
- Sketchy
- Cartoon
- Masculine
- Feminine
- Disquieting
- Light
- Strong
- Geometric
- Abstract
- Tight
- Loose
- Architectural

These flags communicate information while adding visual interest to this carefully designed page. They are from copyright-free rub-on sheets.

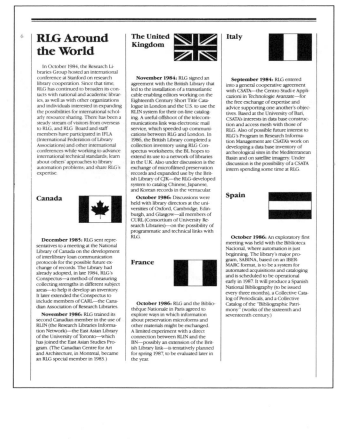

or transparencies. Often you pay a second fee, based on how the photograph is going to be used (one amount for an ad, for example, another for a booklet). Look under *Photographers, Stock* in the Yellow Pages of the phone book. These photo-find services are more likely to be available in larger cities than in smaller communities. Stock photos are also available in clip art books.

Rights, Permissions, and Fees

There are several points to be made regarding rights, permissions, and fees for original illustration and photography. They are as follows:

You can get double use out of a single photograph.
For example this picture could be used full frame on a cover,
then "zoomed in on" and used in place of an initial cap or as a spot illustration.

Permissions

You must get permission to use someone else's illustrations and photographs. This may be from the person who created them, or it may be from someone else who owns the copyright. Remember that permissions take time, so allow for it.

Fees

The range of fees for illustrations and photographs is as broad as the level of talent available, and that is *very* broad. There is almost always a correlation between the two.

Many different arrangements are made for reimbursement; there is no single way it's done. For example, a photographer might charge an hourly rate, or a day rate, or for time and materials. Sometimes more than one print is included, sometimes extras must be puchased at additional cost.

Some illustrators charge by the hour, others by the drawing. Keep in mind that what really matters to you is the *sum total* of what you'll have to pay to get the drawings you want.

Each agreement is between you and the individual. Whatever arrangement you make, be sure it is clearly understood at the outset. For more on hiring and estimate gathering, see pages 44 and 64.

Rights

Illustrations and photographs are usually sold with one-time use rights, unless of course you negotiate a different agreement. Try to think through your future needs for the pictures at the very beginning.

Obligations

If you give an assignment to an illustrator or photographer and end up not using the work, you are still obligated to pay for it. To avoid hassles and headaches, be sure to clarify your understanding in writing, and stay in touch throughout the project.

Credit

Give the illustrator or photographer credit for their work in your piece as often as you possibly can. All publications are joint efforts, and photographers and illustrators appreciate the recognition.

Whether you are creating graphic images from scratch or using existing ones, they will improve the effectiveness of your printed piece if you select them with care. Don't compromise on art and photography. Good taste is essential.

Photographs that are taken "straight on" really show the design of the object. This pineapple was shot on seamless background paper.

Chapter 21

Logos and the Graphic Image

Companies spend a lot of money on their corporate image. The cost of the design of a logo or trademark and the development of a *corporate identity* can be as much as $30,000; Fortune 500 companies spend considerably more. These enterprises are run by some sharp cookies—they don't spend money needlessly. The size of the expenditure says something about the value of the graphic image.

Political candidates also pay whopping sums to get themselves packaged, and a lot of that packaging is in print. It is not uncommon for national congressional and senatorial candidates to spend $4 million or more. Some candidates in my area—a community of 57,000—spend $10,000 to run for a local school board election.

We live in an intensely competitive society. Add this fact to the over-busyness people feel these days, and you see why the packaged impression—absorbed at a glance—has so much force. The graphic image is fast (sometimes instantaneous), powerful, and often subliminal.

Rightly or wrongly, people make judgments on the character of a person, an organization, or a business based on what they see in print. Every printed piece you issue creates an impression, whether it's the one you intend or not. Your letterhead, your business card, and every other printed piece you issue creates and maintains that impression. So if that's the way it's going to be, you may as well *choose* the impression your printed materials make.

The Graphic Image

Your *graphic image* is the visual impression that is made by the printed pieces you produce. A logo (described in detail later in this chapter) is often a part of it. The color, the art or photography, the type, their arrangement on the page, the size, and the paper the piece is printed on are the elements that go into creating the graphic image.

When these same elements are used uniformly on all printed pieces produced by the same organization, you've got what's called a *visual communication system*. In plainer language, the pieces match. All print that carries the same graphic image are also referred to as a *family of pieces*.

Printed pieces that are part of the same communication system do not all have to look *exactly* alike. Good "identities" provide plenty of room for variations on the theme. Individual publications can and often do have some distinct variation, but they are still recognizable as belonging to the same family.

*The logotype for a corporate health
communication program has been consistently applied
to many kinds of pieces. Ink colors are teal and violet on bright white.*

Advantages of a Good Image

You may already have a strong image for the printed pieces you produce. If you don't, there are some good reasons for developing one. A uniform look can do several things for you. A good graphic image:

• *Creates a professional look.* Pieces that match have a more professional look, and a professional look carries more weight. A uniform graphic image implies that an organization is serious and has its act together. It also suggests reliability.

• *Helps keep costs down.* Pieces that match are often less expensive to produce. Many print producers don't realize this fact, or take advantage of this important benefit. The initial establishment of a uniform look is an investment, but once the system is in place, it can actually save you money. By utilizing preestablished formats, colors, type, paper, and so on for new pieces, ones that might otherwise call for outside professional help can often be produced in-house. When a publication is especially complicated, a designer can be called in for a consultation.

• *Makes production faster.* Pieces that match can be produced more quickly. This is because all of the basic design decisions have already been made.

• *Makes designing new pieces easier.* Pieces that match are easier to produce. Trial and error is eliminated once a common look is established, so new pieces can be put together with confidence.

• *Keeps the image consistent.* Pieces that match make it easier to control your image. This is especially important if your organization has a large (or particularly independent) staff. Once the look is developed, guidelines can be written up so everyone knows how to apply the image uniformly.

• *Reinforces your identity.* Pieces that match are more quickly identifiable. Every new piece that comes out is recognized as coming from the same source, and each piece serves to promote the others.

• *Creates pride in your look.* Pieces that match are more satisfying to send out. You will probably be using some printed piece on a daily basis—a letterhead, business card, or brochure, for example. If the design is weak, materials can be an embarrassment and a handicap. If they are done well, they are a source of pride and a pleasure to work with.

Creating Your Image

Condensing an entire organization into one graphic image requires a great deal of skill. If you are not a professional yourself, I encourage you to hire one to develop your graphic image and logo. The time you most need an experienced person's help is now. An amateurish image will not serve you well. Hiring a pro to develop a strong, consistent graphic style for your product or service is the wisest investment you can make with your design dollars.

If your budget is limited, tell a designer at the outset how much you have to spend, and ask what he or she can do for that amount. (For more on working with designers, see Sidebars 43, 44, and 45; for ideas for quick and easy and inexpensive logos, see Sidebars 61 and 62.)

If you do decide to take on the challenge yourself, consider getting some professional advice. Even an hour can make a difference. Designers can give you more helpful advice when they have something concrete to respond to, so a consultation will probably be most useful *after* you have developed some preliminary sketches. Don't get too attached to any one idea. You'll come out with a better image if you maintain an open and flexible attitude throughout the whole graphic design process.

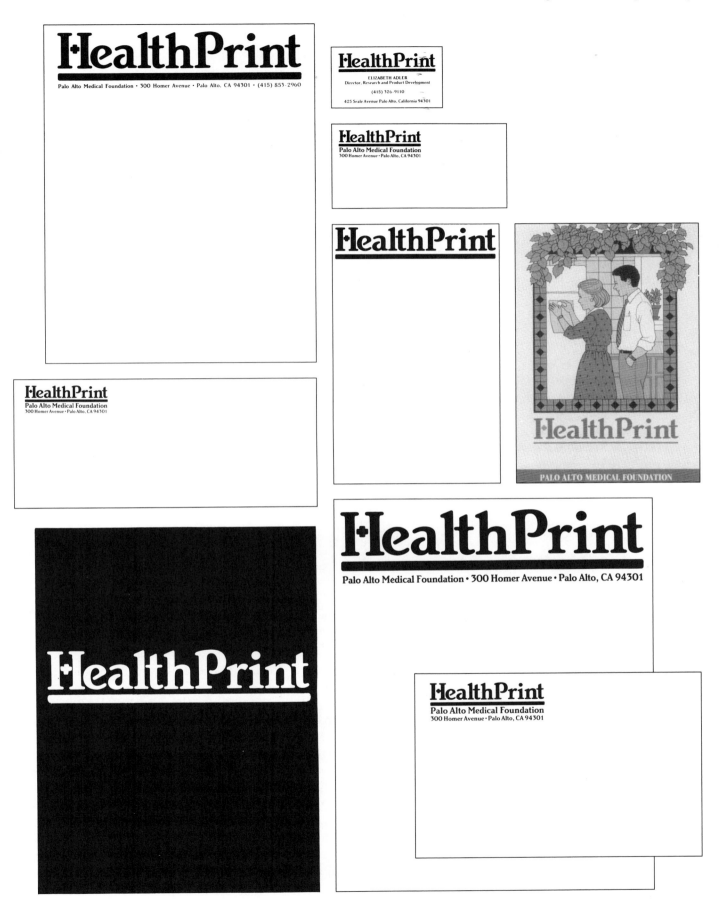

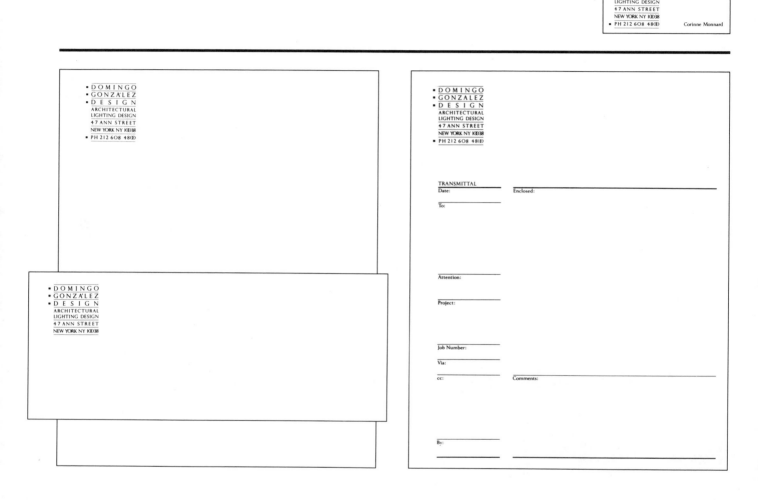

Corinne Monnard

When to Create a Graphic Image

Many visual communication systems owe their creation to a new employee who wants a strong letterhead, or to someone in a new organization who understands the value of a good graphic image. This is often the point at which the question of a logo arises: Do we need a logo? Should we update the old one? Or should we start all over from scratch?

So the creation of a whole graphic image often accompanies the creation of a new logo. This forces the VIPs to think about what image they want to project. The designer will create that image by making decisions about color, type, layout, and so on, but those decisions will be based on the kind of look the VIPs want.

The sooner you get a logo, the better (if you are starting from scratch), because you can then take advantage of the many benefits mentioned earlier. There is, however, one exception: when you don't yet know who you are (organizationally speaking, of course), and therefore cannot yet know what image you want to project. Don't waste a lot of time and effort creating a look that could be inappropriate for the organization.

I was once asked to design a logo for a new group that was struggling to define itself. As usual, I started by asking questions about such things as how the or-

This graphic image for an
architectural lighting design firm uses a clean,
contemporary style, and bright red and gray ink on white paper.

DOMINGO
GONZÁLEZ
DESIGN
ARCHITECTURAL
LIGHTING DESIGN
47 ANN STREET
NEW YORK NY 10038
PH 212 608 480

ganization saw itself, what its goals were, and what kind of image it wanted to project. The group had few answers. In fact, each question I asked generated expressions of real differences of opinion among the group's managers. The only consensus was that there was no consensus. I suggested that the development of a graphic image and logo might be premature, but the director was determined to have one right away.

With some effort over many weeks we finally hit upon a reasonably common direction. But the graphic image could have been much stronger (and the process more pleasant) if the group had given themselves a bit longer to sort themselves out. Frankly, I'm not sure they ever did.

When to Change a Graphic Image

If your graphic image is fundamentally good, keep it. Sometimes it just needs updating and a few minor revisions.

Other times there are good reasons to change a look entirely. It might be inherited from a prior regime whose vision and philosophy was entirely different, or perhaps it is no longer appropriate for the organization, or it could be outdated, amateurish, or just plain ugly.

Sometimes a weak graphic image hangs on out of inertia. Users may feel ambivalent or even dissatisfied with it, but no one has the time or energy to put into developing a new one. And there always seems to be just enough letterheads left over to perpetuate the old design.

Occasionally there is a lone but forceful voice defending a not-so-good image—a voice that's just strong enough to block a new rendition from being created. When even *one* person defends a weak image, it can be enough to cause a stalemate. Then each new publication is burdened with the old look, and is greeted with ambivalence rather than enthusiasm.

If the graphic image for your business or organization is wrong, boring, bad, or all of the above, it is unlikely to improve with the passage of time. Make an effort to change it or get it changed. A fresh new image gives everyone a boost.

The Planned Image: An Example

A lot of time, money, and effort can be saved when the design and production of an organization's printed pieces are carefully planned. Let me give you an example. A few years ago I worked with a large corporate division of a community hospital to create a uniform system for their printed pieces. This division sends health professionals from four different programs into corporate worksites to provide a variety of health-

This letterhead and business card for a builder/developer uses different but related illustrations on each. Colors are brown and gray on ivory.

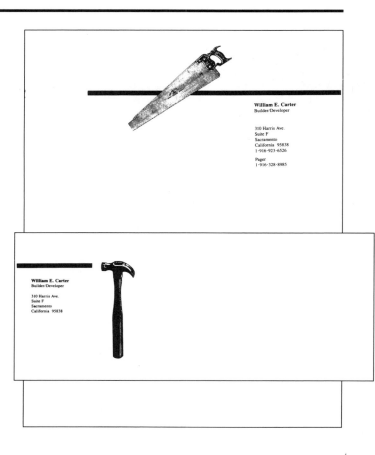

related services. Its staff regularly produces proposals, reports, brochures, flyers, and other printed materials as a part of their on-going responsibilities. My task included rethinking and reorganizing all of the pieces into a new order. In this case, both writing and design were involved.

A quick glance through a stack publications revealed that each was as different from the others as the people who produced them. The skills of these professionals were in areas other than print communication, so their ability to come up with effective print was understandably limited. These highly-individualized pieces were serving neither their creators, the division, nor the hospital as effectively as they might. But fortunately the division had a director who understood the value of strong printed communications and a uniform system.

A common structure for materials *within* each of the four programs was needed, and the four programs needed to *match each other* as well. The task began with reading a mountain of reports, proposals, data sheets, updates, and so forth to become more familiar with the organization, and to identify common denominators among the pieces.

The second step was to conduct interviews with members of the staff and with their clients. The main objective was to collect opinions of what was working and what wasn't. I asked the staff for their ideas for what would make the pieces easier to produce; I asked the clients how the pieces might be made more useful, and I solicited ideas for improving them from everyone concerned. This kind of input is a valuable part of the redesign process.

For the content, I developed an outline based on regularly recurring topics. It would serve as the outline from which staff members could write copy. This would insure that all of the pieces covered the same key topics consistently. For example, proposals would regularly cover five important areas and the final reports would address exactly the same ones. A stan-

dardized outline would also make writers' jobs easier and less time-consuming since they do not have to reinvent each piece every time they sit down to write.

Next, I designed a flexible grid (pattern) to be applied to all of the printed pieces. This would identify them as coming from the same common source. One of the challenges was to find ways to give the division a distinct look and still reflect the one that had already been established by the hospital.

The hospital had assigned this division green as its identifying color. To make this color more distinctive, we chose a particularly beautiful and unusual shade of silver-green. Two typefaces had also been previously prescribed, so we selected one of them and

*Standardizing both writing and design
for these hospital pieces increases efficiency, saves
time, and enables different people to put out consistent publications.*

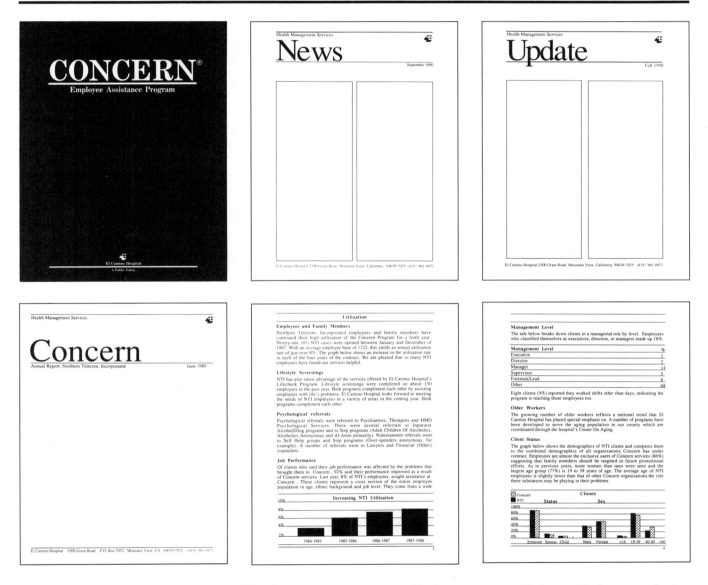

used it particularly large, to give it added distinction. By using a striking color and an ordinary typeface larger than usual, we were able to create a distinguishing look that matched the preestablished one, and at very little cost.

I recommended that the division invest in a desk-top publishing system. This enabled me to design templates (patterns or style sheets) for the layout of the pieces that would be produced most often on the computer. These templates could be used by everyone. By carefully thinking the system through and making it easily accessible via computer, printed

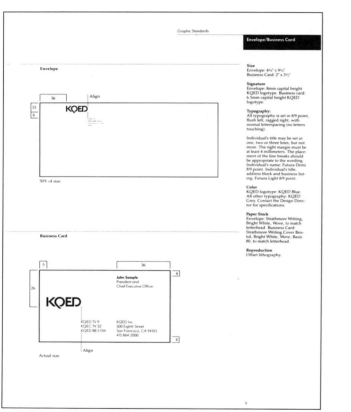

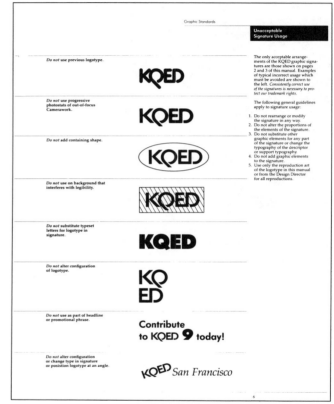

pieces would be consistent, of higher quality, and easier to produce.

The last phase was to conduct a workshop for the staff. Its purpose was to explain the system, offer tips on how to use it, and answer questions. Follow-up consultations gave us time to work out any unanticipated problems.

Finally a *style guide* was developed. This three-ring binder contained guidelines and detailed information for producing the division's publications. All staff members received a copy.

A year later a meeting was held to assess the value of the new publications system. Following is the staff's evaluation:

Standardization of materials

- Provides consistency in communication pieces

- Eliminates redundancy

- Gives a more professional look to all materials

- Provides good guidelines—gives parameters without being restrictive

- Saves time and increases efficiency because publications aren't created from scratch

If you put out publications regularly, consider developing a similar system for them.

*A style quide is helpful when
many people in an organization use
the same design.These pages, left, from KQED's
Graphic Standards show users how to apply the logo.*

The Logo

A *logo* is a symbol used by a group or organization to represent itself visually. It is called a *trademark* when it is applied to a product. The logo is often a central element of a group's graphic image; the graphic image is often developed to work in harmony with a logo.

The logo—an organization's stamp—adds value to whatever it appears on (how much, of course, depends on the reputation of the organization behind it). It assures a certain standard of quality and degree of reliability.

Just as marks were once used by medieval guilds and samurai clans, logos are widely used today. They appear on brochures and business papers instead of on swords and shields; instead of on horses, they are placed on cars, trucks, buses, trains, and planes. Today, logos are also commonly used on T-shirts, buttons, signs, and uniforms; buildings, pencils, displays and greeting cards; banners, plates, machinery and decorations.

The logo, although commonly printed in ink on paper, also appears on wood, steel, cloth, and concrete; neon, and the electronic lines on a television or computer screen, and on just about anything else you can think of. You'd be surprised at the number of logos you see in a day if you counted them.

What Makes A Good Logo

As I mentioned earlier, the development of a good logo requires quite a bit of skill. And a strong logo has many distinctive characteristics. Following is a discussion of many of them. They are summarized in an evaluation checklist in Sidebar 64 to help you assess any logos you are considering.

• *A good logo has impact.* A strong logo has immediate impact. There should be nothing wishy washy about it. This doesn't mean that it has to be *bold* to be

Ideas for Logos   59

Here is a list of images and shapes commonly used as themes in logo design. Run through it to get ideas for your logo. You can also use the list as a starting point for a logo brainstorming session.

Motifs

• Indian	• Japanese
• Pre-Columbian	• Americana
• Antique	• Tropical
• Ancient	• Patriotic
• High-tech	• Sport-related
• Fantasy	• Southwestern
• Regional	• Traditional

Shapes & Characters

• Circle	• Rectangle
• Triangle	• Oval
• Polygon	• Letter forms
• Hexagram	• Free forms
• Diamond	• Numbers
• Square	• Dingbats

Images

• Arrow	• House
• Bird	• Boat
• Fish	• Car
• Insect	• Plane
• Animal	• Train
• Flower	• Bike
• Tree	• Tool
• Sun	• Figure
• Star	• Face
• Moon	• Hand
• Eye	• Fruit
• Shell	• City building
• Mineral	• Vegetable

*Japanese family crests date back to the
11th century. These designs, like corporate logos today,
are based on objects, geometric shapes, and images from nature.*

good. A logo made up of very thin lines, for example, or one that is refined or delicate can be as effective as a bolder one. But it does mean that it has to have enough *style* to make a strong impression.

• *A good logo is good to look at.* This statement may seem self-evident until you start paying attention to what's out there. A good logo is aesthetically pleasing.

• *A good logo is understandable.* If people look at your logo with puzzled expressions on their faces, or if they ask "what is it?" it needs more work. A good logo doesn't make people ask questions or feel dumb or annoyed because they can't figure it out. It certainly does not have to be a literal translation, but neither should it be confusing.

• *A good logo is distinctive.* A logo needs its own distinctive character to distinguish it from all others. It is especially important that it be distinctly different from those of your competitors in both color and form. Your logo should reflect the uniqueness of what it is *you* are offering.

• *A good logo creates a positive image.* Obviously you don't want a logo that creates a *bad* image, but neither do you want one that is *neutral*. Many logos leave the viewer cold, or with no response whatsoever. Good logos please their viewers.

• *A good logo accurately represents your business or organization.* Your logo should be compatible with the nature of your business or organization. Logos sometimes incorporate the subject of the product or service into the design. The creation of these marks usually requires the highest level of skill (especially when the topic is abstract, like *health* or *prosperity*). When done well, they're among the strongest.

• *A good logo is simple.* There are exceptions, but on the whole, many of the strongest logos are the simplest. Logos closer to symbols than signs, for example, tend to be the most direct. They have a purity and power that more complex logos lack. The Red Cross logo and the peace symbol, for example, are direct and powerful symbols.

• *A good logo is memorable.* Another important reason to keep your logo simple is because simpler ones are easier to remember. A good logo is grasped at a single glance and leaves a lasting impression.

• *A good logo is flexible.* You need a logo that will work in many different ways. It has to look good small enough to go on a business card and large enough to cover the front page of a folder or a conference banner. It has to look good in black as well as in color. And it has to look good if it is used on surfaces other than paper—for signs, on pencils, on trucks, and in electronic images, for example.

*These contemporary logo designs, below
and left to right, are for a photographer, a West Coast
regional park, a health promotion center, and a golf equipment retailer.*

• *A good logo copies well.* In this era of fax machines and copiers, printed pieces with your logo will undoubtedly be copied. And based on the quality of the copier, it will turn up in any number of shades of gray. A logo that copies well is a real plus, so take that into consideration.

• *A good logo wears well over time.* Weak logos are continuously being replaced with other logos; good ones stay around awhile. *Coca Cola* (the logotype), for example, has been with us for nearly a century; other familiar ones (on utilities and trains and boxes in kitchens) are several generations old. They have been through periodic updates, but all the same, that's *endurance.* Although you may not need your logo to last a century (but then, who knows), ask yourself how it will look a couple of years from now.

• *A good logo is one you're proud of.* When you evaluate a potential logo, envision yourself in a variety of situations, and ask yourself how you would feel about showing it. For example, picture yourself giving a presentation with the logo on the podium in front of you, or on your booth at a fair or conference. Or imagine giving a printed piece with the logo on it to someone whose respect you'd like. Imagine yourself signing a letterhead displaying it, and your clients or constituency noticing it as they read your letter. If these thoughts give you a good feeling, you've probably got a winner.

How to Design a Logo

If you're not a designer, again I advise you to hire one to do your logo and graphic image. If however you want to go ahead and design your own, the following steps offer some guidance. They will familiarize you with the order of procedure. This sequence is also useful to know if you are hiring a designer.

Although the steps involved may differ from designer to designer, the same basic ground is covered. Logo development includes: interviews and meetings, research, design, feedback, and the application of the logo to sample pieces.

A new logo is usually applied to a new letterhead, business card, and other printed pieces as soon as it is designed. As we go through the development of a logo, keep in mind that the whole graphic image often evolves along with it (the sum total of the new look is what creates the graphic image). Here's what is involved in the development of a logo.

• *Interviews and meetings.* Translating the character of an organization into a graphic symbol is a big responsibility. The designer needs to be familiar with the nature of the organization, its history, and its future aspirations.

All experienced designers agree: only one person should be in charge of the development of a logo. Design by committee is not a very effective way to come up with a good logo (or much else, for that mat-

269

Choose logos that work well in both positive and negative, as shown below. The darker version is good in color; the lighter one copies well. Right: Insist on seeing sketches for a logo before the designer takes any one idea very far. If you're the designer, get several ideas down before perfecting any one.

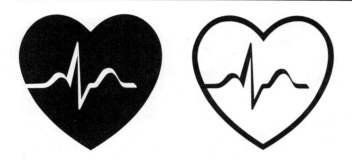 

ter). But gathering the thoughts and opinions of others is another matter. That is an important part of the design process.

Good logo designers often interview everyone with an interest in the image of the organization, and make use of the collective experience and opinions. You can do this one on one, or hold a meeting or brainstorming session.

A logo brainstorming session can be enormously productive. When it is well-run it gives the designer a lot to work with, and it's fun for the participants. Include the entire staff. Don't exclude anyone, even the non-visual types. You never know who will come up with a great idea. If you don't have a staff, get together with some imaginative friends.

A good session often takes between one and two hours. Meetings with some structure are usually most productive, so plan it ahead (see Sidebar 10, *How To Run a Good Meeting,* page 51).

Someone (probably you) should write what is said on a blackboard or a flip chart for all to see as you go along. It is also helpful to have someone taking notes.

Start by writing your organization's name very large. Ask everyone to write down five images that come to mind as they look at the name. Why ask for five? Because most people come up with one or two fairly quickly. You want to push them past these easy first thoughts and get them to dig a little deeper.

Next, talk about the organization: its purpose, its plans, and its goals for the future. Someone at the blackboard can summarize the comments for all to see. Discuss the current image the organization is thought to have, and how this differs from the one the group would like it to have.

Try not to get bogged down in debates. The purpose of a brainstorming session is to come up with as much input as possible, not to analyze and critique. When differences do come up, write down each point of view on the list, and *keep moving.*

Once you get this information up so that everyone can see it, ask participants for new images that fairly and accurately represent the organization. You might want to copy Sidebar 40, large enough for all to read. It will help to stimulate more interesting ideas. You can also use Sidebar 59 to trigger more ideas. Ask what objects or themes best represent the images people come up with.

Now the images should be getting more interesting. Encourage free discussion and generate as much input as possible. You can sift, sort, evaluate, and establish priorities later. Be sure to let all participants know that you value their time, energy, and contribution to the project.

• **Research.** Collect as many samples of your organization's past and present publications as you can. Look through them to get a feeling for how its image has been represented to date. Ask anyone who was involved with their production what worked well and what didn't, and critique them yourself.

Expose yourself to good logos. Books devoted entirely to the subject can be found in bookstores, art

The Good Ol' Rubber Stamp

60

Consider getting your logo made into a rubber stamp—they are surprisingly inexpensive. A stamp with your logo on it is a good way to extend the possibilities for its use without the expense of printing. You can stamp your logo onto books, cardboard boxes, film or video cases, and many other surfaces that might not otherwise carry it.

A stamp can be made from any simple image, and they come in a wide variety of typefaces and sizes. Stamped images have another positive bonus: ink pads are available in great colors (everything from shocking pink and emerald green to brilliant turquoise, red, and chrome yellow). Look in the Yellow Pages for sources of rubber stamps, and call to get cost estimates.

*The first two rows of these logos are based
on initial letters, row three on living things and an object,
and the fourth row on carefully worked out geometric shapes.*

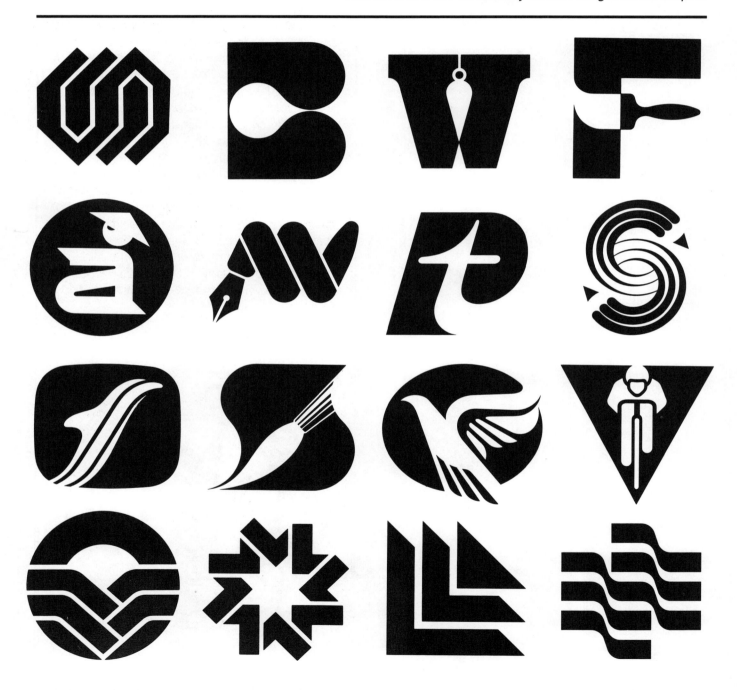

A copyright-free design could work well for your logo—if you find the righ tone. These designs are from T/Maker's ClickArt® Business Images.

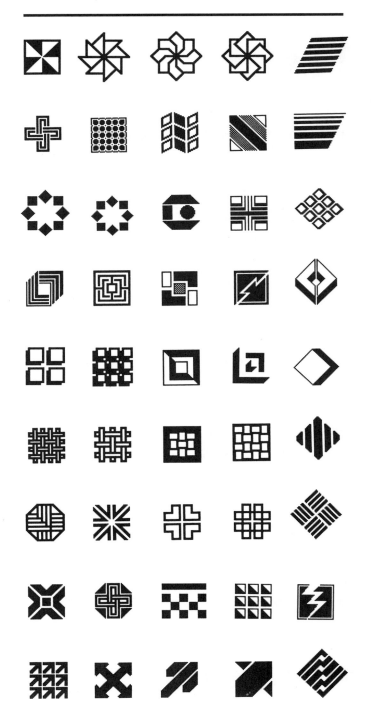

Quick and Easy Logos   61

There are ways to come up with a logo quickly when you need to. It may not be the timeless symbol that strikes a deep responsive chord, but it may serve your purpose well enough. Use:

Clip Art

Clip art is copyright-free illustrations that any-one can legally use free of charge.It comes in books and computer software. There are liter-ally thousands of copyright-free designs and motifs that can become a strong logo; it's a matter of looking until you find the right one. Designs from different cultures can make es-pecially good logos: those from Africa, Asia, South America, or Scandinavian countries, for example. Or consider images from differ-ent eras in history.

Typeface Designs

Your name in a special typeface may be all the logo you need. There are many typefaces that are so highly distinctive that they can work as a logo on their own. Decide on what image you want for your organization first, then look at different typestyles until you find the right one. Look through catalogs of rub-on type at an art supply store, or other books of type.

Calligraphy

If the look suits your organization, consider hiring a calligrapher to write out the name of your business. He or she might also be able to draw a symbol to go along with it.

Color

Color alone acts as a unifying element when it is unusual or distinctive. Use color in a simple bold shape, and you've got a logo, or use it on your name with distinctive lines under it for a logotype. Be sure the color fits the nature of the organization and suits the image you want to convey.

Good logos work well in different sizes.
Imagine yours small enough for a business card
and large enough for a poster, a truck, or a conference banner.

years, and every culture has its own versions (a librarian or bookseller can help you find what you're looking for). Whatever image you're after, find examples of ways it has been done before.

• **Design.** Now you're ready to turn your collection of ideas into a graphic image. Here are some suggestions for things to try:

- Combine more than one image
- Try it both large and small
- Try the image thicker and thinner
- Try enlarging different sections of the image
- Base the design on a letter
- Base the design on a number
- Combine the image with a strong shape, such as a circle or square
- Flip the image and combine it with the first un-flipped one
- Try the image at different angles
- Try repeating the image several times
- Try it in positive and negative (light background, dark foreground, and vice versa)

Play around with the possibilities, and try the ones suggested above. If you hit a dead end, go back to your notes from the brainstorming session and try a new tack. Logo design involves a lot of noodling around. (If you're doing it on a computer, the possibilities are infinite. Don't forget to eat and sleep).

• **Feedback.** A common mistake is to develop a single image too far before you get others' comments. It's better to take several sketches part of the way than

supply stores, and libraries (look under *trademarks, logos,* and *symbols*). These images will inspire you and extend the range of possibilities beyond your current thinking. Even if you are turning the logo design over to someone else, it's time well-spent. You'll be able to pass on your ideas, setting him or her off in the right direction. Remember that you're looking for *inspiration*, not something to copy.

Research often continues throughout the development of the logo design. Say you decide to base your logo on the image of a bicycle. Get as many pictures of bikes as you can. Sources might include catalogs and magazines as well as books. Or say your logo will be based on the image of a star. People have been drawing representations of stars for thousands of

Inexpensive Logos

62

Why Designers Will Help

If you are working for a non-profit organization or if you have a small business or start-up, you may be able to get a logo at little or no cost, but you'll have to have something to offer the designer instead of money. And you may indeed have something else to offer. Here are some reasons why you may be able to get help with your logo for below market cost:

- Beginning designers need printed pieces for their portfolios.

- Art students are interested in taking on "real" assignments.

- Designers are interested in having logos with name recognition in their portfolios. If your organization is well-known (or if you're headed that way) there could be interest.

- Some ad agencies and design studios—even top ones—are willing to contribute to their community. Especially if the assignment is interesting.

- Designers who are experiencing a slowdown in business or are between jobs will sometimes take on a project *gratis* (for no payment) to keep their hand in design.

What to Do

Start with a letter. Explain your proposal and describe your organization, but keep it short. Spell out what compensation you are offering (propose a competition to a design class, for example, and offer a certificate of award). Follow up your letter with a phone call. If you go this route, read about working with volunteers, page 66. Here are some possible candidates:

- Students at colleges of art or design or university art departments (high school students are too inexperienced—trust me)

- People at local advertising agencies or design studios

- Freelance graphic designers (ask everyone you know for names)

- People who work in the design department at a local newspaper

- Designers who work in community services or other organizations

If the people you talk to can't help you, ask them who might be able to. Nothing ventured, nothing gained.

63 The Logo: Sign or Symbol?

Carl Jung, the brilliant Swiss psychologist in the early part of this century, made a distinction between a sign and a symbol. He saw a sign as being superficial. It evokes a more shallow response than a symbol, which triggers a deeper one. And he meant much deeper—right down to our very archetypal cores.

Examples of signs are what hung over shop doors in the old days to announce what was sold inside, such as a bean kettle or a shoe or a tea pot. Images on road signs are another example.

Symbols, on the other hand, have a more ancient, deeply rooted, and powerful meaning. Circles (which suggest wholeness, for example) or a cross or the sun are powerful symbols. These timeless images evoke the strongest response when they have not been so trivialized that they lose their strength.

Take a really good look at logos and trademarks. They're everywhere around you. Notice the ones that look more like signs, and the ones that have the power of symbols. You may want to keep this distinction in mind when you select your logo.

Type alone can be used for a logo, or art can be integrated into the type as shown below.

These logos are both imaginative and appropriate. The one below is for Hospital Rentals (movie rentals).

to refine one too fully. When you come up with something you like, get feedback by showing it around. You can count on the design going back to the drawing board (or screen) more than once. So as soon as you've got a few decent possibilities, get the impressions of others. What strikes people first when they see your logo might never have occurred to you.

If someone else is designing the logo, insist on seeing preliminary sketches. A lot of time and money can be wasted on refining the wrong image. You may need to see the logo at several stages of development before it's what you want.

• ***Application.*** When you've got some good contenders, try the logo in color. If your computer has color, now comes the fun (some can generate millions of colors). Show the logo in as many different ways as possible: in color, in black and white, small and large, and in positive and negative, for example.

Finally, apply the logo to several pieces, such as a letterhead, a business card, a brochure, or a flyer. You will need to make decisions on type, ink, and paper. Make up some dummies (three-dimensional samples) on the paper you are considering so you can get the *feel* as well as the look. Once you've got what you want (and the blessing of the significant others), you're on to production.

As mentioned earlier, enormous sums are spent on creating the right impression in print. And although the amount spent isn't always reflected in the quality or strength of the graphic image, it does say something about its value in our world today. Put some thought into the impact your printed piece will have, and make up what you lack in dollars with resourcefulness and imagination. It's a wise investment. The more attention you give your graphic image now, the better it will serve you over time.

Logo Evaluation Checklist

64

The following questions will help you evaluate a logo you are considering for your organization. You can also use them as a basis for group discussion. A worksheet version of this sidebar appears on page 364.

- ☐ Does this logo have immediate impact?
- ☐ Is it good to look at?
- ☐ Is it distinctive?
- ☐ Does it create a positive image?
- ☐ Does it accurately represent your organization or business?
- ☐ Is it straightforward?
- ☐ Is it comprehensible?
- ☐ Is it memorable?
- ☐ Is it flexible?
- ☐ Does it copy well?
- ☐ Will it hold up both large and small?
- ☐ Will it wear well over time?
- ☐ Will you be proud to use it?

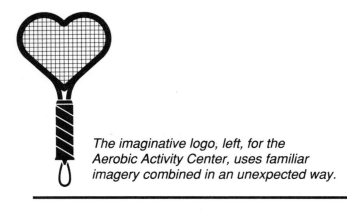

The imaginative logo, left, for the Aerobic Activity Center, uses familiar imagery combined in an unexpected way.

Notice how beautifully the type and art go together in the logo immediately above.

These logos, above, appropriately reflect the kinds of organizations they represent. The one in the upper left is for Fat Chance Records, the one to its right for a bicycle shop, the lower left is for an open space developer, and the one on the lower right is for a manufacturer of children's apparel.

Production and Distribution

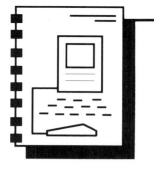

Chapter 22

Desktop Publishing

This chapter will introduce you to desktop publishing (DTP) if you are new to it; if it's familiar to you, it offers another perspective. We'll look at some of the popular myths about desktop publishing, and examine its strengths and shortcomings. We'll discuss computers, monitors, scanners, printers, software and fonts. Sidebar 70 will familiarize you with DTP-related terms (you may want to read through it before you read this chapter, or refer to it when you do). There are tips and recommendations at the end of the chapter, and sidebars to help you evaluate your needs and select the right software.

Desktop publishing involves producing printed pieces on a computer. It enables the user to combine text and graphics on a page, and to choose from many fonts (type styles) that print out high-quality type on a laser, linotronic, or other printer.

You don't have to do the desktop publishing yourself to benefit from its advantages. There are commercial centers that offer complete desktop publishing production services from design through camera-ready art. If you want to do the desktop publishing yourself, you need a personal computer such as a Macintosh or an IBM PC (or compatible), a mouse (a device that controls what's on the screen), and software (i.e., a word processing program and a desktop publishing program, at the minimum).

Those who are comfortable with computers jump right into desktop publishing and are in their glory; the rest of us approach it a bit more tentatively. But once you realize what you can do with desktop publishing, the reason for all the enthusiasm is clear.

There is a great deal of mystique surrounding desktop publishing. If you are confused as to what desktop publishing is, where it's going, what you should be learning , and what you should be buying, you've got a lot of company. There is confusion on every level, from developers to dealers to users.

We're in a period of transition, and the confusion is the result of change. Old, familiar ways of producing publications are becoming obsolete; new ways are not yet firmly established. High tech companies scramble to make their products the first, the best, and the most comprehensive. Computers and printers are upgraded continuously. They get faster, more capable, and more powerful. Every month there is new software that does more things more easily. Larger and larger libraries of fonts and computer clip art are published.

Although the most dramatic desktop publishing innovations may have already happened, major battles are still being waged over which companies will set

Once you come up with a design you like, a computer enables you to try it in positive, in negative, and in different weights of both very quickly.

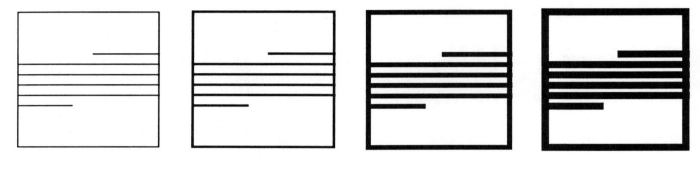

the industry standards. The field is like pick-up-sticks that have been tossed up in the air—we can see that there are lots of them and they're brightly colored, but we don't know what configuration they'll take when they land. This accounts for both the anxiety and the excitement.

The field of desktop publishing is replete with options, alternatives, high-tech language, and hard decisions. No wonder the "early adopters" feel continuously behind and the rest feel overwhelmed. Keeping pace with this change is a full-time job!

In spite of the flux, the number of people using computers to design publications is growing dramatically. Eventually the dust will settle, but for the moment, you have to muddle through with the rest. It's worth the effort if your work involves producing print—desktop publishing is not going away. In one form or another, it's here to stay.

Designing on a Computer

In desktop publishing, the computer becomes an electronic drawing board upon which anyone can draw a straight line. Not only can you draw a line quickly, perfectly, and easily, you can change its weight and place it anywhere. The same with shapes. You can create boxes, circles, patterns, and borders. You can move elements around singly or in groups. You can choose from a number of fonts (typefaces) in a wide range of sizes. You can duplicate each element

(or a whole page) as many times as you like, or get rid of what you don't want instantly and start again.

With a page layout program you can design a printed piece—a newsletter, for instance—and manipulate all of the parts: the masthead, the text, the page numbers, photographs, captions, and illustrations. You can choose the number of columns you want on a page and *zap*—there they are, precisely in the widths you specify. The same is true with margins. Pick the sizes, and they're instantly there.

There are rulers on the screen that make measuring easy. You can *import* the text from a word processing program and watch it *flow* into the columns. You can set up *master pages* and *style sheets* that automatically repeat a format you specify. You can look at your page as a whole sheet or zoom in on it at different enlargements.

With *draw* and *paint* programs you can create every conceivable kind of image, including 3D images. There are programs that enable you to make graphs and charts, and some that let you retouch or combine photographs. Some programs enable you to use both PANTONE and process colors, and to make color separations. Others enable you to work with more than 16 million colors and 1,200 fonts. You can import photographs or illustrations or commonly used images (such as logos) with a scanner. Pages can be prepared ready for the printer, or text can be sent over telephone wires to a typesetter.

For all of these wonderful capabilities, there are

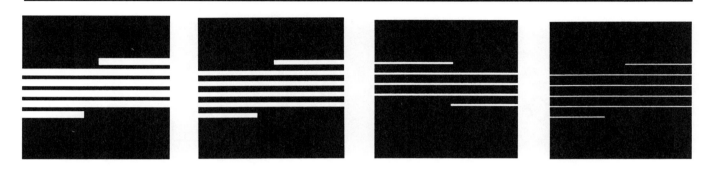

some myths about desktop publishing's Herculean feats. The major ones have to do with time, money, ease, and the final appearance of the piece. Let's take a look at some of these myths.

Great Expectations: Four Myths of Desktop Publishing

1. Desktop Publishing Is Fast

It takes a while to learn how to use desktop publishing efficiently. The truth is desktop publishing *can* be fast, but it isn't always, especially at the beginning. There are several reasons.

Designing on an electronic screen is a whole new way of working, and it requires new skills. Once you master the basics, tasks can indeed be performed quickly. But until you do, the going can be slow.

Let's say you get yourself a desktop publishing system on Tuesday. On Wednesday you sit down at the computer with your new page layout program, and plan to have your four-page newsletter at the printer's by Friday. But on Friday night you're still trying to figure out where page two disappeared to. On the following Monday you find out, and by Tuesday you're really beginning to get the hang of it.

At the end of the week the newsletter is at the press. One week late. Not bad. By the end of that week you know you've really accomplished something.

Next time the newsletter will be on time.

Here's another common scenario: The boss goes to a conference or learns from a friend about the astounding capabilities of the magic box. The boss comes back to the office, buys a desktop publishing system, and announces the end of production headaches. Someone is appointed to figure out how to adapt the equipment to the needs of the organization (or the organization to the needs of the equipment). The appointed person is up to his or her ears in manuals trying to figure out how to make the system work. It seems as if something that's supposed to take no time at all is taking forever. Disillusionment sets in. The appointee is frustrated; the boss is mad. What's going on?

The fact is that learning takes time. Knowing what desktop publishing *can* do is different from knowing *how to do it.* Learning takes practice. It takes trial and error. It takes effort. Desktop publishers do not have to be technical wizards, but they do need the willingness, ability, and patience to learn. That means they have to switch over to "beginner" mode, and that's sometimes hard to do, especially if the beginner is used to being an expert.

But say you love technology and you love learning new programs, or it just comes easy to you. Or say you're just determined, and you finally master a program. For all the computer's speed and power, desktop publishing can still be more time-consuming than you might think. Why?

You can actually spend more time designing a logo on a desktop publishing system rather than less because endless versions can be created instantly and easily from one idea.

The noodle factor. You get involved. You futz with this and you futz with that. You try different versions. One easy-to-make change gives you three new ideas, and you're not satisfied until you try out each one. Each new version can be endlessly modified, a bottomless pit for a perfectionist. No buzzer goes off when the piece is "done," so desktop published pieces tend to get worked on right up until the last minute, and beyond. Desktop publishing can take up more time, not less.

And although computers are fast and getting faster, we quickly adapt to their speed and want them to go *even faster*. The several seconds it takes for a certain function to be performed can seem interminable once you get used to moving quickly.

Another reason why desktop publishing may not save you quite as much time as you expected: you may be taking on new tasks such as design and typesetting. As designer of the piece, you must make decisions about type: its size, weight, placement, and spacing. You must make the page look good as an integrated whole, and make it easy to read. As typesetter, you must "create" the type, produce the proofs, and do the proofreading. And you'll be running your piece through some kind of printer. You may also find yourself spending more time getting agreements and approvals and on pick ups and deliveries—going to the copy shop or service center, and going to the printer.

Obviously, the kinds of printed pieces you put out have a lot to do with the amount of time that's required. A letterhead, flyer, or business card can be put together quickly; a newsletter takes more time, especially when you're setting up the format. A manual or booklet takes still longer. As one designer commented, "for something so fast, sometimes it sure seems slow." "It" isn't; we are, especially in the beginning. But after that initial investment of time, repeat or similar work goes a whole lot faster.

2. Desktop Publishing Saves Money

Desktop publishing does not automatically or immediately save money. First of all, there is the capital outlay. If you're starting from scratch, a DTP system is expensive. A computer, a large screen monitor, and a laser printer can cost in the neighborhood of $10,000. Software packages are also not cheap; many are several hundreds of dollars.

Then there is the cost of your time: the time it takes you to learn how to make the computer and its programs work, the time to make the design decisions, and the time to perform the tasks.

On top of that there are the continuously seductive opportunities for buying upgrades and expansions. This is especially tempting if you like to stay at the state of the art, or reasonably close behind it. And then there's the cost of all that extra time you put in just because you're hooked.

Nevertheless, desktop publishing can save you the costs of typesetting, illustration, design, and paste-up. So desktop publishing saves money—eventually—but not in the beginning.

3. Desktop Publishing Is Easy

Desktop publishing, like anything else, is easy after you know how to do it. But getting to easy can be difficult. Some software programs can be learned in a few hours; others may take a week or more. There are some things that make sense right away; other things stay fuzzy for a while.

It is entirely possible to reach the level of expertise you need to put out your publication fairly quickly, and stay there. You only need to master the kinds of skills that are necessary to do the kinds of publications you put out regularly. A computer is, after all, just a tool to be used to make your work easier and your printed pieces look better. That work may entail something as simple as creating a few columns of text with headlines and some clip art. But if your task is more complex, such as putting out a slick full-colored magazine, there are software packages that offer the capabilities to handle it.

Whatever your level of technological expertise, life with a computer is unpredictable. The cover of this book was designed by a very knowledgeable designer on his up-to-the-minute desktop publishing system. He and I were working on it one night when the computer flatly refused to print a certain font he wanted to try. "Now *that's* never happened before!" he said. "You think you've seen it all and there are still more surprises." On the whole, the functioning usually does go smoothly, but every now and then some things crop up to stump you.

4. DTP Improves the Look

As Peter Lewis, writer on personal computers for the *New York Times* said, "Giving so many powerful graphics tools to casual users can be dangerous, at least from an aesthetic sense. Many beginners have the urge to create circus posters when a clean and simple report will do." Desktop publishing *can* help to improve the look of your piece, but it isn't going to do it automatically.

Knowing how to use the computer is not the same as knowing how to design or how to set type. Desktop publishing systems make millions of design elements available to many people, but they don't give them the ability to know what looks good or communicates well. The products of desktop computers run the whole gamut of visual appearance from the cluttery, junky "circus poster" look to the arresting look of first-rate design.

You can learn how to communicate information dynamically using desktop publishing *if* you have a mind to do so. You can develop the eye of a designer *if* you have the interest and *if* you have the time to develop the skill. No computer can do these things for you. One desktop publisher put it this way: "Anyone can throw anything up on the screen and print it out. That doesn't make it good."

A desktop publishing system only does what you tell it to do. You still have to do the thinking and make the decisions. With desktop publishing, the responsibility for the look of the piece is entirely yours.

Business pieces are not the only things you can do on a desktop publishing system. The invitation, left, and this family's holiday card were designed on a computer. The photograph was scanned in.

Desktop Publishing: Advantages

With the kinds of qualifications described above, desktop publishing really can make producing publications faster, cheaper, and easier, and *can* make them look better. And there are other pluses to producing your publications on a desktop system. Here are some of the important ones.

Immediate Gratification

Desktop publishing is *fun*. There is an infinite number of shapes, sizes, patterns, and graphic devices to play with. You can see your ideas immediately, and change them quickly and easily. You can print out many variations and choose the best.

Control

The thing that desktop publishers like best about producing print electronically is the amount of control it gives them. You don't have to count on anyone else, and you don't have to wait for others. You are free to develop your own piece your own way, and to do it on your own time schedule.

Desktop publishing enables you to refine your product for as many hours as you have to put in on it. You control the whole process (with perhaps the exception of printing), and that convenience and satisfaction is worth a lot.

Control over the type is especially important and satisfying. Specifying type in the traditional way is considered a hassle by most designers. The text has to be precisely and thoroughly specified, which requires a lot of calculating. It has to be sent out to a typesetter and it often goes back and forth for several rounds of corrections.

The process can take days or weeks. And no matter how carefully it is specified, there are almost al-

Desktop publishing makes tools available for producing highly professional printed pieces. The pages below were created with Aldus PageMaker® 3.0. In the piece on the left, illustrations were made in Aldus FreeHand™ and the photograph was taken with Aldus SnapShot®. In the piece on the right, the graph was imported from Aldus Persuasion®; the spreadsheet was created in Microsoft Excel®.

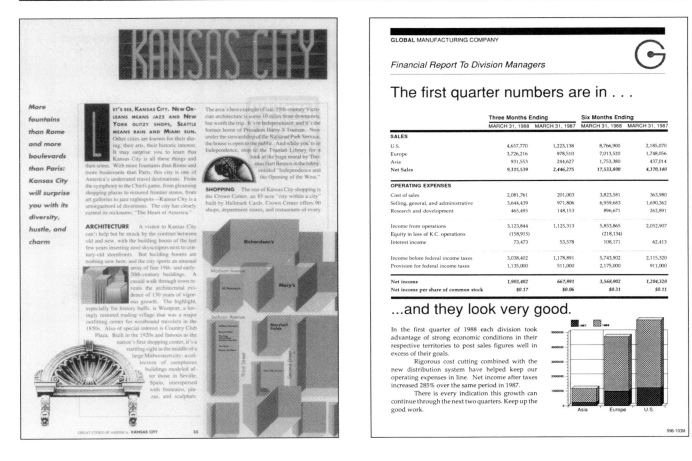

ways surprises. Designers often end up with something less than they envision because of the time and expense involved in making changes. With desktop publishing you can see the type instantly, and work with it until it is precisely the way you want it.

Experimentation

The ability to change designs easily leads to more experimentation. Let's say you're designing a logo. You can duplicate your first version with a keystroke and put the two logos side by side. Seeing the images together gives you a new idea, and you make modifications based on the new idea. These modifications further stimulate your thinking. The design evolves more rapidly (and differently) than it would if you did it by hand. First versions on computers have a more finished look, so you run though a series of ideas in a shorter period of time. The design develops faster.

Or at least you have more versions. The down side of the quickly evolving design is the tendency to create more and more images rather than develop any one in depth, and *quantity* does not replace *quality*. Nevertheless, computers make experimentation easy and fun, and strong images can be created that would otherwise never appear.

Graphics-related software invites experimentation. These illustrations were developed with a drawing program. The pictures below show variations of the same image. The ones on the next page are for different publications in the same series.

Quick and Easy Changes

When you produce a publication using DTP, you can make changes right down to the wire. This is a great advantage in cases where information or images are slow in arriving and deadlines are tight. Last-minute changes no longer throw the whole procedure into crisis (or at least not as often).

Savings on Supplies

Some computers enable you to put everything in place, so you can hand the job to the printer ready to go (as camera-ready art). Color monitors eliminate the need for magic markers and other paraphernalia. Even color separations are now done on the computer. Gone is the need for T-squares and triangles, rulers in picas and points, rub-on type, ink, and huge quantities of wax or rubber cement.

Spell-checkers

At last, something for the poor spellers of the world. Many programs come with a spell checking capability that lets you correct your mistakes before someone else does. Spell checkers aren't foolproof—they only catch the non-words. If you type *he*, for example and meant *the*, the computer misses the mistake; if you type *jhe* instead of *the*, it catches it.

Investing in the Future

Not very long from now the phrase "desktop publishing" is likely to be synonymous with producing print. Traditional typesetting and some methods of preparation will continue on as highly-skilled or specialized crafts, as calligraphy is today, but the vast majority of printed images will be produced electronically. So one advantage of producing your publications on a

desktop publishing system now is that you won't have to switch over later. You'll have the fundamental skills down, and you can get on with doing whatever else it is you do best.

Limitations and Frustrations

For all of the advantages, desktop publishing has its share of limitations and frustrations. Following are the ones that users report most commonly.

Time for Learning

Time out for exploration and education is not built into most people's schedules. Finding time to get up to speed and staying there is a frustration experienced by many desktop publishers. Becoming familiar with alternative systems and software is time-consuming, and, as mentioned earlier, it takes time to learn how

Keeping Up with DTP   65

There are many ways to keep yourself updated with desktop publishing—choose the ones that are most comfortable for you. Here are several possibilities.

- Your best source of information about desktop publishing is from people who use it to produce pieces like yours

- Look for these people through friends, colleagues, or computer users' groups

- Talk with more than one user to get a range of experiences and a well-rounded picture

- Ask users what computer stores are good, and visit them

- Write out your DTP questions ahead, and bring them with you

- Become familiar with basic desktop publishing terms (see Sidebar 70)

- Go to a bookstore and look at books or magazines on desktop publishing

- Read magazines like *Publish!* (for both the Mac and the PC), *MacUser* and *MacWorld*, *PC* and *PC World*

- Use magazines and indexes at the library (a back issue may have just the information you're looking for)

- Attend users' groups and conferences

- Visit service centers, and ask about services and costs

- Go to computer shows, look at everything, and ask lots of questions

- Borrow manuals on software you're interested in from friends or colleagues, or take them out of the library

66 Your Desktop Publishing Needs

Before investing in a desktop publishing system, analyze your situation. You're after a match between your needs and the products that are currently available. Knowing what you want will enable others to be more helpful. The following questions will help you sort out the relevant issues.

- What kinds of publications do you want to produce?

- How often will you be producing them?

- How many pages are involved?

- What computer equipment do you currently have?

- How important is it that these pieces look good?

- What are your requirements for type?

- Will you need graphics? What kind?

- Do you want to use photographs?

- Do you need color?

- Do you have the time to learn about desktop publishing?

- Do you have the enthusiasm for it, and the ability to take on new skills?

- Where will the money come from to pay for the costs involved?

A worksheet version of this sidebar is on page 366.

to use them. Many users of desktop publishing systems feel they could get more out of the computer and software they *already* have if they had the time to learn more about them. One desktop publisher summed it up well when he said "The technology changes so fast. No matter how much I try to keep up, I always feel behind."

System Limitations

For all of a desktop publishing system's complex innards, surprisingly few technical problems arise. But when something does go wrong, it can ruin your day. Our expectations of the system and application software become very high very fast, and so does our dependency on them.

One of the biggest frustrations desktop publishers experience is losing work—minutes, hours, or days worth. This can happen when the system *crashes* and you've forgotten to *save* your work (permanently store it by hitting a *save* key) or to back it up (make a copy on another disk). Hard disk crashes are especially devastating (a hard disk also has to be backed up). Other common annoyances are:

- Getting something out of the printer that looks different from what's on the screen

- Waiting for commands to be completed

- Waiting for something to print out

- Time spent moving to different areas on a small screen (a problem that can be solved by buying a larger monitor)

- Insufficient computer memory to run particular programs

- Not fully understanding how to use a program

- Insufficient storage (a problem that can be solved by getting a larger hard disk)

- Programs that have *almost* everything you want, but not quite, so you have to switch back and forth between two or more

Compatibility

As manufacturers struggle for dominance in the field of desktop publishing, energy goes into this mercantile competition instead of solving users' problems. Compatibility between two systems such as the Macintosh and the PC is still limited. This lack of compatibility is especially frustrating for those who work in a "dual environment." And there are many program incompatibilities in the DOS (PC disk operating system) world. These problems are likely to be worked out over time, but meanwhile, you have to pay attention to what goes with what.

Expense

As mentioned earlier, a new desktop publishing system can be very expensive. So can software. The expense makes it imperative to consider carefully what to buy before you buy it. Become familiar with what's available and compare prices before you plunk down your money.

The Bottom Line

For all the limitations and frustrations of desktop publishing, no one who uses a computer to produce printed pieces would consider going back to the old way. The advantages, quite simply, outweigh the disadvantages.

In addition, desktop publishing has already brought about several positive changes. It has stimulated a new interest in graphic design, and accounts for greater awareness of printed communications. There are already many fine examples of newsletters, brochures, annual reports, flyers, and other printed pieces that

Buying DTP Equipment   67

Purchasing desktop publishing equipment is a big step. Read up on it and talk with people who use it. Here are more suggestions.

- Avoid computer-buyer's paralysis: the fear of making a commitment because what you buy will soon be outdated. Improvements in DTP will continue for some time, so you may as well jump in.

- Buy a system that can be upgraded later. You will be better able to upgrade it if it's based on your own experience with your own publications.

- Each software program has certain hardware requirements. Be sure your hardware will support (work with) software you select.

- Decide on your priorities, such as ease of use, speed, cost, graphs, text handling, design, illustration, and so on.

- Think through which of these features you would use the most.

- Remember that salespeople often work on commission, and that some have little or no direct experience in desktop publishing.

- Ask to speak with the salesperson who is most knowledgeable in desktop publishing.

- Bring a sample of the kinds of pieces you want to produce. This will orient sales people to your needs quickly.

- Consider buying a large-screen monitor. It will save scrolling time, which adds up.

- When you make a purchase, make sure it will do the job adequately. People are more apt to *underestimate* their needs than *overestimate* them, especially for memory or storage capacity.

This brochure for Quark XPress® 2.12 (page design software with commercial-quality typography, color support and integrated word processing) was designed using the software it promotes.

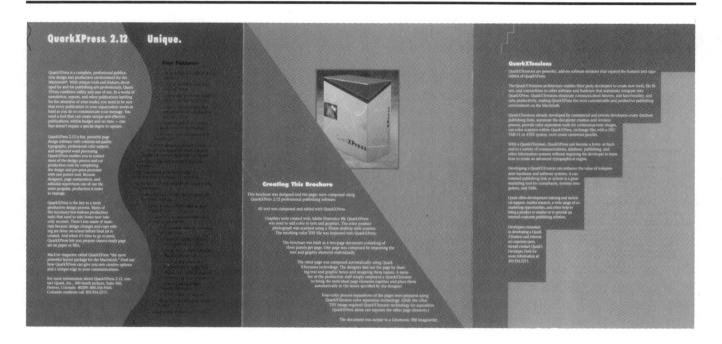

have been created entirely electronically. And it is getting harder and harder to distinguish pieces produced on desktop systems from ones produced on more expensive equipment.

There is a difference of opinion among computer-using print producers as to how much technical expertise is necessary to use the tools effectively. Some feel you have to be pretty knowledgeable in computer technology, but I tend to agree with the designer who said "Doing desktop publishing is like driving a car: you don't have to know how a car works to get it to take you where you want to go." On the other hand, knowledge is power. The more you know about it, the more in control you are.

Computer whizzes, experts, and ordinary users are all trying to figure out how to use the vast potential of this electronic drawing board. As one man strategically placed in the crossroads of users, manufacturers, and program developers said of desktop publishing, "No one totally understands what they're

doing yet. Not even the people in the business." And that's what makes it interesting.

Hardware

Because changes are taking place so rapidly, it is difficult to talk about hardware or software in a book. For up-to-the-minute information and in-depth analyses, your best bet is to read computer-related magazines (several are mentioned in Sidebar 65), and talk with users.

Nevertheless, it is possible to present an overview of hardware (the actual pieces of equipment or components of a computer system) and software (any program that tells the computer what to do). This overview describes equipment, lays out options, and points out what to take into consideration when you're shopping around. This section is intended for people who are exploring desktop publishing, who are are relatively new to it, or who use it to a limited extent.

Selecting Software 68

You don't need software with features you won't use. By the same token you don't want to be without the ones you need. Consider the following issues when you set your priorities.

- Price

- Document length: the maximum number of pages

- Image handling: the ease of design

- Style sheets

- Design templates

- Color

- Compatibility between DTP programs and word-processing programs

- The environment you plan to work in

- A good match between your level of sophistication and the program

- Compatibility between your DTP program and other programs you plan to use

- Fonts, letterspacing (kerning), and line spacing (leading)

- Speed: the time it takes to pour text into columns, to format a page, to move from one page to another, to save a page, to print out

- Help: documentation, on-line help, and telephone technical support

- Compatibility: between computer fonts and printers; between programs and scanners

Computers

If you don't yet have a computer, the first question is what to get. For desktop publishing there are two main camps: the IBM PC (and compatibles) and Apple's Macintosh. There are devotees of both. People are often fiercely loyal to whatever system they are most familiar with, and that one tends to be the one they learned on.

If you're starting from scratch, I think the Macintosh is the superior system for desktop publishing (I've worked on both). You will hear of people switching from the PC to the Mac for desktop publishing, but you are unlikely to hear of anyone switching from the Mac to the PC for that purpose unless they have to. Here's why.

IBM's products are basically business machines; they're number-oriented. And for these needs they are firmly established in the market. The Mac, on the other hand, was visually oriented from the start, and continues to evolve in that direction. From its very beginning the Macintosh was designed for working with images. This makes it an ideal publishing tool, and it is fast becoming established as the standard in the publishing world.

There are other reasons why the Macintosh is the better system for desktop publishing at the present time. There is more compatibility within the system. There is more compatible software for DTP on the Mac, more clip art, and more fonts (although this will most likely be changing). Applications have a common interface, which makes them easier to learn. And people who have used both systems say the Mac is more fun to work on (I agree).

I'm sure Macintosh users could come up with many more reasons; IBM users would understandably debate them. Still, if you have the choice and can afford it, I think you'll be happier with a Mac for desktop publishing.

But let's say you're in a DOS (IBM compatible)

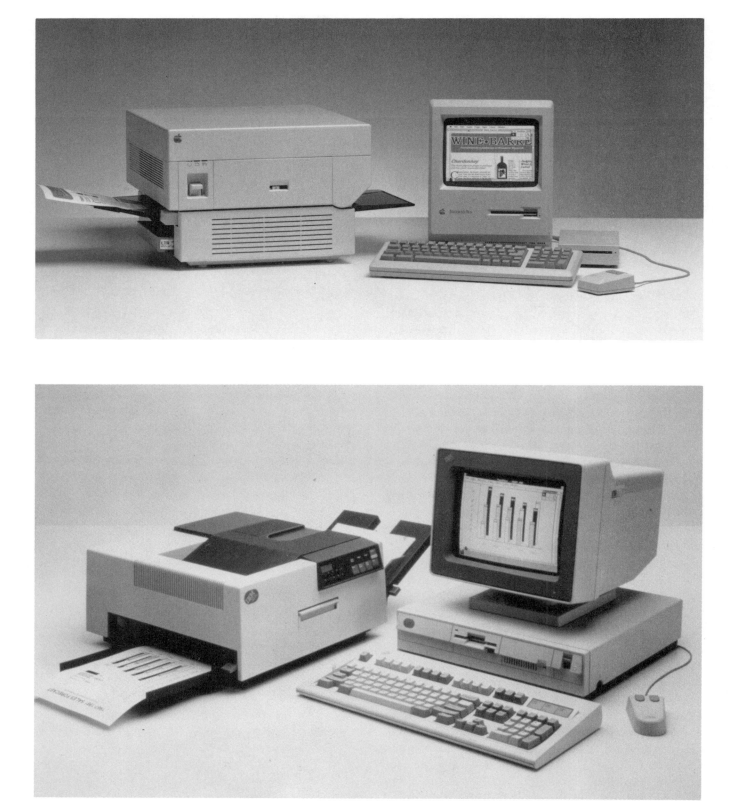

Apple's basic Desktop Publishing System, upper
left, consists of a Macintosh computer and a LaserWriter® printer.
Below left is IBM's Solution Pac Personal Publishing System. A selection of IBM hardware
and software products can be used with IBM Personal Computers and IBM Personal System/2 Computers.

world, which is often the case. Do you buy a Mac (which is like swimming upstream), or do you go with what's already there? One criterion is the amount of publishing you do. What proportion of your day is spent on producing publications? If it's not much, a PC could suit your needs quite well.

Sometimes the advantages of staying in the PC world outweigh the advantages of switching, and circumstances sometimes make that the best choice. Or you may be in a situation in which you have no choice. Organizations with PCs already in the office can use the same equipment as a part of a desktop publishing system. People use PCs and compatibles very successfully for desktop publishing, and they are swiftly evolving in the Macintosh direction.

But if you put out a lot of printed materials, don't automatically build a desktop publishing system with PC components before you take a serious look at the Mac. Many organizations decide to use the PCs for other things and buy a Macintosh for producing print.

Convenient compatibility between the Mac and DOS worlds would, of course, make many people's lives easier. It will come, but it's not here quite yet. Meanwhile software such as Microsoft Corporation's Microsoft®Word (used primarily for word processing) and Aldus Corporation's PageMaker® (for desktop publishing) bring us the closest to compatibility yet. Files can be created, opened, and worked on in either system.

One thing that is important to have for desktop publishing is a hard disk—the bigger the better. It is important because desktop publishing involves importing text, graphics, and information from other applications. And graphics, scanned images, and paint files take a lot of storage space.

Scanners

One kind of hardware that may be of use to you is a scanner. A scanner (or "imaging device") enables you to convert photographs and illustrations into digitized images (tiny black and white dots) so that they can be stored in your computer. With the right software they can be manipulated and modified on the screen, integrated into your page layout, and printed on the output device (printer) of your choice.

Some scanners can also be used as OCR (optical character recognition) devices. These scan typewritten copy on paper so you don't have to key in the words. They go directly into the computer enabling you to edit them on the screen.

Some scanners have different operating modes for three kinds of images: black and white mode for black and white line art (solids such as a woodcut or silhouette drawings); gray-scale mode for black and white continuous tone images (images with shading such as photographs or watercolors); and color mode for color photographs. Gray-scale mode produces 16, 64, or 256 shades of gray (as opposed to all black dots). Some scanners can be hooked up to video cameras to capture video images.

Scanners are handy to get your logo and other much-used imagery on to your computer screen, and they are easy to use. If you don't want to buy one, you can use one at a service center.

Monitors

If you do a lot of desktop publishing, you will spend a lot of time looking at your computer screen. Having the right monitor will make your work easier and faster. Features and capabilities of the screens you can purchase vary widely. There are three major categories of monitors:

Monochrome monitors

These one-color monitors simulate shades of gray. They display text and line images very sharply, but not color.

Gray-scale monitors

These monitors are useful if you work with photographs or other shaded images as part of your DTP tasks. They come with a number of shades of gray: 16, 24, or 256 at the moment. Capabilities are reflected in the price.

Color monitors

These are the most sophisticated monitors on the market today, and are used to produce every kind of graphic publication. They are also used as retouching tools for color photographs. Currently the number of colors they display are 32, 256, 768, or 16.7 million; there may be more by the time you read this.

Other considerations

What else should you consider when you are shopping for a monitor? Here are six important variables.

• *Size.* One reason to buy another monitor is to get a bigger screen (larger screens are much more convenient to work on). Tests show that larger screens can save you time because you don't spend so much of it wandering around looking for an area you want to work on. 19″ and 21″ are standard sizes. Some monitors are *landscape* (horizontal); others are *portrait* (vertical). There are one-page displays and two-page displays. Find out whether or not a monitor you are considering displays a whole 8-1/2″ x 11″ page, and if it is presented at full size. Some monitors chop off the edges of the page, others reduce it.

• *Resolution.* The sharpness of the image on a screen is described by the number of *dots per inch* (dpi) it displays. Compare the dpi on different monitors, and look carefully at how sharply letters and lines are represented.

• *Glare.* Notice the amount of glare that comes from the screen. If you work on it for long hours at a time, you'll care about the glare. Anti-glare screens are available.

• *Distortion.* Some screen images are truer than others. Compare the amount of distortion on different screens.

• *Contrast.* Compare the range of contrast on different screens. The higher the better.

• *Flicker.* Nothing is more annoying than a nervous, flickering screen. Look for a monitor with a flicker-free image.

Printers

There are many printers on the market today. The printer you select will have a lot to do with how good your printed piece looks. Dot-matrix printers may be fine for working on documents and proofing, but they lack professional quality. Their resolution isn't high (sharp) enough for reproduction.

Printers range, for example, from the 300 dpi laser printer, to the Linotronic 300 with 2,540 dpi. The more dpi a printer has, the sharper the image and the higher the cost of producing each page.

You don't necessarily need the sharpest possible image or the most expensive printer for every job you do. Allow yourself time to try out different printers before you have to produce the final output.

Match the quality of the printer's output to the importance of the specific printed piece. What printer you select also depends on your budget and the typeface you're using. Stouter ones like Helvetica, Palatino, and Avant Garde will reproduce well at lower resolutions; finer ones with thinner lines look better at higher resolutions. Halftones and other complicated graphics will also look better at higher resolutions.

And take the kind of paper your piece will be printed on into consideration as well.

If you want what the printer produces to look like what you see on the screen, check for compatibility between your screen fonts and the printer fonts. A printer that supports Adobe PostScript®, for example, will run Adobe typefaces; a clone will not. (PostScript® is the computer language developed by Adobe Systems. It converts a design on a screen into hard copy, driving a printer to reproduce it.)

Software

All computer programs are software. Software refers to the individual programs that tell the computer exactly what to do. When you buy a computer, it comes with a software operating system to control the basic functions of the computer. For the IBM PC and compatibles, for example, the system is called DOS (disk operating system).

Desktop publishing usually depends on several different kinds of programs (also called *applications*) to produce a printed piece. The central program in desktop publishing is called a page layout (or page makeup or desktop publishing) program. It is the one that enables you to combine text and graphics. Different elements can be created in other programs, and imported into the DTP program.

Think of a DTP program as a clean sheet of paper into which you bring all of the components you need for your publication (text, a logo, illustrations, charts, and so on). Each of these elements is often created in its own program, which is designed specifically to accomplish some particular task. The text, for example, may be developed in a word processing program like Microsoft® Word, and drawings created in a "draw" or "paint" program like MacDraw®. Clip art images are usually imported from clip art software such as T/Maker®'s Click Art (although some also come with some programs). Data can be imported

Desktop Publishing Reminders

69

The field of DTP is large, complex, and continuously changing, but there is a lot of help around if you look for it. Here are some tips and reminders.

- Stay updated. Take classes at local community colleges or at stores that sell DTP equipment.

- Look for classes in local newspapers. They are also listed in the Yellow Pages under *Computers* and *Training*.

- One-on-one instruction is the most efficient way to learn at any stage.

- You can find a tutor the same way you find a class, or ask other desktop publishers for recommendations.

- Remember to keep the design of your electronically produced pieces simple.

- Keep fonts, shadows, and other gizmos on your page to a minimum.

- Don't forget to "save" your work continuously (at least once every half hour), and back it up regularly.

- Have a back-up plan for producing your piece in case of an emergency, such as a power failure.

- Don't expect to be proficient at desktop publishing overnight. New programs take several hours or a week or more to learn.

- Once you are familiar with your basic desktop publishing system, learning new programs becomes easier, faster, and more fun.

*These spreads from a brochure
for Aldus PageMaker® show the steps involved
in putting a printed piece together using desktop publishing.*

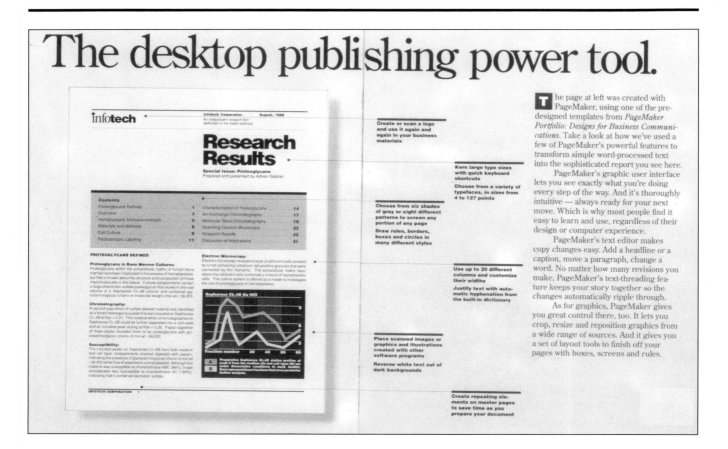

from a database or spreadsheet program. Photographs are imported into a page layout program by using a scanner.

Once all the elements are brought into the desktop program (or on to your "blank sheet") from the other ones, they can be modified, cropped, organized, adjusted, and laid out on the screen (or "page") as the user pleases. That is the major function of a desktop publishing program.

Ordinary word processing software is evolving closer and closer to DTP software. There are now word-processing programs that integrate text and graphics, offer many fonts, and have page layout features. One of these may be sufficient for your desktop publishing needs. At the same time, the newest desktop publishing programs include the capability for creating text. The two types of software are merging. But for the moment, many DTP programs still depend on importing components from elsewhere for anything but the simplest of layouts.

Let's take a closer look at the kinds of software that are used for desktop publishing. The following descriptions will give you the basic lay of the land, but keep in mind that this is a rapidly changing area. New programs are instantly dated when newer ones come out, and newer ones are coming out all the time. Check with computer magazines, friends, and software stores for the latest.

From start to finish in four easy steps.

Begin your publication by preparing text and graphics.

Write and edit copy with your favorite word-processing program. Create illustrations and graphics using electronic clip art, computer-created graphics or scanned images.

PageMaker is your link to more word-processing and graphics programs, for a wider selection of computers and printers, than any other desktop publishing application on the market.

Next, develop a format for your publication with PageMaker's master page feature.

Define the margins, number of columns and column widths. Then add standing design elements like headers, page numbers and non-printing guidelines, and you'll have your publication format — one you can use for this project only or save as a template for repeated use. PageMaker's built-in flexibility lets you modify these individual page formats any time you choose.

Now, select your text or illustration with PageMaker's powerful "Place" command, position the pointer and click your mouse button.

PageMaker flows your word-processed text onto the page. You adjust the position of your text and resize your graphics to fit any space. Adjustable rulers and non-printing guidelines help you put everything in its place with accuracy and ease.

When the pages look the way you want, you're ready to print.

Laser printers produce fine-looking pages for immediate use or masters for multiple copies of your materials. For true typeset-quality output, you can print to a PageMaker-compatible typesetter.

Page Layout Programs

There are currently well over fifty page layout programs for the Macintosh and DOS-based systems. They range in price from $40 for a program primarily for school use to over $40,000 for one used for professional magazine layout. Most programs fall somewhere between $100 and $800.

Aldus Corporation publishes almost identical versions of PageMaker® for both the Macintosh and the PC. It is one of the most widely used desktop publishing programs. Here are some of the things it does (you might use this list as a basis to compare other programs):

- Imports images
- Justifies text
- Produces columns automatically
- Adjusts sizes of type from 4 to 650 points
- Handles up to 99 pages depending on disk space
- Has search and replace capabilities for text, fonts, point sizes, etc.
- Rotates text and condenses or stretches characters
- Wraps text around irregular shapes

This cover of Aldus Magazine was created in Aldus FreeHand™. It demonstrates the kind of sophisticated publication that can be produced on a desktop publishing system

- Allows you to crop, scale, and kern

- Has handy pull-down rulers

- Has spelling and hyphenation dictionaries

- Comes with page-design templates

- Allows you to do text writing and editing in a window overlaying the pulication window

- Imports style sheets defined in Microsoft® Word

- Produces overlays for solid color, tints, and screens

- Prints out camera-ready art

- Supports all PostScript® and QuickDraw® printers

- Enables you to work with PANTONE colors and process colors with a software extension

Each desktop publishing program has its own unique features and advantages. Another DTP program, Quark XPress®—made by Quark, Inc. for the Macintosh— came out after PageMaker®, but is rapidly gaining popularity. Some professionals prefer QuarkXPress®, others prefer PageMaker®. Desktop publishing programs seem to leap-frog in popularity as more and more capabilities are added.

Ready, Set, Go!® (by Letraset USA), also for the Mac, is another popular DTP program. It has global search and replace capabilities, word processing, spell-checking, and a useful "grouping" capability.

For the PC, Xerox's Ventura Publisher® is one of the most widely-used desktop publishing programs. Ventura has many strengths, among them the capability of handling very long documents. Type-Set-It® (from Good Ideas, also for the PC) has 1,296 font styles and 96 sizes of each, giving the user over 124,000 fonts

to choose from as of this writing. By the time you read this, there may be more.

There is as much competition among "entry level" desktop publishing software as there is for the more sophisticated packages. Springboard Publisher puts out DTP software for both the Mac and the PC; it offers many good features for the price. Quark also makes QuarkStyle®, a less-complex (and less expensive) program than QuarkXPress®. With over 70 templates, it is geared toward the business person.

Desktop publishing software is evolving fast. Manufacturers work to include a feature in a competitive program in their new upgrade; a capability missing in their earlier version is often built into the

*The image below is used to demonstrate
the capabilities of Adobe Illustrator 88 ™, one of
the first sophisticated illustration programs. There are now
several good ones that enable you to create professional-looking graphics.*

next. The best place to find in-depth comparisons of the latest in software is in computer magazines like *MacUser*, *MacWorld*, *PC*, *PC World*, and *Publish!*.

Word Processing

As discussed earlier, you may want to work on your text in a word-processing program first, and then import it into your DTP program. So make sure that the DTP program you select is compatible with your word-processing program, and vice versa.

And as mentioned earlier, Microsoft® Word is a widely-used word processor for both the Mac and the PC. Other DOS word processing programs that can be imported into DTP programs include WordStar®, WordPerfect®, MultiMate®, and GEM Write®. Examples of word processing programs for the Mac include MacWrite®, WriteNow®, and FullWrite Professional®.

Not all programs have spell checkers and global searches, so if these features are important to you, be sure your word processing program has them.

Graphics Programs

There are many programs on the market that enable you to "draw" and "paint." You do this by choosing from among many *tools* offered on the side of the computer screen in the *tool box*. *Draw* and *paint* programs work differently. Images made in paint programs are *bit-mapped*—that is, made up of tiny black squares. Paint images are changed by filling in or "erasing" squares on the screen. Draw programs are *object oriented*. That means that individual "objects" such as lines, curves, or geometric shapes are created and manipulated as *whole units* (reduced, enlarged, expanded, rotated, and so on).

With these two kinds of programs, you can create just about any kind of image you can imagine. You can draw "freehand" with a pencil tool, for example, or create predefined shapes such as circles, rectangles, or squares by selecting the appropriate tool. You can fill in areas with different patterns or colors selected on the screen. You can erase parts of your image. The more sophisticated the program, obviously, the more you are able to do with it.

Examples of draw and paint programs are Claris Corporation's MacDraw® and MacPaint®. PixelPaint®, Aldus Freehand® (for the Mac) and Adobe Illustrator® (the latter for both Mac and PC) are more sophisticated versions. FullPaint® is a Macintosh program that combines both drawing and painting capabilities. When you're doing DTP on the PC, graphics can be imported from programs like CorelDraw!®, PC Paintbrush®, and Windows Paint®.

For doing presentation graphics, viewgraphs, and slides, there are programs like PowerPoint® and Persuasion® and Cricket Graph® for pie charts, line charts, and so on for the Mac. Equivalents for the PC are programs like Harvard Graphics®, Xerox Presents®, and Chart-Master®. Base the selection of your programs on the features you will be using most.

The availability of clip-art packages is increasing

Clip art copyright-free illustrations anyone can use is widely available for the computer. Below is a sampling of software images from T/Maker®'s ClickArt®.

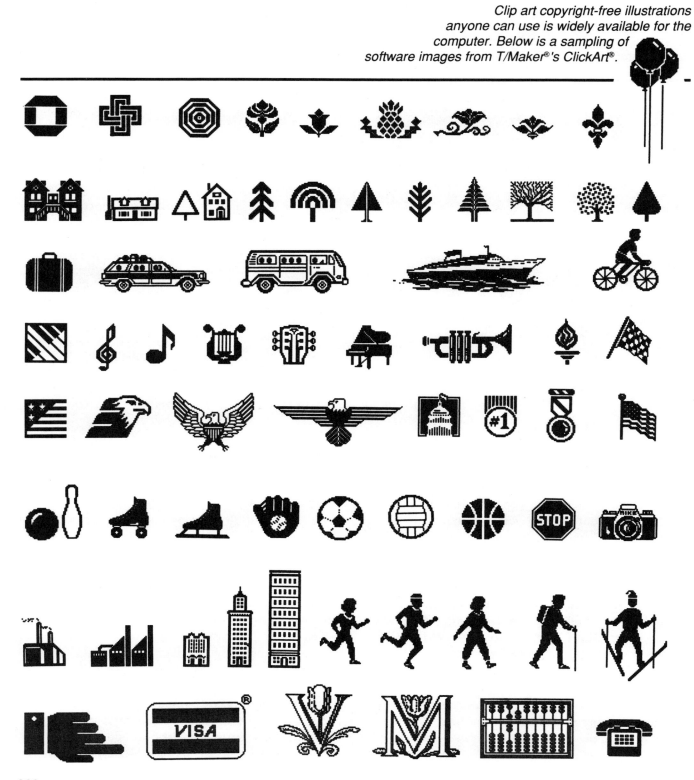

*Desktop publishing has taught computer
users more than they ever thought they'd know
about type. Below is a spread from the AdobeType Library Catalog,*
Font & Function. *This issue shows more than 600 typeface for the Mac and PC.*

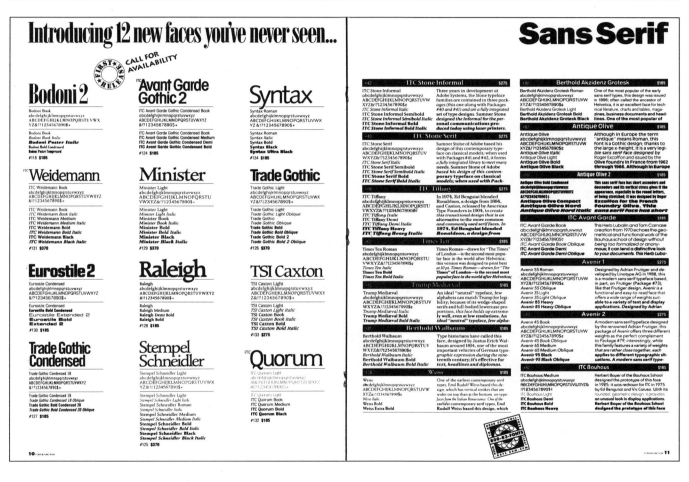

steadily. Clip art purchased on computer disks enables you to import copyright free illustrations into your desktop publishing program. The quality of the drawings in these packages varies widely—be sure to choose illustrations that will really *enhance* your printed piece. Examples of clip-art programs are Click Art® by T/Maker and the WetPaint Series® for the Mac; there is Springboard's Clip Art Collection® and Art Gallery I and II® for the PC.

New software comes out continuously. You will find that each program has strengths and weaknesses, and no program is likely to have everything you want.

Again, the best way to select software is to read computer magazines, look at software manufacturers' printed materials, talk to users, and try out several kinds at a software store.

Desktop Publishing Fonts

One of the things that makes desktop publishing powerful is access to so many fonts, weights, and sizes. Working with *scalable* fonts that you can make any size you want (not just the standard 10 point, 12 point, 14 point, and so on), is especially convenient.

Desktop Publishing Terms

Application: Software program that performs a particular kind of task, such as word processing, page layout, accounting, illustration, database retrieval, and so on.

Backup: To make a copy of your work for protection in case the original is accidentally changed or lost.

Bit: Stands for **bi**nary digi**t**, the smallest unit of digital information, represented electronically as either 1 (on) or 0 (off).

Bit-map: The screen is divided into a grid ("map") of tiny white or black squares ("bits"). Characters or images that are stored as a pattern of squares are "bit-mapped."

Byte: Unit of digital information (set of 8 consecutive bits). Memory and disk capacity are measured in thousands (K) of bytes. One byte is roughly equivalent to one character of text. If a piece has 2000 characters, it needs about 2K (kilobytes) of storage.

Clip art: Copyright-free art that can be used and modified by anyone without permission. Comes both on disk and in books.

Desktop publishing: The integration of text and graphics on a computer.

Desktop publishing system: The hardware required to do desktop publishing.

Disk: Storage medium for programs and files, either "hard" (usually not removable) or "floppy" (removable).

Disk drive: A device that holds a disk, gets information from it, and saves information on it.

Display: Screen. A Color display is a screen with color.

Document: Whatever piece you create on the computer.

Documentation: The printed material that explains how to use a particular program or piece of hardware.

Dot-matrix printer: A low resolution (and relatively inexpensive) printer that prints out computer-generated information and images.

Download: Moving information from one place to another, often from one computer to another over an electronic network.

Downloadable font: A set of instructions defining a family of letters (a font) that is stored in a computer and sent (downloaded) to an output device (such as a laser printer) for printing.

dpi: Dots per inch. The more dpi, the sharper the image (also described as having a *higher resolution*).

Floppy disk: Removable storage medium with low-to-medium capacity (generally about one MB [megabyte] per disk).

Font: A complete set of characters in a particular typeface.

Hard copy: The paper version of what's been generated on a computer.

Hard disk: Storage medium (usually fixed) with medium-to-high storage capabilities (often from 10 to 100 or more MB [megabytes] per hard disk).

Hardware: The physical components of a computer system, such as a computer, monitor, disk drive, and printer.

Icons: Symbols on a computer screen.

Interface: Compatibility between computer software and hardware; also software that transfers data from one piece of equipment to another.

K: Kilobyte (1024 bytes). Common measure of memory capacity (a double-spaced typewritten page uses about 1.5 K).

Laser printer: A high resolution printer that prints out computer-generated type (near-typeset quality) and graphics.

Desktop Publishing Terms

70

LPI: Refers to the resolution of halftones. LPI is the number of lines of dots per inch. The more lines per inch, the higher the resolution (the sharper the image).

Megabyte (MB): Unit of measure of computer memory, equal to 1024 kilobytes or roughly one million bytes.

Memory: The place where information is stored in the computer. Memory is measured in thousands (K) of bytes.

Menu: The lists of options on a computer screen.

Modem: Device enabling communication between computers over telephone lines.

Monitor: Display screen.

Mouse: Pointing device that sits next to the keyboard. It enables you to manipulate what is on the computer screen.

Online: When the connection between one computer and another in a network is "on."

Operating system: The program that enables you to run the computer.

PCL (printer command language): The commands for operating printers.

PDL (page description language): A program such as Adobe's PostScript® or Xerox's Interpress® that tells printers what to do.

Pixel: Short for "picture element," a pixel is the smallest graphic dot on a computer screen.

PostScript®: A computer language that describes letter forms and graphics for laser printers and other output devices.

Program: The coding that tells the computer what to do. Often used interchangeably with the words "software" or "application."

RAM (random access memory): The amount of memory in a computer (measured in K—thousands of bytes), or memory that stores information temporarily while you're working on it.

Resident font: A font that is permanently stored in a laser printer.

Resolution: The level of refinement of an image, depending on how many dots there are per inch (dpi). High resolution has more dots per inch and is a better reproduction; low resolution has fewer dots per inch and has rougher edges.

ROM (read only memory): Programs or instructions that are permanently stored or "hard wired" in a computer.

Save: To store information on a disk.

Scanner: An imaging device that enables you to convert line art, photographs, or text from paper into electronic form so that they can be used in a computer.

Service bureau: A center or shop that has computers, printers, and other desktop publishing-related equipment that you can use for a fee. Some service bureaus also offer instruction and expert help.

Software: Any program that tells the computer what to do.

Template: A pre-designed pattern or grid for printed pieces such as newsletters, brochures, and manuals.

Toner: "Ink" for a laser printer (fine plastic particles).

Windows: In some programs, sections of the screen (sometimes overlapping) that enable you to work with multiple applications at once.

WYSIWYG (Pronounced wizzy-wig): Stands for "what you see is what you get." Refers to whether or not what you see on the computer screen is the same as what you will see on the hard (printed) copy.

With the advent of laser printers the computer font market has exploded. There are thousands of fonts available from a wide variety of vendors—Adobe Systems, Hewlett-Packard, VS Software, and Bitstream Inc., to name a few. You can also buy font-editing programs that enable you to customize your own fonts. The quality of fonts varies greatly, so check them out carefully. Look at sizes and ask about other limitations. Fonts use a lot of disk space, so be sure you have the capacity to store the number you want.

Another important issue: If you want to see the type on your computer screen that corresponds to what comes out of the printer, the fonts on your screen and the ones in the printer you intend to use *have to match*. Each font consists of a *screen font* and a *printer font*. Laser printers come with a certain number of fonts already in them. You can buy additional "downloadable" fonts (such as the ones from Adobe and Bitstream), and install them in your computer. If you use a printer at a service center, shop personnel will sometimes give you corresponding fonts for your computer.

Go For It

If you are already producing your printed pieces on a computer, update yourself when you can find the time. If desktop publishing is new to you, I urge you to explore it. The only way to be an expert is to be a beginner first. Don't get intimidated or overwhelmed if others are ahead of you. There will always be people who know more, and more who know less.

Desktop publishing is still in its infancy; exciting possibilities lie ahead. Greater capabilities and improvements in both hardware and software are coming rapidly.

And in spite of all the myths and misconceptions about desktop publishing, it is likely to save you time, money, and headaches in the long run.

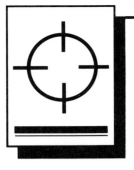

Chapter 23

Preparation for Printing

Preparing your printed piece for reproduction is making it *camera-ready*; what you give to the printer to produce it from is called *camera-ready art.* A printed piece is camera-ready when all its parts (except halftones) are placed precisely in position, as they are to finally appear. It is then ready to go before the camera—hence the name.

If you produce your printed piece on a computer, the pages may be camera-ready when they come out of the printer. If you prepare your piece in the traditional way, all the parts—type, line art, rules, so on— are drawn or pasted up on *art boards.* They are also called *illustration boards*—thick rigid cardboard that is usually white on one side. They can be purchased at art supply stores.

Sometimes jobs that have been desktop-published and laser-printed are also placed on boards. This enables you to indicate accurate placement of the image on the final sheets (laser-printed images don't always come out with the margins exactly where you want them). Camera-ready art should be covered with a protective flap or put in a folder to keep it clean. Putting the work on art boards may also make it easier for press people to work with, and for you to store after it is printed.

By the time your printed piece is ready for final preparation, you should already have cost estimates (Sidebar 17), type set (page 201), and a printer selected (page 325). At this point there are five steps remaining in the production process. You'll need to:

- Discuss camera-ready preparation with the printer

- Prepare the camera-ready boards (if necessary)

- Take the boards to the printer and go over the job together

- Check bluelines and color separations (when relevant)

- Do a press check (if appropriate)

Preparing camera-ready art in the traditional way is a highly meticulous job. Every measurement must be precise. All the type and every line must be perfectly straight. Line (solid) illustrations must be in their exact positions. Photographs have to be cropped and marked with a number corresponding to their exact location on the board. The boards must be neat and perfectly clean. And whether your camera-ready art is prepared in the traditional way or comes straight out of a printer, it is always wise to accompany it with detailed written instructions.

Paste-up is the process of gluing or waxing all elements into position on the art boards. This step is skipped in desktop publishing because all parts can be placed in position on the computer screen.

You may be producing your printed piece in the traditional way and need paste-up. If you don't have paste up skills, you can save yourself a lot of grief by hiring someone who does. This precise work requires manual dexterity, patience, and preferably, experience. Sometimes it can be done at the print shop, or the printer may be able to recommend a freelancer to do it for you.

It is important to discuss the camera-ready preparation with your printer *before* you begin. Most printers prefer to receive the pages or boards prepared in a particular way. And this discussion can also save you enormous amounts of time and effort. Color separations are often done with the camera, for example, rather than on separate overlay sheets by hand. Printers may also be able to show you some valuable shortcuts. They can save you from making mistakes that are expensive or time-consuming to fix.

Here are some of the questions to ask your printer or printer's representative (rep) regarding your camera-ready preparations:

- How would you like this job made camera-ready?

- Do you have some examples I can look at?

- How should I handle color separations?

- Any special way you'd like the photographs handled?

- The illustrations?

- How would you like folds indicated?

- Is a gripper edge required?

- Do you have other suggestions for preparing the camera-ready art?

It is a good idea to make up a *dummy* (a three-dimensional model) of your printed piece before you take the job to the printer. This enables you to discuss your job in detail with a sample both of you can look at. Be sure to leave the dummy with the printer along with the camera-ready art. Questions that come up during the printing are often answered with a quick glance at a dummy.

Traditional Paste-Up

You may decide to prepare the camera-ready boards yourself in the traditional way. If so, here's how to do it. Start by pulling together the basic materials you will need to work with. They are available at any art supply store.

Basic Materials

This list covers the most basic supplies you will need to do paste-up. Although there are other products designed to make paste-up more convenient, you don't really need them.

Art boards. Described on previous page.

T-square, drawing board, and angle, or C-Thru® ruler. Some device is needed for getting things straight. A C-Thru® ruler is clear plastic with a grid pattern on it. It makes paste up easier because you can see through the ruler to check alignments.

Rubber cement or waxer. You need something to stick the parts of your printed piece (such as type and art) on to the board. Waxed elements can be lifted and repositioned repeatedly. You have only a few seconds to reposition rubber-cemented pieces, but you can do it if you work fast. After the glue sets, rubber-cemented elements can only be lifted with solvent (rubber cement is the kind of glue used for paste-up).

This brochure is camera-ready. Note the fold and trim lines, the register marks for the screen overlay, and the color and paper samples below it. The brochure outline and panel divider lines are drawn with non-photo blue pencil.

Scissors and/or a knife. Scissors or an X-acto® knife are essential. A paper cutter is also very useful. It's worth getting one if you do a lot of paste-up.

Paper or acetate. You need paper or acetate for overlays and cover flaps.

Non-photo blue pencil. The printer's camera will not "see" non-photo blue pencil marks, so you can write directly on the type, art, or boards with them.

Rubylith or Autopaque. Rubylith, Autopaque, or the equivalent are commonly used for making *windows* which show the exact size and location of halftones (photographs or other multi-toned images).

Camera-Ready Elements

Next, gather together all of the elements that go into your printed piece. They may include:

- Any and all type, including rub-on type if you're using it
- Photographs
- Art: original illustrations, graphic devices, and/or clip art
- Maps, charts, graphs, or any other diagrams
- Logos, seals, signatures, or other customized graphic elements

Register marks placed on camera-ready art guide cropping and assure accuracy on overlays. They come on tape, as rub-ons, or you can make your own.

Doing the Paste-Up

Finally, here's what to do to prepare the camera-ready art. The order in which you do things is not critical.

Be certain the type is correct

Before you paste down the type, make sure that it has been approved, and that it has been proofread (at least once) by someone other than the writer.

Prepare the boards

Draw the correct size pages on the art boards in non-photo blue pencil, and place crop (cut) marks out to the sides of the sheet if necessary. If your piece is to be printed on larger sheets and trimmed to size after printing, the printer will follow these crop marks. If the piece is printed on the same-sized paper, the crop marks show the position of the image relative to the edges of the paper.

Put in windows

Define halftone or screen tint areas (the windows) in one of two ways: 1. By placing Autopaque or another self-adhesive material on the art boards, or Rubylith (an overlay material usually cut out with a knife) on acetate overlays, or 2. Put in a *keyline* (a box in black ink) to show where they go. Either way they must be perfectly measured and positioned on the board. If you do a keyline, the printer makes the windows. This is more accurate but usually costs a bit more. It is better to have the printer put in screens, but you must mark their positions and percentages precisely.

Put in graphic elements

Put in any lines, frames, solid graphic designs, or boxes that are to appear on the finished piece (use

black ink). Make sure you differentiate between a frame around an illustration or photograph (which is to print) and a keyline. If it is a keyline, write on the board *Keyline only. Do not print.*

Lay out the pieces

Cut around all of the elements to be placed (except photographs or illustrations which will be halftoned). Lay them out where they go on the boards *before you stick anything down to see if everything fits.*

Stick the pieces down

Firmly attach every piece of type exactly in position. Be sure it's straight. Burnish it down so all edges adhere to the board.

One easy way to align it precisely is to draw a straight line under the first line of type in a column using a non-photo blue pencil. Then draw another line on the board exactly where the type is to sit. Cut the right and left edges off the type unit so that you can lay it directly on the board. Align it with your blue guidelines underneath.

If you are using rubber cement, here is a good way to get it on the pieces. Take an old magazine, and put the piece to be glued—face down—on a clean page. Go around all four edges with the rubber cement applicator brush, and glue the piece in position (giving yourself some blue guidelines might help). Then turn to a fresh page in the magazine and repeat the process with the next piece to be glued. Turn to a clean page for each piece you glue.

*Below is a photograph of the
two-page spread you are currently looking at.
It was desktop-published and printed out on a Linotronic®
Imagesetter, after which it was camera-ready (ready to go to the printer).*

Section 6: Production and Distribution

Register marks placed on camera-ready art guide cropping and assure accuracy on overlays. They come on tape, as rub-ons, or you can make your own.

Doing the Paste-Up

Finally, here's what to do to prepare the camera-ready art. The order in which you do things is not critical.

Be certain the type is correct

Before you paste down the type, make sure that it has been approved, and that it has been proofread (at least once) by someone other than the writer.

Prepare the boards

Draw the correct size pages on the art boards in non-photo blue pencil, and place crop (cut) marks out to the sides of the sheet if necessary. If your piece is to be printed on larger sheets and trimmed to size after printing, the printer will follow these crop marks. If the piece is printed on the same-sized paper, the crop marks show the position of the image relative to the edges of the paper.

Put in windows

Define halftone or screen tint areas (the windows) in one of two ways: 1. By placing Autopaque or another self-adhesive material on the art boards, or Rubylith (an overlay material usually cut out with a knife) on acetate overlays, or 2. Put in a *keyline* (a box in black ink) to show where they go. Either way they must be perfectly measured and positioned on the board. If you do a keyline, the printer makes the windows. This is more accurate but usually costs a bit more. It is better to have the printer put in screens, but you must mark their positions and percentages precisely.

Put in graphic elements

Put in any lines, frames, solid graphic designs, or boxes that are to appear on the finished piece (use

310

black ink). Make sure you differentiate between a frame around an illustration or photograph (which is to print) and a keyline. If it is a keyline, write on the board *Keyline only. Do not print.*

Lay out the pieces

Cut around all of the elements to be placed (except photographs or illustrations which will be halftoned). Lay them out where they go on the boards *before you stick anything down to see if everything fits.*

Stick the pieces down

Firmly attach every piece of type exactly in position. Be sure it's straight. Burnish it down so all edges adhere to the board.

One easy way to align it precisely is to draw a straight line under the first line of type in a column using a non-photo blue pencil. Then draw another line on the board exactly where the type is to sit. Cut the right and left edges off the type unit so that you can lay it directly on the board. Align it with your blue guidelines underneath.

If you are using rubber cement, here is a good way to get it on the pieces. Take an old magazine, and put the piece to be glued—face down—on a clean page. Go around all four edges with the rubber cement applicator brush, and glue the piece in position (giving yourself some blue guidelines might help). Then turn to a fresh page in the magazine and repeat the process with the next piece to be glued. Turn to a clean page for each piece you glue.

Below is a photograph of the two-page spread you are currently looking at. It was desktop-published and printed out on a Linotronic® Imagesetter, after which it was camera-ready (ready to go to the printer).

reduced art goes here

Final Stages: DTP and Traditional

Whether you are preparing your camera-ready art on a computer or pasting it up by hand, the steps are pretty much the same from this point on. A bold **DTP** indicates preparation for desktop published sheets; a bold **T** applies to traditional paste-up. If neither appears, information applies to both.

Put in line art and other elements

T: Get line art (solid art as opposed to halftoned, or multi-toned) enlarged or reduced to the size needed. Burnish it down in position just as you do the type.

DTP: By this point let's assume you've got your text laid out in a desktop publishing program. (How to do that is the subject of many books and software manuals, so I won't repeat it here.) Now draw in any remaining boxes, rules, or other graphic devices, and import any line art you plan to use from other programs or a scanner. Size and place the art.

Check for straightness and alignment

Make certain all elements are straight both horizontally and vertically, and that everything that is supposed to line up does so. Headline type, for example, may need to align with a column or a line beneath it;

311

Final Stages: DTP and Traditional

Whether you are preparing your camera-ready art on a computer or pasting it up by hand, the steps are pretty much the same from this point on. A bold **DTP** indicates preparation for desktop published sheets; a bold **T** applies to traditional paste-up. If neither appears, information applies to both.

Put in line art and other elements

T: Get line art (solid art as opposed to halftoned, or multi-toned) enlarged or reduced to the size needed. Burnish it down in position just as you do the type.

DTP: By this point let's assume you've got your text laid out in a desktop publishing program. (How to do that is the subject of many books and software manuals, so I won't repeat it here.) Now draw in any remaining boxes, rules, or other graphic devices, and import any line art you plan to use from other programs or a scanner. Size and place the art.

Check for straightness and alignment

Make certain all elements are straight both horizontally and vertically, and that everything that is supposed to line up does so. Headline type, for example, may need to align with a column or a line beneath it;

Linotronic® is a registered trademark of Linotype A.G. and/or its subsidiaries.

311

The pieces below are examples of line art— art that the desktop publisher or the paste-up person can put in place before handing the job over to the printer.

captions may need to align with photographs or illustrations; columns of type or bullets or numbers should also be straight.

T: Use an angle and a T-square or C-thru® ruler.

DTP: Put your page in the most enlarged version possible. Use the guides to check alignment.

Check the sequence

Read through your piece carefully to make sure all type is in the right position. Pay special attention to areas where you may have cut between lines or paragraphs, and from one page to the next.

Check the content

Check to see that page numbers, running heads, titles, and captions are accurate and placed correctly. Make sure chapter divisions and all other pages are where they should be.

Crop photographs

Cropping is indicating the section of a photograph you want to appear in your piece. Draw crop marks on the margins (not on the photograph itself), or on a copy of it, or cover it with tracing paper and mark the desired

*The illustrations in these pieces will be halftoned,
so the printer places them in position. The person preparing
the camera-ready art indicates their precise location with windows.*

area. If you want the image to face in the opposite direction, write *Flop* in the margin.

Photographs must be cropped proportionally to fit into the space indicated for them on the camera-ready art board. Various gadgets for scaling photographs—on a diagonal or by percentage—can be bought at art supply shops, and come with instructions.

Key photographs to boards

Number photos in the margin, on the back, or on *peel-off* stickers or tape. Key them to their correct location on the camera-ready art.

Package illustrations and photographs

Stack all marked illustrations and photographs neatly, put them in an envelope, and identify the contents clearly on the front. Put the name of the piece on it along with your own name and telephone number.

Identify areas of color

Spot color (color in specified areas) is usually indicated in one of two ways. The work on the camera-ready board (or first sheet) is usually the one printed in black (although it could be any color). Each addi-

Here is the cover of this book, ready for printing.
Ink colors are indicated to the printer on the upper left.

tional color is separated on to its own overlay sheet. The colors must register precisely when placed on top of the camera-ready board or first sheet.

Alternatively, the printer does the color separations. You simply mark where the areas of color go on a tissue (tracing paper) that covers the board. If you're using a computer to make color separations, check with your program manual (each program has its own version) and discuss your plans with your printer.

Indicate color placement

Clearly show where the colors go (inks are covered in the *Color That Works*, page 221). Write the correct

colors and their numbers on the board as well. For example, you might write: INKS—Pink: 212. Turquoise: 307. Brown: 4625.

Indicate the gripper edge

Ask the printer if you need a gripper edge (an ink-free margin on your printed piece that can be gripped by the printing press), and if so, how large it should be. You don't need a gripper edge when it is to be printed on an over-sized sheet that will be trimmed (cut) to its final size after printing. If you do need one (such as for a letterhead), indicate the edge you planned for the printing press to grip.

Camera-Ready Checklist · 71

It is important to check over camera-ready boards very carefully. Mistakes after this point are expensive. This checklist will help you make sure you haven't missed anything.

☐ Nothing is missing

☐ There is nothing extra

☐ Instructions are accurate and specific

☐ Illustrations to be made into halftones and photographs are organized

☐ They are keyed to the right spots

☐ The boards or pages are covered with a protective flap or folder

☐ The name of the job, your name, and your phone number are on all pieces

☐ The camera-ready art is accompanied by the instruction and production sheets

☐ The dummy is also included (if you have one)

☐ The delivery address is given

A worksheet version of this sidebar is on page 364.

Write clear instructions

Good *written* instructions are extremely important. To insure that all goes well at the print shop, directions should be spelled out as clearly and in as much detail as possible. Keep a copy of your instructions and the print production sheet in your files. It will come in handy should a dispute arise later over what was or was not communicated. This kind of information is also valuable to have when you do your next job, or when you want information later on this one.

Write your notes carefully and neatly on the camera-ready boards or attach them to your computer-generated pages. Accompany them with the typed letter that goes over the printing instructions in detail. Include a print production sheet (page 316).

Mention any special instructions you have (for example, you might want one third of the order to be 3-hole punched, two-thirds not). State the agreed-upon delivery date, locations, and the names and phone numbers of people who will receive the order. Some part of it may be shipped to the office, for instance, another part to a mailing house, and a third part to storage.

Write out where you can be reached for blueline and press checks or in case of an emergency. Be sure to include the billing name and address if it is different from your own.

Check over boards or pages carefully

When it comes to preparing camera-ready art, *you can't be too careful.* It is better to err on the side of repeating yourself too much than to leave something out.

Mistakes at this point are relatively inexpensive to correct. Changes on camera-ready art after it goes to the printer are much more costly, and even the most experienced and highly skilled people can make mistakes. If someone else has done the paste-up, you

P. O. Box 208
Palo Alto, CA 94302-0208
(415) 322-2855

September 1990

TO: Printer
FROM: Helen O'Donnell
RE: Printing instructions for *PRINT THAT WORKS*

GENERAL INSTRUCTIONS:

```
Trim Size:       8-1/2 x 11"
Page Count:      416 pages
Gutter Margin:   3/4"
Head Margin:     3/8" to top of running head
Paper:           60# Finch Opaque
Text Ink:        Black
Cover Stock:     12 pt Carolina C1S
Cover Ink:       4 PMS colors; covers to be film laminated
                 Black and PMS 286 (blue), PMS 116 (yellow),
                 PMS 032 (red)
```

Text prints a very rich black. We are looking for a very high
contrast.

Shoot halftones at percentages indicated using 133 line screens.

Part Openers (see pages listed below) 1/4" black rule bleeds to
outside edge and bottom of page.

80 pages with sidebars bleed to outside of page (see sidebar table
of contents for page numbers).

PAGING INSTRUCTIONS:

PAGE
i-xii   Front matter (all pages have blind folios)

i	Title page	vi-viii	Sidebar Table of Contents
ii	Copyright page	ix	Thank you
iii	Dedication	x	blank
iv	blank	xi	Preface
v	Table of Contents	xii	blank

PAGE		**PAGE**	
1	Part 1 (blind folio)	279	Part 6 (blind folio)
2	blank	280	blank
3-13	text	281-303	text
14	blank	304-305	text bleeds into gutter
15-24	text	306-344	text
25	Part 2 (blind folio)	345	Part 7 (blind folio)
26	blank	346	blank
27-68	text	347-366	worksheets
69	Part 3 (blind folio)	367-368	resources
70	blank	369-380	glossary
71-114	text	381-388	photo/illustration credits
115	Part 4 (blind folio)	389-402	index
116	blank	403	order form
117-170	text	404	blank
171	Part 5 (blind folio)	------	
172	blank	416	total pages

*It's a good idea to write out updated instructions
for the printer just before the job goes to press (instructions
for this book are at left). Then go over each page carefully. Below
is page 268 before it was checked (the right column is one line too short).*

standings can be prevented when you discuss the job thoroughly, and in person. Call ahead to arrange a time to meet with the printer. Don't forget to bring a dummy if you have one, and leave it with the rest of the materials.

Ownership

There are standard trade customs in the printing business. The camera-ready art—pages or boards—is yours, and should be returned to you after the job is printed.

The negatives and plates from your job generally are considered to belong to the printing company unless you have an agreement to the contrary. They are usually stored at the print shop for up to three years, although the length of time often varies from printer to printer. (Check with yours to find out what the policy is.) Your printed piece can be reproduced only with your permission.

There are advantages of staying with the same printer. He or she already is familiar with your job, and having been through it before, should be able to do it better. And you know that the shop has the right equipment to handle the original negatives. The disadvantage of staying with the same printer is that he or she may take you for granted. You could be overcharged for reprinting, or you could receive less than a top-notch job.

If you think you're going to want the film yourself, negotiate this in advance and be prepared to pay for it. It's best to discuss it at the time of the original quote. Be sure to spell out the details of your agreement in the purchase order.

Storing Your Camera-Ready Art

You may want to reproduce your printed piece again. If you keep your camera-ready art, you can easily make changes for an updated version.

go over it carefully too. Check over each board with an eagle eye—several pairs of eagle eyes if possible. Make sure that every element is in the right spot, and that no piece is missing. Check to see that there is nothing extra. Go over the instructions to be sure they are clear, specific, and accurate.

Photographs and illustrations to be made into halftones should be organized and keyed to the right spots on the boards. Cover the boards with a protective flap or put the pages in a folder, and write the name of the job, your name and phone number on all pieces. You can use the checklist in Sidebar 71 when you check over your camera-ready art.

Plan on spending some time with the printer (or sales rep) going over your job together. Misunder-

When the boards or pages are returned to you, wrap them well to keep them clean, and label and date them. It is best to store them flat, in a dust-free environment away from heat (it may melt the wax).

And by the way, don't leave boards that have been waxed in a hot car. On more than one occasion camera-ready work headed for printing has gone back to the drawing board because pieces have melted or popped off the boards.

Camera-ready art can mount up faster than you think, so develop a system for keeping track of it. If the printer forgets to return it to you, follow up and get it back as soon as possible. If you wait you may easily forget about it yourself, or it may get messed up or misplaced at the print shop. You can forget about it after it's safely stored away.

Chapter 24

Printing

By the time your printed piece is ready to be printed, it has already been through many stages. Its goals have been defined, its audience identified, and its concept developed. The piece has been written, proofread, designed, checked, made camera-ready, and checked again. Each of these stages represents time, energy, attention, and hard work, and often reflects the effort of several people. If your piece is going to be worth this kind of investment, it is important to keep up the vigilance throughout printing.

This chapter will help you see the production of your printed piece successfully through to the end. We'll look at the business of printing, different methods of reproduction for your piece, and when to use them. We'll also discuss selecting and working with printers, and how to handle bluelines and press checks. Your rights and responsibilities throughout the printing stage will be described, and we'll end with reminders and tips for getting the best printing job possible.

The Printing Business

If you are buying printing, it is helpful to know something about the nature of the business you're dealing with. The printing industry in America is one of the largest, involving billions of dollars and employing large numbers of people. Printing is a fast-paced, high-pressure business. Printers compete for clients in a crowded market while contending with the daily hassles and headaches of a highly technical trade.

Printers must keep up with rapid and continuous technological change on the one hand, and customer demands for greater speed, price-savings, and quality on the other. And although the printer's task is to mass-produce publications in large quantities, every job that comes in the door is unique. Each customer's printed piece is a custom order for paper, inks, and binding, and so requires special attention.

Just as you rely on the printer to do a good job with your piece, your printer relies on other people to get it successfully through a complicated series of steps. For things to go right, employees have to carry out their work correctly and in the right sequence, paper and other supplies have to arrive on time, and sensitive equipment has to work properly.

Printers operate on tight, carefully-coordinated schedules. They handle many jobs simultaneously, each of which is at a different stage of production at any given time. They rely on their customers to get the work in on time; late arrivals or rush jobs can and do throw schedules out of kilter. Bad weather can keep the ink from drying which can cause back-ups;

*Bright-colored stickers come in a wide
range of subjects and shapes. They can add
interest to a small quantity of photocopied or printed materials.*

so do jobs that turn out to be more complicated than expected.

When you add up all the situations in which things can go wrong—custom jobs, multiple steps, simultaneous projects, and rapidly changing and complex technology, not to mention human frailties—it's easy to see why printing is a difficult business. It's hard to imagine one that is more detailed or complex. One printer summed it up well when he said, "There are a thousand ways to do it wrong, and only one way to do it right."

Because there are so many possibilities for problems and so many of them are beyond your control, choose your printer *very carefully*. Good communication with a printer is your best assurance for ending up with the kind of printing job you want.

Reproduction Alternatives

There are four commonly-used methods of reproduction: photocopying, quick or instant printing, offset printing, and silkscreening. Each of these methods can be the best one. It's a matter of matching the capabilities of the method to your needs and the requirements of the piece. Here are some of the major strengths and limitations of these alternative reproduction methods.

Photocopiers

Photocopying is a quick, easy, and relatively inexpensive method of reproduction. There are times when reproducing your piece on a Kodak, Canon, Xerox, or other copier makes the most sense. The capabilities of these machines have improved dramatically in recent years, making it possible to get surprisingly good results.

Different copiers offer different features. There are copiers that can enlarge and reduce, some that staple (from one to three staples per piece), some that put on front and back covers, and some that glue pages together. Some copiers collate. As collating is an added step in offset printing, this photocopier capability could save you time. There are photocopiers that can produce up to 10,000 copies from one original, and there are some that perform multiple tasks. Ask shop personnel to direct you to the machine that is most suitable for your job.

Photocopiers also have some obvious limitations. Size is usually restricted to 8-1/2" x 11" or 11" x 17", although there are oversized copiers that use rolls of paper three feet wide by just about any length you want. Most "print" only in black. Copiers do not reproduce photographs well and aren't particularly good with bleeds and reverses.

But say you're on a very tight budget, or perhaps you need only a small quantity of a flyer, invitation, data sheet, announcement, or other such piece. If you *design it with the copier's capabilities in mind*, you can produce some very satisfying results. Especially when you think creatively.

Copy shops have several papers to choose from in a variety of colors, weights, and textures. When you design your piece, keep in mind that your "ink" will be black, and select a paper that goes well with it. White, bright, or deep colors tend to look better with black than pastels. You may want to choose the paper before you begin design.

There are several ways you can add color and interest to a small quantity of printed pieces. If you can find an appropriate image, again you can use stickers. Place them in a key position as an illustration, or use them to close the piece. Stickers come in a wide variety of designs and shapes such as stars, circles, hearts, cars, stop signs, sports equipment, flowers, balloons, holiday motifs, and even pottery. They are available at stationery stores and gift shops (including museum gift shops). Stickers are considerably less expensive when you buy them by the roll. It is also possible to have them custom made (in an image such as your logo, for example). Call an advertising specialty company (see pages 84–85) for costs.

Or attach a blue ribbon and gold seal or penny to your piece, or add a spot of glue and glitter—whatever is appropriate to your topic. Use your imagination. This handwork can be done painlessly at lunch time in the conference room or in an evening in front of the TV. A little something extra can really make a difference. It helps your piece get attention, gives it distinction, and makes it memorable.

Color copying is also much improved recently on such copiers as the Canon Color Laser. The quality of the color is better, and can be adjusted by the copier operator. Images can be cropped, and spot color can be added to black and white originals. These machines can make prints from positive color images as well as from negatives and slides.

Some copiers can be connected to computers, tying them in directly with the production of the material.

If you want an enlargement of a brochure, newsletter, cover, report or similar piece for a sales meeting, conference, or other occasion, color copying may be the solution. These copiers have the ability to enlarge images as much as 400%. You can also get color pieces reduced. This is a handy way to prepare printed pieces for a presentation or a portfolio.

Because the capabilities of color copiers are relatively new, their potential for the printed piece has not yet been fully explored. There is lots of room for imaginative use. Experiment.

Quick Printing

A step up from photocopying is quick or instant printing. The kinds of pieces reproduced at quick print shops include business cards, envelopes, letterheads, announcements, forms, flyers, invitations, price lists, note pads, and simple brochures. Quick printers use offset presses, but they make the plates (the press master upon which the image is etched) directly from your original, thus eliminating the time and expense of camera work. This makes them considerably less expensive and faster than regular offset printing shops, but it also means that your camera-ready art must be perfect. There are no intermediary check or correction points between when you hand it over and the final product.

There are, of course, other limitations. The majority of pieces that come from a quick print shop are black. You can also specify a color, but it is usually limited to one (ask about the additional cost for color). Some quick print shops have *color days* during which you can get a color other than black at little or no extra charge. For example Mondays might be blue, Tuesdays red, Wednesdays green, and so on.

The maximum size is usually 11" x 17" and paper selection is limited compared with what is available through a regular printing shop. Photographs are not usually handled by quick printers. If they are, you often must get them screened (converted to halftone dots) yourself.

Since the services of a quick print shop do not include improvements or corrections to your camera-ready boards (described in *Preparation For Printing*, page 307), you are more likely to be satisfied with the results if you keep the design simple and clean. Also it is not possible (or not advisable) to use special effects such as large areas of solid ink, *reverses* (ink in the background, image in the paper color), or *bleeds* (ink to the edge of the paper). But again, if you take the strengths and limits of the shop into account from the beginning, you can come out with a very effective printed piece.

Some quick printers can handle quantities upwards of 50,000, but most do much smaller runs. Jobs usually take two to three days, depending on what's involved and how busy the shop is. Leave yourself as much time as possible to get your piece printed. Unexpected surprises can and do turn up.

Printing Terms

Blanket: A rubber coated fabric clamped to the cylinder of a printing press. It transfers the inked image from the the plate to the paper.

Bleed: Ink that goes to the edge of the page.

Blueline: Printer's proofs (made from negatives shot from your camera-ready boards) to be checked before a piece is printed. Bluelines (also called brownlines, silverprints, and Van Dyke prints) show text, position, cropping, size, and folds.

Camera-ready art: The final piece as assembled by the designer, paste-up person, or desktop publisher, so that it is ready to go to the printer. Every element must be precisely in place, perfectly clean, and ready to be photographed. Overlays for different colors or instructions may also be attached. Also called a *mechanical.*

Comp: A layout or drawing that shows as closely as possible what the finished piece will look like when printed.

Crop marks: Lines indicating where a photograph or illustration should be cut to eliminate parts of it and so it fits into a particular size and shape.

Color separations: The separate sheets upon which each individual color is indicated.

Dummy: A mock-up or model of what the final printed piece is to look like. Photographs are sketched in (or copied or glued in); type is either *greeked* (made up of meaningless characters) to show where it goes, or a copy of the final type is used.

Grippers: The clamps in a printing press that control the flow of paper through it. Some jobs require a *gripper edge*—a margin in which no ink can be printed.

Halftone: A photograph or art (with gradually changing shades) which has been converted into solid dots. Converting a photograph or continuous tone image into a halftone enables it to be printed to look like the original.

Line art: Solid art with no range of tones. Less expensive to reproduce than halftones.

Overlay: A transparent or tissue sheet covering the camera-ready art board showing color breaks, instructions, or corrections.

Overrun: Extra pieces printed in addition to the specified quantity.

Plate: A thin sheet of metal on a printing press that transfers the image to the paper. The surface is treated so that only the part that is to print receives the ink. Quick printing shops often use disposable paper plates.

Proof: A preliminary sample by which work to be printed is checked.

Reverse: Usually type or an image is printed in dark on light (positive on negative). When they are *reversed*, the type or image appears in white (or a light color) on a dark background (negative on positive).

Signature: A group of pages printed together on a large sheet.

Trim marks: Marks on the camera-ready art which show where the piece is to be cut.

Offset Printing

The majority of substantive printed materials are reproduced on commercial offset printing presses. These are capable of the highest-quality work and can produce stunning results. Any of the kinds of pieces already mentioned for photocopying or quick printing can also be printed at a regular printing company, as well as every other kind of printed matter including booklets, annual reports, posters, catalogs, newsletters, presentation folders, and menus.

Offset presses are highly sophisticated machines and have multiple capabilities. They can produce both simple and complex jobs equally well. If your piece includes black and white photographs or other halftone work, you probably need a regular commercial offset printer to do the job.

Other capabilities of standard offset presses include color reproduction, both spot-color (page 222) and full color (four-color process, page 223). Offset presses can run one color at a time or several, and some can print two sides at once. They have the ability to lay down large flawless areas of ink; they can print bleed edges and reverses. Registration can be precisely controlled. You can also get pieces produced in odd sizes, and you'll have the widest selection of inks and paper colors, weights, and textures.

Two common kinds of offset presses are *sheet-fed* and *web*. Sheet-fed presses run individual sheets of paper through the press. The kinds of pieces covered in this book are mainly printed on sheet-fed presses. Web presses use rolls of paper, and are used for newspapers, magazines, and other pieces that are produced at high speeds in very large quantities.

Traditional offset printing includes three distinct phases: 1. Pre-press work involving camera and film, 2. Printing, and 3. Binding. Being familiar with these steps and what's involved in each of them enables you to do a better job preparing the boards. It also helps you to communicate more effectively with the printer,

and helps to insure that you are not taken advantage of. Here are the three phases your printed piece will go through at a regular offset print shop:

1. Pre-press work

The goal of pre-press work is to get the image from your camera-ready board onto the plate accurately. Pre-press efforts are demanding and precision is essential. A plate is the master image-carrier that goes on the printing press. This is done photo-mechanically by exposing a negative of your board to the light-sensitive plate (the negative image creates the area that won't print).

Several people may work on your piece at this stage. Large printing companies have separate pre-press departments with highly-skilled experts who handle different parts of the job. There are those who do the camera work, which includes converting photographs and illustrations to halftones and making film negatives from your camera-ready boards. *Strippers* place or *strip* the negatives into precise position on the *film flats*. You will be asked to check the proofs—often called *bluelines*—at the end of this phase of the process (more on bluelines later). *Platemakers* etch the plates from the film flats.

2. Printing

The term *offset* comes from the way the image is set on the paper in the printing press. It is transferred from the plate to a rubber cylinder (or blanket) which then *offsets* the image on to the paper. There are many books available that go into printing in detail if you are interested in learning more about the technical aspects.

During the printing phase, the *pressman* is the person in charge. This person operates, regulates, and adjusts the printing press. You may be called in to check proofs on the press at this stage.

3. Binding

In this last phase of the process, your printed piece undergoes finishing and binding work. This is done either at the printing plant (if all the work is done in-house) or it is subcontracted out to another shop. During this stage, flat sheets are made up into booklets, directories, catalogs, manuals, programs, and so on, and newsletters, brochures, menus, and such are folded. Binding and related functions are covered on pages 190–192.

Silkscreening

Silkscreening is used for printing on surfaces such as fabric, vinyl, glass, metal, wood, pottery and plastic as well as paper. It is known for its refined look, saturated colors, and slightly thicker texture. Fine posters and prints are silkscreened; so are T-shirts, binders, and specialty items such as buttons and mugs. This custom work is usually done in relatively small quantities and is labor-intensive. Silkscreening is done either by hand (by cutting stencils), or photo-mechanically, using a light-sensitive stencil.

Choosing a Printer

Once printers (or their sales reps) have responded to your request for an estimate (covered in *Watching Your Money*, page 61), you are ready to begin an important evaluation process. For anything but the smallest jobs, get more than one bid. The process of finding a printer begins with identifying promising candidates, as described on page 44. The purpose of this section is to help you choose the best printer for your particular needs. Here are five criteria upon which to base your decision:

- Price
- Quality

Money Saving Tips　73

It is possible to do effective printed pieces without spending a fortune. Keep your design simple and straightforward, and produce it carefully. Here are suggestions to help keep costs low:

- Avoid using photographs or shaded illustrations; use all line art instead

- Stick with standard sizes

- Avoid using bleeds (ink that goes to the edge of the page)

- Avoid reverses (large areas requiring heavy ink coverage are harder to print)

- When you use black ink, think of it as you would a color

- See if your quick printer has "color days" when a color costs little or nothing extra

- Use black ink on a white, brilliant, or deep shade of paper instead of two inks

- Use a brilliant or deep-colored ink on colored paper instead of two inks

- Select one magnificent color instead of two common ones

- Use a handsome paper and one ink color instead of two

- Use your printer's *house stock*

- Find an honest and reliable printer

- Move through each production step carefully (mistakes are expensive)

- Plan to give yourself the time you need (rush jobs cost more)

- Ask the printer for ways to save money on your particular job

- Service and convenience
- Reputation
- Communication

Price

Like every good business person, you want the best possible job for the least possible cost. So let's take a closer look at those bids you get.

Are there great variations in the estimates you receive, or are they close in price? Wide variations in price can suggest something is wrong. Were the printers bidding on *exactly* the same specifications? You can't compare them if they weren't. Variations in bids are often traced to changes in the description of the job. Did the printer interpret your request accurately? Whether an estimate seems too good to be true or outrageously high, go over it carefully with the person who gave it to you.

Negotiation is common in the printing business, and there are a wide variety of styles and approaches. Some people ask a preferred printer who bids him or herself out of the picture for a better price, some ask for suggestions for how the cost can be lowered. Others take the first bid as final because they don't want the printer to get into the habit of assuming they'll get another chance.

When estimates are close in price, there are several things upon which to base your decision. As you may have learned already, going with the cheapest bid is not always the smartest. It can mean continuous headaches and a disappointing job.

If you made any changes on your job since you submitted your original request for bids, ask the printer to revise the quote to reflect those changes. You might also ask if there are any hidden or unexpected costs you should anticipate. Find out what taxes and shipping or delivery charges will do to the bottom line. When the cost of your job is updated to reflect the

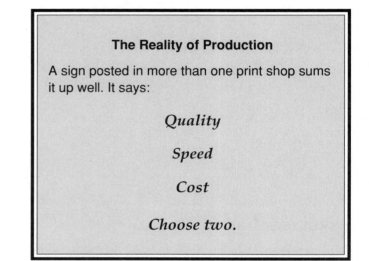

The Reality of Production

A sign posted in more than one print shop sums it up well. It says:

Quality

Speed

Cost

Choose two.

piece you will be handing over and the printer has reviewed your camera-ready art, get the final estimate in writing. Ask for the agreed-upon delivery date to be written in too.

Payment arrangements should also be agreed on in the beginning. Unless you or your organization set up an account with the printing company in advance, the work is C.O.D.

Quality

Ask to see samples of pieces that have been produced recently by the print shops you are considering. The more the samples reflect the kind of piece you are doing, the better. Would you like your piece to look like the examples you see?

Obviously, a good printing job looks good. The reader is not distracted from the content of the message by any flaw. Type and images are crisp, ink is solid, even, and as dark as it's supposed to be, photographs are sharp, colors are true, registration is accurate, and margins are even.

There is no ironclad guarantee, but you will have a better sense of the likelihood of a good job if you visit

---

Questions to Ask the Printer

Printing is a highly skilled craft, and a good printer is a wonderful source of information. Organize your questions ahead of time. Write them down (you can use this list as a starting point) and bring it to the print shop, or go over your questions on the phone.

- What kinds of pieces is this print shop especially good at producing?

- Do you have the right equipment to do my job efficiently?

- How much of the job is done in-house? What is farmed out?

- Is there any reduction in price for long-term contracts? (Such as a year's worth of newsletters)

- How can I achieve the look I want and stay within my budget?

- Do you anticipate any problems with this job? If so, what?

- Do you have a house stock?

- Can you recommend a less-expensive but similar-looking paper?

- What are the options for folding?

- (If you're in a hurry): Is there anything you can do to speed up the process?

- (If you are concerned about how the ink will look on a particular shade of paper): Do you have any samples that show colors on this sheet? Can you make me a sample? What will it cost?

- (If you are considering using special effects such as duotones, metallic inks, die cuts, or embossing): Do you have any examples? Does this make sense for my job?

- How long will it take to produce the job?

- When can I expect delivery?

- When do you expect the blueline to be ready?

- (In relation to delivery): How will the job be packaged? How many pieces come in a box? Do you shrink wrap?

- (If reprinting is a likely possibility): How do you charge for reprints? (Ask about them in the beginning, when agreements are easier to work out.)

- If this were your job, what questions would you be asking?

---

the print shop. It's a good idea to tour any plant that you are seriously considering. You'll learn a lot. Most printing businesses welcome the opportunity to show you what they can do and have a chance to get to know you. They're looking you over too. Call ahead to set up a mutually convenient time.

When you go on site, be a sharp observer. Notice the atmosphere and observe the employees. Do they look productive and focused on their work? Notice the customers, and the interactions between them and the employees. Are people getting along? Pay attention to how neat or messy the place is. Is it well-organized? Do you like the look of the work you see coming off the presses? Do you like what you see stacked up, waiting for the next step? Are you comfortable in the shop? How are you treated? Do you feel okay about asking questions? Are they answered clearly?

These observations give you clues as to the level of quality you can expect from the place. They also suggest how the shop will respond if there are problems or difficulties with your job. You can count on at least one.

Wise print producers take the advice of printers,

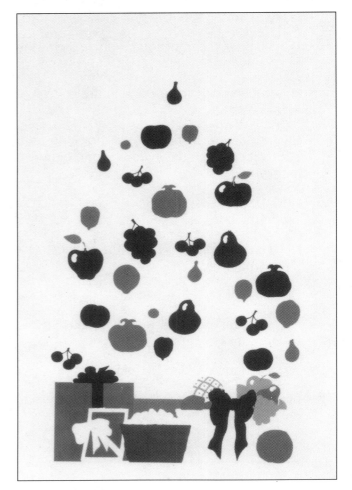

sales reps, designers, and others experienced in the business. If you're advised against a particular paper, line thickness, ink, or some special effect, pay attention. If any of these folks question whether some part of the work you bring in is do-able and you go ahead anyway, you're courting trouble. Explain what effect you are after, and ask how you can achieve it.

It's your job is to make sure that your printing request matches the capabilities of the shop. Keep in mind that the printing will be only as good as the camera-ready art and instructions you give to the printer. It is also up to you to provide clean boards with clear instructions and to check proofs carefully. It is up to the team at the print shop to turn the piece into a quality product.

Service and Convenience

Find out what customer services the printing companies you are considering offer. Do they offer paste-up or other technical services? Do they provide pickup and delivery? Is someone readily available to answer

*Here is the color proof for
this Christmas card. Each of the three images
on acetate, left, shows one ink color (one with its lighter shades).
They are layered and stapled together, far right, to create the final effect.*

questions? Can they handle special procedures such as die-cutting or embossing? What is the policy on rush jobs? What is the additional fee?

Another convenience you may want to weigh in the balance is location. All other things being equal, a handy print shop is better than one at a distance.

Reputation

A printer's reputation is a good indicator of the kind of quality and service you can anticipate. Do check

references—both ones the printer gives you and others you hear about. Ask such questions as: Are the jobs completed on time? Have you been satisfied with the work? What kinds of problems have you had? How have they been resolved?

Communication

When your work includes producing print, one of your most valuable resources is an experienced printer or printer's representative (rep). He or she can save you time, money, and frustration, and increase the odds that you'll be happy with how your printed piece turns out. Ideally, you find a friendly and knowledgeable printer and establish a good relationship; he or she does great work for you at reasonable prices, and you live happily ever after.

But as in every other line of work, there are good printers, bad printers, and mediocre printers. There are those who are truly skilled and those who are klutzes; those with integrity and those without it. Get to know printers and evaluate their character. You're looking for someone you can trust and rely on.

When you do find the right printer, you can look forward to a mutually beneficial relationship. Production is simpler and a lot more enjoyable when you have a printer you like. And shops in which you're a "regular" are more apt to be responsive to your needs. If they aren't, or if you feel taken for granted, it's time to look elsewhere.

The importance of establishing a good working relationship with someone at a printing company cannot be overemphasized. Relationships are based on the good will of *two* people: yours and theirs. In terms of your attitude, a friendly but business-like approach is likely to serve you best over time. Your understanding and recognition that printing is a high stress and complex business will go a long way to establishing good rapport. Printers don't want to be taken for granted or treated insensitively any more than you do. Every successful collaboration requires give and take. Be flexible, and you'll find that most printers will want to please you.

Stay in touch with the printer or the printer's rep throughout the production process. Go over the job together at the outset. Talk through each point and make sure your instructions are clear. There are many places for misunderstandings in this business, *so do not make any assumptions.* Let the printer know your priorities. If there is something you are particularly concerned about, say so.

If any changes are made, ask how they will affect the cost (don't put this off). Let the printer or rep know that you want to be called (if you do) when a question arises—preferably before the first 2,000 copies have been run. Take notes at your meetings, and keep them to clear up any confusion later.

If something seems wrong at any point in the process, stay calm and ask about it. Printing can be confusing; don't be afraid to ask questions. If your concerns are not addressed, complain. If your complaints are ignored, look for another printer. Expect occasional problems, but if they become regular, it's a sign to go elsewhere.

Ask for reasonable periodic updates on big or complex jobs, and to be notified if the schedule slips. Keep others in your organization informed as to the status of the piece.

Sometimes questions arise as to who relates to whom in this business. *One person* from your organization should represent you. Instances in which more than one person is involved can cause unnecessary complications and frustration. This person may be a designer or an ad agency you hire, or a print broker who works independently and collects his or her fee from either you or the printer, or it may be you yourself. Whoever it is, this person should keep in touch with the printer or the rep.

I know of one situation in which three people from an organization interacted with the printer—the project director, the art director, and the production manager. Work was duplicated and made more confusing. Everyone did schedules and updates, for example, and everyone gave the printer instructions. He didn't know who he was working for or whose requests to follow. The situation was further complicated by pickups and deliveries made by the printer's son, an independent young man upon whom all depended to carry communications back and forth. When the less-than-well-produced job arrived, everyone had someone else to blame.

This was a messy and uncomfortable situation for all involved. You can avoid your own version of it by clearly defining who will represent your organization, and requesting that a single contact person from the printing company be named.

Finding a good printer takes time. There are many of them out there, and many issues to consider in addition to price. Look for someone who can give you the quality you want, and be a good partner in the process at the same time.

Checking Proofs

When you bring your camera-ready art to a quick printer, your production tasks are over. The next time you see your piece it will be printed. But if you turn it in to a regular commercial offset printer, there are one or possibly two more check points. One of them is checking the blueline; the other is looking at the work on the press.

The Blueline Check

The image of your piece is transferred to photo-sensitive paper by exposing it to a light source through photographic negatives of your camera-ready art. The photo-sensitive paper reproduces the image exactly, often in blue, and is therefore called a *blueline* (or brownline or whatever color it happens to be).

The purpose of the blueline is to check the accuracy of the image (you will not see real ink and paper at this stage). If your job has more than one color, each will be shown as a different shade of blue on the blueline. You will also see a color key. A color key simulates the colors you have specified. If you are using four-color process for photographs or other images, you will also see these proofs.

It is very important to check the bluelines and to check them *carefully*. This is your last chance to catch problems or errors before the piece goes on the

Things That Go Wrong | 75

Because there are so many details and so many steps in printing, things can and do quite regularly go wrong. Here are some of the many things that typically happen.

- Something slips past you on the blueline
- The paper doesn't come in on time
- The ink takes longer to dry than expected
- Some critical person gets sick
- There are bindery or folding problems
- The black ink isn't black enough
- The colors are wrong
- The color turns out darker than you expected
- The color turns out lighter than you expected
- The color looks awful on the paper
- Solid areas of ink are streaky
- The piece comes out crooked
- Your job shows up on the wrong paper
- The piece wasn't scored (cut half-through), so it is cracked at the fold
- Something is left out
- You don't ask how much a change will cost before it is made
- The job is delivered to the wrong place
- You made an assumption you should not have made

76 | Press Checklist

Press time is precious. If you arrange to check your printed piece on the press, you have to go when you are called. Here are things to pay attention to when you do a press check:

☐ Have the changes and corrections you made on the blueline and color key been carried out as specified?

☐ Is your job being printed on the right paper?

☐ Is the sheet absolutely clean? There should be no specks in either the inked or uninked areas.

☐ How is the ink density?

☐ Are solid areas consistently solid?

☐ Is the registration accurate?

☐ Is the black ink black enough?

☐ Are the colors right?

A worksheet version of this Sidebar is on page 365.

press. Although you may want more than one person to look them over, one person from your organization should have the authority and the responsibility for checking and signing off on these proofs. Let the printer know who the responsible person is.

The only purpose of the blueline and color key checks is to *compare them* to your camera-ready boards, and *not to make changes*. Any change you make at this stage will be expensive. The check is to see that the images on your boards have been accurately transferred (through the negatives) to the blueline proofs (these same negatives will be used to make the plates), and to make sure that your instructions have been accurately followed.

Take your time going over a blueline. Keep it overnight if you can. If you do make changes, find out how much they will cost *before* they are made. Circle or mark anything you question *directly on the blueline*, and write on it how it is to be fixed.

Sidebar 77 has a blueline and color key checklist to help you go over your proofs. You may want to keep it handy and use it every time you check proofs.

After you review the proofs thoroughly, sign and date them. Sign *okay as is*, or *okay, with revisions as shown*, or *not okay—need to see second proof* (or something similar). If there are many changes, it's a good idea to see another set of bluelines. Your signature on the blueline puts the responsibility for uncaught mistakes clearly on your shoulders, so take this signing seriously.

It is important to differentiate between the printer's mistakes (these are the printer's responsibility and should not be charged to you), and any changes you decide to make (you must pay for these). You might want to use two different colors—say red for printers' errors and blue for your changes. Go over all changes with your sales rep or printer to make sure they are clearly understood. Then carefully check your bill to be sure it accurately reflects your understanding of which corrections were the printer's mistakes and which ones were your changes. The person tallying up the printer's bill sometimes assumes all the mistakes are yours.

Press Check

Sometimes a printed piece is also checked on the printing press, although not always. It depends on the job. Discuss this possibility with your printer when you submit the camera-ready boards. Some printers charge for a press check, so ask what the policy is.

If you do a press check, alterations at this point will be strictly limited (your printer will tell you what the parameters are). Keep your input limited to what is actually changeable.

If you do a press check, you have to be ready to respond when you are called. This is your final chance to see your piece before it is printed. Sidebar 76 has a press checklist. When you sign off on a press check, your production tasks are over.

Accepting The Job

At last—the moment that makes you either ecstatic or sick. Your piece is printed. Hopefully it is a terrific job, and you sign off on the delivery slip, which means you accept it as is.

But before you do that, dig down through the cartons or open several packages and pull some samples out at random. How do these pieces look? Is the printing quality consistent on all pieces?

If there is a problem, don't formally accept delivery, and call the printer right away. Stay calm and ask questions. Understand what happened before you start to complain. Communication now is as important as it ever was. Who is responsible? This should be decided before you accept delivery.

Do you want to see the bluelines or color keys, to be reminded of what you signed off on? Is the mistake your fault? If it is, it is better to admit it up front. No one is perfect.

Blueline and Color Key Checklist

77

Check through the entire proof for one thing at a time, then go back and go through it again for the next. Check it against the camera-ready art, mark errors, and say how you want them corrected. Ask yourself:

☐ Is the type sharp?

☐ Are there any broken characters?

☐ Is any type missing or in the wrong place?

☐ Is everything squared and centered as it should be?

☐ Are photographs and art cropped right?

☐ Are they in the right spots?

☐ Do they butt up against a frame as they are supposed to?

☐ Are there any marks, specs, flaws, or flecks on the blueline? Circle all.

☐ Is anything missing?

☐ Is anything there that's not supposed to be there?

☐ Is the size right?

☐ Are the folds correct? (try folding it to make sure)

☐ Is the registration accurate?

☐ Are color breaks right?

☐ How is the color alignment?

☐ Do colors butt up against each other accurately?

☐ Are the colors where they're supposed to be?

A worksheet version of this Sidebar is on page 365.

78 | Tips for Working with a Printer

Good print producers must find ways to work effectively with printers, and experienced ones know just how important that relationship is. Here are some tips to facilitate yours.

- Keep a file of pieces that represent the quality of printing you want, and discuss them with the printer

- Different shops do different things best, so keep track of who does what well for future reference

- Bring in a sample dummy with your camera-ready art

- Ask printers for cost-saving ideas

- Let your printer know as soon as possible if the job is being delayed at your end

- When placing an order, confirm the proofing and delivery dates

- Ask for good ink coverage

- Anticipate problems before they arise

- The earlier a change is made, the less expensive it is, so do each check carefully

- Stay in touch with your printer or rep during the printing process

- Don't get too comfortable with any one printer (watch your costs, and get other bids regularly)

- If you use the same printer for many jobs, make sure the quality doesn't slip

- If you buy a lot of one kind of printing, find a printer who specializes in this work

- Pay attention to reprint costs

- Give yourself as much time as possible to avoid a last minute rush

- All good relationships are based on mutual give and take, so be flexible

The mistake may not be as bad as you initially think. An important question to ask is: "What kind of impact will this error have on the audience?" Imperfection can be greatly magnified at this moment. It is better to separate your own disappointment from what may or may not be your audience's.

If the fault is on the part of the printing company, was it something beyond anyone's control, or was it carelessness? Give them a chance to explain it or make it up to you. Either get the job reprinted or get a reduction in the price. If you have legitimate complaints, put them in writing and send them to the printing company right away.

When you do accept a job, ask what quantity is being delivered. It can be 10% over or under unless a specific number is guaranteed at the outset. Have the art boards been returned to you? Will the printer keep the negatives? If so, for how long?

Make an effort to maintain a good relationship with your printer. By the same token, don't ever feel obliged to stay with one whose performance or service is not satisfactory.

Take every opportunity learn about production. The better you understand the process the more comfortable you'll be with it, and the more likely you are to get a first-rate printing job.

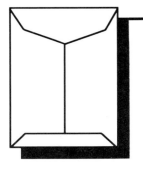

Chapter 25

Distribution Points

Distribution is the process by which the printed piece gets to its readers. This is the important last step for every print producer. Now it is critical to get the publication into the right hands; otherwise the entire effort—the development, the writing, the design, and the production of the printed piece—will all have been wasted.

There are essentially three ways to get a printed message from you to "them." You can:

1. Send it through the mail

2. Drop it off at key locations

3. Piggyback the piece along with something else in print, such as an ad in a newspaper or magazine, or a piece stuffed in a paycheck envelope, or sent with a bill or letter.

If you mail the piece, there are postal regulations you need to be aware of. If you hand-distribute it to key locations, you'll need the cooperation of those on site. If your piece is to piggyback on something else, arrangements need to be made. All have cost implications of one kind or another. We'll cover each of these methods in this chapter.

How do you decide on the best method of distribution for your printed piece? They say that the three most desirable features in real estate are location, location, and location. When it comes to effective print distribution, the three things that count the most are *convenience, convenience, and convenience.* The most effective method of print distribution is the one that maximizes the ease with which recipients get your piece.

In a society in which leisure time is an abstract concept for many, reading your printed piece is unlikely to be anyone's highest priority. The easier you make it for people to get your printed piece, the more likely they'll be to read it. And there may be more effective ways to get the word out than the first one that comes to your mind, or than the way you've always done it before.

Each of the three methods of distribution—direct-mail, hand or drop-off distribution, and piggybacking—has its own set of strengths and drawbacks. Familiarity with each one will help you select the best way. Also, knowledge of your target audience is useful (see *Tailoring the Piece to Your Audience,* page 71). Before you decide, imagine sending your piece out in several different ways first. And you may want to test alternative methods to see what works best for your particular audience.

1. Mailing Your Piece

The number of printed pieces mailed directly to constituents, clients, and customers has increased dramatically in recent years. L.L. Bean, the Maine mail-order company, is an example of just how effective direct mail can be. The company sends out more than 90 million copies of 22 different catalogs a year (four are shown on page 72). L.L. Bean's 3,200 employees increase to over 5,000 during the Christmas season to handle the response. Total annual revenues in recent years were in excess of $600 million, 87% of which came from direct mail sales.

Many other direct mail merchandisers are also doing well. What accounts for their success? Convenience, for one thing. Recipients of their mailings can consider, reject, or accept what is offered in the convenience of their own home. For busy people, ordering or responding through the mail saves time and gas and the hassles of parking, crowds, and waiting in line. If the material is sensitive and the wrapper is plain (in any color), the mail also offers privacy. You can't make a printed piece much more convenient than putting it in someone's mailbox.

When a piece comes through the mail, it receives a moment of the recipient's undivided attention. In that moment you have the opportunity to capture and hold their attention. *That instant* is what you're paying for when you mail your printed piece. Section 3, *Getting and Holding Attention*, pages 69–114, describes how to make the most of it.

Another big advantage of direct mail to you, the sender, is that you can carefully select your audience, and tailor the piece specifically to it. You can plan the best time for the mailing (see Sidebar 15 for ideas). And you can reach people who otherwise might be hard to reach, such as seniors or the handicapped or teenagers. Mailing lists are so precise these days that you can get them to include just about anyone from Swedish cat fanciers in North Carolina to Phi Beta

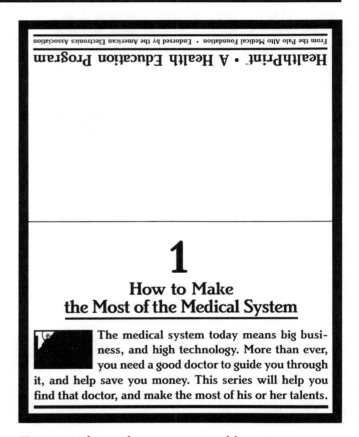

Kappas with sons between two and four. You can rent mailing lists for a specified number of mailings, or buy them (look in the Yellow Pages under *Mailing Lists*). Or you can build your own.

If you create your own mailing list, your local library is an excellent resource. There are directories for just about every kind of organization, and there are even directories of business directories. Local Chambers of Commerce have mailing lists of their members. These are often for sale. Consider whether a piece should be sent to a name or to a title (titles change less frequently than names, but are less personal).

If you decide to use a mailing house to send out your printed piece, ask printers and others you know

*This series of self-mailers went through the mail
folded once. Ample space was left to introduce the subject on
the outside. It leads in to information on the other side. (Insides on page 124.)*

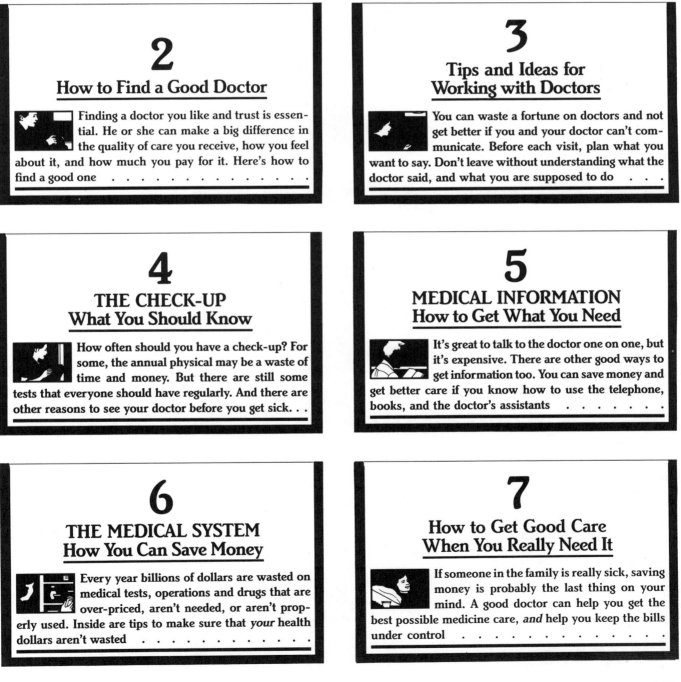

2

How to Find a Good Doctor

Finding a doctor you like and trust is essential. He or she can make a big difference in the quality of care you receive, how you feel about it, and how much you pay for it. Here's how to find a good one . . . .

3

Tips and Ideas for
Working with Doctors

You can waste a fortune on doctors and not get better if you and your doctor can't communicate. Before each visit, plan what you want to say. Don't leave without understanding what the doctor said, and what you are supposed to do . . .

4

THE CHECK-UP
What You Should Know

How often should you have a check-up? For some, the annual physical may be a waste of time and money. But there are still some tests that everyone should have regularly. And there are other reasons to see your doctor before you get sick. . .

5

MEDICAL INFORMATION
How to Get What You Need

It's great to talk to the doctor one on one, but it's expensive. There are other good ways to get information too. You can save money and get better care if you know how to use the telephone, books, and the doctor's assistants . . . .

6

THE MEDICAL SYSTEM
How You Can Save Money

Every year billions of dollars are wasted on medical tests, operations and drugs that are over-priced, aren't needed, or aren't properly used. Inside are tips to make sure that *your* health dollars aren't wasted . . . .

7

How to Get Good Care
When You Really Need It

If someone in the family is really sick, saving money is probably the last thing on your mind. A good doctor can help you get the best possible medicine care, *and* help you keep the bills under control . . . .

For this direct mail campaign, the first in a series of tip sheets was mailed in an envelope, below. It included a magnet for posting the sheet on the refrigerator. Thereafter tip sheets were sent as self-mailers, right (insides on page 88).

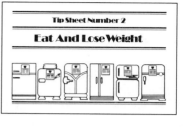

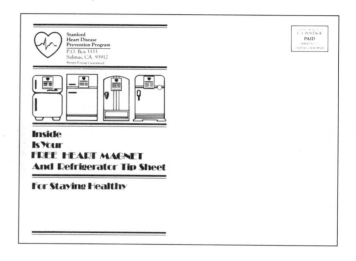

to recommend a good one. Mailing houses offer services in addition to mailing, such as sorting and stuffing. And as mailing is their business, mailing house personnel can also provide valuable advice.

Is it better to use an envelope or not? It depends on the nature of the piece. Obviously you have to use one if there's more than one enclosure. There is a real advantage to sending a piece through the mail (called a *self-mailer*) without an envelope. The piece itself then ends up in the recipient's hands. The envelope can be a barrier—you're counting on the recipient to have enough interest to take the time to open it. The other advantage of using a self-mailer is that you save the cost of buying the envelopes, and the time and cost of stuffing them.

If you decide to go with a self-mailer, the paper needs to be heavy enough to withstand the mails. You may or may not save money on postage—that's something to check out with the mailing house or post office. The piece may need to be folded, but avoid using staples. They tear it when it is opened.

An envelope, on the other hand, does offer some protection against your piece arriving torn, bent, or dirty. If you do use one, take advantage of the envelope's printing surface, and say something about what's inside to motivate the reader to open it. Most envelopes that do this have really dumb or uninteresting messages printed on the outside. You will come up with something better by directing a message or question that is personally tailored to your audience.

There are many kinds of ready-made envelopes to choose from. Your printer has charts and samples of what's available. They come in different bonds and text-weight papers with matching stock for enclosures, and in a wide variety of colors. You may want to try a bright colored envelope to attract attention. You can also have envelopes custom made. There are companies that specialize in producing them; printers can direct you to a good one. There is a description of envelopes in Sidebar 80.

The biggest disadvantage of mailing is, of course, the expense. You might consider trying it on a limited basis. If you've got a piece that is tailored, written, and designed well, you may find the benefits of sending it through the mail outweigh the costs.

Post Office regulations

The Post Office has very specific guidelines to insure that their personnel and machinery can handle the mail efficiently. These parameters must be taken into consideration when the piece is being designed. The Post Office specifies the way a piece can fold, and the thickness of postcard stock. There are specific measurements and rules for business reply cards. There is a minimum size for envelopes, preferred standard sizes, and regulations on shapes. It's wise to discuss any piece you plan to mail with the postmaster early in its development.

Post Office officials are very knowledgeable resources who can help you figure out the best way to use the system for your particular piece. Or they can help you tailor your piece to make the best use of the system. Discuss whether your piece should be hand stamped, metered, or preprinted. Decide what mail-

Ways To Distribute Your Printed Piece

79

There are many good ways to get your printed piece into the right hands. Direct mail is one; many others are suggested below. Consider *using some new and unusual channels. Tune in to your audience for ideas that are likely to be most successful with them.*

Places	Events	Piggybacking
• At work sites	• Meetings	• Newspapers
• Near copiers	• Conferences	• Magazines
• Near the coffee	• Lectures	• Newsletters
• In restrooms	• Classes	• In-house communiques
• On bulletin boards	• Fairs	• Pay checks
• At schools	• Shows	• Yellow Pages
• At colleges	• Sporting events	• Invoices
• At shopping centers	• Cultural affairs	• Updates
• In waiting rooms	• Picnics	• Presentation folders
• On store counters	• Parades	• Church bulletins
• At churches	• Outdoor markets	• School flyers
• In grocery stores	• Open houses	• Yearbooks
• At clubs	• Community events	• Proposals
• At libraries	• Social gatherings	• Annual reports
• On kiosks	• Grand openings	• Trade journals

ing class makes the most sense (each has benefits and drawbacks). Bulk mail, for example, is cheaper, but more of it goes in the trash; first class is faster and gets better response, but you pay for it.

Call the Post Office for advice on the phone, or schedule a mutually convenient time to meet. Bring a sample of the kind of printed piece you have in mind. Since Post Office regulations have been known to change, it is important to do this at the outset of each new project, or on some regular basis.

2. Key Location Distribution

One good way for coming up with ideas for where to distribute your printed piece is to hold a brainstorming session. It could be part of the agenda for other meetings on your piece, like the planning meeting in which you define goals, or one in which you develop an audience profile (Sidebar 5 helps focus on goals; Sidebar 10 is on holding meetings; Sidebar 21 helps you define your audience).

These nutrition tips on bright-colored paper have English on one side, Spanish on the other. They were put into grocery bags, one a week, at checkout counters. Envelopes enable entire packets to be sent out at once.

To choose good locations for distributing your piece, write down where members of your audience go—daily, weekly, and monthly. I knew for sure, for example, that people would be going to the market regularly when I came up with the idea for grocery bag stuffers for a health promotion project. The plan was to distribute a series of short nutrition-related sheets to food stores. They would be packed in bags along with customer's groceries, one a week, over several weeks. This way tips on eating less salt and fewer eggs, for example, would be unpacked in the kitchen along with the salt and the eggs.

What kinds of places relate to the content of your printed piece? Where do you find your clients or constituents? Which waiting rooms do they sit in or which lines do they stand in? Most of us would read just about anything we were handed while waiting in line for tickets or to get a license renewed. What stores or shopping centers do they go to? Are they involved in particular clubs? Churches? Do they read community or dormitory bulletin boards? Do they use libraries? What worksites would you find them in? Where are they likely to congregate? The water cooler? The lunch room? The copy machine? The coffee pot? Don't forget about rest rooms.

In addition to places, there may also be events at which your printed piece is relevant, or at which you will find your audience. What activities are they likely to attend? What activities relate to your topic? Most professions have conferences. Which ones do your audience members go to?

Remember to come up with ways of adding extra value to your piece, as covered in *Ideas to Make Your Piece More Interesting*, page 83. For example, you might make your piece more valuable to conferees by printing a good map of the convention area on one side of a sheet and your message on the other. Suggestions for good local restaurants, shopping, or other attractions would also be of interest.

Will the members of your audience be attending citizens groups or city council meetings? Classes or workshops? Cultural or sports events? Open houses, parades, grand openings, or picnics? Tie your message into the activity, or co-produce a piece with event sponsors. It doesn't matter if it hasn't been done before. You can be the first to do it. A list of location possibilities is in Sidebar 79.

Your distribution plan may require getting permissions or working out agreements with the management or others whose locations you would like to

*This evaluation sheet makes it easy
to fill in—you just check the appropriate boxes.
It is also easy to mail (you fold it in half and drop it in the mail).
A certificate is offered as further incentive for returning the printed piece.*

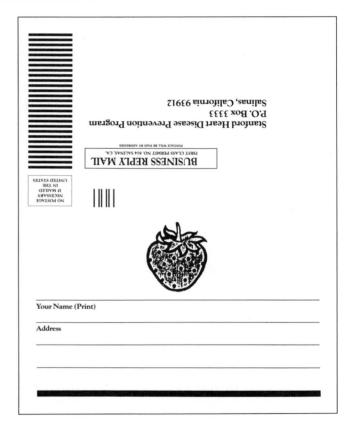

THE FIFTH STEP

When you have completed the four steps, record all your food changes here. Add your name and address, fold this sheet, drop it in the mail, and we will send you your "Certificate of Good Nutrition."

DID YOU MAKE THESE CHANGES?	Made Change	Didn't Make Change	No Change Needed
Limit egg yolks to three a week	☐	☐	☐
Cut down on high-fat specialty meats	☐	☐	☐
Pick lean meats, discarding all possible fats	☐	☐	☐
Eat chicken or fish three times a week	☐	☐	☐
Switch to lowfat, then to nonfat milk	☐	☐	☐
Cut down on high-fat cheeses	☐	☐	☐
Cut down on cream, ice cream	☐	☐	☐
Read labels to avoid saturated fats	☐	☐	☐
Eat unsweetened foods for breakfast	☐	☐	☐
Buy bread made with whole wheat	☐	☐	☐
Eat a starchy food at every lunch and dinner	☐	☐	☐
Increase the amount of vegetables you eat	☐	☐	☐
Cut out sugary desserts and snacks	☐	☐	☐
Eat breakfasts without eggs or breakfast meats	☐	☐	☐
Eat dishes where meat is used as a flavoring	☐	☐	☐
Try out dishes with no ingredients of animal origin	☐	☐	☐
Salt Changes: Did You			
Move the salt shaker off the table?	☐	☐	☐
Cut down on salt used in cooking?	☐	☐	☐
Cut down on salty-tasting foods?	☐	☐	☐
Stop buying prepared soups, stews, sauces?	☐	☐	☐

BUSINESS REPLY MAIL
FIRST CLASS PERMIT NO. 814 SALINAS, CA.

POSTAGE WILL BE PAID BY ADDRESSEE

Stanford Heart Disease Prevention Program
P.O. Box 3333
Salinas, California 93912

NO POSTAGE
NECESSARY
IF MAILED
IN THE
UNITED STATES

Your Name (Print)

Address

---

use. If you figure out some benefit to them (such as thanking them in the piece), you'll be surprised at how many people are open to a new idea. In fact they're often glad you thought of it. Nothing ventured, nothing gained.

This kind of drop-off distribution requires some ingenuity, so everyone doesn't do it. And that's precisely why it is such an effective way to get your message across. But it does take careful planning, good management, and conscientious follow-through to pull it off successfully. Someone needs to deliver the pieces, enlist the aid of people on site, and stay on top of the situation.

And on-site people may need to be motivated to participate. For example, the grocery bag stuffers needed the cooperation of store clerks—the nutrition tip sheets had to be put into grocery bags. You may have a similar request, or you may want to suggest specific locations on site for distribution (otherwise your pieces could end up in a corner). Someone needs to keep on-site personnel supplied with the materials, and to see that they do what they agreed to do. Incentives help. People like being rewarded for their cooperation. You might bring a T-shirt, magnet, muffins, or some other goodie when you visit the site.

As the woman who managed the grocery bag distribution program said: "Dissemination plans like this one have impact because they are unique. They

A perforated tear-off card encourages response, especially when it is prepaid and preaddressed. Leave plenty of space for writing on it.

really get the word out. It takes planning and work. You have to go back and check that it's being done and that the pieces are ending up in the right place. But the results are definitely worth the effort."

You may find a volunteer to oversee key location distribution, or hire someone to do it. Who ever takes the task on needs to be enthusiastic and reliable.

This kind of distribution could be less expensive and more effective than buying mailing lists or paying for postage. To find out what works best for your particular printed piece, try some of both.

3. Piggybacking Your Piece

Whether you buy the space in another publication or work out a deal for piggybacking your printed piece on another, start by thinking about what kinds of printed pieces your target audience already receives. There is plenty of opportunity for freer and more imaginative thinking here as well.

Does the content of your printed piece relate to the interests of students? Of parents? Can you reach your constituency through schools? Most day-care centers and elementary schools send regular communiques home to parents. Could your message go in the school newsletter or along with it? Children up to about fifth grade can be relied upon to bring messages home. High schools often mail report cards and other printed pieces home.

If your message is directed to people "in house," can it go along with a pay check or newsletter or other mailing, either delivered on site or to the home? If you represent a non-profit organization, is there a city government or other community mailing you could piggyback on? Or a local business or utility mailing? Think of organizations with whom you have common interests.

Department stores have figured out that they can put more than the bill in their envelope. Can you do the same? If you send out invoices, consider including

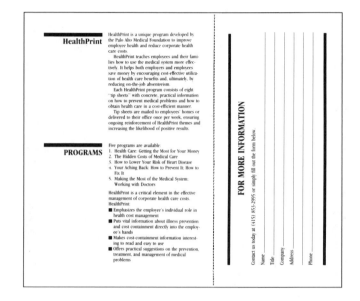

some new information about your product or service along with them.

Do you use presentation folders? Can you add unexpected pieces to them, such as fact or data sheets or catalogs? If you are sending out directories or manuals or proposals or annual reports, what other printed pieces can go with them? Don't let anything go out the door without asking yourself whether something else can be piggybacked along with it.

Or consider placing an ad in a newspaper or magazine. What newspapers do members of your audience get? If you don't know, how can you find out? What magazines do your clients or constituents read? The array of special interest magazines is vast—they include the spectrum of human interest from auto mechanics to high finance. Newspapers and magazines can give you circulation data and descriptions of their audiences if you ask them for it; they also will tell you their specifications, deadlines, and fees. Or track down this information in library directories. If you do, you may come across some good prospects you hadn't thought of before.

Choices for Envelopes

80

There are many different kinds of envelopes to serve different kinds of purposes. Printers have *charts and samples to choose from. Several of the possibilities are described below.*

Commercial. These are the familiar business correspondence envelopes, known as No. 10 (4-1/8" x 9-1/2"). They also come in No. 11 (4-1/2" x 10-3/8") and No. 9 (3-7/8" x 8-7/8"). They are produced in many kinds of papers with matching sheets for enclosures. Commercial envelopes can also be custom-made.

Baronial. Baronial envelopes are the handsome and more square-shaped ones. They are traditionally used for announcements, invitations, and greeting cards. These envelopes also come in a variety of colors and textures, and in a series of standard sizes. They are accompanied by matching papers.

Window. Window envelopes are used mostly for bills and statements. These envelopes save time because the name and address appear through the window. They too come in a variety of sizes and papers.

Metal Clasp. Clasp envelopes are of heavier weight and are used mainly for mailing papers, reports, and other large or heavy publications. These utilitarian envelopes can be opened and closed more than once with the metal clasp, as can the button and string version. They are usually tan.

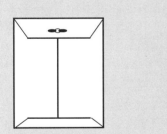

Open End. These are the rugged envelopes with gummed closings at one end. Directories, catalogs, manuals, papers, and booklets are among the kinds of publications regularly sent in these envelopes. They are usually made out of sturdy kraft paper.

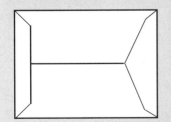

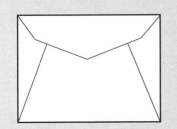

Open Side or Booklet. These envelopes open on the long side. They are used for mailing booklets, reports, and other pieces when a nice look is desired. They commonly come in white or gray, but they can also be custom-made from a number of different papers. Booklet envelopes can be printed on both front and back, offering advertising opportunities. Standard sizes are 6" x 9", 6-1/2" x 9-1/2", 7" x 10", 7-1/2" x 10-1/2", 8-1/4" x 11-1/4", and 9" x 12".

This over-sized envelope in a beautifully-textured paper helps get attention. When the quantity is large enough, consider getting your envelopes custom-made.

Involve the Reader

Giving readers something concrete or specific to do helps get them involved. One enterprising publishing company recruiting magazine subscriptions enclosed a gift card in the magazine. Givers could send the gift card to the recipient at the same time they ordered the subscription.

You might try requesting an opinion or a vote—it can encourage response, especially when accompanied by a prepaid reply envelope. They are especially important if you want a questionnaire or other important piece returned. You can also engage readers with self-scoring tests or quizzes. They also like to punch out, stick on, tear off, fill in, and check boxes.

Other time-tested methods to motivate participation involve readers by offering them something. It might be something for free, or for so much off, or two-for-one. Or it might be a "get-acquainted" offer. Coupons also can be effective when they are the right ones directed to the right audience. And a short, attention-getting fact sheet may generate interest in an otherwise ordinary mailing such as a report or a fund-raising letter.

Whatever you can do to inspire, involve, motivate, or encourage the reader will help to elicit the response you are after. The possibilities are unlimited.

Everything Else
7

Sidebar Worksheets

Sidebar 5   Questions for Planning Your Printed Piece 348

Sidebar 13   Week-by-Week Schedule 350

Sidebar 14   Backwards Schedule 351

Sidebar 16   The Cost of Print: A Checklist 349

Sidebar 17   Printer Cost Estimating Form 352

Sidebar 18   Subcontractor Cost Estimating Form 353

Sidebar 19   Budget Checklist 349

Sidebar 21   Audience Profile 354

Sidebar 24   Idea Lists: Your Audience 355

Sidebar 24   Idea Lists: Your Product or Service 356

Sidebar 24   Idea Lists: Your Printed Piece 357

Sidebar 28   Adding Interest with Questions 360

Sidebar 29   Selecting a Writing Tone 358

Sidebar 31   Writer's Checklist 358

Sidebar 35   Proofreading 359

Sidebar 37   Editor's Checklist 359

Sidebar 44   Selecting a Graphic Designer 361

Sidebar 54   Specifying Paper 362

Sidebar 55   Getting Dummies 363

Sidebar 64   Logo Evaluation Checklist 364

Sidebar 66   Your Desktop Publishing Needs 366

Sidebar 71   Camera-Ready Checklist 364

Sidebar 76   Press Checklist 365

Sidebar 77   Blueline and Color Key Checklist 365

Questions for Planning Your Printed Piece

1. What is the purpose of your piece?

_____

2. Who is your message for?

_____

3. What image do you want to project?

_____

4. What will make your piece more attractive to your audience?

_____

5. Are there any special requirements?

_____

6. What are your limitations?

_____

7. What are the unknowns?

_____

8. What are the possible formats? (Suggestions: pages 9–14)

_____

9. What is the best method of distribution to your audience? (Suggestions: Sidebar 79)

_____

10. If you mail your piece, will anything else be mailed with it? What?

_____

11. How will you know if your piece has achieved its goals?

_____

12. What else can you do to reinforce your message?

_____

The Cost of Print: A Checklist

People	Supplies and Services
☐ Ad agency or P.R. firm	☐ Graphic supplies
☐ Consultant	☐ Software
☐ Writer	☐ Photocopying
☐ Editor	☐ Stats
☐ Secretary	☐ Type
☐ Desktop publisher	☐ Laser or linotronic printing
☐ Art director	☐ Offset printing
☐ Designer	☐ Mailing lists
☐ Illustrator	☐ Mailing house
☐ Photographer	☐ Postage
☐ Typesetter	☐ Delivery
☐ Proofreader	☐ Distribution
☐ Paste-up person	☐ Storage

Budget Checklist

Expense	Cost
☐ Writer	$_____
☐ Editor	$_____
☐ Art Director	$_____
☐ Designer	$_____
☐ Desktop publishing	$_____
☐ Illustrator/photographer	$_____
☐ Typesetting	$_____
☐ Proofreading	$_____
☐ Secretarial/typing	$_____
☐ Pretesting/evaluation	$_____
☐ Software/supplies	$_____
☐ Copying/stats	$_____
☐ Paste-up	$_____
☐ Printing	$_____
☐ Mailing/postage/distribution	$_____
☐ Delivery charges/storage fees	$_____
☐ Staff time	$_____
☐ P.R. firm or ad agency	$_____
☐ Other	$_____
Total	$_____

Week-by-Week Schedule

The Piece : _____   **Date:** _____

Week of	Action to be taken	By whom

Backwards Schedule

The Piece: _____

Goal	Time required	Target date
In reader's hands		
Distribution		
Printing		
Proofreading, resetting, check		
Typesetting		
Design, photography, illustration		
Research, writing, data entry		
Production schedule, hire help		
Time and cost estimates		
Refine concept		
Audience (market) research		
Concept development		

Printer Cost Estimating Form

Printer's Name: **Phone:**

Name of piece: Date:

Quantity:

Trim size:

Cover stock:

Inside stock:

Ink colors:

Halftones (no. and size)

Bleeds:

Reverses:

Folding or binding:

Additional description:

Requested delivery date:

Cost:

© 1991 Bull Publishing Co. from *Print That Works* by Elizabeth Adler

Subcontractor Cost Estimating Form

Subcontractor: **Phone:**

Printed piece: Date:

Job description:

Time needed:

Dates needed:

Number of hours:

Estimated cost for job:

Overtime plan:

Opinion of work:

Person's strengths; weaknesses:

Action taken:

Source of name:

References:

Audience Profile

General description:

_____

Mostly male or female:

_____

Age:

_____

Living environment:

_____

Income level:

_____

Education level:

_____

Skill & knowledge level:

_____

How they are like you:

_____

How they are different:

_____

Attitude toward your product or service:

_____

Background:

_____

Values and tastes:

_____

How leisure time is spent:

_____

What they read:

_____

How they are unique:

_____

When most likely to get their attention:

_____

Where most likely to get attention:

_____

Impression you want to make:

_____

What action you want them to take:

_____

Idea Lists: Your Audience

Potential clients, in order of priority:

_____

_____

_____

Client characteristics (use your Audience Profile):

_____

Where they go:

_____

Where they're most likely to pay attention to the piece:

_____

When they're most likely to pay attention to the piece:

_____

Design styles most likely to appeal (Suggestions: Sidebar 40):

_____

Writing tones most likely to appeal (Suggestions: Sidebar 29):

_____

Idea Lists: Your Product or Service

Benefits to users (What it will do for them):

_____

_____

_____

Features (What's good about your product or service):

_____

_____

_____

Components of your service or product (What goes into it):

_____

_____

_____

Experience, authority and expertise (Why someone should trust you)

_____

_____

_____

Idea Lists: Your Printed Piece

Ways to make the piece personally relevant to this group:

_____

Ways to make the piece useful:

_____

Ways to make it authoritative:

_____

Ways you can suggest what to do or how to do it:

_____

Ways you can motivate your audience to respond:

_____

Ways you can break your information up:

_____

Ways to make your piece easy to remember:

_____

Ways to make the piece easy to get:

_____

Ways to keep your message coming:

_____

Possible formats:

_____

Selecting a Writing Tone

- ☐ Direct
- ☐ Light
- ☐ Friendly
- ☐ Fun
- ☐ Witty
- ☐ Honest
- ☐ Serious
- ☐ Strong
- ☐ Authoritative
- ☐ Bold
- ☐ Lively
- ☐ Intimate
- ☐ Punchy
- ☐ Adventuresome
- ☐ Sincere

Writer's Checklist

- ☐ The piece is simple and direct
- ☐ The words look easy to read
- ☐ It has a strong title
- ☐ The headlines are descriptive
- ☐ Important information is at the beginning
- ☐ The piece is interesting
- ☐ The information is accurate
- ☐ The tone is positive
- ☐ It motivates the reader
- ☐ It is aimed at the right level
- ☐ Examples are given when needed
- ☐ No premature dating
- ☐ The piece is as short as it can be
- ☐ The piece says what is intended

Editor's Checklist

☐ The piece is clear and understandable

☐ It is well thought out

☐ The piece holds interest

☐ Points are well made

☐ There is no redundancy

☐ It delivers the intended message

☐ The tone is professional

☐ The grammar is correct

☐ The punctuation is consistent and correct

☐ The spelling is accurate

☐ All numbers have been double checked

☐ All names and addresses have been double checked

Proofreading

☐ Check over all page and reference numbers to make sure they are right

☐ Double-check all other numbers

☐ Mistakes tend to be clustered, so if you find one, be on the lookout for others around it

☐ Make sure the information is in the right sequence

☐ Notice paragraph lengths; note when they're too long (shorter is better)

☐ If the writer refers to a page or section, be sure the reference is accurate

☐ Check spelling

☐ Check grammar

☐ Be sure that brackets, quotes, and parentheses are used correctly

☐ Check punctuation

☐ Watch for repeated words, like "of of"

☐ Look for missing punctuation, like commas or periods

☐ Look for missing words (often small ones like "a" or "the" are left out)

Adding Interest with Questions

Fill in the blanks for questions relevant to your organization, business, product or service.

What is the most common _____ ?

What do _____ and _____ have in common?

How many Americans (Europeans, Japanese, etc.) _____ ?

Can you name _____ ?

What is the most _____ ?

People from _____ have (own) the most _____ ?

What is the best selling (most popular) _____ in (city, stage, country) _____ ?

At what age _____ ?

What is _____ ?

What is the most unusual _____ ?

Selecting a Graphic Designer

Name: _____   **Date**: _____

Yes	No	
_____	_____	1. Does this person have the specific skills you need?
_____	_____	2. Do you like most of the pieces in the designer's portfolio?
_____	_____	3. Would you like your printed piece to look like these?
_____	_____	4. Does the designer have relevant experience?
_____	_____	5. Is this person available when needed?
_____	_____	6. Does the designer charge a rate you can afford? Is it negotiable?
_____	_____	7. Was the designer on time for your interview?
_____	_____	8. Does this person strike you as reliable and conscientious?
_____	_____	9. Would this person fit in with your organization?
_____	_____	10. Would you enjoy working with this person?

Comments:

_____

_____

_____

_____

Specifying Paper

Name:

Weight:

Line:

Grade:

Color:

Finish:

Getting Dummies

_____

Size:

_____

Number of pages:

_____

Binding or folding:

_____

Inside sheets:

_____

Cover sheet:

_____

Pocket height:

_____

Spine width:

_____

Other description:

_____

Logo Evaluation Checklist

☐ Does this logo have immediate impact?

☐ Is it good to look at?

☐ Is it distinctive?

☐ Does it create a positive image?

☐ Does it accurately represent your organization or business?

☐ Is it straightforward?

☐ Is it comprehensible?

☐ Is it memorable?

☐ Is it flexible?

☐ Does it copy well?

☐ Will it hold up both large and small?

☐ Will it wear well over time?

☐ Will you be proud to use it?

Camera-Ready Checklist

☐ Nothing is missing

☐ There is nothing extra

☐ Instructions are accurate and specific

☐ Illustrations to be made into halftones and photographs are organized

☐ They are keyed to the right spots

☐ The boards or pages are covered with a protective flap or folder

☐ The name of the job, your name, and your phone number are on all pieces

☐ The camera-ready art is accompanied by the instruction and production sheets

☐ The dummy is also included (if you have one)

☐ The delivery address is given

Blueline and Color Key Checklist

☐ Is the type sharp?

☐ Are there any broken characters?

☐ Is any type missing or in the wrong place?

☐ Is everything squared and centered as it should be?

☐ Are photographs and art cropped right?

☐ Are they in the right spots?

☐ Do they butt up against a frame as they are supposed to?

☐ Are there any marks, specs, flaws, or flecks on the blueline? Circle all.

☐ Is anything missing?

☐ Is anything there that's not supposed to be there?

☐ Is the size right?

☐ Are the folds correct? (try folding it to make sure)

☐ Is the registration accurate?

☐ Are color breaks right?

☐ How is the color alignment?

☐ Do colors butt up against each other accurately?

☐ Are the colors where they're supposed to be?

Press Checklist

☐ Have the changes and corrections you made on the blueline and color key been carried out as specified?

☐ Is your job being printed on the right paper?

☐ Is the sheet absolutely clean? There should be no specks in either the inked or uninked areas.

☐ How is the ink density?

☐ Are solid areas consistently solid?

☐ Is the registration accurate?

☐ Is the black ink black enough?

☐ Are the colors right?

Your Desktop Publishing Needs

What kinds of publications do you want to produce?

How often will you be producing them?

How many pages are involved?

What computer equipment do you currently have?

How important is it that these pieces look good?

What are your requirements for type?

Will you need graphics? What kind?

Do you want to use photographs?

Do you need color?

Do you have the time to learn about desktop publishing?

Do you have the enthusiasm for it, and the ability to take on new skills?

Where will the money come from to pay for the costs involved?

Resources

There is a growing number of good books and magazines on just about every topic related to publications. Figure out what kind of information you want, and go to a bookstore or library to see what's new. *Find it Fast: How to Uncover Expert Information on Any Subject* by Robert Berkman (Harper and Row, 1987) may be a good place to start. Here are some topics to look under.

- Planning
- Management
- Marketing
- Creativity
- Writing
- Newsletters
- Graphic Design
- Typography
- Color
- Time Management
- Desktop Publishing
- Paper
- Art
- Illustration
- Clip Art
- Photography
- Logos
- Trademarks
- Symbols
- Printing
- Production
- Direct Mail

Writing

The Elements of Style by William Strunk, Jr. and E.B.White (MacMillan Publishing Company, Inc., 1979).

Writing with Style by John R. Trimble (Prentice-Hall, 1975).

Mark My Words: Instruction and Practice in Proofreading by Peggy Smith (Washington, D.C. Editorial Experts, 1987).

On Writing Well by William Zinsser (Harper & Row, 1985).

Marketing

Successful Direct Marketing Methods by Bob Stone (National Textbook Company, 1988).

Direct Marketing: Strategy/Planning/Execution by Edward L. Nash (McGraw-Hill Book Company, 1982).

Secrets of Successful Direct Mail by Richard V. Benson (The Benson Organization, Inc., 1987).

The Regis Touch by Regis McKenna (Addison-Wesley Publishing Company, Inc. 1985).

Advertising Pure and Simple by Hank Seiden (American Management Association, 1976).

1001 Ways to Market Your Books, Third Edition by John Kremer (Ad Lib Publications, 1990).

Book Publishing Resource Guide by John Kremer (Ad Lib Publications, 1990).

The Self-Publishing Manual, Fifth Edition by Dan Poynter (Para Publishing, 1989).

Literary Market Place, R.R. Bowker, New York (updated annually).

Design and Production

Pocket Pal: a graphic arts production handbook (International Paper Company, 1983).

The Graphic Designer's Handbook by Alastair Campbell (Running Press, 1987).

Handbook of Practical and Ethical Guidelines (Graphic Arts Guild, 1987).

Designer's Guide to Creating Charts and Graphs by Nigel Holmes (Watson-Guptil, 1984).

Complete Guide to Pasteup by Walter B. Graham (PO Box 369, Omaha, Nebraska 68101, 1987).

Looking Good in Print by Roger C. Parker (Ventana Press, 1988).

The Makeover Book by Roger C. Parker (Ventana Press, 1989).

How to Spec Type by Alex White (Watson Guptil, 1986).

Magazines

Communication Arts
P.O. Box 10300
Palo Alto, CA 94303
(415) 326-6040

Print
6400 Goldsboro Road
Bethesda, MD 20817
(301) 229-6700

Step-by-Step Graphics
PO Box 1901
Peoria, IL 61656-9979
(800) 255-8800

How
6400 Goldsboro Road
Bethesda, MD 20817
(800) 229-6700

Catalog of books with copyright-free art

Dover Publications
31 East Second Street
Mineola NY 11501

Desktop Publishing

New books are continuously coming out on desktop publishing. Guides and handbooks are often written in relation to specific computers and software, so for the most up-to-date information, your best bet is to go to a bookstore with a good desktop publishing section. If you want an overview, the library is a good source. Here are some books and magazines to get you started.

Barron's Dictionary of Computer Terms (Barron, 1986).

Publishing from the Desktop by John Seybold and Fritz Dressler (Bantam, 1987).

Chicago Guide to Preparing Electronic Manuscripts (University of Chicago Press, 1987).

Desktop Publisher's Guide to Pasteup by Tony Middleton (Plusware, 1987).

Magazines

Personal Publishing
P.O. Box 3240
Harlan, IA 51537
(800) 727-6937

Publish!
501 Second Street
San Francisco, CA 94107
(800) 222-2990

Glossary

Words in italic refer to the area of the graphic arts in which the term is most commonly used.

For a description of specific kinds of printed pieces, see pages 9 through 13.

DTP: desktop publishing.

A

A.A.s: *Typesetting, Printing*—**A**uthor's **A**lterations. Changes or corrections made on either the typesetter's or printer's proofs. These expensive changes are charged to the client; they are not the typesetter's or printer's mistakes.

Accordion fold: *Binding*—Folding paper back and forth into parallel panels like an accordion. Brochures sometimes have accordion folds.

Airbrush: *Art, Photography*—A small pencil-shaped ink sprayer powered by compressed air. It creates even, smooth, and graduated tones, light to dark.

Alignment: *Layout*—Lining elements up exactly. Commonly aligned elements are columns of type, rules (lines), headlines, photographs, and artwork.

Antique finish: *Paper*—Paper with a rough surface, usually in shades of naturals, whites, and ivories.

Application: *DTP*—A software program that performs a particular kind of task, such as word processing, page layout, accounting, illustration, database retrieval, and so on.

Art director: *Graphic design*—The creator and supervisor of the visual aspects of a printed piece. This person usually selects art and photographs and oversees the design.

Art work: *Graphic design*—All forms of illustration used in printed materials, including drawings, photographs, graphs, maps, hand lettering, charts, and graphic devices.

Ascender: *Type*—The part of a letter that rises above the main body (the x-height) of a letter (see page 207). Letters such as b, f, and h have ascenders.

B

Backup: *DTP*—An additional copy of work done on a computer. Used for protection in case the original is accidentally lost or changed.

Baseline: *Type*—The invisible line upon which a row of letters sits (see page 207). The x-height of a letter sits on the baseline, its ascender (as in b) rises above it; its descender (as in g) drops below.

Basis weight: *Paper*—The weight of a ream (500 sheets) of a particular paper cut to its standard size. A 60 pound paper means that a ream of that paper weighs 60 pounds; a ream of a 100 pound paper weighs 100 pounds.

Bindery operations: *Printing*—Usually refers to the operations that put the printed piece together into its final form. Binding can include collating, folding, perforating, and binding pages of a booklet or book together by gluing, sewing, stitching (stapling), wire binding, or other method.

Bit: *DTP*—Stands for **bi**nary dig**it**. The smallest unit of digital information. It is represented electronically as either 1 (on) or 0 (off).

Bit-map: *DTP*—When the computer screen is divided into a grid ("map") of tiny white or black squares ("bits"), characters or images are stored as a pattern of squares and are referred to as being "bit-mapped."

Blanket: *Printing*—A rubber coated fabric clamped to the cylinder of a printing press. It transfers the inked image from the plate to the paper.

Bleed:*Graphic design, Printing*—Ink that goes to the edge of a page. To get a bleed edge, ink must be printed on paper larger than the final size of the piece. It is then trimmed (cut) back to the final size.

Blind embossing: *Graphic design, Printing*—Embossing involves pressing a metal die into the surface of paper to raise an image in the shape of the die. When a surface is *blind* embossed, the image appears without ink.

Blueline: *Design, Printing*—The printer's proofs made from the client's camera-ready art. The blueline is checked over carefully against the camera-ready art before it goes to press (see page 331). Bluelines are also called brownlines, silver prints, and Van Dyke prints.

Boards: *Design, Paste-up, Printing*—The art or illustration boards with all elements (type, art, etc.) precisely in position (also called *camera-ready art*).

Body type: *Type*—The type that makes up the main part of the text (as opposed to headline or display type which is larger, and used to attract attention).

Boldface (BF)**:** *Type*—A heavy version of a typeface used for headlines and other words intended to stand out. The first word of each entry in this glossary is in boldface type.

Bond paper: *Paper*—A kind of paper commonly used for letterheads, matching envelopes, and other business papers.

Book paper: *Paper*—A group of coated and uncoated papers with a wide variety of finishes (glossy, dull, matte, and so on) available in a number of different weights.

Bullets: *Writing, Design*—Typographic characters used to set off units of type (usually solid bold circles, but can be other shapes as well).

Byte: *DTP*—Unit of digital information (a set of 8 consecutive bits). Memory and disk capacity are measured in thousands (K) of bytes. One byte is roughly equivalent to one character of text. If a printed piece has 2000 characters, it needs about 2 K (kilobytes) of storage.

C

C/lc: *Type*—Typographic specification indicating that the first letter of the word should be in capitals, the rest in lower case.

Calligraphy: *Art, Type*—Highly refined or artistic handwriting, sometimes used in place of machine-set type.

Camera-ready art: *DTP, Paste-up, Printing*—The printed piece as prepared by the designer, paste-up person, or desktop publisher. Every element must be precisely in place, perfectly clean, and ready to be photographed in preparation for printing. Overlays for different colors and instructions are often attached. Also called a *mechanical*.

Caption: *Writing*—The text that accompanies illustrations or photographs, and usually describes or explains them.

Cast coated: *Paper*—Coated paper with a high-gloss enamel finish.

Character: *Type*—Any letter, number, or symbol in a typeface (font). When doing a character count, each blank space is also counted as a character.

Chroma: *Color*—Pure color, without any white or gray mixed in.

Clip art: *Design*—Copyright-free drawings, illustrations, and photographs purchased in books, rub-on sheets, and on computer software.

Coated paper: *Paper*—Paper coated with white clay or acrylic to create a smooth printing surface. Coated paper often has a glossy surface but it can also be dull, matte, eggshell, etc.

Cockle finish: *Paper*—Paper with a hard, rough surface, common in bond papers.

Cold type: *Type*—The most common method of setting type. It includes phototypesetting, hand lettering, computer-generated, and typewriter type. Hot type uses melted lead to form the letters.

Collate: *Printing*—To gather together into the right sequence.

Color key: *Printing*—A light-sensitive film (made by 3-M) used to check colors before printing.

Color-process work: *Printing*—See *Process color*.

Color separations: *Paste-up, Printing*—The sheets onto which the images of a printed piece have been separated by color.

Composition: *Type*—The process of producing the type to be used in printed materials.

Comprehensive (Comp): *Design*—A layout or drawing that shows (as closely as possible) what the finished piece will look like when printed. A *tight comp* has details; a *loose comp* is rougher.

Crop marks: *Paste-up, Printing*—Lines indicating where a photograph, illustration, or sheet is to be cut.

Condensed type: *Type*—A narrow version of a typeface (font), designed to get more characters into a smaller space.

Continuous tone: *Art, Photography*—An unscreened picture with many gradually changing shades of gray, from white to black.

Contrast: *Art, photography*—The gradation in tones ranging from highlights through middle tones to shadows.

Copyfitting: *Type*—Figuring out how much space a particular typeface in a certain size will take up; or changing the typeface and size to fit a certain space.

Copyright: *Writing, Art*—For an artist, writer, or designer, etc., exclusive rights to their work for a limited period of time. Protection is authorized by the U.S. Constitution.

Cover paper: *Paper*—A wide variety of heavier weight papers mainly used for covers of printed materials, but also used for brochures, business cards, and other printed pieces.

Crop: *Design, Photography*—To cut. Crop marks are lines indicating where a photograph or illustration should be cut to eliminate parts of it, or so it fits into a particular size and shape.

Cyan: *Printing*—One of the four inks in four-color process printing. Also called *process blue* (it is actually turquoise in color).

D

Deckle edge: *Paper*—The soft torn-looking edge on some fancy papers.

Descender: *Type*—The part of a letter that extends below an invisible baseline upon which the main body (x-height) of the type sits (see page 207.) The tails in letters like g, p, and y are descenders.

Desktop publishing: The integration of text and graphics on a computer.

Desktop publishing system: The hardware and software required to do desktop publishing.

Die-cut: *Design, Printing*—A shape cut out of paper.

Disk: *DTP*—Storage medium for programs and files, either "hard" (usually not removable) or "floppy" (removable).

Disk drive: *DTP*—The device that holds a disk, gets information from it, and saves information on it.

Display: *DTP*—A screen. A color display is a screen with color.

Display type: *Type*—Large type (usually 14 points or more) used to attract attention.

Document: *DTP*—Whatever piece you create on the computer is called a *document*.

Documentation: *DTP*—The printed material that explains how to use a particular program or piece of hardware.

Dot: *Printing, Photography*—The individual elements that make up a halftone (a picture with gradually changing shades).

Dot matrix printer: *DTP*—A low resolution (and relatively inexpensive) printer that prints out computer-generated information and images in dots.

Download: *DTP*—Moving information from one place to another, often from one computer to another over an electronic network.

Downloadable font: *DTP*—A set of instructions defining a family of letters (a font) that is stored in a computer and sent (downloaded) to an output device (such as a laser printer) for printing.

dpi: *DTP*—**d**ots **p**er **i**nch. The more dpi, the sharper the image (which is also described as having a *higher resolution*).

Draw-down: *Printing*—Refers to a glob of ink that has been "drawn-down" a sheet with a putty knife to see what the printed ink will look like on the paper.

Drop-out: *Design, Printing*—Designers often specify that type or images be *dropped out*. This means that they appear in the color of the paper with the ink color surrounding them in the background. It is also called *reversed*.

Dull coated: *Paper*—Paper that has a smooth, dull surface.

Dummy: *Design, Printing*—A mock-up or model of what the final printed piece will look like. Photographs are sketched in or copied and glued in place; type is either *greeked* (made up of meaningless filler characters) to show where it goes, or a copy of the final type is used.

Duotone: *Design, Photography, Printing*—Halftones made by separating a photograph or art work into two negatives—one with the light tones, the other with the dark. Each is printed in a different color of ink to create a rich effect. In a *double black* duotone, each negative is printed separately in black.

Duplex paper: *Paper*—Paper with a different color or finish on each side.

E

Em: *Type*—A unit of measure based on the largest letter in a typeface. It is equally high and wide (in 10 point type, an em is usually 10 points wide). The word comes from early typography when the letter "M" was cast on a square body.

Embossed finish: *Design, Printing*—A surface pattern made by pressing paper against an engraved steel roll to create a textured look (pebble, leather, wood, etc.).

Embossing: *Design, Printing*—Pressing an image into paper to create a raised surface (also see *blind embossing*).

En: *Type*—Half the width of an em.

Estimate: *Printing*—A tentative price developed by a vendor at a client's request.

Extended type: *Type*—a variation of a regular typeface (font) designed to take up more horizontal space. It is also called *expanded* type.

F

Fax (Facsimile transmission): *Communication*—Graphic images or words that have been scanned and sent electronically over telephone wires.

Family of type: *Type*—All sizes and weights, and variations of the same type design (typestyle, font). Variations include regular, bold, Roman, italic, and so on (see page 203).

Felt side: *Paper*—The "right" side of a sheet of paper; the one that gets better printing results.

Finish: *Paper*—The surface texture of paper, such as antique, vellum, wove, etc.

Flat: *Printing*—In offset printing, the photographic negatives or positives from which the press plates are made (usually using goldenrod masking paper).

Flop: *Design, Photography, Printing*—An instruction to the printer to reverse the direction of a photograph or piece of art.

Floppy disk: *DTP*—Removable storage medium with low-to-medium capacity (generally about one MB (megabyte) per disk).

Flush: *Design, Type*—An instruction to set something in line with something else. For example, a column set flush right and left has both edges aligned (also called *justified*); a column that is set flush left and ragged right has an aligned left side and an unaligned right side.

Foil: *Printing*—A colored, metallic, tissue-like material stamped on paper. Used instead of ink.

Folio: *Design*—A page number. Also refers to a sheet that has been folded once.

Font: *DTP, Type*—A complete set of characters in a particular size and style of type.

Format: *Design*—The overall design of a printed piece. Format decisions include the size, layout, type, margins, printing requirements, etc.

Four-color process: See *Process color.*

FPO: *Printing Preparation*—Photographs or art work placed "For Position Only," and not for reproduction.

French fold: *Design*—Paper printed on one side, then folded vertically, then horizontally (as traditional greeting cards are folded).

G

Galley proofs: *Type*—Typesetter's preliminary proofs of type to be checked over for errors or problems.

Gatefold: *Design*—Describes the way a printed piece is folded. A gatefolded piece has three panels; one opens left, the other right, to reveal a center spread.

Gathering: *Printing*—Bringing together folded signatures (pages of a printed piece) in the right sequence.

Gloss: *Paper*—Surface shine.

Gloss ink: *Printing*—Ink with extra varnish added to make it extra shiny.

Graphic artist: *Art*—A person who produces art through graphic methods (such as lithography, serigraphy, aquatint, etching, engraving, dry point, and so on). Often confused with graphic designer.

Graphic designer: *Design*—A design professional whose work is usually produced on a printing press. Tasks include designing the layout of a printed piece as well as specifying the size, type, art, colors, and paper for printed materials.

Graphic device: *Art*—All visual elements other than original illustrations and photographs. They include such things as typographic ornaments and characters, borders, lines, symbols, geometric shapes, and enlarged letters and numbers.

Gravure: *Printing*—A printing process in which the image is etched below the surface of the printing plate, and is pressed directly into the paper.

Gray scale: *Photography, Printing*—Standardized tones of gray, from white to black.

Gripper edge: *Printing*—The edge of the paper that is held by the printing press as it passes through it. No ink can be printed in the gripper edge space.

Grippers: *Printing*—The clamps that hold the paper as it goes through the printing press.

Guillotine: *Printing*—A large paper cutter with a single cutting blade.

Gutter: *Design, Printing*—The inside margins of a booklet or book, from the printing area to the binding.

H

Hairline registration: *Printing*—The meeting (butting) of two or more colors with no color overlap.

Halftone: *Printing*—Photographs or art with gradually changing shades that have been converted to solid dots. Converting these continuous tone images into halftones enables them to look like the original when they are printed.

Halftone screen: *Printing*—The engraved glass through which photographs or other shaded images are reduced to a series of dots and photographed.

Hard copy: *DTP*—The paper version of what has been generated on a computer.

Hard disk: *DTP*—Storage medium (usually fixed) with medium-to-high storage capabilities (often from 10 to 100 or more MB (megabytes) per hard disk).

Hardware: *DTP*—The physical components of a computer system, such as the computer, monitor, disk drive, and printer.

Head (headline): *Writing, Design*—Type intended to get attention. It is often larger than the body copy (type that makes up the main part of the text).

Hickey: *Printing*—An unwanted speck or imperfection on a printed sheet.

Hue: *Color*—The color itself (red, blue, purple, yellow, and so on).

I

Icons: *DTP*—Symbols on a computer screen.

Initial cap: *Design*—A large or decorated letter (or number) at the beginning of ordinary lines of type, used to get attention and add interest to the design.

Intaglio: *Printing*—A printing process in which ink goes into etched-in areas of a metal plate. The surface is wiped clean, and the plate is pressed directly on to the paper. Intaglio is one of the major methods of printing (letterpress and offset printing are others).

Interface: *DTP*—Compatibility between computer software and hardware. Also software that transfers data from one piece of equipment to another.

Italic: *Type*—Type that slants to the right *(this is italic type)* in contrast to Roman (which is straight up and down, like this). Most typefaces have an italic.

J

Justify: *Type*—To set the left and right margins of a column of type so that both edges are perfectly even.

K

K: *DTP*—Kilobyte (1024 bytes)—common measure of memory capacity (a double-spaced typewritten page uses about 1.5 K).

Kerning: *Type*—Removing space between characters to make a word look and read better.

Key: *Design*—Identifying photos, art, or other elements by a letter or number which is matched (keyed) to its appropriate position on a dummy or camera-ready art.

Keyline: *Paste-up*—An outline drawing specifying the exact shape, position, and size of a photograph or art work.

Kraft: *Paper*—Tan or brown paper made from unbleached wood pulp.

L

Laid: *Paper*—Paper with a tiny parallel line pattern through it in the same color.

Laser printer: *DTP*—A high resolution printer that outputs computer-generated type and images.

Layout: *Design*—The designer's sketch for the arrangement of type, art, etc., for a printed piece.

lc: *Type*—Used by type specifiers to indicate **lower case** type to the typesetter (as opposed to capitals).

Leaders: *Writing, Design*—A row of dots used to guide the eye across a page.

Leading: *Type*—The amount of space between lines of type, measured baseline to baseline.

Ledger paper: *Paper*—A tough grade of business paper often used for keeping records.

Letterpress: *Printing*—A printing method in which the printed image is on a surface raised above the non-printed areas. The raised areas touch the inked rollers and transfer the image to the paper. One of three major methods of printing (intaglio and offset printing are the other two).

Letterspacing: *Type*—Adding more space between the letters in a word to make it look and read better (as opposed to *kerning*, which subtracts space from between the letters in a word).

Line (line art or line drawing): *Design, Art*—A solid black image that can be reproduced without using a halftone screen (and is therefore less expensive).

Lithography: *Printing*—Any printing process in which the image and non-image areas are separated by chemical repulsion.

Logo: *Design*—A sign or symbol used by an organization to represent itself (it is called a trademark when applied to a product).

Logotype: *Design*—A typeface selected to be used for the name of a business or organization. The same typeface (or one that is harmonious with it) is often used in its printed pieces.

lpi: *Photography, DTP*—lpi is the number of lines **per** inch, referring to the resolution of halftones. The more lines per inch, the higher the resolution (and the sharper the image).

M

M: *Printing*—Used to indicate a quantity of 1,000.

Magenta: *Printing*—A bright pink-purplish red; one of the four-process colors (yellow, cyan, and black are the other three).

Makeready: *Printing*—The work done at the print shop to prepare a piece for printing.

Markup: *Paste-up, Printing*—Instructions given to the printer on the camera-ready art.

Matte finish: *Paper*—A paper surface with no gloss or shine.

Mechanical: *Paste-up, Printing*—Another name for *camera-ready* art (page 307).

Megabyte (MB): *DTP*—A unit of measure of computer memory, equal to 1024 kilobytes or roughly one million bytes.

Memory: *DTP*—The place where information is stored in the computer. Memory is measured in thousands (K) of bytes.

Menu: *DTP*—The lists of alternative commands on a computer screen.

Modem: *DTP*—A device making communication between computers possible via telephone lines.

Monitor: *DTP*—Display screen.

Mouse: *DTP*—Pointing device that sits next to a computer keyboard enabling the user to manipulate what is on the computer screen.

N

Non-photo blue: *Print preparation*—Refers to the blue pencil or pen used on camera-ready art because it will not reproduce (also called *non-repro blue*).

O

Offset paper: *Paper*—An uncoated paper which comes in a variety of finishes. It is especially good for offset printing because it repels water absorption.

Offset printing (offset lithography, photolithography): *Printing*—A printing process in which both the image area and the non-image area exist on the same surface (the plate). Of three major methods of printing—intaglio, letterpress, and offset—offset is the most commonly used by print producers.

Online: *DTP*—When the connection between one computer and another in a network is "on," permitting communication between them.

Opacity: *Paper*—The degree to which printing ink shows through on the second side of a sheet (referred to as *show through*).

Operating system: *DTP*—The program that enables you to run the computer.

Overlays: *Paste-up, Printing*—Transparent sheets prepared by the paste-up person for camera-ready art, showing one color per overlay. Each layer must be perfectly registered to the one below it. This work is often done photographically by the printer. Instructions are also written on overlays.

Overrun: *Printing*—Additional copies beyond the number originally specified.

P

Paste-up: *Printing preparation*—The process of preparing camera-ready art (a mechanical). It involves organizing all the elements for a printed piece (type, photos, lines, etc.) and waxing (or gluing) them down perfectly into their final position. Rubber cement may be used instead of wax.

PCL: *DTP*—**P**rinter **C**ommand **L**anguage—the commands for operating printers.

PDL: *DTP*—**P**age **D**escription **L**anguage—a program such as Adobe's PostScript® or Xerox's Interpress® that tells printers what to do.

P.E.s: *Printing*—Printer's Errors, as opposed to A.A.s (author's alterations). The client pays for A.A.s. The printer pays for P.E.s.

Pebble: *Paper*—Paper with a pebbly textured surface.

Photocomposition: *Type*—Photographically set type.

Photostat (stat): *Design, Paste-up*—A copy of a solid black image. Any line art can be photostated and enlarged or reduced to specification.

Pica: *Type*—A unit of measure in printing. There are six picas to an inch. One pica has 12 points.

Pixel: *DTP*—Short for "picture element," a pixel is the smallest graphic dot on a computer screen.

Plate: *Printing*—A thin sheet of metal on a printing press that transfers the image to the paper. The surface is treated so that only the part that is to print receives the ink. Quick printing shops often use disposable non-metal plates.

PMS colors: *Design, Printing*—PMS stands for the PANTONE MATCHING SYSTEM. It includes 747 standardized ink colors from which the designer chooses. There are also additional metallic inks.

Point: *Type*—A unit of measure in printing. One inch has 72 points; one pica has 12 points.

PostScript®: *DTP*—A computer language that describes letterforms and graphics for laser printers and other output devices.

Press proofs: *Printing*—First sheets run on the press for a final check before an entire job is printed.

Process color: *Printing*—Also called *four-color process*. A means of achieving full color with four inks: yellow, magenta (pink-purplish red), cyan (turquoise blue) and black. Each color is separated onto its own negative. A full color effect is created by overlapping these four transparent ink colors.

Program: *DTP*—The instructions that tell the computer what to do. Often used interchangeably with the words *software* or *application*.

Proof: *Printing*—A preliminary copy of the printed piece used for checking accuracy. Corrections are written on the proof.

R

Rag paper: *Paper*—Paper containing at least 25% rag or cotton fiber. The more rag content, the more elegant (and the more expensive) the paper.

Ragged right (or left): *Type*—A column of type that does not line up evenly on the right (or left) side.

RAM (**R**andom **A**ccess **M**emory): *DTP*—The amount of memory in a computer, which is measured in K (thousands of bytes), or memory that stores information temporarily while you're working on it.

Readers: *Type*—Preliminary samples of type to be proofread by the client.

Ream: *Paper*—500 sheets of paper.

Register marks: *Paste-up, Printing*—Guidelines used for the exact positioning of a printed piece.

Resident font: *DTP*—A font that is permanently stored in a laser printer.

Resolution: *DTP, Photography*—The level of refinement of an image, depending on how many dots there are per inch (dpi). Images with higher resolution have more dots per inch and reproduce better; lower resolution images have fewer dots per inch and their edges are rougher.

Reverse: *Design, Printing*—Type or an image is usually printed in ink and appears in the foreground.

When they are *reversed*, the ink makes up the background and surrounds the type or the image (they are the color of the paper beneath them). The usual situation is therefore reversed.

ROM (Read Only Memory): *DTP*—Programs or instructions that are permanently stored or "hard wired" in a computer.

Roman: *Type*—Regular type that sits straight up and down, as differentiated from italic (slanted) type. The first part of this sentence is in Roman; *this is italic.*

Roughs: *Design*—Preliminary sketches.

Rub-on type: *Design, Type*—Sheets of type that are transferred to paper by rubbing on the surface (also called *transfer type* and *instant lettering*).

Rules: *Design*—In the graphic arts, lines are called *rules*. They can be drawn by hand, rubbed on from a sheet of transfer type, or computer-generated.

Run: *Printing*—The total number of copies printed at one time (for example, a *run* of 5000 pieces).

Run-in head: *Writing, Design*—A headline, usually in bold face, which is part of the first line of type.

Running head: *Writing, Design*—A title that is repeated on the left or the right side of each page (or both) to help orient the reader.

S

Saddle stitching: *Printing*—Stapling through the middle fold of a booklet to hold it together.

Sans serif: *Type*—Type designed without serifs ("feet"), as opposed to *serif* type (with "feet"), which has a more traditional look (see page 202).

Satin finish: *Paper*—Paper with a smooth, satin-like finish.

Save: *DTP*—To store information on a disk.

Scaling: *Design, Photography*—Figuring out how much a picture must be reduced or enlarged to fit a specified area. Usually indicated as a percentage of the original.

Scanner: *DTP*—An imaging device that enables you to convert line art, photographs, or text from paper into electronic form so that they can be used in a computer.

Score: *Printing*—An indent or slight cut (not all the way through) put into heavy paper along a fold line so that it folds easier, neater, and cleaner.

Screen: *Photography*—Dots (in patterns or rows) used to create halftones.

Self-cover: *Design, Printing*—A cover made out of the same paper as the inside pages.

Serif: *Type*—Type designed with serifs ("feet"), as opposed to sans serif type (without "feet," page 202).

Service bureau: *DTP*—A center or shop that has computers, printers, and other desktop publishing equipment that can be used on site for a fee. Some service bureaus also offer expert help.

Set solid: *Type*—Type with no extra space (leading) between the lines. A 12 point type without extra leading, for example, is verbalized "12 on 12," and is written 12/12.

Sheet-fed press: *Printing*—A press that uses precut sheets of paper, as differentiated from a press that takes paper from a continuous roll (a web press).

Signature: *Printing*—A group of pages printed together on a large sheet.

Small caps: Small capital letters about the height of lower case letters.

Software: *DTP*—Any program that tells the computer what to do.

Solid: *Printing*—An area completely and solidly covered with ink (in 100% of the specified color).

Spiral binding: *Printing*—The binding in a book or booklet made up of spiral wire inserted through a series of holes along the spine.

Spot varnish: *Printing*—Varnish put in specified areas on a printed page (instead of over the entire surface).

Spread: *Design*—Two facing pages in a booklet, book, catalog, etc.

Stamping: *Design, Printing*—Pressing an image into paper with a metal die; embossing. Metal or colored foil or ink is stamped on to paper to give the image color. When there is no color, it is called *blind embossing.*

Stat: *Design, Printing*—A photographic copy in solid black.

Stock: *Paper, Printing*—A term used for paper or other material to be printed.

Suede finish: *Paper*—Paper that has a velvety-suede surface.

T

Template: *DTP*—A predesigned pattern or grid. Used for several kinds of printed pieces such as newsletters, brochures, and manuals.

Text: *Writing, Design*—The body or main part of the information on a page, as opposed to headlines.

Text paper: *Paper*—A high quality paper used for brochures, booklets, invitations, etc.

Thumbnails: *Design*—Small sketches used to show possibilities for layout or illustration.

Toner: *DTP*—"Ink" for a laser printer (actually fine plastic particles).

Trim: *Printing*—To cut away. Guidelines for cutting are indicated by *trim marks.*

Trim size: *Printing*—The final size of the printed piece after it has been trimmed (cut).

Typo: *Type*—An error in the type.

U

Unjustified: *Type*—A column of type in which one side (usually the right) is not aligned. Also called *ragged.*

UC (Upper case): *Type*—Type specifier's mark to indicate capital letters (caps).

V

Varnish: *Printing*—A coating applied like ink to the paper's surface. Although usually glossy and clear, varnish can also be dull or tinted. It is used to protect the surface as well as to add aesthetic interest.

Vellum: *Paper*—A good quality paper. It is uncoated, relatively absorbent, and has a slightly rough surface.

Velox: *Photography, Printing*—A trade name for a printing paper made by Kodak. Commonly refers to a screened black and white print of a halftone.

W

Waxer: *Paste-up*—A gadget commonly used in paste-up. It coats paper (type, art, etc.) with a thin layer of melted wax so that it will stick to the art board.

Web press: *Printing*—A high-speed press that prints on rolls of paper (called *webs*).

Widow: *Type*—A word on a line by itself. A typesetter will often space type to avoid a widow.

Window: *Printing*—Cut out or masked off areas on a negative to expose only the desired image.

Windows: *DTP*—Some programs have *windows*. They enable users to work in different applications at the same time.

Wire-O binding: *Design, Printing*—A binding made of double wire loops which weave in and out of holes punched along the side of a booklet.

Wove: *Paper*—Surface with a soft, smooth finish.

WYSIWYG: *DTP*—Pronounced "wizzy-wig," stands for "**W**hat **Y**ou **S**ee **I**s **W**hat **Y**ou **G**et." Refers to whether or not what you see on the screen will be the same as what you see on the hard (printed) copy.

X

X-Acto knife: *Paste-up*—A pencil-sized cutting tool with a sharp blade. Often used in preparing camera-ready art.

x-height: *Type*—Refers to the body of the lowercase letter (the fat part that sits on the baseline as opposed to the *ascender*, which goes above the x-height (as in b), or the *descender* which goes below it (as in g).

Illustration and Photograph Credits

This page is a continuation of the copyright page. We wish to gratefully acknowledge the permissions granted to reproduce images in the text.

Chapter 2: Your Competitive Edge

Page 18 *Left*: *The Book of Kells*, Dover Publications, Inc., Mineola, New York. *Right*: Xyvision 1987 Annual Report, Art director: Roy Hughes, Hughes Communication, Boston, Massachusetts; designer: Samantha Murray; photographer: Brian Smith. Used with permission.

Page 19 HealthPrint poster. Designer: Elizabeth Adler; illustrator: Margaret Sanfilippo. Used with permission of the Palo Alto Medical Clinic.

Page 20 Quit Smoking ad. Print director/designer: Elizabeth Adler; illustrator: Margaret Sanfilippo. Used with permission of the Stanford Center for Research in Disease Prevention. All materials developed and used by permission of the Stanford Center for Research in Disease Prevention are copyrighted by the Board of Trustees of the Leland Stanford Junior University.

Page 21 Quit Smoking campaign booklet. Designer: Elizabeth Adler. Used with permission of the Stanford Center for Research in Disease Prevention.

Page 22 Donald M. Vickery/James Fries, *Take Care of Yourself*, ©1989, Addison-Wesley Publishing Co., Inc., Reading, Massachusetts. Reprinted with permission of the publisher.

Page 23 *What Color Is Your Parachute*, by Richard N. Bolles, Ten Speed Press, Berkeley, California. Used with permission.

Page 24 *About Your Company*, courtesy of International Business Machines Corporation.

Chapter 8: Tailoring the Piece to Your Audience

Page 72 Magazine covers courtesy of L.L. Bean, Inc.

Page 74 Used with the permission of the American Cancer Society, Inc.

Page 75 Earthquake Map, figure 1 of Borcherdt, Gibbs, and Lajoie, 1989, U.S. Geological Survey Map MF-709.

Page 76 Maternity Infant Care Project brochure. Designer: Elizabeth Adler. Used with permission.

Page 80 Promotion for the *San Jose Mercury News*. Writer: Garey De Martini; art director: Stuart English; typesetter: Graphic Arts West, Campbell; printer: Imperial Printing, Cupertino. Used with permission.

Page 81 Guia para Dejar de Fumar. National Cancer Institute. Designer: Elizabeth Adler; photographer: Alex Viranes.

Page 82 Blood Pressure brochures. Designer: Elizabeth Adler. Used with permission of the Stanford Center for Research in Disease Prevention.

Chapter 9: Ideas to Make Your Piece More Interesting

Page 84 Brochure for Leaf and Petal (clothing shop). Designer: Carol Cruikshank.

Page 85 Blood pressure pad. Print director/designer: Elizabeth Adler. Used with permission of the Stanford Center for Research in Disease Prevention.

Pages 86-87 Energy Awareness Program of the Facilities Department at Stanford University Medical Center. Creative director: Elizabeth Adler; designer: John Stoneham; writer: Prudence Breitrose. Used with permission.

Page 88 Tip Sheets. Print director/designer: Elizabeth Adler. Used with permission of the Stanford Center for Research in Disease Prevention.

Page 89 Clip-a-Tip Mailer. Print director/designer: Elizabeth Adler; writer: Mia Clark. Used with permission of the Stanford Center for Research in Disease Prevention.

Pages 90-91 No-smoking policy announcement posters and letterhead for Stanford University Hospital. Designer: Elizabeth Adler; illustrator: John Stoneham. ©1987 Elizabeth Adler. Used with permission.

Page 92 Guia para Dejar de Fumar. National Cancer Institute. Designer: Elizabeth Adler; photographer: Alex Viranes.

Page 95 Guia para Dejar de Fumar. National Cancer Institute. Designer: Elizabeth Adler; photographer: Alex Viranes.

Page 96 Parental Stress Hotline bookmark and Stanford University postcard. Designer: Elizabeth Adler. Used with permission.

Chapter 10: Tapping Your Creativity

Page 98 Depression brochure. Reprinted with permission from The Kelly Group, Charlottesville, Virginia, ©1984.

Page 99 *Left*: Poster for the University Art Museum, Berkeley, California. Designer/illustrator: Elizabeth Adler. Used with permission. *Right*: Self-promotion poster. Designer: Robert Cook, Jr., Smith/Cook Design, Houston, Texas. Used with permission.

Page 100 Self-promotion poster for Monte Dolack Graphics. Designer/illustrator: Monte Dolack, Missoula, Montana. Used with permission.

Page 101 Fish drawings courtesy of Ms. McCall's 5th grade class, El Carmelo School, Palo Alto, California.

Page 102 *Left*: Christmas card for European Auto Techniks. Designer: Phil Chrzanowski, Chrzanowski Design, Houston, Texas. Used with permission. *Right*: MADD 1987 Annual Report Cover. Designer: Bryan L. Peterson, Peterson & Co., Dallas, Texas. Used with permission.

Page 103 *Left*: Kennedy/King memorial concert poster. Design firm: Larson Design Associates, Rockford, Illinois; art director: Jeff Larson; designer: Scott Johnson. Used with permission. *Right*: "How To Build a Snow Bronco," cover for *Contemporary*, magazine of the *Denver Post*. Designer: Gerry Chapleski, Gerry Chapleski Design, Broomfield, Colorado. Used with permission.

Page 104 Brochure for D. Larson, D.D.S., Designer: Lauren Smith, Lauren Smith Design, Palo Alto, California. Used with permission.

Page 112 Poster for Utah's Hogle Zoo. Courtesy of Fotheringham & Associates, Salt Lake City, Utah. Used with permission.

Chapter 11: A Way to Make Writing Easier

Pages 121-122 Illustrator: Carolyn Hammond

Chapter 12: Guidelines for Reader-Friendly Writing

Page 124 HealthPrint Tip Sheets. Creator/designer/writer: Elizabeth Adler; illustrator: Margaret Sanfilippo. Used with permission of the Palo Alto Medical Clinic.

Page 126 *The Exercise Book*. Print director/designer: Elizabeth Adler; writer: Prudence Breitrose. Used with permission of the Stanford Center for Research in Disease Prevention.

Page 129 Blood pressure brochure. Designer: Elizabeth Adler; writer: Prudence Breitrose. Used with permission of the Stanford Center for Research in Disease Prevention.

Page 130 Allen Memorial Art Museum brochure, 1970s. Designer: Elizabeth Adler. Used with permission.

Page 132 *Food for Health* booklet. Print director/designer: Elizabeth Adler; writer: Prudence Breitrose; illustrator: Margaret Sanfilippo. Used with permission of the Stanford Center for Research in Disease Prevention.

Page 135 Nurse's Checklist, Kaiser/Stanford Heart Attack program. Designer: Elizabeth Adler. Used with permission.

Page 136 Smoking Quit Kit. Print director/designer: Elizabeth Adler; writer: Prudence Breitrose; illustrator: Margaret Sanfilippo. Used with permission of the Stanford Center for Research in Disease Prevention.

Page 140 *Basics of Birth Control* brochure. Reprinted by permission. Planned Parenthood® Federation of America, Inc.

Page 141 Materials brochure. Designer: Elizabeth Adler. Used with permission of the Stanford Center for Research in Disease Prevention.

Page 142 Reprinted with permission of The Research Libraries Group, Inc., from "The Research Libraries Group News," No. 15 (January 1986), editor Hilary Hannon.

Chapter 13: Making Writing More Readable

Pages 144-145 *The Cook's Book*. Designer: Elizabeth Adler. Used with permission of the Stanford Center for Research in Disease Prevention.

Pages 146-147 *The Exercise Book*. Print director/designer: Elizabeth Adler; writer: Prudence Breitrose; illustrator: Margaret Sanfilippo. Used with permission of the Stanford Center for Research in Disease Prevention.

Page 149 Guia para Dejar de Fumar. National Cancer Institute. Designer: Elizabeth Adler; photographer: Alex Viranes.

Page 151 Strawberry Festival flyer, First Parish Federated Church, South Berwick, Maine.

Page 153 Courtesy of the International Business Machines Corporation.

Chapter 14: How to Write a Basic Brochure

Page 158 *Top*: Health Promotion Resource Center brochure. Designer: Elizabeth Adler. Used with permission of the Stanford Center for Research in Disease Prevention. *Bottom*: HealthPrint brochure. Designer: Elizabeth Adler. Used with permission.

Page 159 Oberlin College brochure, 1970s. Designer: Elizabeth Adler. Used with permission.

Page 162 *Agenda 90* brochure. Designer: Halleck Design Group, Palo Alto, California. Used with permission.

Pages 163-169 Laura Richards Property Improvement brochure. Designer/writer: Elizabeth Adler.

Page 170 *Left to right*: Fairhaven Inn brochure; Smiling Hill Farm; "Insured Plus Account" brochure created by Calvert Group Ltd., 1987. Used with permission. The Medieval & Early Modern Data Bank brochure. Reprinted with permission of The Research Libraries Group, Inc., editor Hilary Hannon.

Chapter 15: What's Good Design?

Page 174 Brigham Young Financial Aid poster. Designer: McRay Magleby, Provo, Utah. Used with permission.

Page 175 *Agenda 90* brochure. Designer: Halleck Design Group, Palo Alto, California. Used with permission.

Page 176 *Top*: T-Shirt Design for Buster's Bowl. Designer/illustrator: Van Hayes, Van Hayes Design, Dallas, Texas; Client: Buster Moore. Used with permission. *Below*: Package design for PRESIDIO Gourmet Sauces. Designers: Roger Christian and Elaine Lytle, Taylor Christian & Co., San Antonio, Texas. Used with permission.

Page 177 Posters for Acme Bread Company and Mirage. Courtesy of David Lance Goines, Berkeley, California.

Page 178 Photographs of rooms. Courtesy of Laura Ashley, Inc.

Page 179 *Left*: *The Book of Kells*, Dover Publications, Inc., Mineola, New York. *Right*: Birthday Card. Designer: Georgia Deaver, San Francisco, California. Used with permission.

Page 180 Dustjacket for *The Silver DeSoto*. Designer: Carol Haralson; publisher: Council Oak Books, Tulsa, Oklahoma. Used with permission.

Page 181 *Top*: Cover for Champion papers. Designer: Koppel & Scher, New York, New York. Used with permission. *Bottom*: Spread from *THIS PEOPLE* magazine. Art Director: Ron Stucki, Salt Lake City, Utah. Used with permission.

Page 182 *Left*: Woodcut by Jost Amman, *The Annals of Printing*. *Right*: CalTrans Annual Report Cover. Art Director: Lindy Dunlavey, The Dunlavey Studio; illustrator: David Stevenson. Used with permission.

Page 184 *Left*: *Chairs Through the Ages*, Dover Publications, Inc., Mineola, New York. *Right*: Mies van der Rohe, Ludwig. *"Barcelona" Chair*. 1929. Chrome-plated flat steel bars with pigskin cushions, 29-7/8" x 19-1/2" x 19-5/8". Collection, The Museum of Modern Art, New York. Gift of Knoll International. Used with permission.

Chapter 16: Basic Design Decisions

Page 190 Promotional brochure for International Paper Co. Designer: Rex Peteet/Sibley, Peteet; illustrator: Jack Unruh. Used with permission.

Page 192 Tragon brochure. Designer: Halleck Design Group, Palo Alto, California. Used with permission.

Pages 196-197 Stanford University Libraries Annual Report. Designer: Elizabeth Adler. Used with permission.

Page 198 *Left*: Booklet for Children's Hospital at Stanford. Designer: Elizabeth Adler; photographer: Jane Wattenburg. *Right*: Shortwood Tennis Club brochure. Design firm: Weber Design Partners, Inc.; art director: Christina Weber; designer: Monique Davis. Used with permission.

Page 199 *Left*: Ad for Springfield Mall. Designer: Richards Brock Miller Mitchell & Associates/The Richards Group; art director/illustrator: Ken Shafer; client: Fischer McLeod. Used with permission. *Right*: Promotional brochure for International Paper Co. Designer: Rex Peteet/Sibley, Peteet; illustrator: Jack Unruh. Used with permission.

Page 200 Brigham Young University Registration Poster. Designer: McRay Magleby, Provo, Utah. Used with permission.

Chapter 17: Understanding Type

Page 203 Type family variations from *Letraset Graphic Materials Handbook*. Used with permission from Letraset USA.

Page 210 Xyvision 1987 Annual Report. Art director: Roy Hughes, Hughes Communication, Boston, Massachusetts; designer: Samantha Murray; photographer: Brian Smith. Used with permission.

Page 211 Poster for the American Institute of Graphic Arts. Designer: Bryan L. Peterson, Peterson & Co., Dallas, Texas. Used with permission.

Page 213 A sample of type styles available. Taken from *Letraset Graphic Materials Handbook*. Used with permission from Letraset USA.

Page 214 *Left*: Announcement for Fortress Chair. Designer: Ms. Carson Pritchard, Carson Pritchard Design; illustrator: David Hockney. Used with permission. *Right*: Tragon brochure. Designer: Halleck Design Group, Palo Alto, California. Used with permission.

Page 217 Rub-on type sample. Used with permission from Letraset USA.

Page 218 Poster for Jacksonville Landing. Designer: Sullivan/Perkins, Inc., Dallas, Texas. Used with permission.

Chapter 18: Color That Works

Pages 220-223 PANTONE Products and PANTONE by Letraset Color Products. Used with permission.

Page 224 Logo for National Park Academy of the Arts. Designer/illustrator: Lee Riddell, Riddell Advertising & Design, Jackson Hole, Wyoming. Used with permission.

Page 225 Christmas Card. Print director/designer: Elizabeth Adler. Used with permission of the Stanford Center for Research in Disease Prevention.

Page 226 Logo for New England Accents. Art Director/Designer: Geraldine Greenberg; copywriting: Tom O'Connor; agency: Geraldine Greenberg & Company; illustration: Tom Barrett; photography: Jack Richmond Studio; typography: Arrow Composition; stationary printing: Graphic House; brochure printing: Chadis Printing; client: New England Accents. Used with permission.

Page 228 Oberlin College Conservatory of Music brochure, 1970s. Used with permission.

Chapter 19: Selecting and Specifying Paper

Page 232 Relational Technology brochure. Designer: Lauren Smith, Lauren Smith Design, Palo Alto, California. Used with permission.

Page 234 Paper samples courtesy of Sylvia Louis, Zellerbach.

Page 236 Wheat and pumpkin drawings. Illustrator: Elizabeth Adler. Used with permission.

Page 238 *Top*: Business card. Used with permission. *Bottom*: Paper samples courtesy of Sylvia Louis, Zellerbach.

Page 239 Dieta Tradicional Para Su Corazon. Designer: Elizabeth Adler. Used with permission of the Stanford Center for Research in Disease Prevention.

Page 240 Planned Parenthood Invitation. Designer/illustrator: Brenda Bodney, Bodney+Siedler Design; copywriter: Cindy Weigle; client: Planned Parenthood of Riverside and San Diego Counties. Used with permission.

Chapter 20: Art and Photography

Page 242 Photograph of Yosemite. Photographer: Richard Adler. Used with permission.

Page 243 Illustration for Behavioral Health Systems. Print director: Elizabeth Adler; illustrator: Margaret Sanfilippo. Used with permission.

Page 244 *Left*: Dover catalog cover. Dover Publications, Inc., Mineola, New York. Used with permission. *Right*: Sample of rub-on art available from Letraset USA. Used with permission.

Page 245 ClickArt® disk and samples. Courtesy of ClickArt®. ClickArt® is a registered trademark of T/Maker Co. ©1987 T/Maker Company.

Page 246 Booklet endsheets. Designer: Elizabeth Adler. Used with permission of the Stanford Center for Research in Disease Prevention.

Page 247 *Left to right*: Annual Report for the Palo Alto Medical Foundation. Designer: Elizabeth Adler. Used with permission. Health Promotion Resource Center How-to Guide. Designer/writer: Elizabeth Adler. Used with permission of the Stanford Center for Research in Disease Prevention. Tragon brochure. Designer: Halleck Design Group, Palo Alto, California. Used with permission. Sample design. Designer: Elizabeth Adler. Used with permission.

Page 250 *Left*: Brochure for Heritage Press. Design firm: Richards Brock Miller Mitchell & Associates/ The Richards Group, Dallas, Texas; designer/illustrator: Robin Ayres. Used with permission. *Right*: Awards booklet for Atlanta Advertising Club. Designer: Don Trousdell, Trousdell Design, Inc., Atlanta, Georgia. Used with permission.

Page 251 *Left*: Booklet for the Palo Alto Medical Foundation. Designer: Elizabeth Adler. Used with permission.

Page 252 *Top left*: Oberlin College Bulletin, 1970s. Designer: Elizabeth Adler. *Top right*: Recipes for Your Heart's Delight. Art director/designer: Elizabeth Adler; illustrator: Margaret Sanfilippo; writer: Mia Clark. Used with permission. *Bottom Left*: Brochure for Stanford Court Hotel. Designer: Halleck Design Group, Palo Alto, California. Used with permission. *Bottom right*: Clip art.

Page 253 Photograph of Vermont fair and Maine coast. Photographer: Richard Adler. Used with permission.

Pages 254-255 Photograph of mid-western farm. Photographer: Richard Adler. Used with permission.

Page 256 RLG Around the World. Reprinted with permission of The Research Libraries Group, Inc., from "The Research Libraries Group News," No. 12 (January 1986), editor Hilary Hannon.

Page 257 Photograph of kitten. Photographer: Hilary Hannon. Used with permission.

Page 258 Photograph of pineapple. Photographer: Richard Adler. Used with permission.

Chapter 21: Logos and the Graphic Image

Page 261 Corporate Health Communication Program materials. Creator/designer: Elizabeth Adler. Used with permission of the Palo Alto Medical Foundation.

Pages 262-263 Communication materials for Domingo Gonzalez Design. Designer: Ms. Perry Defino. Used with permission.

Page 264 Communication materials for William E. Carter Construction. Designer: Michael Kennedy, Michael Kennedy Associates, Sacramento, California. Used with permission.

Page 265 Materials for Health Management Services, El Camino Hospital. Designer: Elizabeth Adler. Used with permission.

Page 266 KQED Graphic Standards Manual. Design director: Jane E. Tierney. Used with permission.

Page 269 *Left to right*: Logo for Phillip Cooke Photography. Designer: Scott Ray, Peterson & Co., Dallas, Texas. Used with permission. Logo for a regional park. Designer: Elizabeth Adler. Used with permission. Logo for the Health Resource Center. Designer: Elizababeth Adler. Used with permission of the Stanford Center for Research in Disease Prevention. Logo for Geared for Golf. Designer: John Stoneham. Used with permission.

Page 270 *Left*: Logos for the Stanford Heart Disease Prevention Program. Print director/designer: Elizabeth Adler. Used with permission of the Stanford Center for Research in Disease Prevention. *Right:* Health care logos. Designer: Elizabeth Adler. Used with permission.

Page 271 *Left:* Sketches for logos. Designer: Elizabeth Adler. Used with permission. *Right:* Hegstrom Stamp. Designer: Ken Hegstrom. Used with permission.

Page 272 Logos based on initial caps and geometric shapes. Designer: John Stoneham. Used with permission.

Page 273 Examples of computer clip art. Courtesy of ClickArt®. ClickArt® is a registered trademark of T/Maker Co. ©1987 T/Maker Company.

Page 274 Symbol for Phoenix Little Theater. Designer: Ann Morton Hubbard, Hubbard & Hubbard Design, Phoenix, Arizona. Used with permission.

Page 276 *Top to bottom:* Logo for Yokota. Designer: John Stoneham. Used with permission. Logo for Shadowgraph. Designer: Art Chantry, Seattle, Washington. Used with permission. Logo for Sportimes. Designer: John Stoneham. Used with permission. Logo for Syllabus. Designer: John Stoneham. Used with permission. Logo for Galardi's Pizza. Designer: Patrick Sooho Designers, Los Angeles, California. Used with permission.

Page 277 *Top to bottom:* Logo for Library of Congress "1989-Year of the Young Reader." Used with permission. Symbol for Hospital Movies (movie rentals). Designer/illustrator: Michael Connors; art director: Phillip Poole, Poole2, Inc., Fort Worth, Texas. Used with permission.

Page 278 *Top to bottom:* Symbol for Aerobic Activity Center. Design firm: Richards Brock Miller Mitchell & Associates/The Richards Group; designer: Gary Templin, Dallas, Texas. Logo for The Closet Organizer. Designer/illustrator: Lana Fuqua, Vaughn Weeden

Creative, Albuquerque, New Mexico. Logo for Fat Change Records. Designer: Lane Evans, Southwest Design Associates, Irving, Texas. Logo for CycleCraft. Designer: John Stoneham and Ken Hegstrom. Logo for American Widgeon. Designer: John Stoneham. Logo for Open Space. Designer: Elizabeth Adler. All used with permission.

Chapter 22: Desktop Publishing

Pages 282-283 Computer generated logos. Designer: Elizabeth Adler. Used with permission.

Pages 284-285 Computer generated logos. Designer: Elizabeth Adler. Used with permission.

Page 286 *Left:* Picnic invitation. Designer: Elizabeth Adler. Used with permission. *Right:* Seasons Greeting from the Clarks. Designer: Tim and Mia Clark. Used with permission.

Page 287 © Aldus Corporation 1989. Reprinted courtesy of Aldus Corporation. Aldus PageMaker, Aldus FreeHand and Aldus Persuasion are registered trademarks of Aldus Corporation. All rights reserved.

Pages 288-289 Computer generated illustrations. Designer: Elizabeth Adler. Used with permission.

Page 292 Brochure. Used with the permission of Quark, Inc., Denver, Colorado.

Page 294 *Top:* Desktop publishing hardware. Courtesy of Apple Computer, Inc. *Bottom:* Courtesy of International Business Machines Corporation.

Pages 298-299 PageMaker brochure. © Aldus Corporation 1989. Reprinted courtesy of Aldus Corporation.

Page 300 Aldus Magazine. © Aldus Corporation 1990. Reprinted courtesy of Aldus Corporation.

Page 301 Illustration. Used with the permission of Adobe Systems, Mountain View, California.

Page 302 Samples. ClickArt® is a registered trademark of T/Maker Co. ©1987 T/Maker Company.

Page 303 Type catalog *Font & Function*. Used with the permission of Adobe Systems, Mountain View, California.

Chapter 23: Preparation for Printing

Page 309 Camera-ready art for *Child of Mine: Feeding with Love and Good Sense* brochure. Used with permission of Bull Publishing Company, Palo Alto, California.

Page 312 Mastheads for Drop it Off and Sabor y Salud. Designer: Elizabeth Adler. Used with permission of the Stanford Center for Research in Disease Prevention.

Page 313 *Left*: Ecology Action Report. Designer: Elizabeth Adler. *Right*: CycleCraft letterhead. Designer: John Stoneham and Ken Hegstrom. All used with permission.

Chapter 24: Printing

Pages 328-329 Christmas Card. Designer: Elizabeth Adler. Used with permission of the Stanford Center for Research in Disease Prevention.

Chapter 25: Distribution Points

Pages 336-337 HealthPrint Tip Sheets. Creator/designer/writer: Elizabeth Adler. Used with permission of the Palo Alto Medical Clinic.

Page 338 Stanford Heart Disease Prevention Program tip sheet and envelope. Print director/designer: Elizabeth Adler. Used with permission.

Page 340 Grocery bag stuffers. Print director/designer: Elizabeth Adler; illustrators: Elizabeth Adler and Margaret Sanfilippo; writer: Mia Clark. Used with permission of the Stanford Center for Research in Disease Prevention.

Page 341 The Fifth Step Evaluation Sheet. Designer: Elizabeth Adler. Used with permission of the Stanford Center for Research in Disease Prevention.

Page 342 HealthPrint reply card. Designer: Elizabeth Adler. Used with permission of the Palo Alto Medical Clinic.

Page 344 Over-sized business envelope for Young Craig & Co. Designer: Halleck Design Group, Palo Alto, California. Used with permission.

The chapter icons were illustrated by Elizabeth Adler and Carolyn Hammond.

This book was created and produced on a Macintosh using Adobe Illustrator88™ 1.6 and Aldus PageMaker® 3.02 and 4.0.

Index

abbreviations, using, 149
absolute statement(s), avoiding, 150
acronyms, using, 149
active voice, 146
ad(s), 12
address, on a brochure, 168
advertising specialties, 12, 84, 85
alignment, of type, 211
analogy(ies), as writing technique, 148
anecdote(s), as writing technique, 133
angle(s), 308, 312
appendix(es), 187
application(s),defined, 304. *See also* software
approval people, 52
art, 39, 250-252. *See also* illustration(s);
   photograph(s)
      choosing and using, 241-243
      copyright-free, 244
      permissions for, 39
art board(s), 307
art director(s), 48
article(s), 11
ascender(s), 207
audience(s), 29-30
      broad, 82
      tailoring printed pieces to, 71-82
audience profile, 77
Autopaque, 309
Avant Garde, 209
award(s), 95-96

backup, defined, 304
backwards schedule(s), 57-58, 60
bar(s), as graphic device, 247
baseline, of type, 205, 207
basis weight, of paper, 233
Bauhaus style, 178, 184
binder(s), 11
      printing covers of, 191

binding, 190-192, 325
      mechanical, 191
      perfect, 191
      plastic, 191
      ring, 191
      saddle stitching, 190-191
      side stitching, 191
      wire, 191
bit, defined, 304
bit-map, defined, 304
bit-mapped graphics, 301
black and white mode, of scanners, 295
blanket(s), defined, 323
bleed(s), 224, 324
      defined, 226, 322, 323
blind embossing, 192
blueline(s), 50
      checking, 41-42, 324, 331-333
      checklist for, 333
      defined, 41-42, 323, 331
board(s), 50
body copy, defined, 146
body type, 202
boldface type, 203, 226
bond paper, 235-237
booklet(s), 10
book paper(s), 237
border(s), as graphic device, 248, 251
box(es)
      alternatives to, 249-250
      as graphic device, 248-250
      screened, 248
brochure(s), 10, 17
      cover of, 163
      format and content of, 161-162
      writing, 157-170
budget(s), 65-68
      checklist for, 67
      common mistakes in, 65-66
      limitations to, 31

budget(s), *(continued)*
     making the most of, 68
budget and production notebook(s), 68
bullets, to improve ease of reading, 149-152
business card(s), 9, 157
business papers, 9
byte, defined, 304

calendar(s), 12
camera-ready art, 307. *See also* camera-ready
  board(s)
     defined, 323
     ownership of, 317
     storing, 317-318
camera-ready board(s), 50. *See also* camera-ready art
     checking, 41
     checklist for, 315
     defined, 307
     preparing, 307-318
capital letters, 210-211
caps and lowercase, 210
caption(s), 150
catalog(s), 10
certificate(s), 95-96
chapter division page(s), 187
chart(s), 250
checklist(s)
     for bluelines, 333
     for budgets, 67
     for camera-ready boards, 315
     for color keys, 333
     for editors, 155
     for logos, 277
     for press checks, 332
     for production costs, 62
     for writers, 139
     as writing technique, 135
checks, as graphic device, 247
C/lc. *See* caps and lowercase

clip art, 48, 244-245, 273, 298, 301-303
     defined, 304
collating, 190
color(s), 219-230
     combinations of, 227, 229-230
     hue of, 226
     identifying on camera-ready boards, 313-314
     PANTONE, 222-223
     of paper, 238
     photocopying in, 322
     PMS, 222-223
     preferences in, 220
     process, 223-224
     saturation of, 226
     selecting, 226-230
     trends in, 220-221
     and type, 228-229
     using one effectively, 226-228
     value of, 226
color key(s), defined, 331
     checklist for, 333
color mode, of scanners, 295
color proof(s), 329
color separations, defined, 323
column(s), 199
commercial artist(s), 48
comp(s), defined, 323
compacted type, 203
comparison(s), as writing technique, 134
compatibility, in desktop publishing, 291
compressed type, 203
computer(s)
     designing on, 282-283
     for desktop publishing, 293-295
computer clip art, 244-245, 298, 301-303
comstock type, 203
concept developer(s), 47
concept development, 37-38
condensed type, 203
consultant(s), 50-51

content expert(s), 47
content research, 38
contents, table of, 143-144, 187
contrast, in monitors, 296
copy, defined, 146
copy approval stage, of print production, 39
copyright page, 187
corrections
    of copy, 39
    of design, 40
    of type, 40
cost, of producing printed pieces, 61-68
    checklist, 62
cost estimating form for printers, 63
cover(s)
    of brochures, 163
    designing, 189
    inside front and back, 187
    outside front and back, 187
    self, 189
cover paper(s), 235
creative director(s), 48
creativity, tapping, 97-113
credits page(s), 187
crop marks, defined, 323
cropping, 253, 254, 255, 312-313
    defined, 312
C-Thru® ruler(s), 308, 312

data sheet(s), 11
decorative type, 202
demi bold type, 203
descender(s), 207
design, 173-200. *See also* graphic design; graphic
    image
    on computers, 282-283
    of covers, 189
    defined, 173
    defining good, 173-184

discipline in, 179
inspiration for, 174-176
integrating with writing, 125
of the page, 187
process of, 186
standardizing, 265
design approval, 40
design decisions, 185-200
    at the beginning, 187-192
designer(s), 39. *See also* graphic designer(s)
    role of, 185-186
design stage, of print production, 39
design style, 174
    current trends in, 182-184
    origins of, 176-179
    types of, 183
desktop publisher(s), 48
desktop publishing (DTP), 40, 212-215, 281-306
    advantages of, 285-289
    compatibility in, 291
    defined, 304
    for designing, 282-283
    determining your needs for, 290
    buying equipment for, 291
    fonts for, 303
    hardware for, 292-297
    keeping up with, 289
    limitations of, 289-291
    myths of, 283-285
    paste-up in, 311-317
    software for, 293, 297-303
    terms, 304-305
desktop publishing equipment, 292-297
    buying, 291
desktop publishing system, defined, 304
die cut(s), 192
dingbat(s), as graphic device, 246
direct mail distribution, 335, 336-339. *See also*
    distribution
directory(ies), 10

disk(s), defined, 304
disk drive(s), defined, 304
display(s), defined, 304
display type, 202
distortion, in monitors, 296
distribution, of printed pieces, 32-33, 42, 335-344
    defined, 335
    direct mail, 335, 336-339
    drop-off, 335, 339-342
      choosing good locations for, 340
      methods of, 339
      piggybacking, 335, 339, 342
distribution plan(s), 340
document, defined, 304
documentation, defined, 304
dot-matrix printer(s), 296
    defined, 304
dots per inch (dpi), 296, 304
double black duotone(s), 255
download, defined, 304
downloadable font, defined, 304
dpi (dots per inch), 296
    defined, 304
draw computer programs, 282, 301
drawing board(s), 308
drop-off distribution, 335, 339-342. *See also*
  distribution
dropped out type, 226
DTP. *See* desktop publishing
dummy(ies), 235, 308
    defined, 239, 323
duotone(s), 255
Duplex paper, 235

editing stage, of print production, 39
editor(s), 48
    checklist for, 155
em(s) (type measurement), 205
embossing, 192

envelope(s), 344
    choices for, 343
    vs. self-mailers, 338
estimate(s)
    getting, 187-192
    for printing, 62-63, 187
    from subcontractors, 64-65
evaluation, of printed pieces, 33, 42
example(s), as writing technique, 140
expanded type, 203
extended type, 203

fact(s), startling, as writing technique, 131
fees, publishing, 162
film flat(s), 324
finishing, of printed pieces, 189-192
flicker, in monitors, 296
floppy disk(s), defined, 304
fluorescent ink(s), 224
flush left and right, 208
flyer(s), 12
focal length, of a photo, 255
folding, 189-190
folio(s), 144
follow-up evaluation, 42
font(s). *See* type, type font(s)
form(s), business, 9
format(s)
    choosing, 30
    of basic brochures, 161-162
    types of, 7, 8-13
four-color process, 223-224
frame(s), as graphic device, 251
free-form shape(s), as graphic device, 247
fund-raising letter(s), 13

galley(s), 50
geometric shape(s), as graphic device, 247

glare, in monitors, 296
glossary(ies), 187
gopher(s), 51-52
graph(s), 250
graphic artist(s), 48
graphic design, 39. *See also* design
    defined, 173
graphic designer(s), 48. *See also* designer(s)
    interviewing, 191
    selecting, 193
    working with, 195
graphic device(s), 244-250
    copyright-free, 244-245
    placement of, 245
    size of, 245
    types of, 245-250
graphic image, 30-31, 125, 259-266
    advantages of good, 260
    creating your own, 260-266
    example of planning, 263-266
    when to change, 263
    when to create, 262-263
graphics software, 288, 301-303
gray-scale mode, of scanners, 295
grid
    creating, 194-198
    defined, 194
gripper edge, indicating, 314
grippers, defined, 323
gutter, defined, 199

halftone, defined, 241, 242, 323
handbill(s), 12
handbook(s), 10
hand distribution, 335, 339-342. *See also* distribution
hard copy, defined, 304
hard disk(s), 295
    defined, 304

hardware
    defined, 304
    for desktop publishing, 292-297
head(s)
    levels of, 152-154
    writing strong, 128, 145
headline(s). *See* head(s)
head type, 202
Helvetica, 209
"however," avoiding awkward constructions with, 150
hue, of a color, 226

icon(s), defined, 304
idea lists, 101-113
idea notes, 118, 119-120
illustration(s), 39, 250-252
    copyright-free, 302
    credit for, 258
    fees for, 257
    permissions for, 257
    rights to, 258
illustration board(s), 307
illustration style(s), 252, 256
illustrator(s), 48
    working with, 251-252
image, of printed pieces. *See* graphic image
ImageWriter output, 216
imaging device(s), 295
index(es), 145, 187
interface, defined, 304
initial cap(s), as graphic device, 245, 247
ink(s), printing, 221-225
    coverage of, 228
    fluorescent, 224
    metallic, 223, 224
    varnish, 225, 228
insert(s), 162
inside covers, 187

interview(s), as writing technique, 137
invitation(s), 13
invoice(s), 9
italic type, 202

jargon, avoiding, 146-147
joint venture(s), 66-68
justified type, 208

K (kilobyte), defined, 304
kerning, defined, 204, 206
keyline(s), defined, 310
key location distribution, 335, 339-342. *See also*
    distribution

label(s), 9
landscape (horizontal) monitor(s), 296
laser printer(s), 296
    defined, 304
laser printer output, 216
layout
    defined, 194
    doing, 194-200
    for writers, 149-155
leading, 205-206, 207
    defined, 205
leave-behind, 159
length, of printed pieces, 188
letterform(s), as graphic device, 245-246, 248, 250
letterhead(s), 9, 157
letterspacing, 206
life span of printed pieces, 32
light type, 203
line(s), as graphic device, 247, 249, 251
line art, 51
    defined, 241, 243, 323
line length, 208-210

optimum, 206
Linotronic output, 216
logo(s), 260, 267-278
    criteria for good, 267-269
    defined, 267
    designing, 269-277
    evaluation checklist for, 277
    as graphic device, 248
    ideas for, 267
    inexpensive, 275
    quick and easy, 273
logotype. See logo(s)
long-term planning, 34
lowercase, 207
LPI (lines per inch), defined, 305

mail distribution, 335, 336-339. *See also*
    distribution
mailing house(s), 336-338
mailing list(s), 336
manual(s), 10
map(s), 250
margin(s), 194, 198-199
marketing, 19
marketing director(s), 47
market research, 38
marking up copy, 50
master page(s), 282
mechanical binding, 191
meeting(s), running, 51
megabyte (MB), defined, 305
Melior, 209
memory, defined, 305
memo sheet(s), 9
menu(s), 11
    defined, 305
message
    deciding on, 120-121
    unstated, 29

metallic ink(s), 223, 224
modem(s), defined, 305
modern type, 202
money. *See* cost of producing printed pieces
monitor(s), 295-296
    color, 296
    defined, 305
    gray-scale, 296
    landscape, 296
    monochrome, 295
    portrait, 296
    resolution of, 296
    size of, 296
mouse, defined, 305

newsletter(s), 10
non-photo blue pencil(s), 309
notebook(s), budget and production, 68
notepad(s), 9
number(s), as graphic device, 246

object-oriented graphics, 301
OCR (optical character recognition) device(s), 295
odd sizes, 188
offset paper(s), 237
offset printing, 324-325
oldstyle type, 202
online, defined, 305
opacity, of paper, 232
operating system, defined, 305
optical character recognition (OCR) device(s), 295
Optima, 209
overlay(s), defined, 323
overrun(s), defined, 323
overview(s), 145
outline(s), organizing for writing, 119-120
outline type, 203

page(s)
    number of, 188-189
    parts of, 187
page layout software, 299-301
page number(s), 144
paint computer programs, 282, 301
Palatino, 209
pamphlet(s), 10
PANTONE Color Formula Guide, 220, 222
PANTONE MATCHING SYSTEM (PMS), 222-223
paper(s), 231-240
    bond, 235-237
    book, 237
    coated, 222, 225, 228, 239
    color of, 221, 238
    cost of, 232
    cover, 235
    criteria for choosing, 231-233
    Duplex, 235
    finish of, 238-239
    grade of, 235-237
    name(s) of, 233-235
    offset, 237
    opacity of, 232
    samples of, 239
    specifying, 233-239
    text, 237
    Two-sheet, 235
    uncoated, 222, 239
    weight of, 232-233
paragraph(s), construction of, 155
passive voice, 146
paste-up, 41, 50
    basic materials for, 308-309
    defined, 308
    in desktop publishing, 311-317
    doing, 310-317
    final stages of, 311-317
    traditional, 308-317
paste-up artist(s), 50

paste-up person(s), 50
PCL (printer command language), defined, 305
PDL (page description language), defined, 305
perfect binding, 191
perforations, 192
permissions, for art and photographs, 39, 257
photocopying, 63-64, 321-322
photograph(s), 39, 253-256
    choosing and using, 241-243
    credit for, 258
    cropping, 253, 254, 255, 312-313
    fees for, 257
    focal length of, 255
    permissions for, 39, 257
    placement of, 254
    rights to, 258
    scaling, 313
    size of, 254-255
    stock, 49, 255-256
photographer(s), 49
photostat(s), 245
pica(s) (type measurement), 205, 208
piggybacking, 335, 339, 342. *See also* distribution
pixel(s), defined, 305
planning, of printed pieces, 27-36
    alone, 35
    long-term, 34
    with others, 35
    personal style of, 34-35
    questions for, 35
    value of, 29
plastic binding, 191
plate(s), for printing, 50
    defined, 323
platemaking, 324
PMS colors, 222-223
point(s) (type measurement), 204, 205
polka dots, as graphic device, 247
portrait (vertical) monitor(s), 296
postcard(s), 12, 87

Post Office regulations, 338-339
PostScript, 297
    defined, 305
poster(s), 12
pre-press work, 324
presentation folder(s), 13
press(es)
    sheet-fed, 324
    web, 324
press check, 42, 333
    checklist for, 332
press type, 217
pretesting stage, of print production, 39-40
printed piece(s)
    adding appeal to, 83-96
    advantages of, 20-22
    cost of producing, 61-68
    determining purposes of, 28-29
    distribution of, 32-33, 42, 335-344
    evaluating, 33, 42
    examples of good, 22-24
    family of, 259
    format of, 7, 8-13, 30
    goal of, 17
    improving quality of, 15-24
    length of, 188
    life span of, 32
    mailing, 336-339
    making them look easy to read, 123-125
    planning, 27-36
    size of, 187-189
    standardization of, 266
    steps in producing, 37-42
    tailoring to audiences, 71-82
    timing arrival of, 59
    types of, 7, 8-13
    unstated message of, 28
    writing for, 117-170
printer(s), 50
    choosing, 325-331

questions to ask, 327
tips for working with, 334
printer(s), computer, 296-297
print medium, 4-5
    defined, 6
printing, 41-42, 156, 319-334
    alternative methods of, 321-325
    estimates for, 62-63
    money-saving tips for, 325
    offset, 324-325
    photocopying, 63-64, 321-322
    preparing for, 307-318
    quick, 63, 322
    silkscreening, 325
printing estimates, 62-63
printing ink(s), 221-225
print production. *See* production
process color, 223-224
production, 281-334
    desktop publishing, 281-306
    people involved in, 43-52
    preparation for printing, 307-318
    printing, 319-334
    roles in, 44
    steps in, 37-42
production manager(s), 49
production staff, 43-52
    finding, 44-45
    managing, 46
    selecting, 45, 49
program(s), computer, 11
    defined, 305
progress update memo(s), 54
project director(s), 45-47
promotion pieces, 12
proof(s), defined, 323
    checking, 331-333
proofreader(s), 50
proofreader's marks, 153
proofreading

of copy, 39
    guidelines for, 152
    marks for, 153
    of type, 40-41
proposal(s), 13

question(s), as writing technique, 131-133
question-and-answer format, as writing technique,
    135-137
questionnaire(s), 13
quick printing, 63, 322
quiz, as writing technique, 135

ragged right, vs. justified, 208
RAM (random access memory), defined, 305
readability
    improving, 143-156
    of type, 208
reader(s), 50
reader-friendly writing, 123-142
report(s), 13
repro copy, 50
reproduction, methods of, 321-325. *See also*
    printing
research
    content, 38
    market, 38
resident font, defined, 305
resolution
    defined, 305
    of monitors, 296
reverse(s), 224, 324
    defined, 226, 322, 323
rights, to illustrations and photos, 258
ring binding, 191
risk, communicating, 151
ROM (read only memory), defined, 305
roman numerals, avoiding, 150

Roman type, 202
rub-on type, 217
rubber stamp, for logos, 271
Rubylith, 309
rule(s)
    around photographs, 255
    as graphic device, 247
running heads, 144

saddle stitching, 190-191
sans serif type, 202
saturation, of a color, 226
save, defined, 305
scalable type fonts, 303
scaling, photographs, 313
scanner(s), 295
    defined, 305
schedule(s), 53-60
    backwards, 57-58, 60
    creating, 51-58, 60
    explaining, 53-55
    rush, 55
    week-by-week, 56, 57
scoring, 189
screen tint(s), 225, 248
script type, 202
self-cover(s), 189
self-mailer(s), vs. envelopes, 338
sentences, writing strong, 146
serif type, 202
service bureau, defined, 305
set solid, type, 205
shaded type, 203
shadow type, 203
sheet-fed press(es), 324
"should," avoiding, 150
sidebar(s), 187
side stitching, 191
signature(s), defined, 323

silk-screening, 191-192, 325
sink, defined, 197
size, of printed pieces
    determining, 187-188
    odd, 188
    standard, 187-188
slash(es), avoiding, 150
slice-of-life, as writing technique, 134
software
    clip art, 244-245, 298, 301-303
    defined, 305
    desktop publishing, 293, 297-303
    graphics, 288, 301-303
    page layout, 299-301
    word processing, 298, 301
specifications, determining, 61-62, 187-192
spell-checkers, 288
square serif type, 202
standard sheet size, of paper, 233
standard size(s), 187-188
stapling, 190-191
stat(s), 51, 245
stereotyping, guarding against, 81
stitching, 190-191
stock. *See* paper
stock photograph(s), 49, 255-256
sticker(s), 321
stripes, as graphic device, 247
stripping, 50, 324
style(s)
    Bauhaus, 178, 184
    design, 174, 176-179, 182-184
    illustration, 252, 256
    type, 201, 202
    writing, 30, 137
style guide(s), 266, 267
style sheet(s), 282
subcontractor(s), getting estimates from, 64-65
summary(ies), 145
swatch book(s), 238, 239
symbols, as graphic device, 248

table(s) of contents, 143-144, 187
target audience, 29-30, 73
technical information, conveying, 141-149
template, defined, 305
testimonial(s), as writing technique, 134-135
text
    defined, 146
    writing, 146-149
text paper(s), 237
text type, 202
thin type, 203
time limitations, 31
Times, 209
timing arrival of printed pieces, 59
tint(s), 225, 248
tint guide(s), 225
tip sheet(s), 11
title page(s), 187
titles, writing good, 126-127
tone, writing, 137, 138
toner, defined, 305
topic sheet(s), 119-120
trademark(s), 267
transfer lettering, 217
transitional type, 202
trim marks, defined, 323
trim size(s)
    defined, 187
    standard, 187-188
T-square, 308, 312
Two-sheet paper, 235
type, 201-218. *See also* typeface(s); type font(s)
    alignment of, 211
    black, 203
    body, 202
    boldface, 203, 226
    and color, 228-229
    common mistakes with, 217
    compacted, 203
    comparing sources of, 216
    compressed, 203
    comstock, 203
    condensed, 203
    decorative, 202
    demi bold, 203
    display, 202
    dropped out, 226
    expanded, 203
    extended, 203
    families of, 202-204
    head, 202
    italic, 202
    light, 203
    measurement of, 205
    medium, 202
    modern, 202
    normal, 202
    oldstyle, 202
    outline, 203
    parts of, 207
    plain, 202
    preparing, 40
    press, 217
    proofreading, 40
    readability of, 208
    regular, 202
    Roman, 202
    rub-on, 217
    sans serif, 202
    script, 202
    selecting, 202-212, 215
    serif, 202
    setting, 212-218
    size of, 204-205
    square serif, 202
    shaded, 203
    shadow, 203
    text, 202
    thin, 203
    transitional, 202
    ultra black, 203

typeface(s), 201
    list of popular, 209
type family(ies), 202-204
type font(s), 201
    defined, 304
    for desktop publishing, 303
    mixing, 211, 218
    scalable, 303
type measurements, 205
typesetter(s), 49-50
typesetting, 212-218
    desktop publishing, 40, 212-215
    traditional, 40, 212
    typewriter, 215, 216
typesetting machine output, 216
type size, 204-205
type style(s), 201, 202
typewriter, 215, 216
typist(s), 47
typographical character(s), as graphic device, 246
typographical ornament(s), as graphic device, 246

ultra black type, 203
underlining, avoiding, 217
unjustified type, 208
unstated message, of printed pieces, 29
uppercase, 207

value, of a color, 226
varnish, 225, 228
vertical space, 154-155
"very," avoiding, 150
visual(s), to convey technical information, 148
visual communication system, 259
visual image(s), choosing and using, 241-243. *See also* illustration(s); photograph(s)
visual impression, of printed piece(s), 125, 259-266.
    See also graphic image

volunteer help, 66

waxer, 308
web press(es), 324
week-by-week schedule(s), 56, 57
white space, 159, 198, 200
window(s)
    in computer programs, 305
    in paste-up, 309, 313
wire binding, 191
word choice, 146
word processing software, 298, 301
word processor(s), 47
wordspacing, 206
writer(s), 47
    checklist for, 139
    giving assignments to, 138
writing, 117-170
    brochures, 157-170
    headlines, 128, 145
    integrating with design, 125
    making it easier, 117-122
    making it interesting, 131-137
    making it more readable, 143-156
    making it reader-friendly, 123-142
    text, 146-149
    titles, 126-127
    standardizing, 265
writing stage, in print production, 38
writing style, 30, 137
writing tone, 137, 138
WYSIWYG, defined, 305

Zapf Dingbats, 246

Order Form

To Order This Book

To order additional copies of *Print That Works: The First Step-By-Step Guide that Integrates Writing, Design, and Marketing,* send $23.95 plus shipping and handling ($3.00 for the first book; $.75 for each additional book). California residents add $1.73 sales tax per book. All orders must be prepaid.

Other Information

For more information about other books in the Bull Publishing catalog, send your name and address on the form below.

(check areas of interest)

- ☐ Women's Health
- ☐ Nutrition and Fitness
- ☐ Mentor Health Promotion Programs
- ☐ Parenting and Child Nutrition
- ☐ Cancer Education

Send _____ copies of *Print That Works: The First Step-By-Step Guide that Integrates Writing, Design, and Marketing* by Elizabeth Adler.

Form of payment:

☐ Personal Check ☐ Company Check

☐ Send catalog information only

Fill in Master Card or VISA number below:
(circle one)

_____

Expiration Date: _____

_____

Signature

(___)_____

Name

(Area Code) Telephone number

Company Name

Address

City State Zip Code

Send $23.95 plus shipping and handling, (California residents add $1.73 sales tax per book ordered), to Bull Publishing Company, P.O. Box 208, Palo Alto, California 94302 or call (415) 322-2855. Please allow four to six weeks for delivery.

Order Form

To Order This Book

To order additional copies of *Print That Works: The First Step-By-Step Guide that Integrates Writing, Design, and Marketing,* send $23.95 plus shipping and handling ($3.00 for the first book; $.75 for each additional book). California residents add $1.73 sales tax per book. All orders must be prepaid.

Other Information

For more information about other books in the Bull Publishing catalog, send your name and address on the form below.

(check areas of interest)

- ☐ Women's Health
- ☐ Nutrition and Fitness
- ☐ Mentor Health Promotion Programs
- ☐ Parenting and Child Nutrition
- ☐ Cancer Education

Send _____ copies of *Print That Works: The First Step-By-Step Guide that Integrates Writing, Design, and Marketing* by Elizabeth Adler.

Form of payment:

☐ Personal Check   ☐ Company Check

☐ Send catalog information only

Fill in Master Card or VISA number below:
(circle one)

_____

Expiration Date: _____

Signature

(___) _____
(Area Code) Telephone number

Name

Company Name

Address

City   State   Zip Code

Send $23.95 plus shipping and handling, (California residents add $1.73 sales tax per book ordered), to Bull Publishing Company, P.O. Box 208, Palo Alto, California 94302 or call (415) 322-2855. Please allow four to six weeks for delivery.